Martin Luther

as Prophet, Teacher, Hero

Texts and Studies in Reformation and Post-Reformation Thought

Caspar Olevianus, *A Firm Foundation: An Aid to Interpreting the Heidelberg Catechism,* translated, with an introduction by Lyle D. Bierma.

John Calvin, *The Bondage and Liberation of the Will: A Defence of the Orthodox Doctrine of Human Choice against Pighius,* edited by A. N. S. Lane, translated by G. I. Davies.

Law and Gospel: Philip Melanchthon's Debate with John Agricola of Eisleben over Poenitentia, by Timothy J. Wengert.

Martin Luther as Prophet, Teacher, and Hero: Images of the Reformer, 1520–1620, by Robert Kolb.

Martin Luther

as Prophet, Teacher, Hero

Images of the Reformer, 1520–1620

Robert Kolb

a Labyrinth Book

Published by Baker Books
a division of Baker Book House Company
P.O. Box 6287, Grand Rapids, MI 49516-6287

and

Paternoster Press
P.O. Box 300, Carlisle, Cumbria CA3 0QS
United Kingdom

Printed in the United States of America

Library of Congress Cataloging-in-Publication Data

Kolb, Robert, 1941–
Martin Luther as prophet, teacher, hero : images of the reformer, 1520–1620 / Robert Kolb.
p. cm. — (Texts and studies in Reformation and post-Reformation thought)
"A Labyrinth book."
Includes bibliographical references and index.
ISBN 0-8010-2214-2 (pbk.)
1. Luther, Martin, 1483–1546. I. Title: Martin Luther. II. Title. III. Series.
BR325.K64 1999
284.1′092—dc21 99-049291

British Library Cataloging-in-Publication Data

A catalogue record of this book is available from the British Library.

ISBN 0-85364-997-9

For information about academic books, resources for Christian leaders, and all new releases available from Baker Book House, visit our web site:
http://www.bakerbooks.com

Contents

Abbreviations

CR Philip Melanchthon. *Corpus Reformatorum. Philippi Melanchthonis opera quae supersunt omnia*. Edited by Karl Bretschneider and Heinrich Bindseil. 28 vols. Halle and Braunschweig: Schwetschke, 1834–60.

Ulrich Zwingli. *Corpus Reformatorum. Huldreich Zwinglis Sämtliche Werke*. Edited by Emil Egli et al. 14 vols. (88–101). Zurich: Berichthaus, 1959–68.

LW Martin Luther. *Luther's Works*. 55 vols. St. Louis and Philadelphia: Concordia and Fortress, 1958–86.

WA Martin Luther. *Dr. Martin Luthers Werke*. 65 vols. Weimar: H. Böhlau, 1883–1993.

WA Br Martin Luther. *Luthers Werke. Briefwechsel*. 18 vols. Weimar: H. Böhlau, 1930–85.

Illustrations

Introduction

In an attack published in 1529, Johannes Cochlaeus, Martin Luther's fierce foe and first biographer, characterized the Reformer as having seven heads.[1] Throughout the almost five centuries since then, Luther has been depicted by friend and foe alike as having many more than seven faces. The image makers of his own age began immediately to project into public view a picture which reflected their experience of Luther. Their successors have taken the raw material of his life and thought and cast it into forms which would serve their own purposes—with varying degrees of historical accuracy. Few public figures have enjoyed and suffered the process of publicity as has Martin Luther.

Most ages seize historical personalities as clay from which they mold icons of mythical proportions to embody their values and aspirations. Into the apocalyptically charged atmosphere of late medieval Germany stumbled Martin Luther, whose career coincided with the invention of the medium of print. At the outset of his career, historical and religious conditions, medium, and man came together in a unique manner to begin fashioning a public persona which soon loomed larger than life over the German and western European ecclesiastical landscape. Read in the streets of towns and discussed in the taverns of villages, his own publications and the representations of his thought and person by other pamphleteers produced a cultural paragon which his followers in the sixteenth century put to use in several ways.

In the conclusion to his pioneering assessment of the changing views about the Reformer from Wittenberg, Horst Stephan observed that new images of Luther are always "born out of a new encounter with the testimony of the original image, and they are reflections of his form in water of different depths and different hues."[2] To a degree perhaps unique in the history of the church since the apostolic age, the image of this single person, Martin Luther, has directly shaped the institutions and life of a large body of Christendom. He has influenced his followers both as churchman and as teacher of the church. Calvinist churches, of

1. Johannes Cochlaeus, *Septiceps Lutherus, vbique sibi, suis scriptis, contrarius in Visitationem Saxonicam* (Leipzig: Valentin Schumann, 1529).

2. Horst Stephan, *Luther in den Wandlungen seiner Kirche* (Giessen: Töpelmann, 1907), 127.

course, look to John Calvin as model and magister for their ecclesiastical life. John Wesley exercises a continuing role in the Methodist churches. To a far greater extent, however, Lutheran churches have found in Luther not only a teacher but also a prophetic hero and authority. Heinrich Bornkamm's observation extends beyond the borders of the German cultural realm which he was sketching: "Every presentation and assessment of Luther and the Reformation means a critical engagement with the foundations of our more recent history. Like no other historical figure, that of Luther always compels anew a comprehensive reflection on the religious, spiritual, and political problems of our lives."[3]

Since Stephan's study others have examined the interpretation of Luther's thought and work both within and outside Lutheranism.[4] None of these, however, has focused in detail on the ways in which Luther's image and thought shaped Lutheran thinking and action during the century following his appearance on the stage of Western history. From the very beginning Luther's students and friends regarded him as a figure of more than normal proportions. Some saw him as an illustrious hero of the faith. Others regarded him as a powerful doctor of the church in line with Moses, Paul, and Augustine. Many also regarded him as a unique servant of God, a prophet and the eschatological angel who is depicted in Revelation 14 as the bearer of the gospel in the last days and whose authority could be put to use in governing and guiding the church, particularly in the adjudication of disputes over the proper and correct understanding of biblical teaching.

Without taking into account the conceptual framework of biblical humanism on the one hand, and that of late medieval apocalyptic on the other, such images seem strange to us moderns. Within the context

3. Heinrich Bornkamm, *Luther im Spiegel der deutschen Geistesgeschichte* (Heidelberg: Quelle & Meyer, 1955), 11.

4. E.g., see Ernst Walter Zeeden, *Martin Luther und die Reformation im Urteil des deutschen Luthertums: Studien zum Selbstverständnis des lutherischen Protestantismus von Luthers Tode bis zum Beginn der Goethezeit,* 2 vols. (Freiburg/B: Herder, 1952); and Bernhard Lohse, "Zur Geschichte der Lutherdeutung," in *Martin Luther: Eine Einführung in sein Leben und sein Werk,* 2d ed. (Munich: Beck, 1983), 210–48. For material on the more recent views of Luther, see Bornkamm, *Luther im Spiegel,* 13–19 (a very brief introduction regarding the period "from the Reformation to the Enlightenment"); *Interpreters of Luther: Essays in Honor of Wilhelm Pauck,* ed. Jaroslav Pelikan (Philadelphia: Fortress, 1968), a series of essays which does not treat any of the sixteenth- or early-seventeenth-century German Lutherans; *Luther in der Neuzeit: Wissenschaftliches Symposion des Vereins für Reformationsgeschichte,* ed. Bernd Moeller (Gütersloh: Gerd Mohn, 1983), a series of essays concentrating on the last two centuries; and Ulrich Michael Kremer, "Martin Luther in the Perspective of Historiography," in *Seven-Headed Luther: Essays in Commemoration of a Quincentenary, 1483–1983,* ed. Peter Newman Brooks (Oxford: Clarendon, 1983), 207–29.

of Luther's time, however, they provided vehicles by which people could make sense of Luther's impact on their lives and his role on the stage of human history. With such images of Luther in mind his followers set about to reshape the institutions and ideas which held their world together.[5]

This inquiry will review how Luther's message and his career reshaped sixteenth-century German Lutherans' views of God and human history. Three conceptions of the Reformer emerge, reflecting a variety of needs in his society, which was organized around religious ideas and ecclesiastical institutions and practices. Although all three of these conceptions appeared in the first few years of public comment on Luther, they developed in different ways as the years passed. Their influence can best be presented through a chronological tracking of their evolution as exhibited in representative writings from the pens of his disciples. To be sure, historians' analyses always oversimplify: the categories are not so distinct and discrete that they can be neatly separated from each other. Thus our discussion of each motif will reveal aspects of the others.

First, for some of his followers during the subsequent decades, the Reformer functioned as a prophet who replaced popes and councils as the adjudicating or secondary authority (interpreting the primary authority, Scripture) in the life of the church. Like almost every age, the late Middle Ages were a period of crisis, and people were rethinking questions of authority in various aspects of life. Within the church Luther's challenge to the medieval papacy heightened the crisis by confirming doubts about the old religious system. Although Luther and his adherents did not discard the ancient fathers of the church nor disregard their usefulness, they did affirm the primacy of biblical authority; for them Scripture was the sole primary source of truth. The church, however, always needs a more elaborate system of determining the meaning of the biblical message; and the tradition, in the hands of popes, bishops, and councils, could no longer suffice to adjudicate differences in interpretation of the Scripture. To replace the medieval au-

5. This study will not address the success or failure of the Reformation, a debate generated by Gerald Strauss's *Luther's House of Learning: Indoctrination of the Young in the German Reformation* (Baltimore: Johns Hopkins University Press, 1978). Conclusions based on the application of twentieth-century standards to source materials with naturally negative biases (such as the law sections of Lutheran sermons and visitation reports intended to focus on the problems of local congregations) must be compared to evidence which suggests that the public mentality of central Europe did change under the impact of the Reformation. On the other hand, we must also acknowledge evidence which tends to confirm the presupposition of Luther's theology of the cross that the gospel is likely to fail in a world hostile to its message.

thorities who had interpreted biblical dicta regarding truth and life, Luther emerged as a prophet of God in whose words a secondary level of doctrinal authority could be found. Those who believed that this Wittenberg professor was God's special agent—a voice of divine judgment upon the corruption of the old system—were able to ascribe such authority to him without difficulty. When the living myth had disappeared into his tomb, and could no longer adjudicate disputes by composing letters or formal faculty opinions, his writings—widely available in print—were used as a secondary authority by some of his disciples.

Second, over the years Luther functioned as a prophetic teacher whose exposition of the biblical message supported and guided the biblical exposition of his followers. Luther based his perception of life and truth upon his conviction that God had spoken reality into existence and shaped human life through his Word. Teaching—the content of the Word—thus was paramount in Luther's conception of the way in which God came to people in the sixteenth century and functioned as their God. While the Reformer was still alive and writing, his vast literary output enabled him to influence a broad circle of readers and of nonreaders who heard his ideas from them. When he died, his adherents continued to learn and to teach others through the published corpus of his thought. In elaborating Luther's role as teacher, we must pay attention to the ways in which his writings were reproduced and used in the Lutheran churches of Germany after his death. For his heirs not only reprinted his complete corpus and individual treatises in it; they also repackaged and organized Luther's thought topically for handy reference in the pastor's library. In this manner Luther continued his teaching activity after his death through citations, reprintings, and the organizing of his thought for consumption in a new era.

Third, for his German followers Luther remained above all a prophetic hero whom God had chosen as a special instrument for the liberation of his church—and of the German people—from papal oppression and deceit. As a heroic prophet, Luther symbolized the divine Word which brought God's judgment upon the old papal system, and he embodied the hopes of the people and the comfort of the gospel which brought new heavenly blessings upon the faithful children of God. In their troubled times his followers saw in Martin Luther the assurance that God would judge their enemies and intervene eschatologically in their behalf with the salvation he had promised.

After an initial overview of the images of Luther current during his lifetime and at his death (ch. 1), we will address the development of the three major images in the period between his death and the eve of the Thirty Years' War (chs. 2–4). Our historical overview will conclude with a glance at fresh presentations in the first years of the seventeenth century (ch. 5). To assess Luther's prophetic authority, we will survey appeals to it in treatises of his disciples as they disputed over his legacy (ch. 2). We will analyze his role as a prophetic teacher through a brief overview of the way in which his works were used to address the new generation's controversies over the Lord's Supper (ch. 4) and through a survey of the republication of his writings in various forms (chs. 6–8). We will also combine a look at the heroic status assigned to him in the general treatments of his life and the particular arguments that Lutherans used against the Roman Catholic party regarding his teaching and person (ch. 3).

Out of these reflections will emerge an understanding of how Luther after his death continued to function as an authority, as a teacher, and as a hero for those who claimed his name. We will see how his image as an authority disappeared during the course of the sixteenth century, his image as a teacher became limited, and his image as a hero continued into the critical period before the outbreak of the Thirty Years' War. Through this discussion will come insights into the nature of authority within the church—as Luther's followers and heirs conceived it—into the ways in which they defined and delivered the biblical message according to Luther's tradition, and into their conception of their church in the midst of a changing society.[6]

6. These ideas took form originally in my essay "'Perilous Events and Troublesome Disturbances': The Role of Controversy in the Tradition of Luther to Lutheran Orthodoxy," in *Pietas et Societas: New Trends in Reformation Social History: Essays in Memory of Harold J. Grimm,* ed. Kyle C. Sessions and Phillip N. Bebb (Kirksville, Mo.: Sixteenth Century Journal, 1985), 181–201, and were expanded in "Die Umgestaltung und theologische Bedeutung des Luthersbildes im späten 16. Jahrhundert," in *Die lutherische Konfessionalisierung in Deutschland: Wissenschaftliches Symposion des Vereins für Reformationsgeschichte 1988,* ed. Hans-Christoph Rublack (Gütersloh: Mohn, 1992), 202–31. I am grateful to Rublack for urging me to develop my ideas further, first in the lecture for the symposium of the Verein and thereafter in book form; to Irene Dingel for many suggestions for improvement of the manuscript; and to Richard Muller for the encouragement and support of his careful editorial eye and hand.

Part One
Theander Lutherus
The Man of God as Prophet, Teacher, and Hero

1

The Living Prophet

Luther in the View of His Contemporaries

In 1520 Ulrich Zwingli—later no friend of Luther at all—wrote that he and others in the circles of south German and Swiss humanists regarded Martin Luther as a contemporary Elijah.[1] Fifteen years earlier this same Martin Luther had entered the Observant Augustinian monastery in Erfurt as a terrified sinner. In 1507 his fear of God's awesome power overcame him as he was consecrating the elements of the mass. Five years later, in 1512, he reluctantly completed his studies for the degree of doctor of Bible as he continued the routine of monk and university instructor. By 1520 he had acquired a European reputation and had been commandeered as a vehicle of the eschatological longings of the German populace.

The reason why Luther was being hailed as a prophet by Zwingli and others, educated and uneducated, lay not in the faithful and effective service he in fact did perform as an administrator in his order, nor in his engaging lectures to his students. His rapid rise to fame and intellectual influence had been propelled both by his ideas and by the course of events which they had unleashed. Ideas and events in tandem had thrust Luther's name into prominence throughout ecclesiastical circles in every European land and throughout the German populace.

Luther's was an age of urgent and ardent expectations. Humanists longed for the restoration of good learning—and thus for societal order and well-being. Exhibiting various degrees of apocalyptic dreaming, the common people yearned for a new age.[2] A crisis of pastoral care also

1. Ulrich Zwingli, letter to Oswald Myconius, 4 January 1520, in *Huldreich Zwinglis Sämtliche Werke* 7:250 (*CR* 94); Ulrich Zasius, letter to Zwingli, 13 November 1519 (ibid., 222), cites another reference in Zwingli's correspondence that is similar but no longer extant.

2. Robin Bruce Barnes, *Prophecy and Gnosis: Apocalypticism in the Wake of the Lutheran Reformation* (Stanford: Stanford University Press, 1988), esp. 19–30.

gripped Western Christendom, and many were listening and looking for God's direct intervention in their lives.

Onto such a stage stumbled this terrified sinner, the reluctant student mounting the steps of academe at the order of his superiors. He had become a moderately successful young man at an undistinguished university at the edge of civilization. He was beginning to gain the respect of other scholars across Germany.[3] In 1515 and 1516 he advanced suggestions for a reshaping of academic theology in both form and content. To test his ideas, he composed theses on Aristotelian theology and Pauline thought for academic disputations.[4] These theses called into question fundamental paradigms of the theological establishment which had shaped his mind. That mind was on the move, and he hoped to bring the church with him through the normal professorial channels of academic debate.

The Beginnings of the Reformation

Luther himself would later regard another set of theses prepared for academic disputation as the first and critical step on the path which led to his recognition as a prophet—and a host of similar images. He prepared those theses, the famous Ninety-Five, on the subject of indulgences at the end of October 1517, and thus, in his words, "I got into these turmoils by accident and not by will or intention."[5] In the preface to the first volume of the Wittenberg edition of his Latin works, published in 1545, he sketched the beginnings of his Reformation. There he pointed to the theses on indulgences as the juncture at which his ideas generated events which changed the Western world.[6] There he made it clear that these events were set in motion by his conflict with the papacy.

It is impossible to determine whether Luther in these theses was fully and forthrightly setting forth his convictions regarding indulgences. He was under no compulsion to do so as he composed theses for academic disputation. This genre was designed by intellectuals who used it to

3. Helmar Junghans, *Der junge Luther und die Humanisten* (Göttingen: Vandenhoeck & Ruprecht, 1985), 288–91; and Leif Grane, *Martinus Noster: Luther in the German Reform Movement, 1518–1521* (Mainz: Zabern, 1994), 147–87.

4. Above all, the theses Luther prepared for Bartholomaeus Bernhardi, "Quaestio de viribus et voluntate hominis sine gratia disputata," *WA* 1:145–51, and those which at Luther's prompting Franz Günther composed for his own promotion, "Disputatio contra scholasticam theologiam," *WA* 1:224–28.

5. *WA* 54:180.2–4; *LW* 34:328.

6. *WA* 54:180.5–20; *LW* 34:329. On reactions to the publication of the Ninety-Five Theses, see Junghans, *Der junge Luther,* 292–93.

provoke discussion and to search for the truth, not to express it definitively. In addition, however accurate a picture of Luther's current theological development the theses may offer, they are not particularly significant as a milestone in that development.

But the Ninety-Five Theses are critically important in the unfolding of Luther's career—as well as in the advance of Western cultural history. They represent the first major use of the medium of print to alter the course of society. Although, as Elizabeth Eisenstein points out, the medieval church had already attempted to use the printing press to help promote the crusade against the Turks, Luther's was the first movement "fully to exploit its potential as a mass medium. It was also the first movement of any kind, religious or secular, to use the new presses for overt propaganda and agitation against an established institution."[7] As he wrote the theses, however, Luther did not realize that they were to become the first modern media event.

The dimensions of that inaugural explosion of printed material remain difficult to grasp even today. As he was fulminating against Johann Tetzel, little did Luther in his cell at the Black Cloister realize that these theses would be published and would bring him an international audience within weeks. By 1520 Luther had published some thirty tracts or books, and they had sold over six hundred thousand copies, according to one estimate.[8] Quickly his ideas were being read and digested, refashioned for and resold to clergy and laypeople alike. While Luther may not have always been understood as he wished to be understood, he was the "dominant publicist" during the crucial years of the early Reformation; more than 20 percent of the pamphlets published in Germany between 1500 and 1530 came from his pen (all obviously stemming from the latter half of that period).[9]

And yet Luther's call for reform could not have won widespread public support in sixteenth-century society simply through the new medium of print. Mark Edwards's observation is correct: the Reforma-

7. Elizabeth L. Eisenstein, *The Printing Press as an Agent of Change: Communications and Cultural Transformations in Early-Modern Europe,* 2 vols. (Cambridge: Cambridge University Press, 1979), 1:303–4.

8. Bernd Moeller, *Deutschland im Zeitalter der Reformation,* 2d ed. (Göttingen: Vandenhoeck & Ruprecht, 1981), 62; on the spread of Luther's message inside and outside Germany, see idem, "Das Berühmtwerden Luthers," *Zeitschrift für historische Forschung* 15 (1988): 65–92; idem, "Die Rezeption Luthers in der frühen Reformation," *Lutherjahrbuch* 57 (1990): 57–71; and idem, "Luther in Europe: His Works in Translation, 1517–46," in *Politics and Society in Reformation Europe: Essays for Sir Geoffrey Elton on His Sixty-Fifth Birthday,* ed. E. I. Kouri and Tom Scott (New York: St. Martin's, 1987), 235–51.

9. Mark U. Edwards Jr., *Printing, Propaganda, and Martin Luther* (Berkeley: University of California Press, 1994), 1–2, 172.

tion was an oral event—most of Luther's contemporaries heard the message rather than read it.[10] Often (in German lands, at least) preachers spread the new insights in some form or other before Luther's writings arrived.[11] Nevertheless, Edwards is also correct when he concludes that "the printed word played a crucial role in the early Reformation, and when multiplied by the effects of preaching and conversation, can be said to be a major factor in spreading a relatively coherent message throughout the German-speaking lands."[12] For "it broadcast the subversive messages [of Luther and other Reformers] with a rapidity that had been impossible before its invention. More than that, it allowed the central ideological leader, Martin Luther, to reach the 'opinion leaders' of the movement quickly, kept them all in touch with each other and with each other's experience and ideas, and allowed them to 'broadcast' their (relatively coordinated) program to a much larger and more geographically diverse audience than had ever been possible before."[13]

The printing press not only aided the spread of Luther's message, but also introduced him to the broader public. As the Ninety-Five Theses on indulgences appeared in print, Luther claimed with one stroke a place in the public eye of all Germany, of all of Western Christendom. Edwards asserts that Luther "is not simply one publicist within a larger constellation" but instead "the dominant publicist" of his era. And, Edwards continues, "he dominated to a degree that no other person to my knowledge has ever dominated a major propaganda campaign and mass movement since."[14] The printing press enabled a single intellectual with provocative ideas to play a public role never before possible. Colleagues and commoners could address and absorb his ideas because they circulated in print in an unprecedented manner. Luther's proclamation became more than the sharing of ideas; it became—his contemporaries observed—a historical watershed.

In later autobiographical observations Luther distinguished between the event, which led others to acclaim him as hero and prophet, and the ideas, which he came to believe were indeed a prophetic message from God. Those ideas, he recalled, were not yet completely shaped by the autumn of 1517. After rehearsing the battles which he

10. Ibid., 11, 37.

11. That this was not always the case is demonstrated by David P. Daniel, "Publishing the Reformation in Habsburg Hungary," in *Habent sua fata libelli, Books Have Their Own Destiny: Essays in Honor of Robert V. Schnucker,* ed. Robin B. Barnes, Robert A. Kolb, and Paul L. Presley (Kirksville, Mo.: Thomas Jefferson University Press, 1998), 47–60.

12. Edwards, *Printing*, 172.

13. Ibid., 7.

14. Ibid., xii.

had fought with officials of the church during the following two years, Luther noted, "Here, in my case, you may also see how hard it is to struggle out of and emerge from errors which have been confirmed by the whole world."[15] In 1519, as he began to lecture on the Psalms a second time (the first series had been delivered in 1513–15), he was leaving old misconceptions behind and finally coming to understand the concept of the righteousness of God, and the distinction between two kinds of human righteousness (in God's sight and in relation to other human creatures), which he claimed as late as 1535 was the heart of his theology.[16] So even before his prophetic message had assumed its mature form, his ideas had generated events which made him a hero to many.

The events which flowed from the posting of the theses on indulgences made Luther a figure of great renown. His contemporaries recognized the key role which the Ninety-Five Theses played in propelling Luther to this prominence. Almost without exception, his followers' reflections on the roots of the Reformation agreed with Luther's assessment of what had caused his rise to heroic status. The most important exception is Georg Spalatin, Luther's close friend and supporter, who was serving as secretary to Elector Frederick the Wise of Saxony at the time. His "Annals of the Reformation" began the story in the year 1518, when he accompanied Elector Frederick to the imperial diet at Augsburg. Thus he failed to comment on the Ninety-Five Theses. This may be due to the fact that Spalatin had had no direct involvement in the posting of the theses; he had been at the electoral court, not at the university, at the time. However, he was present at Augsburg. There, as a councilor of the prince, he had witnessed Luther's encounter with the papal representative Cardinal Cajetan and could place it in the larger context of the confrontation between the German nation, assembled in its diet, and the papacy. Part of this context was the diet's consideration of a set of grievances against Roman "oppression." Spalatin's account depicts Luther as a hero, advancing into Augsburg without a safe conduct, boldly defending the truth while deferentially respecting the cardinal. For Spalatin the Reformation—defined as the conflict between Luther and the papal party which refused to let God's Word rule in his church—began in the political setting of the German diet at Augsburg.[17]

15. *WA* 54:183.21–23; *LW* 34:333–34.

16. *WA* 40.1:40–51; 54:186.3–29; *LW* 26:4–12; 34:337.

17. "Georgii Spalatini, Annales Reformationis, oder Jahr-Buecher von der Reformation Lutheri," ed. Ernst Salomon Cyprian, in Wilhelm Ernst Tentzel, *Historischer Bericht vom Anfang und ersten Fortgang der Reformation Lutheri* (Leipzig: Gleditsch and Weidmann, 1718), 2:1–7.

A series of Spalatin's contemporaries presented another picture, however. For example, in his very brief introduction to the "state of religion and the commonwealth" under Charles V the Strassburg historian Johannes Sleidanus reported on the publication of the Ninety-Five Theses.[18] Friedrich Myconius, pastor in Gotha and, like Spalatin, a confidant of the Wittenberg Reformers, also dated the beginning of the Reformation in 1517 and expanded his recital of the events around the theses far beyond Sleidanus's short comment. After an introductory chapter on "how the papacy arose and how the Antichrist led Christianity astray," Myconius's account of the Reformation sketched the beginnings of Luther's career "as a learned monk devoted to the papistic doctrine." In reaction to the sale of indulgences arranged by Pope Leo X for the sake of Archbishop Albrecht of Mainz, however, Luther began his critique of the papacy. Luther's reaction to the peddling of indulgences arose out of his concern for his people, out of pastoral sensitivity. Luther alone was bold enough to voice the concerns which many held regarding the practice, Myconius suggested, but he did so in an orderly fashion, in letters to bishops and in academic disputation. However, within two weeks all of Germany and within a month all of Christianity had read his theses "as though the angels themselves carried the message."[19] This reflection of a devoted follower reveals more than merely Myconius's own conviction at a distance of twenty years. Almost immediately an electric excitement framed popular reactions to Luther's accidental intrusion into the public square. Luther's Reformation had begun with an air of the supernatural about it. In a world which had no experience of the potential power of the printing press, his instant impact on German ecclesiastical and political life seemed miraculous.

Luther's theology of the cross also shaped Myconius's reflections on the beginning of the Reformation. This theology taught that God reveals himself in the hiddenness of crib and cross, in the lowliest of human circumstances. Myconius pointed out that at the time of the indulgence controversy Luther was preaching in the humble structure of a tiny chapel on the grounds of the Augustinian monastery in Wittenberg. That chapel resembled artists' depictions of the stall in Bethlehem where Christ was born. "In this poor, miserable, wretched chapel God let his dear, holy gospel and the dear child Jesus be born again in these last times," Myconius wrote.[20] The parallels between God's decisive inter-

18. *Commentariorvm de statv religionis & Reipublicae, Carolo Quinto Caesare, Libri XXVI* (Strassburg: Theodosius Rihel, 1559), 1–2.

19. "Friderici Myconii, Historia Reformationis vom Jahr Christi 1517. bis 1542.," ed. Ernst Salomon Cyprian, in Tentzel, *Historischer Bericht,* 2:1–23.

20. Ibid., 24–25.

vention in human history in Jesus Christ and God's contemporary intervention in restoring Christ's message through Martin Luther's prophetic action were not to go unnoticed.

Luther's colleague Philip Melanchthon interpreted the initial stages of Luther's Reformation much as Luther had. He composed a brief overview of the Reformer's career for the second volume of the Wittenberg edition of Luther's Latin works (1546). He focused on Luther's struggles of faith as monk and professor in the 1510s, and he traced the beginning of the dawning of the gospel in his colleague's consciousness to Luther's encounter with an anonymous old monk who took Brother Martin aside and directed him to the words of the creed, "I believe in the remission of sins." The monk also pointed Luther to the comments of Bernard of Clairvaux on forgiveness through God's grace in Christ. Luther proceeded to study Paul and Augustine, Melanchthon wrote, but he continued to hang on to the Scholastic theologians Gabriel Biel, Jean Gerson, and William of Occam, whom he preferred to Thomas Aquinas and Duns Scotus.

Melanchthon sketched Luther's theological development as he lectured on Romans and then on Psalms in 1513–15 and again in 1519 (his second series of lectures on the Psalms). These latter lectures reveal "how, in the judgment of all pious and prudent people, after the long, dark night of the novel doctrine [of the papacy] the light arose." Luther had revived the proper distinction between law and gospel. He had refuted the terror which had reigned under the papacy's teaching that human works merit the remission of sins. After an extensive summary of Luther's proclamation of the gospel, Melanchthon wrote that "in the course of all this" Luther, provoked by "that most impudent sycophant, Tetzel," issued his propositions on indulgences. Melanchthon continues with a recounting of the conflicts which arose out of the dispute over indulgences in the succeeding years.[21] Thus his emphasis in this biographical sketch fell first on Luther's theological development and then on the course of events which it engendered. Those events flowed, Melanchthon was certain, out of the indulgence controversy. Thus the *Chronicle* of world history which his student Johannes Carion began, and which the Preceptor and his son-in-law Caspar Peucer continued to edit and update, gives October 31, 1517, as the beginning of the Reformation.[22]

Nikolaus von Amsdorf had shared the heady days of the indulgence controversy with Luther and Melanchthon as their colleague on the Wittenberg faculty. In 1555 he took pen in hand to introduce the second

21. *CR* 6:155–70.
22. Johannes Carion, *Chronica* (Wittenberg, 1532), fij^{r}.

attempt to issue Luther's collected works, the Jena edition. It was conceived as a corrective to the Wittenberg edition, in which the prefaces of Luther and Melanchthon mentioned above had appeared. Amsdorf did not offer his own biography of Luther in his preface to the Jena edition's first volume, but he did explain why its chronological presentation of Luther's writings was superior to the Wittenberg edition's topical ordering. The Reformer had not come to his most mature understanding of the gospel by 1517, the year of Luther's first significant publication, the Ninety-Five Theses. In the period covered by the first Jena volume, 1517–21, Luther had still taught "in papistic fashion," specifically, Amsdorf recalled, on the power of the popes and bishops, on the mass, and on communion in both kinds.[23] Nonetheless, Amsdorf concluded that even though Luther's prophetic message had not fully developed by that time, the events of 1517 had been critical in the course of the Reformation.

This opinion apparently was shared by Luther's students who had struggled through the events of the 1510s in Wittenberg. A decade later one of the brightest and best among them, Johann Agricola, ascribed the outbreak of the Reformation to the year 1517.[24] The next generation of Wittenberg students did the same.

Luther's later student and amanuensis Johann Aurifaber, the first editor of the Reformer's correspondence, drew a similar picture of the beginning of the Reformation. In the preface to the first volume of his collection of Luther's letters, he placed Luther in the line of proclaimers and witnesses of the Word of God that stretched through Isaiah the prophet and Paul the apostle into the sixteenth century. Preachers of the Word are always under attack by the enemies of the truth, Aurifaber observed; Luther's students had learned well that conflict between God and Satan is always being played out in the history of the church.[25] Methodius had had to fight Origen; Augustine had had to battle Pelagius; Bernard of Clairvaux had not been able to avoid his opponents among the monks. Luther could not have expected anything but conflict as a teacher of God's Word.

Aurifaber began his sketch with Luther's receiving his doctorate. Thereafter, "Luther did not spend his time in leisure; rather, he spent his time meditating and reading Scripture, so that he weakened his body with his studying, vigils, fasting, and prayer, until the contro-

23. *Der Erste Teil aller Bu[e]cher vnd Schrifften des thewren/seligen Mans Doct: Mart: Lutheri/vom XVII. jar an/bis auff das XXII.* (Jena: Christian Rödinger, 1555), preface.

24. *Epistola S. Pavli ad Titum . . .* (Hagenau: Johannes Secer, 1530), E3^r.

25. On Luther's understanding of the conflict between God and Satan in human history, see John M. Headley, *Luther's View of Church History* (New Haven: Yale University Press, 1963), 19–41, 59–69.

versy over indulgences was set in motion by Tetzel, during which he was liberated by God from the prison and torture chamber of consciences." Aurifaber paused to remind his readers of the state of Christendom when Luther "was raised up to cleanse the church from the doctrines of demons" (1 Tim. 4:1) which had plagued it during its "Egyptian and Babylonian captivity." The showdown with Tetzel had initiated the process of Luther's liberation, although that confrontation was important only because it led to the confrontation between Luther and the papal theologians, above all Cajetan at Augsburg in 1518.[26]

Aurifaber, like Amsdorf, saw Luther's theology as developing along with his career. He recognized as well that the events which followed the publication of the Ninety-Five Theses initiated Luther's rise to prominence as a hero in the battle against the papacy. He also recognized that it was during this controversy that Luther's theological liberation released him from the torture chamber in which medieval doctrine had placed his conscience. This liberation permitted him to function as a prophet of God's Word.

For Aurifaber, like Myconius and Melanchthon, the ideas and the events which made Luther God's tool were inseparably linked. These earliest accounts of Luther's life focus on the unfolding events of the Reformation, not on the development of his thought. In the view of his contemporary followers and their immediate heirs Martin Luther's conflicts with papal opponents had thrust him onto the public stage as a hero, a man of prophetic action; he was not a secluded monastic thinker. His dramatic advent paved the way for him to play a decisive leadership role in church and society. For he presented his message as a challenge to the old paradigms for theology and for ecclesiastical life and organization.

From Monk and Teacher to Prophet and Angel

The course of events which gushed forth from Luther's critique of indulgences propelled him to center stage in the view of European intellectuals and the German populace. The reasons for his fame or notoriety differed from one group to another. The older humanists were attracted to his call for reform because they believed any call for reform would support their own. At first the scholars of Erasmus's generation had no idea that their concept of moral and institutional reform would not coincide precisely with Luther's concept of doctrinal reform. So the

26. *Epistolarvm Reverendi patris Domini D. Martini Lutheri, Tomus primus* (Jena: Christian Rödinger, 1556), aij–[*v][r].

senior representatives of the humanist movement praised Luther with the rhetorical forms at their disposal during the later years of the 1510s. They thus influenced his own self-consciousness as well as the intellectual leaders' general appreciation for his position.[27]

In similar fashion the German populace enthusiastically greeted Luther's expression of grievance against Rome as the same as their own. On the eve of the Diet of Worms in 1521 the papal legate Jerome Aleander commented, "All of Germany is in an utter uproar; nine-tenths of the people are shouting 'Luther,' and the other tenth—if Luther is of no consequence to them—at least have 'Death to the Roman court!' as their slogan."[28] It is likely that most did not see a significant difference between their position and that of Luther. Luther was acting as a leader of reform, and neither intellectuals nor common people were at that point too concerned about his definition of reform. Initially quite unaware, he was connecting with the deeply felt apocalyptic hopes of peasants and humanists alike.[29] Both were beginning to codify his image.

Robert Scribner suggests that there were three aspects to the earliest glimpses afforded to most Germans of their new hero and prophet, glimpses given by illustrations published in popular tracts. Luther was depicted "as monk, as doctor, as man of the Bible."[30] Alongside these religious themes, and intertwined with them in the sacralized culture of late medieval Germany, were the themes of national educator and liberator. Humanists and political leaders alike were delighted to ascribe these roles to Luther as they hailed him as hero and phoenix. The poet Hans Sachs looked to Luther as the Wittenberg Nightingale whose song had awakened Christendom to the threat from the wolf, the papacy, and had called sinners to repentance and the comfort of the gospel. The painter Albrecht Dürer praised him as "a man gifted with the

27. Junghans, *Der junge Luther,* 288–318; Grane, *Martinus Noster,* 147–66. On the differences between the humanists of Erasmus's generation and those of Melanchthon's, see Lewis W. Spitz, "The Third Generation of German Renaissance Humanists," in *Aspects of the Renaissance: A Symposium,* ed. Archibald R. Lewis (Austin: University of Texas Press, 1967), 105–21. Junghans (p. 316) points out that Erwin Mühlhaupt's dating of Luther's realization of his prophetic role (Mühlhaupt finds no such self-consciousness before 1521 and only a gradual acceptance of this role before 1530) is much too late. See Erwin Mühlhaupt, "Martin Luther oder Thomas Müntzer—und wer ist der rechte Prophet?" *Luther* 45 (1974): 55–71.

28. Martin Brecht, *Martin Luther: His Road to Reformation, 1483–1521,* trans. James L. Schaaf (Philadelphia: Fortress, 1981), 439.

29. Will Erich Peuckert, *Die Grosse Wende, Geistesgeschichte und Volkskunde* (Darmstadt: Wissenschaftliche Buchgesellschaft, 1966), 25–474.

30. Robert W. Scribner, *For the Sake of Simple Folk: Popular Propaganda for the German Reformation* (Cambridge: Cambridge University Press, 1981), 15.

Holy Spirit."[31] Hans Holbein hailed him as the "German Hercules" in an illustration published in 1523. Dressed in monk's habit but equipped with a lion's pelt and a club reminiscent of the mythical hero Hercules, Luther is depicted assaulting Jacob von Hochstraten, a Dominican professor at Cologne. He has already laid low Aristotle, Thomas Aquinas, William of Occam, Nicholas of Lyra, Peter Lombard, and Duns Scotus. The accompanying tract developed in greater detail the heroic acts of the German Hercules in opposing papal oppression.[32] Similar treatises echoed this theme and placed it in starkly national terms, feeding on German grievances against Italian exploitation which had become a common feature of German public discussion in the late Middle Ages.[33] "Hero" is a word with many meanings. Luther himself developed a concept of the *vir heroicus* as a chosen instrument to whom God gives a special assignment to accomplish divine goals, particularly in times when the normal functioning of human institutions does not serve human need.[34] For many of his followers Luther clearly fit this description.

Luther with Nimbus and the Dove (1520)
(Lutherhalle, Wittenberg)

Indeed, inseparable from—but even more important than—these strains of humanistic praise and proud national accolades heaped on Luther were the attributes accorded him as a man of God. To return to Scribner's categories: "Luther as a monk is he who lives a pious Christian life; as doctor he who is a pious teacher; as man of the Bible he who points to saving doctrine."[35] Scribner comments, "So powerful

31. Hans Preuss, *Martin Luther: Der Prophet* (Gütersloh: Bertelsmann, 1933), 59–63; on Sachs's poem of 1523, see *Hans Sachsens ausgewählte Werke* (Frankfurt/Main: Insel, 1961), 1:12–21. On Sachs and the Reformation, see Bernd Balzer, *Bürgerliche Reformationspropaganda: Die Flugschriften des Hans Sachs in den Jahren 1523–1525* (Stuttgart: Metzler, 1973).

32. Scribner, *Simple Folk,* 32–34.

33. Ibid., 34–36; see also Andrea Körsgen-Wiedeburg, "Das Bild Martin Luthers in den Flugschriften der frühen Reformationszeit," in *Festgabe für Ernst Walter Zeeden zum 60. Geburtstag am 14. Mai 1976,* ed. Horst Rabe, Hansgeorg Molitor, and Hans-Christoph Rublack (Münster: Aschendorff, 1976), 162–64.

34. Gustaf Wingren, *Luther on Vocation,* trans. Carl C. Rasmussen (Philadelphia: Muhlenberg, 1957), 156–61.

35. Scribner, *Simple Folk,* 17.

are these signs that they identify Luther even when any likeness is lacking."[36]

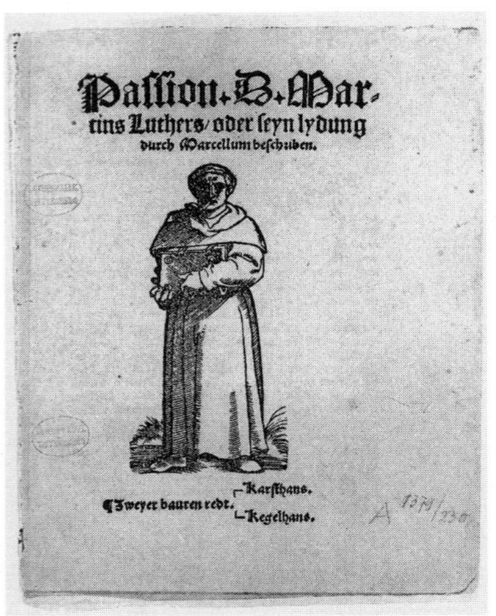

Passion D. Martins Luthers . . . (1521) (Lutherhalle, Wittenberg)

Both in illustrations and in the narrative of early tracts Luther was depicted as a monk who could be ranked with the saints. His likeness appeared with nimbus and with the Holy Spirit in the form of a dove, the symbol of divine inspiration associated with Saint Gregory and other great teachers of the church.[37] The tracts described his personality and character in saintly terms.[38] In 1521 a tract appeared which drew parallels between Luther's trial at Worms and the passion of Christ.[39]

Few went that far. Nonetheless, the apocalyptic restlessness of the late Middle Ages seized on Luther as the fulfilment of its hopes for dramatic change in church and society. Already in the period before and directly after his appearance at the Diet of Worms, various tracts identified him as God's chosen vessel, God's instrument and tool, the herald of true teaching, the true pope and apostle, the good shepherd who Ezekiel had prophesied would tend the people of Christ (Ezek. 34:22–23). He was greeted as a new Daniel and above all a new Elijah.[40] Comparisons of Luther with the biblical prophets were particularly notable, for they fed on a medieval tradition of expectation of prophet-led deliverance from woes of all kinds. The grand historical design promulgated by Joachim of Fiore was only the most prominent of several eschatological plans for a new world under God's rule. In the decades immediately preceding Luther's arrival at Wittenberg, such expectations had been cultivated by popular preachers like Johann Geiler von Kaisersberg and speculative astronomers like Johannes Lichtenberger. Luther fell heir

36. Ibid., 15.

37. Ibid., 17–20. For an elaboration of later regard for Luther as a substitute for the medieval panoply of saints, see Robert Kolb, *For All the Saints: Changing Perceptions of Martyrdom and Sainthood in the Lutheran Reformation* (Macon, Ga.: Mercer University Press, 1987), 103–38.

38. Körsgen-Wiedeburg, "Das Bild Martin Luthers," 154–56. See also Marc Lienhard, "Held oder Ungeheuer? Luthers Gestalt und Tat im Lichte der zeitgenössischen Flugschriftenliteratur," *Lutherjahrbuch* 45 (1978): 56–79.

39. For a summary of this tract see Scribner, *Simple Folk,* 21, or Lienhard, "Held oder Ungeheuer?" 64.

40. Körsgen-Wiedeburg, "Das Bild Martin Luthers," 156–60.

to the yearnings for a prophet which filled many German hearts at the beginning of the sixteenth century.[41]

Scribner cites the treatise published in 1523 by Haug Marschalck of Augsburg as dramatic evidence of how the popular medieval eschatology was applied to the Wittenberg movement. Marschalck associated Luther with the prophecies about Emperor Frederick II, who was widely regarded as an eschatological savior about to return from his grave to reform Christian Europe. The Augsburg pamphleteer depicted Elector Frederick the Wise of Saxony as the legendary Emperor Frederick II, who permits Christ to return from the grave in which the papacy has placed him. Seeking Christ or the Word of God, three Marys come to the grave. These three latter-day Marys, sent forth with God's Word in the Scriptures, are identified as the three Wittenbergers, Luther, Melanchthon, and Andreas Karlstadt. Marschalck developed an acrostic of Luther's name which asserted that he was Elijah and Enoch, who would expose the Antichrist, and the Rabbi who would master all those who had defiled the Scriptures.[42] Reconstruction of the true church would follow the destruction of the false, and both would take place through proclamation of the Word. The prophetic assignment to destroy the enemies of God's truth, the papacy and its followers, was as important in this and similar tracts as was the prophetic assignment to proclaim the Word of God properly.[43] Luther, then, was being defined as both a heroic prophet and as a teaching prophet already in 1523.

Beyond Elijah and Enoch, the angel of Revelation 14:6–7 stood ready for use as a symbol of Luther's significance. In 1522 his fellow Augustinian Michael Stiefel published a song entitled "On the Christ-Formed, Properly Grounded Teaching of Doctor Martin Luther." Luther's message struck a sympathetic chord in Stiefel's mind, strongly influenced by late medieval apocalyptic longing as he was. The first of the thirty-two stanzas of his poetic appeal for Luther's cause played on Luther's name as it recalled the angel that John had described in Revelation 14: "John wrote for us of an angel who would set forth God's Word with complete clarity [gantz luter offenbar]." Stiefel set the stage for an eschatological battle in which this angel was to engage the wolf in God's stall, that is, the pope. A reference to Daniel's apocalyptic visions (8:26) makes it quite clear that Stiefel believed contemporary events were transpiring in an eschatological setting. Nonetheless, Stiefel did not lift

41. Preuss, *Martin Luther,* 4–72.

42. Scribner, *Simple Folk,* 20–21. See also Preuss, *Martin Luther,* 24–36; Peuckert, *Die Grosse Wende,* 606–13.

43. Körsgen-Wiedeburg, "Das Bild Martin Luthers," 160–62.

Luther to the heavenly plane. Instead, he interpreted the angel as someone who would come "with an eternal gospel to proclaim to those who dwell on earth" (Rev. 14:6). For Stiefel, God was working within the context of human history. He was sending his angel to proclaim the gospel and to confront his foes. Luther had done both with his fearless confession of the truth at Worms.

Stiefel then continued with a summary of the message which the angel is proclaiming. His strong voice, free of all deceit, first terrifies the listener by describing "what Adam is." He proclaims the law in order that he might awaken great dread. The following ten stanzas treat the Ten Commandments. Twelve more stanzas then present the angel's gospel of salvation by grace through faith in Christ. A concluding note to the reader emphasizes Luther's faithfulness to the Scriptures.[44] Stiefel's image of Luther included both the apocalyptic backdrop of the prophecy of Revelation and specific reference to his actions and his teaching. He was opposing the pope, and he had confessed the faith boldly at Worms; he was teaching the distinction of law and gospel, of God's wrath and his mercy in Christ. Stiefel's Luther was more than a hero. He was a prophet and more than a prophet. He fulfilled God's promise of angelic power in proclaiming the divine Word.

At the time this Augustinian monk was singing the Reformer's praises, the humanist and cathedral preacher of Augsburg Urbanus Rhegius had begun to engage Luther's ideas. In 1521 he acclaimed Luther an undaunted witness to the truth, an Elijah sent by God; in 1523 he identified him as one who conveyed the light of Christ.[45] Such impressions, fashioned by the force of the Reformer's words in print, Rhegius gained from afar. His first meeting with Luther made an even more dramatic impact upon him. As Rhegius journeyed from Augsburg to assume the post of superintendent of the churches of Braunschweig-Lüneburg in 1530, he stopped to visit Luther at the Coburg. "He remains a theologian for the whole world; of that I am certain. I know him now far better than before I had seen and heard him myself," Rhegius wrote to one friend. To another he simply confessed, "Luther had always been great in my eyes. Then he became the greatest."[46] Luther conveyed to his contemporaries the sense that he was

44. Stiefel's text is found in Philipp Wackernagel, ed., *Das deutsche Kirchenlied von der ältesten Zeit bis zu Anfang des XVII. Jahrhunderts,* 5 vols. (Leipzig: Teubner, 1864–77), 3:74–75; on Stiefel, see Barnes, *Prophecy and Gnosis,* 54, 128, 188–201.

45. Cited in Hellmut Zschoch, *Reformatorische Existenz und konfessionelle Identität: Urbanus Rhegius als evangelischer Theologe in den Jahren 1520 bis 1530* (Tübingen: Mohr, 1995), 32–33, 39, 58.

46. Ibid., 351.

larger than life. Not all of them, of course, accepted his message. Defenders of the old faith sharply criticized his departure from medieval norms, and some of them expressed their conviction that Luther was an agent of the devil, a perversion, and a monster.[47] Their counterattacks, however, failed to convince a sizable readership. The acclamation of intellectuals and common people alike created a positive appraisal which arrested the many negative myths his opponents were fashioning.

This public approbation of Luther as hero and prophet found some echo in Luther's own estimate of himself and his calling from God.[48] He did not regard himself as a Herculean hero. But he did assume the epistolary style of Saint Paul as early as 1522, and he drew parallels between the career of the apostle and his own career, moving out of works-righteousness into the proclamation of the gospel of God's grace.[49] Furthermore, he could call himself the prophet of the Germans, an apostle and evangelist in German territory, an Isaiah or a Jeremiah.[50] Yet Luther did not always possess this prophetic self-confidence. He often engaged in self-examination. He was plagued by repeated doubts about his own person. Yet he could also state, "I do not say that I am a prophet. . . . But if I am not a prophet, I am nevertheless certain for myself that the Word of God is with me and not with them, for I indeed have Scripture on my side."[51]

Luther's concept of himself as a prophet differed, therefore, from the medieval eschatological vision of the prophet who was to come. His claims to the calling of apostle or prophet rested solely on his proclamation of the gospel. For him, what mattered was God's Word. It had brought the universe into being, and it had pronounced the forgiveness of sins upon him. To have the Word was to have the abundant life which Christ restored to the people of God. Luther had no illusions

47. Above all, Johannes Cochlaeus worked on creating such countermyths regarding Luther; see p. 87 n. 28. See also Lienhard, "Held oder Ungeheuer?" On the early Roman Catholic opposition to Luther, see Edwards, *Printing,* 28–37, 57–82, 149–62; and David V. N. Bagchi, *Luther's Earliest Opponents: Catholic Controversialists, 1518–1525* (Minneapolis: Fortress, 1991).

48. Junghans, *Der junge Luther,* 304–13.

49. Timothy J. Wengert, "Martin Luther's Movement toward an Apostolic Awareness as Reflected in His Early Letters," *Lutherjahrbuch* 61 (1994): 71–92. For the later development of Luther's comparison of himself with Paul, see Mark U. Edwards Jr., *Luther and the False Brethren* (Stanford: Stanford University Press, 1975), 112–26; and Preuss, *Martin Luther,* 37.

50. Karl Holl, "Luthers Urteile über sich selbst," in *Gesammelte Aufsätze zur Kirchengeschichte,* vol. 1, *Luther* (Tübingen: Mohr [Siebeck], 1921), 392. This essay is available in English in *Interpreters of Luther: Essays in Honor of Wilhelm Pauck,* ed. Jaroslav Pelikan (Philadelphia: Fortress, 1968), 9–34.

51. Holl, "Luthers Urteile," 382, citing *WA* 7:313.17–29.

about being Enoch or Elijah returned from the grave. In 1522 he claimed, in his Church Postil sermon on Hebrews 1:1–12, that Elijah would not return bodily from the grave. Instead, "it would be his spirit, that is, the Word of God would be brought forward once again, as it is appearing at the present time."[52] What counted for Luther—and what linked him in his own mind with Elijah—was the Word of God in their mouths. He was firmly convinced that his tongue and pen proclaimed the same Word of God which Elijah had proclaimed. Only because of this could he place himself in the ranks of prophets and apostles. Thus, much of the medieval notion of the prophet was not of importance for Luther. He claimed to possess no special gift beyond the Word which had been present in the mouths of the biblical prophets. His estimate of himself, as constructive promoter of the gospel or as destructive critic of false teaching, was always and only connected with the Word of God.

Luther's preface to the Wittenberg edition of his Latin works shows that he saw himself as a prophetic man of action with a positive mission of preaching God's truth embodied in Christ and a negative mission of opposing the enemies of the faith, who were embodied in the papal system. His followers affirmed the negative mission of prophetic criticism against the established ecclesiastical order. They accepted his name as their own badge of faith against the papacy as they spread his teaching, which they believed had been handed down by the prophets and the apostles. They also recognized his positive prophetic powers as they turned to him for precise and specific definition of the gospel as it pertained to a host of problems which they encountered in their own lives and the lives of their congregations or principalities. In letters and memoranda Luther offered authoritative answers to such problems. Alone, or with his Wittenberg colleagues, he gave counsel on marriage, political alliances and resistance, on usury and the doctrine of election, on ecclesiastical policy (as in the case of Martin Bucer's plan for the introduction of the Reformation in Cologne).[53]

For Luther's followers the defining authority of popes and councils and bishops no longer determined the interpretation of the Scripture.

52. *WA* 10.1.1:248.24–28, the Church Postil sermon on the epistle for Christmas Day, Hebrews 1:1–12; see also *WA* 10.1.2:191–97, the sermon for the fourth Sunday in Advent, on John 1:19–28; and *WA* 21:38–39, the Winter postil sermon on John 1:19–28.

53. See, e.g., Luther's counsel to Johann Lüdicke, pastor in Cottbus, 2 February 1539, regarding resistance to secular government, *WA Br* 8:364–68; his counsel on usury to Sebastian Müller of Mansfeld, 26 July 1543, *WA Br* 10:349–52; and his counsel on marriage matters to the city council of Torgau, 8 June 1543, *WA Br* 10:325. Often his colleagues joined him in exercising such authority; see, e.g., *WA Br* 10:103–10, 189–95, 336–42, 347–49; 11:16–19, 250–51.

The old tradition which had adjudicated disputes over the meaning and application of the Bible was laid aside. Luther's opinions assumed adjudicatory authority among his followers. Luther's words replaced the authority of popes and councils to determine disputes among various interpretations of the Scriptures. Eike Wolgast speaks of a "quasi-papalization" of Luther in the drive even before his death to gather the authoritative texts he had composed: "The authority of the living teacher was transformed into the written authority of the corpus of his works."[54] Compilation of his writings was necessary because of the authoritative function which his thought had assumed among some of his followers. For Luther's thought had become a secondary authority[55] which governed the interpretation of the primary authority for teaching in the church, the Bible.

Luther's thought became a secondary authority because his followers shared a humanistic appreciation for the spoken and the written word as presented by contemporaries, and at the same time they shared Luther's view of the nature of God's Word. Luther believed that the words of Scripture were not to be understood in a Platonic sense, as shadows of a heavenly reality, as signposts merely offering information about God's activity elsewhere. He believed that God's power actually rests in the gospel (Rom. 1:16), even as it is spoken or written by contemporaries. That belief permitted the ascription of authority to Luther's faithful repetition and application of the biblical Word. In addition, Luther's heroic confrontation of the Roman church confirmed for his followers that he played a key role in God's directing the life of the church. They had no problems transferring authority to him and to his writings. Luther's prophetic office, his living voice, expressed the gospel for his followers.

54. Eike Wolgast, "Biographie als Autoritätsstiftung: Die ersten evangelischen Lutherbiographien," in *Biographie zwischen Renaissance und Barock: Zwölf Studien,* ed. Walter Berschin (Heidelberg: Mattes, 1993), 43. See also the development of this point in Robert Kolb, "Die Umgestaltung und theologische Bedeutung des Lutherbildes im späten 16. Jahrhundert," in *Die lutherische Konfessionalisierung in Deutschland: Wissenschaftliches Symposion des Vereins für Reformationsgeschichte 1988,* ed. Hans-Christoph Rublack (Gütersloh: Mohn, 1992), 202–31.

55. Throughout this study the term "secondary authority" refers to what Lutheran orthodoxy from the middle of the seventeenth century (according to Arthur Carl Piepkorn, "Suggested Principles for a Hermeneutics of the Lutheran Symbols," *Concordia Theological Monthly* 29 [1958]: 7) called the *norma normata,* the means of adjudicating differences in interpretation of the biblical text, which had primary authority in the church as the *norma normans.* All Christians designate and utilize such an adjudicating authority, even if they do not formally recognize it. The term "prophetic authority" or "authoritative prophet" is here used to designate Luther as the *norma normata* for some of his followers.

Burying and Praising Luther

Then Luther died. With his death, however, the recognition of his prophetic action and his prophetic authority did not die. As they mourned his passing, Luther's followers expressed their confidence that he had been and remained God's chosen tool for the revelation of the gospel in the latter days of the earth's existence. The focus of the myth remained on Luther's person and his status as a prophet—even if the exercise of his authority would shift to the publications he had bequeathed his followers.

Three friends had been with Luther in his last hours as he lay dying in Eisleben. One of them, Johann Aurifaber, referred to Luther's death in terms used at the departure of the prophet Elijah (2 Kings 2:11). He reported to the ecclesiastical superintendent of Leipzig, Johann Pfeffinger, that "this man, the horseman and chariot of Israel," had come to Eisleben to negotiate peace among Mansfeld's feuding counts.[56] The other two friends present at Luther's death, Justus Jonas, former colleague in Wittenberg and at the time pastor in Halle, and Michael Coelius, former student and then court preacher at Mansfeld, preached funeral sermons while his body yet lay in Eisleben. Jonas preached the day following his death, and Coelius preached the day after that. Thereafter his body was taken back to Wittenberg, where his colleagues Philip Melanchthon and Johannes Bugenhagen spoke of their comrade and mentor before a large assembly of students and friends. Familiar themes emerged in these sermons and orations.

Jonas focused first, in good humanistic fashion, on the genius of his friend, which colleagues had recognized at Wittenberg from the beginning of his career there. Jonas singled out Luther's translation of the Bible and his teaching good German to the chancellery. Then he went on to remind his hearers that throughout history the death of the "highest and greatest prophets and men of God" had ushered in evil times and harsh judgment. "Therefore, a terrible judgment upon Germany will certainly follow the death of this man, Doctor Martin, if it does not improve, and that judgment will fall particularly upon the godless, obstinate, despairing papists." Jonas also repeated the long-held contention that "our dear father Doctor Martin Luther" had fulfilled the prophecy which the Czech reformer John Huss had uttered at the Council of Constance as he awaited burning at the stake in 1415: "One hundred years later a swan will come, which they will not be able to roast" as they had the goose ("Huss" in Czech means "goose"). Luther fulfilled

56. The letter is dated the day of Luther's death, 18 February 1546; its text is found in Christof Schubart, *Die Berichte über Luthers Tod und Begräbnis* (Weimar: Böhlau, 1917), 12.

the apocalyptic expectation enfolded in the prophecy attributed to Huss, and he was given place in the line of prophets reaching back to Noah, Elijah, and Elisha.[57]

Coelius agreed with Jonas. He praised Luther as a man who had exercised the same office as had the Old Testament prophets, John the Baptist, and the apostles in their times. "For as indeed these were given certain special gifts by God before him, as far as the office is concerned, he was truly for our time a true Elijah and Jeremiah, a John the forerunner before the day of the Lord, or an apostle." He had stood against the papal Antichrist and all error, heresy, sects, and idolatry. Much like Elijah in his day, so Luther had struck the idol of the papal indulgence to the ground. As Elijah had slain the priests of Baal, so "this man of God" with the sword of the Word overthrew the priests of the popish mass. Like John the Baptist he had proclaimed true Christian repentance. Coelius gave God thanks for enlightening and raising up "this faithful servant."[58]

Similar sentiments echoed from the pulpit in Wittenberg within days. There both Bugenhagen, Luther's pastor and colleague at the university, and Melanchthon, who had joined Luther at Wittenberg and in reformation in 1518, spoke over his bier. Bugenhagen repeated the themes which had been routinely used to describe Luther's work: his opposition to idolatry and to human opinions of the papacy and his proclamation of the gospel of Jesus Christ, which had been God's blessing to German lands and lands far beyond. Bugenhagen called Luther a "great teacher and prophet, a reformer sent by God to the church," and "this holy apostle and prophet of Christ, our preacher and evangelist in the German lands." He did not hesitate to identify Luther with the angel of Revelation 14:16–17, whose message, "Fear God and give him honor," was Luther's message of law and gospel "through which the whole of Scripture is opened and Christ is recognized as our righteousness and eternal life." As Luther's epitaph Bugenhagen repeated a phrase from "our dear Father Doctor Martin" himself: "Pestis eram vivus, moriens tua mors ero, Papa! [Pope, while alive I was your pestilence; dead, I will be your death]."[59]

Philip Melanchthon's oration struck many of the same themes, and yet it was different. Melanchthon did not hesitate to add a note of criti-

57. *Zwo Trostliche Predigt vber der Leich D. Doct. Martini Luther zu Eissleben den XIX. vnd XX. Februarii gethan durch D. Doct: Justum Jonam, M. Michaelem Celium, Anno. 1546* (Wittenberg: Georg Rhau, 1546), Aiij^{v}–C^{r}, Diij^{r}–[Eij]^{r}.

58. Ibid., [Eiij]^{r}–[Iiiij]^{r}.

59. *Eine Christliche Predigt Vber der Leich vnd Begrabnus/Weiland des Ehrwurdigen/ Achtbarn vnd Hochgelarten Herrn D. Martini Lutheri Seeliger Gedechtnis . . .* (Wittenberg: Paul Helwig, 1546).

cism, suggesting that Luther had had his rough edges, negative qualities that were in fact necessary in the time in which God called him to serve. Melanchthon focused above all on Luther's place in the chain of witnesses to God's truth. He traced God's messengers through the patriarchs from Adam to Joseph, who brought pure teaching to Egypt. The chain continued through the prophets from Moses to Elijah and Jeremiah to Jonah, and then to the Maccabees and John the Baptist. Arriving at Christ and the apostles, the witness progressed through patristic and medieval figures down to Bernard of Clairvaux and Johann Tauler.

Melanchthon then reviewed the "great issues of the truth" which Luther had addressed in his proclamation. First, he had brought to the light of day the true, pure Christian teaching of the Scriptures against the darkness of the monks' doctrine of repentance. He had declared the Pauline teaching which explains how human creatures become righteous through faith. He had revealed the proper distinction between law and gospel and the distinction between the righteousness of the Spirit and outward temporal discipline. He had taught the church once again how it should call on God and combat pagan doubt in the heart. He had taught what true works are and how to live the Christian life apart from the ceremonial practices which the papacy had imposed as a way to salvation. He had translated the Scriptures into the German language "so clearly that this translation offers the reader much more light than do many other commentaries." Melanchthon repeated Erasmus's praise of Luther's interpretation of the Bible as well. He also cited Erasmus's suggestion that Luther's coarse ways were necessary medicine for such a time as his.[60]

Within four months of his oration Melanchthon's preface to the second volume of the Wittenberg edition of Luther's Latin works was published. Here he sketched the course of the Reformer's life. He worked very hard to fit Luther into the mold of the biblical humanist. Wherever he did not fit, Melanchthon suggested that the absence of humanist refinement may have caused the rough edges. And as in his funeral oration Melanchthon was once again more willing than others to mention Luther's shortcomings.[61] Nonetheless, for Melanchthon, too, Luther was "our revered father and our most beloved preceptor," and he was "the horseman and chariot of Israel," as Philip said when he informed the student body at Wittenberg of Luther's death.[62]

60. "Oratio in funere D. Martini Lutheri," *CR* 11:726–34. See also James Michael Weiss, "Erasmus at Luther's Funeral: Melanchthon's Commemorations of Luther in 1546," *Sixteenth Century Journal* 16.1 (1985): 91–114.

61. *CR* 6:155–70.

62. *CR* 6:58–59 (19 Feb. 1546).

Frailties and faults were not mentioned in the poetic paeans penned on the occasion of Luther's death. Writing again of his Wittenberg Nightingale, Hans Sachs expressed his sadness over the departure of his "precious hero," the conqueror and "true apostolic battler" who had opposed popes, bishops, kings, and princes.[63] Erasmus Alber, a former student of Luther's and now a pastor in Brandenburg, composed "A New Song, Of the Holy Man of God, Our Dear Father, Doctor Martin Luther, Departed in God," in which he rehearsed the deeds and the message of

> the dear, pious Luther, tender,
> the Germans' true prophet,
> who correctly taught us God's Word.[64]

Other poets expressed similar sentiments.[65] They mourned the loss of the teacher who had opposed Christ's enemies and who had proclaimed his message.

The populace was longing for some sort of apocalyptic interruption of the life they were enduring. The intellectual elite were yearning for signs from God that the golden age was going to return. The printing press enabled a little-known monk's call for reform to stimulate simultaneous discussion among his colleagues even though they were geographically dispersed. It is little wonder that Martin Luther's printed voice stirred up a hornet's nest with those whose interests he attacked. It is also little wonder that this voice could strike chords of response in the common people and in humanist circles. Both were hoping for a prophet, looking for a teacher, and yearning for a hero.

63. The text is found in Ernst Walter Zeeden, *Martin Luther und die Reformation im Urteil des deutschen Luthertums* (Freiburg/B: Herder, 1952), 2:16–19.

64. In Wackernagel, ed., *Das deutsche Kirchenlied,* 3:896–98 (published in 1546).

65. E.g., Johann Friderich Petsch, whose "A Fine Christian Song, on the Worthy Doctor Martin Luther and His Teaching," which reviewed Luther's career of opposition to the papacy and of proclamation of Christ's grace, was published by Georg Rhau in Wittenberg in 1546 (Wackernagel, ed., *Das deutsche Kirchenlied,* 3:975–76). Also worthy of mention are the hymns of Martin Schrot (ibid., 3:974–75) and Leonhart Kettner (ibid., 3:980).

2

The Prophet of God

Luther as the Authoritative Interpreter of God's Word

Therefore, a terrible judgment upon Germany will certainly follow the death of this man, Doctor Martin, if it does not improve.
Justus Jonas, funeral sermon for Luther

In the eyes of contemporaries Justus Jonas had been correct. His prophecy found fulfilment. After Luther's death evil times fell on Germany—on evangelical Germany at least. The opponents of Luther's message gathered their forces and sent armies into the field with the intention of ending once and for all support for the cause of Martin Luther. In 1521 Emperor Charles V had issued his Edict of Worms. In it he had condemned Luther and his followers. The emperor had pledged the powers of his government to the destruction and eradication of the Lutheran pestilence.[1] But other matters had postponed the execution of the edict. Charles had been forced to contend with the Turk and the pope, with France and with the nobles of his Iberian realms. It was not until 1546 that he was able to marshal troops from his Spanish and German domains to march against the princes and cities that were following and defending Luther's reform. In less than a year the Smalcald War had ended, with the leading Lutheran princes in the emperor's chains.

Luther's death resulted in a profound crisis of leadership precisely because he had not only provided leadership, but also exercised a special kind of authority for his followers. Under the best of circumstances no one could have replaced him, for no one else had demonstrated either the heroic prophetic qualities or the ability to teach the Word of God as charismatically as Luther had, and these two factors had supported his

1. *Luther in Worms, 1521–1971: Ein Quellenbuch,* ed. Joachim Rogge (Berlin: Evangelische Verlagsanstalt, 1971), 138–51.

exercise of prophetic authority. The events of and following the Smalcald War (June 1546–April 1547) robbed his colleague Philip Melanchthon of any chance he might have had to assume something like Luther's authority among the broad masses of their followers,[2] and certainly no one else among the Lutherans emerged to exercise that role in the confusion and controversy unleashed by the war and its aftermath.

In less than a year the troops of the emperor had defeated Elector John Frederick of Saxony and Landgrave Philip of Hesse, the leaders of the evangelical Smalcald League, in the battle of Mühlberg on April 24, 1547. Charles imprisoned them and handed over much of the elector's domains to the evangelical Duke Moritz of Saxony, who was both John Frederick's cousin and Philip's son-in-law. Because he had opposed his coreligionists and supported Charles, Moritz received the University of Wittenberg as well as the electoral title by imperial fiat. Charles and his brother, Duke Ferdinand, then proceeded to make arrangements for the religious life of Germany. At the Diet of Augsburg of 1548 Charles had a group of theologians compose a program for moderate—though certainly Roman Catholic—reform which he wanted to impose upon all the evangelical lands of his domains. Because he envisioned this program as an interim solution until the Council of Trent made new provisions for all of Western Christendom, the document has since been popularly known as the Augsburg Interim. The new imperial religious policy provided a program of teaching and practice which set aside many medieval abuses, but retained the heart of medieval Roman doctrine.[3]

The Assertion of Luther's Authority

The Augsburg Interim aroused immediate and fierce opposition among the Lutherans. Intended to bring an end to their faith, if not their lives, it inevitably generated apocalyptic reactions. Its threats fanned the flame of general eschatological expectation, which focused on Luther's legacy. Melanchthon and his colleagues at the University of Wittenberg found themselves in a difficult situation, however. They wished to criticize the Interim—and they did!—but they were bound to support their new lord, Moritz.[4] He, in turn, was bound to support the emperor, who had extended his territories and given him the electoral title. Moritz's ecclesiastical and secular councilors worked out a policy designed to fend

2. See Irene Dingel, "Melanchthon und die Normierung des Bekenntnisses," in *Der Theologe Melanchthon,* ed. Heinz Scheible (Sigmaringen: Thorbecke, 1999), 195–211.

3. *Das Augsburger Interim von 1548,* ed. Joachim Mehlhausen (Neukirchen-Vluyn: Neukirchener Verlag, 1970).

4. Günther Wartenberg, "Philipp Melanchthon und die sächsisch-albertinische Interimspolitik," *Lutherjahrbuch* 55 (1988): 60–80.

off imperial invasion by the appearance of compliance with the Augsburg Interim; at the same time the Lutheran proclamation of the gospel was to be preserved. The new policy was presented but not officially approved at a diet of Moritz's lands held at Leipzig in December 1548.

The new policy was only partially and selectively introduced in electoral Saxony. The entire text of the draft presented to the diet, however, fell into the hands of opponents, who promptly dubbed it the Leipzig Interim. The opposition, centered in Magdeburg but located throughout Lutheran Germany, issued sharp critiques of the route of compromise which Melanchthon and his colleagues had taken.[5] The strife within the Lutheran churches over the two Interims following the Habsburgs' War of Religion led to the formation of two parties, later called the Gnesio-Lutherans and the Philippists by scholars. Centering on the proper interpretation of Luther's message, the strife between these two parties in the quarter century following his death provided the context in which his followers defined Luther's significance.

Even before Luther's death his followers had begun collecting excerpts from his works and republishing entire treatises for various purposes (see chs. 6–7). As the Philippists and Gnesio-Lutherans battled with each other to define Luther's legacy, both parties tried to ground their arguments on the Bible, but quickly they began to reinforce and support their interpretation of Scripture with citations from Luther. For it was his message which they wished to continue to proclaim.

The initial strife which led to the formation of the two parties focused on the Leipzig Interim. There Melanchthon and his associates had conceded the use or reintroduction of certain practices and rites which they considered adiaphora, that is, neither commanded nor prohibited by Scripture. They argued that it was better to make such concessions than to provoke imperial occupation of Saxony. If that were to happen, Charles's troops would replace Lutheran pastors with Roman priests, as he had in areas of southern Germany where his occupation forces had coerced local authorities into imposing the Augsburg Interim.[6] The Gnesio-Lutherans disagreed. They argued that "in a time in

5. On this opposition, which was led by Matthias Flacius Illyricus, see Wilhelm Preger, *Matthias Flacius Illyricus und seine Zeit,* 2 vols. (Erlangen: Bläsing, 1859, 1861), 1:38–204; Hans Christoph von Hase, *Die Gestalt der Kirche Luthers: Der Casus Confessionis im Kampf des Matthias Flacius gegen das Interim von 1548* (Göttingen: Vandenhoeck & Ruprecht, 1940); and Robert Kolb, *Nikolaus von Amsdorf (1483–1565): Popular Polemics in the Preservation of Luther's Legacy* (Nieuwkoop: B. De Graaf, 1978), 69–122.

6. Luther D. Peterson, "The Philippist Theologians and the Interims of 1548: Soteriological, Ecclesiastical, and Liturgical Compromises and Controversies within German Lutheranism" (Ph.D. diss., University of Wisconsin, 1974), 113–24; see also Johannes Herrmann, "Augsburg–Leipzig–Passau (Das Leipziger Interim nach Akten des Landeshauptarchivs Dresden, 1547–1552)" (Th.D. diss., University of Leipzig, 1962).

which a clear confession of the faith is necessary, there is no such thing as an adiaphoron."[7] They believed that any compromise with the papal party would signal both to the Roman Catholics and to their own parishioners that Luther's legacy could be whittled and frittered away.

The Philippists believed that their concessions did no more than Luther had done when he returned to Wittenberg from the Wartburg in 1522. Then, in his "Invocavit" sermons and in his actions thereafter, he had urged caution and compromise for the sake of the weak in the faith. This was the model which the Wittenbergers, led by Melanchthon, claimed to follow.[8] The Gnesio-Lutherans disputed the parallel. They produced copious citations from Luther in which his emphasis on bold and uncompromising confession of the faith against any foe of the gospel was strikingly clear. In 1549 their counterattack began. Matthias Flacius Illyricus had left the Wittenberg instructional staff at Easter 1549 because he could not abide what he perceived to be the compromising tendencies of his preceptor Melanchthon. In 1539 Flacius had fled his native Croatia, leaving behind a member of the family circle, the Franciscan Baldo Lupetino, who had later been executed by the Venetian Inquisition for his adherence to Luther's cause. Luther's gospel had led Flacius through his own spiritual crisis. Thus he was appalled at what he regarded as Melanchthon's apostasy from that gospel in the Leipzig Interim. In addition to other attacks on both Interims, Flacius republished letters which Luther had written at the time of the Diet of Augsburg in 1530. These letters warned against any compromise with the Roman Belial.[9]

7. Robert Kolb, *Confessing the Faith: Reformers Define the Church, 1530–1580* (St. Louis: Concordia, 1991), 71–82; see also Hase, *Gestalt der Kirche,* 47–71.

8. E.g., in the tract *Gruntlicher vnd Warhafftiger Bericht der vorigen vnd jetzigen/für vnd nach dem Kriege ergangen Handlungen/von den Adiaphoris oder Mitteldingen. Sampt eine Christlichen Kurtzen verantwortung* (Leipzig: Bapst, 1550). The analysis presented here was first set forth in Robert Kolb, "'Perilous Events and Troublesome Disturbances': The Role of Controversy in the Tradition of Luther to Lutheran Orthodoxy," in *Pietas et Societas: New Trends in Reformation Social History: Essays in Memory of Harold J. Grimm,* ed. Kyle C. Sessions and Phillip N. Bebb (Kirksville, Mo.: Sixteenth Century Journal, 1985), 185–91; see also Kolb, *Confessing the Faith,* 63–98.

9. *Etliche Brieffe/des Ehrwirdigen Herrn D. Martini Luthers seliger gedechtnis, an die Theologos auff den Reichstag zu Augsburg geschrieben/Anno M.D.XXX. Von der vereinigung Christi vnd Belials/Auss welchen man viel nu[e]tzlicher lehr in gegenwertiger gefahr der Kirchen nemen kan . . .* (Magdeburg: Christian Rödinger, 1549), published also as *Aliquot epistolae reuerendi patris piae memoriae D. Martini Lutheri quibusdam Theologis ad Augustana comitia. Anno 1530. scriptae, de conciliationibus Christi & Belial disserentes* (Magdeburg: Michael Lotther, 1549). Flacius's supporters continued to argue their interpretation of Luther's stand as the controversies between the two parties widened in the 1550s; see, e.g., Johann Stolz, *Brevis defensio viri Dei Martini Lvtheri, in modvm somnij opposite somniatori Adiaphoristico* (Regensburg: Johann Kohl, 1555).

Also in 1549, Joachim Westphal, a former student of the Wittenbergers and at the time a pastor in Hamburg, countered the Adiaphorists' claim with a collection of quotations from Luther which demonstrated that no compromise with Rome was possible for those who wanted to remain faithful to the gospel. In 1551 Westphal reiterated his argument in an analysis of Melanchthon's and his associates' use of the adiaphora argument. Westphal clearly distinguished between Luther's protection of tender consciences in 1522 and the new offense which compromise with the papacy would visit upon such consciences a quarter century later. The context had changed, and Westphal charged that the Leipzig Interim denied the central teachings of the faith. He placed himself with the Luther who in his Galatians commentary had stated that he would not yield a hair's breadth to the world's attacks upon him. He pointed to Luther's defiance of imperial edicts (e.g., the Edict of Worms, which outlawed Luther's teaching, and subsequent edicts which reinforced Worms); these mandates had opposed God's Word. Luther would have continued to be defiant had he lived to see the Interims. And that defiance of Luther's, Westphal claimed, should serve as the model for the present situation. Furthermore, Westphal called into question the good faith of the supporters of the Leipzig Interim, in part because they claimed Luther's name at the same time their settlement had reinstituted liturgical practices which Luther had set aside.

Westphal's opponents accused him and his associates of idolizing Luther and being unwilling to permit any deviation from anything which he had said or done. Such a spirit Westphal could not understand. Picking up apocalyptic language to describe the situation in which he found himself, he preferred to stand with Luther against the "beast of the Babylonian whore." It was clear to him where the theologians in Moritz's employ stood—and that was not at Luther's side.[10] Nikolaus von Amsdorf, who had literally stood at Luther's side in Wittenberg at the very beginning of the Reformation, made much the same argument in a pair of tracts issued about the same time.[11]

For Flacius, Westphal, and Amsdorf it was helpful to cite Luther.

10. *Sententia reverendi viri D. M. Luth. Sanctae memoriae de Adiaphoris ex scriptis illius collecta* (Magdeburg: Michael Lotther, 1549); in German, *Des Ehrwirdigen vnd thewren Mans Doct. Marti. Luthers seliger gedechtnis meinung von den Mitteldingen* (Magdeburg: Michael Lotther, 1550); and *Verlegung des Gru[e]ndlichen Berichts der Adiaphoristen zu diesen bo[e]sen zeiten* (n.p., 1551), Biij^{r}–C^{r}, Ciij^{v}–[Ciiij]^{v}, Dij^{r}, Miij^{v}.

11. *Das Doctor Martinus kein Adiaphorist gewesen ist/vnd Das D. Pfeffinger vnd das buch on namen ihm gewalt vnd vnrecht thut* (Magdeburg: Christian Rödinger, 1550); and *Etliche spruche aus Doctoris Martini Luther Schriften/Darinne er/als ein Adiaphorist sich mit dem Bapst hat vergleichen wollen* (n.p., 1551).

They firmly believed that Luther had given every indication that he would have opposed compromise with the papal Antichrist. Their appeal to Luther's authority was primarily a historical appeal, alongside which, for instance, Flacius could set the authority of Melanchthon himself. To bolster his arguments against Melanchthon's position in the Leipzig Interim, Flacius cited Melanchthon's *Loci communes,* the Augsburg Confession and its Apology, and the preface to Philip's report on the negotiations with Roman Catholic theologians at Regensburg in 1541.[12] At this point Flacius did not accord Luther a special prophetic authority, a privileged role in interpreting God's Word in the Scriptures. Instead, he cited Luther to demonstrate Philippist unfaithfulness to the tradition of Luther's proclamation of the gospel.

The controversy over the Leipzig Interim and adiaphora continued to simmer, but it also gave birth to another controversy. Melanchthon's colleague at the University of Wittenberg, Georg Major, had participated in the composition of the Interim and had casually defended its assertion of the necessity of good works for salvation. Denial of that very phrase had occasioned intense attacks on the Lutheran Reformers of Magdeburg in the 1520s, when Major and Amsdorf had served together in that city. With such memories Amsdorf came to believe that Major had fallen into complete apostasy with his defense of the proposition that "good works are necessary for salvation."[13] In the storm of polemic which followed, Flacius and his colleague in Magdeburg, Nikolaus Gallus, published the memoranda of four north German Lutheran churches on the issue. In their preface Flacius and Gallus recalled how in the 1530s Luther had opposed the concept of the necessity of good works for salvation when it was alleged that Caspar

12. *Eine schrifft widder ein recht epicurisch buch/darin das Leipzische Interim verteidiget wird sich zu hu[e]ten fu[e]r der verfelschern der waren Religion . . .* (n.p., 1549), B^{v}–Bij^{r}, [Biij]^{v}, D; *Widder den ausszug des Leiptzischen Interims/oder das Kleine Interim* (Magdeburg: Christian Rödinger, 1549), Aij^{r}, B, Biij^{v}–[Biiij]^{r}; *Gru[e]ndliche verlegung aller Sophisterey/so Juncker Isleb/D. Interim/Morus/Pfeffinger/D. Geitz in seinem grundlichem bericht vnd jhre gesellen/die andere Adiaphoristen/das Leipsische Interim zu bescho[e]nen gebrauchen* (n.p., n.d.), passim.

13. On the Majoristic controversy see Peterson, "Philippist Theologians," 215–311; Robert Kolb, "Georg Major as Controversialist: Polemics in the Late Reformation," *Church History* 45 (1976): 455–68 (= *Luther's Heirs Define His Legacy: Studies on Lutheran Confessionalization* [Aldershot, Eng.: Variorum, 1996], 4); idem, *Amsdorf,* 123–80; and Timothy J. Wengert, "Georg Major (1502–1574): Defender of Wittenberg's Faith and Melanchthonian Exegete," in Heinz Scheible, ed., *Melanchthon in seinen Schülern* (Wiesbaden: Harrassowitz, 1997), 129–56. That the prominent apostate Wittenberg student and leading Roman Catholic reformer Georg Witzel held views similar to those of Major could only have confirmed Amsdorf's suspicions; see Barbara Henze, *Aus Liebe zur Kirche Reform: Die Bemühungen Georg Witzels (1501–1573) um die Kircheneinheit* (Münster: Aschendorff, 1995), 116–17, with an explicit comparison to Major.

Cruciger had used similar language.[14] For the most part, however, the early stages of the Majoristic controversy witnessed the exchange of biblical arguments, with almost no direct appeal to Luther. Gallus and Flacius seemed to use the Reformer's opposition to the phrase "good works are a sine qua non for salvation" as historical precedent rather than as the deciding voice of prophetic authority.

The year 1553 witnessed a subsidiary dispute over the concept of the necessity of good works for salvation. Major had served briefly as superintendent of the churches of Mansfeld County in 1552, but he resigned because of opposition from the pastors of his ministerium and one of the counts of Mansfeld. He left behind, however, at least one adherent, Stephan Agricola, who later became Roman Catholic. As the ministerium dealt with Agricola's embrace of the necessity of good works for salvation, it issued two memoranda. The first presented its case almost exclusively on the basis of biblical arguments, with only a single appeal to the authority of "our dear master and preceptor, a true instrument of God," Doctor Martin Luther, who had opposed what Major was then teaching.[15] In the second memorandum Luther was cited directly and in detail from his commentary on Galatians of 1535 and his *On Christian Liberty.*[16] These citations were used to prove that Major and Agricola could not claim to be faithful followers of the Reformer. In defending its position the Mansfeld ministerium was claiming Luther's authority as a special instrument of God. Luther had assumed for them a special status in determining and defining the biblical message. His words could be used as a secondary authority to replace the judgments of popes, councils, and bishops concerning the interpretation of the Scriptures. This marks a clear shift from historical argument regarding the proper interpretation of Luther's opinions to reliance on him for authoritative pronouncement. He had become an adjudicatory authority.

14. *Sententia ministrorvm in Ecclesia Lubecensi, Hamburgensi, Lüneburgensi & Magdeburgensi, de corruptelis doctrinae iustificationis, quibus D. Georg. Maior adserit . . .* (Magdeburg: Lotther, 1553), A3v. On the dispute over Cruciger's teaching that contrition was a sine qua non of justification, see Martin Greschat, *Melanchthon neben Luther: Studien zur Gestalt der Rechtfertigungslehre zwischen 1528 und 1537* (Witten: Luther, 1965), 217–30; and the critique of previous analyses of this dispute in Timothy J. Wengert, "Caspar Cruciger (1504–1548): The Case of the Disappearing Reformer," *Sixteenth Century Journal* 20 (1989): 431–37.

15. *Bedencken das diese Proposition oder Lere nicht nu[e]tz/not/noch war sey/vnnd one ergernis in der Kirchen nicht mo[e]ge geleret werden. Das gute werck zur seligkeit no[e]tig sind. Vnd vnmu[e]glich sey, one gute werck selig werden* (Magdeburg: Lotther, 1553), [Aiiij]v, [Diiij]r.

16. *Der Prediger in der Herrschafft Mansfelt antwort/auff Stephani Agricole . . . aussgegangene schlussreden vnd schmeschrifften/die newen lere in vnsern Kirchen/Das gut werck zur seligkeit no[e]tig sein/belangende* (Magdeburg: Lotther, 1553), Bv–Bijv.

His authority had been exalted and intensified. The Mansfeld ministerium was now basing its standards for public doctrine on the words of the Wittenberg professor and prophet.

In the same year Albert Christian, pastor of Saint Ulrich's Church in Magdeburg, the citadel of the Gnesio-Lutheran party, chose Luther's theses on the works of the law and the works of grace (1537) as a weapon against Major's proposition. In introducing his edition of these theses, he set his appeal to this text within the context of the authority which Luther's words possessed: "There can be no doubt for those with sound judgment that the holy man of God, Luther, was moved by the Holy Spirit as he spoke, and that his writing set forth the word of the prophets and apostles made more sure, as he laid waste the empire of the Roman Antichrist."[17] Couched as it was in the language of 2 Peter 1:19–21 with its reference to the Old Testament prophets and Scriptures, this understanding of Luther's proclamation gave him special—unique—authority.

The Perspective of Cyriakus Spangenberg

Albert Christian's regard for Luther's authority was shared by others among Luther's disciples. His esteem for his mentor was echoed in the theological argumentation of, for example, Cyriakus Spangenberg, who was a member of the Mansfeld ministerium and the son of the former superintendent of Mansfeld's churches, Johannes Spangenberg. Since 1550 Cyriakus had been serving as pastor in Eisleben. When he subscribed the Mansfeld memoranda of 1553 on Majorism, he was becoming one of the most articulate exponents of Luther's status as more than a hero of the faith. He saw Luther as a prophet with adjudicatory and interpretative authority in his own right. Eike Wolgast notes, "In contrast to Melanchthon (who placed Luther in the . . . succession of teachers [of the church]), Luther was for the Gnesio-Lutheran Spangenberg a singular phenomenon in the history of the church, in the history of salvation."[18]

Without doubt Spangenberg had learned to appreciate Luther's heroic and prophetic status as he was growing up in the home of his fa-

17. *Disputatio Reverendi patris D. Martini Lutheri de operibus legis & gratiae . . .* (Magdeburg: Lotther, 1553), A3^{v}, in a preface dated 10 August 1553.

18. Eike Wolgast, "Biographie als Autoritätsstiftung: Die ersten evangelischen Lutherbiographien," in *Biographie zwischen Renaissance und Barock: Zwölf Studien,* ed. Walter Berschin (Heidelberg: Mattes, 1993), 68–69, as argued in Robert Kolb, "Die Umgestaltung und theologische Bedeutung des Lutherbildes im späten 16. Jahrhundert," in *Die lutherische Konfessionalisierung in Deutschland: Wissenschaftliches Symposion des Vereins für Reformationsgeschichte 1988,* ed. Hans-Christoph Rublack (Gütersloh: Mohn, 1992), 205–8.

ther, who brought Luther's reform to Nordhausen in 1524, four years before Cyriakus's birth. Cyriakus studied at Wittenberg in the last years of Luther's life and became his devoted disciple. His correspondence reflects his reverence for his preceptor. Luther was clearly the model for Spangenberg's own ministry. As he taught the doctrine which he had learned from Luther, he believed that he was following the example of "my preceptor Dr. Luther" in his proclamation and conduct.[19] Years later, locked in battle with ecclesiastical and political forces which had ousted him from office because of his defense of what he understood to be Luther's teaching on original sin and divine election to salvation, Spangenberg conveyed to Elector August of Saxony his personal estimate of Luther:

> I have, praise God, preached the Word of God purely, clearly, and without adulteration for thirty-two years, as I heard it myself for five years from the holy mouth of the blessed Dr. Luther, my only preceptor, and from his sermons, lectures, and conversations which I heard myself, and from his precious writings, which I thereafter found and still read each day. And in the presence of Dr. Jonas and other theologians, this man of God, knowing that I intended to enter the preaching ministry in time, wished me good fortune and prophesied that I would bear this cross which I must now bear because of what I teach. . . . [My opponents are theologians who] do not daily, in humility and fear of God, diligently read the Holy Scripture and, alongside, its only true interpreter, Luther. But indeed, God did not send Luther to us Germans in vain. He will have Luther, and the gifts which he gave us through that man, used in gratitude, without contempt. But my fears are great in view of the fact that God has let many learned theologians sink and fall to such a low estimate of the writings of this precious man, the true German prophet, Dr. Luther, that they read him very little and follow them not at all.[20]

This was certainly not the case with Spangenberg. He not only read Luther, but also regarded him as an authority second only to Scripture itself—"its only true interpreter." On the one hand, he could cite Luther along with a number of other contemporary Lutheran theologians in defending his views; he claimed to follow "Scripture, Augustine, Luther, Brenz, and others" in his teaching on predestination.[21] On the other hand, in defending his own position on that doctrine, Spangenberg could also accord Luther a special status as his authority. He wrote

19. *Der Briefwechsel des M. Cyriakus Spangenberg,* ed. Heinrich Rembe, 2 vols. (Dresden: Naumann, 1887–88), 2:89–99, a letter of February 1573 to the councilors of the counts of Mansfeld.

20. Ibid., 2:121–22, in a letter of 23 May 1579 to Elector August of Saxony.

21. Ibid., 2:38, in a letter of 21 August 1567 to Hartmann Beyer.

to Duke Johann Albrecht of Mecklenburg that he was simply teaching what he had found in "God's Word, Christ, Isaiah, Paul, and Luther, who, in his book *On the Bondage of the Will,* and on the basis of the Scripture and Augustine, presented this article of faith more powerfully and sublimely than I did in my simple writing on the subject."[22] Both alone and with his colleague Hieronymus Menzel he delivered warnings based on "Scripture and Luther" to his princes, the counts of Mansfeld, and to Joachim Friedrich of Brandenburg, administrator of Magdeburg.[23]

In 1561 Spangenberg published a "reliable report of the benefits which God has shown especially to Germany through Dr. Martin Luther of blessed memory, and of the shameful, uncouth ingratitude for such great gifts." In this tract Spangenberg expressed his conviction that Luther's writings were "a treasure given by God, to be held in all honor next to the Holy Bible, and they should be preserved and presented and brought to our descendants in print without any addition, subtraction, alteration, or admixture of other writings," for Luther had "spoken in good apostolic fashion and had set forth our dear Christ and the true way to heaven on every occasion. Therefore, his theology and writings may rightly be called David's slingshot, Paul's mouth, John's finger, Peter's key, and the Holy Spirit's sword. In summary, he so powerfully internalized the dear apostle Paul, who received such high testimony from God, that Paul is heard from Luther."[24]

In this treatise Spangenberg listed eighteen reasons why the Germans should be grateful to God for Luther's ministry,[25] a list which reappeared nearly thirty years later, in 1589, when Spangenberg reissued twenty-one sermons which during the 1560s and 1570s he had preached on Luther's person and work. In the preface to this collection of sermons, entitled *Luther, Man of God,* he repeated the list of contributions which "in these last times" God has given "our fatherland, the German nation," on behalf of many other people through the gracious visitation of his gospel in the form of Luther's preaching. The eschatological thrust of Spangenberg's view of Luther had not grown weaker

22. Ibid., 2:34, in a letter of 4 July 1567.

23. Ibid., 2:42 (a letter of 17 Nov. 1567 to the counts of Mansfeld), 2:82 (a letter of 31 Jan. 1573 to the counts of Mansfeld), 2:103–5 (a letter of 18 March 1573 to Joachim Friedrich of Brandenburg); for similar expressions see 2:113–14 (a letter of 17 Sept. 1573 to Duke Johann Albrecht of Mecklenburg), 2:115, 116 (letters of 26 Aug. 1574 and 21 Sept. 1575 to Hartmann Beyer), and 2:119 (a letter of 18 Oct. 1577 to Elector August).

24. *Warhafftiger Bericht von den wolthaten/die Gott durch Martin Luther seligen/ fu[e]rnemlich Deudschland erzeigt/vnd von der Schendlichen groben vndanckbarkeit/fu[e]r solche grosse gaben geschrieben* (Jena: Thomas Rhebart, 1561), Aiiij^{r}–B^{v}.

25. Ibid., Cij^{r}–[Cvj]^{r}.

over the intervening decades. Luther remained "the great prophet and third Elijah [John the Baptist being the second], the superior man of God and enlightened teacher." Through him God had given his people a correct understanding of his law and of sin as well as correct teaching regarding the gospel, his grace, the Savior Jesus Christ, and the righteousness which avails before God. No other teacher had ever given clearer and more understandable instruction regarding the proper distinction of law and gospel, and with it a correct understanding of righteousness, good works, and repentance. Luther had restored proper use of the sacraments and a correct understanding of all the articles of the Christian faith. He had restored political authorities to their proper function and honor, and he had clarified how Christian congregations should function as well. He had established good schools and proper procedures for social welfare. He had affirmed Christian freedom for burdened consciences. His translation of the Scripture into German was superior to the best of the Latin and Greek (the Septuagint presumably) translations. He had given all Christians a "particularly precious gem" in his Small Catechism. Spangenberg also praised his hymn writing and concluded his list of reasons to be grateful for Luther's ministry much as he had in 1561.[26]

Luther, Man of God contained the sermons which Spangenberg had preached on Luther between November 11, 1562, and November 11, 1573, at the rate of two each year, generally at the time of Luther's birth and baptism (Nov. 10 and 11) and at the time of his death (Feb. 18). These sermons make it clear how much Spangenberg revered Luther: they contain certain elements found in medieval preaching on the lives of the saints.[27] However, it is misleading to say, as did Wolfgang Herrmann in his study of these sermons, that "the Mansfeld pastor does not present any of his personal impressions of Luther; rather, for him Luther is simply the Saint, to whom only good characteristics may be ascribed, a saint who belongs to a chain of great warriors of God throughout church history and who finally is distinct from everything human."[28] It is indeed regrettable that Spangenberg did not offer more anecdotal material on his personal experiences at Luther's table. None-

26. *Theander Lutherus. Von des werten Gottes Manne Doctor Martin Luthers Geistliche Haushaltung vnd Ritterschaft* . . . (Ursel: Nikolaus Heinrich, 1589), A2[r]–[A6][v].

27. This judgment of Wolfgang Herrmann, "Die Lutherpredigten des Cyriacus Spangenberg," *Mansfelder Blätter* 39 (1934/1935): 23, is confirmed by Spangenberg himself in the third of these sermons, *Die dritte Predigte/von dem heiligen Gottes Manne/Doctore Martino Luthero/Sonderlich von seinem Prophetenampt* . . . (Erfurt: Georg Baumann, 1564), [Aviij][v]; see also *Die Zehende Predigt/Von dem thewren Bekenner Gottes. D. Martini Lvther* . . . (Eisleben: Petri, 1568), a[v]–aij[v].

28. Herrmann, "Lutherpredigten," 59.

theless, Spangenberg was continually presenting his personal impressions of Luther. These impressions convey the sense that this man was larger than life, a prophet of God—indeed, "a saint who belongs to a chain of great warriors of God throughout church history."

Spangenberg's perspective was shared by many of his colleagues who studied at Wittenberg: Luther was a saint, and more than a saint. For Spangenberg, as for Urbanus Rhegius, his mentor was larger than life. The impressions of Luther and his message which had led Spangenberg's father into devoted service for the Wittenberg cause had left an indelible mark on Cyriakus. He believed that Luther was a prophet, evangelist, and apostle of the Lord, and he sacrificed his career in Mansfeld by defending the message and the authority of this new Elijah, John, and Paul. His conviction was shared by the physician Matthaeus Ratzeberger, who had known Luther well, having become acquainted during his service as Elector John Frederick's physician (1537–47).[29] People like Rhegius, Ratzeberger, and Spangenberg believed they had encountered a larger-than-life figure in the Wittenberg theologian Martin Luther.

Prophet and Elijah, apostle, Paul, and the evangelist John were indeed among the images which Spangenberg's series of twenty-one sermons applied to Luther. Other images included Luther as a faithful householder, a spiritual knight, a theologian, the angel of the Lord, a martyr, a pilgrim of God, Jacob, and a priest. To depict Luther's service to God, the concluding eight sermons, preached in the mining community of Mansfeld, developed allegories from the various jobs performed in the mines.[30] Often implicitly, sometimes explicitly, Spangenberg's sermons attributed to Luther, and derivatively to his writings, an authority next to that of Scripture.

Descriptions of Luther as Apostle, Evangelist, and Prophet

Spangenberg agreed with those who at the beginning of the Reformer's career had regarded Luther as a modern-day apostle and evangelist. Three of his sermons on Luther, preached in 1564 and 1565, analyzed his significance in such terms. When the Swiss theologian Heinrich Bullinger disputed the claim that Luther was an apostle for his age, Spangenberg undertook a refutation of Bullinger. He traced Luther's

29. See Ratzeberger's "Warnungschrift" to Elector John Frederick (June 1547), in C. G. Neudecker, *Die handschriftliche Geschichte Ratzebergers über Luther und seine Zeit* (Jena: Mauke, 1850), 268–75.

30. Herrmann, "Lutherpredigten," 19–71, analyzes the production and literary form of these sermons.

struggles as a youth to find Christ. As in the case of Peter, it was not flesh and blood, but the heavenly Father, who revealed Christ to the despairing monk (Matt. 16:17).[31] Like Paul, Luther had been raised by pious parents and sent at an early age to school. Like Paul, he relied on his own works as a Pharisaic monk. Like Paul, he was converted by God's miraculous working. Like Paul's, his teaching was based solely on the Scripture, was absolutely certain, and focused on Christ alone. The two of them shared similar gifts of wisdom, prophecy, disputation, courage, and spirit. They both had the same virtues—faithfulness, zeal, candor, patience, joy in the Spirit, constancy, humility, prudence, and mercy. Both suffered persecution at the hands of the religious and political leaders of their time.[32]

In the next sermon in the series Spangenberg sketched twelve ways in which Luther resembled the evangelist John. He regarded his mentor as a true evangelist, a German Cicero and Demosthenes, because of his skill in presenting the gospel. Like John, Luther could be called "the beloved of the Lord." John had prepared the way for the paschal Lamb, and Luther prepared the way for the Lamb as he was about to return to judge all things (here Spangenberg's references seem to point to John the Baptist rather than the evangelist). Both lay at Christ's breast. As Christ commended his mother into John's care, so the Lord commended the church into Luther's care. Both fought heretics, and both clearly taught the two natures of Christ. Their writings are similar because Luther depended on John to a great extent. Both prophesied the future, both possessed many gifts, both had their own Patmos (to designate the Wartburg during his period of hiding there, Luther chose the name of the island on which the evangelist had spent his last days), and both brought the erring to repentance and faith. Both longed for the second coming of Christ.[33] As artificial as some of these comparisons seem to moderns, they represent an honest effort to convey the significance of a man who had changed the world for the likes of a Cyriakus Spangenberg.

Even more prominent in Spangenberg's picture of Luther was the ascription of the prophetic office. This motif had already been thoroughly

31. *Die Fu[e]nffte Predigt/Von dem Apostelampt des trefflichen Mannes/D. Martin Lvthers* (n.p., 1565). Spangenberg was disputing Bullinger's treatment of Luther in *Repetitio et dilvcidior explicatio consensvs veteris orthodoxae catholicaeque Christi Ecclesiae in doctrina prophetica & apostolica de inconfusis proprietatibus naturarum Christi Domini* . . . (Zurich: Christoph Froschauer, 1564), 63^{r}–64^{v}.

32. *Die sechste Predigt. Von dem werden Gottes Lerer: Doctor Martin Luther/Das er ein rechter Pavlvs gewesen* (Erfurt: Georg Baumann, 1565).

33. *Die Siebende Predigt. Von dem Hocherleuchten Gottesmanne/Doctor Martin Lvther/ Das er ein warer Evangelist/vnd rechter Ioannes gewesen* (Erfurt: Georg Baumann, 1566).

expounded by another of Luther's students at Wittenberg, Andreas Musculus, who as professor at the University of Frankfurt an der Oder was also engaged in transforming the authority of the mythical figure of Martin Luther into authority for his writings. In the preface of a treatise "on the devil's tyranny, power, and might, particularly in these last days," published in 1561, Musculus examined the prophecy of Malachi (4:5) that Elijah would return before the last day. Echoing Luther's own judgment, he explained why that prophecy would not be fulfilled by Elijah himself brought back from the dead, but rather by one who would exercise the same office and responsibility. Just as John the Baptist had been called a true Elijah in his day (Matt. 11:14; 17:10–12), so Martin Luther was a genuine Elijah whose coming had signaled the imminent approach of the end of the world. The figure of Luther had become a commonplace in the eschatological delineation of the era; viewed as a signpost of the horizon of human history, his person and message were already altering the apocalyptic imagination.

Musculus proceeded to compare Luther with the original Elijah, in much the same fashion in which Spangenberg would. The ancient spokesman of God and the contemporary Reformer possessed the same spirit and teaching, and both had stood against the priests of Baal, Luther in his opposition to pope, monks, and priests. They lived in similar times when God's teaching and true worship had been covered by terrible darkness. Both exhibited the strength of God, the strength of one poor individual man with the sword of the Spirit against the four hundred fifty priests of Baal and against the might of popes and emperors. "Since the apostolic era no greater man than Luther, who had so many great and superior spiritual gifts bestowed by God, has lived or come to earth," Musculus concluded.[34]

Expanding Musculus's presentation of Luther as prophet, Spangenberg began by explaining why he treated Luther's life in the manner of his earlier preaching on saints' days. He did not intend to hold Luther up as a mediator for the special veneration of his people. Instead, he wanted to emphasize Luther's teaching, faith, confession, and steadfastness.[35] His sermon on Luther the prophet first established that Luther was not a false prophet. God had given Luther both the gifts of the prophet and a regular, official call to his office. Spangenberg had to be sensitive to Roman Catholic criticism which compared his mentor to Anabaptist preachers who claimed the right to preach without a reg-

34. *Von des Teufels Tyranney/Macht vnd Gewalt/Sonderlich in diesen letzten tagen/ vnterrichtung* (Erfurt: Georg Baumann, 1561), Aij^{r}–[Avij]^{r}; republished in *Teufelbücher in Auswahl,* ed. Ria Stambaugh (Berlin: De Gruyter, 1978), 4:191–95.

35. *Die dritte Predigte,* [Avij]^{v}–[Aviij]^{r}.

ular, orderly call to public ministry. Luther did not deceive his people but faithfully proclaimed the true message of Scripture to them. Luther did not come as a wolf in sheep's clothing; because he was without hypocrisy, none of the epithets given the false prophets in Scripture applied to him.[36]

Spangenberg defined the prophets of the church as those who proclaim God's honor and predict certain things in the future which are necessary for the people of God to know (for instance, that the last day is coming and that the dead will be raised). God gives his gift to interpret Scripture and proclaim Christ more richly to some prophets than to others. Spangenberg concluded that "Luther was the greatest and best prophet the world has had since the time of the apostles, and he was superior to all other teachers since that time, made comparable to the Old Testament prophets by God." God had performed a marvelous work in calling someone from a simple cloister, without the power of council, pope, or prelate behind him, to storm the empire of the Antichrist.[37]

Four pieces of evidence convinced Spangenberg that Luther was truly a prophet. First, he had interpreted the Scripture in powerful fashion, condemning sin and admonishing his hearers to faith and good works. God had sent this prophet, with proper call, to teach his people. The content of Luther's teaching Spangenberg summarized in four points: he preached that Christ alone saves, that good works spring from faith, that troubled consciences find comfort in Christ, and that judgment should be pronounced without regard for the rank of the person under condemnation.[38] Second, Spangenberg regarded Luther as a prophet because he had predicted the future; he had foreseen—Spangenberg asserted—how God's wrath and mercy would fall upon Germany after his death. The student's understanding of his mentor's predictive powers placed them squarely within his ministry of proclaiming law and gospel. Spangenberg cited collections of Luther's prophecies assembled by contemporaries such as Johannes Timann (or Amsterdam), Peter Glaser, and Anton Otto. These prophecies should be used to confirm that Luther's teaching was indeed true and to promote patience and penitence in God's people.[39] Third, Spangenberg was convinced that Luther proved himself a prophet by bringing order to the temporal realm, altering it according to God's command through his admonitions to princes and subjects alike. Fourth, Spangenberg held

36. Ibid., B^{v}–C^{v}.

37. Ibid., C^{v}–Ciij^{v}.

38. Ibid., Dij^{v}–Dv^{r}, [Dviij]^{r}.

39. Ibid., [Dviij]^{r}–Gv^{r}. On collections of Luther's prophecies by his followers, see pp. 178–83.

that the miraculous accomplishments of Luther's ministry—overthrowing the Antichrist and bringing the gospel to light—should convince all that he was truly a prophet of God.[40]

Thus Spangenberg assembled a medley of medieval and evangelical standards for evaluating Luther's status as a holy man of God. Medieval saints had worked miracles and issued predictive prophecies. To reinforce his claim that Luther had served as God's special prophet, Spangenberg produced an evangelical version of predictive prophecy and miracles, stretching their medieval definitions to the breaking point, but using these familiar categories to drive home his conviction that Luther was God's special instrument.

Like Musculus, Spangenberg regarded Luther as a true Elijah. He noted six similarities between Luther and Elijah. Elijah means "strong man" in Hebrew, and Martin is the Latin equivalent of "He(e)rmann," man of hosts. Both received their strength from the Lord and exhibited it. Elijah came from a small, insignificant village just as Luther came from modest Eisleben. Both lived in times of idolatry and persecution. God performed miracles to preserve the lives of both, and just as Elijah had raised the son of the woman of Zarephath (1 Kings 17:21–22), so Luther had raised up those who were in the grip of death under the papacy. Both Elijah and Luther had exhibited the seven gifts of the Holy Spirit. Their greatest similarity in Spangenberg's view, however, was that both proclaimed God's law and God's gospel.[41] Throughout the sermons on Luther, Spangenberg used the simple rhetorical device of comparison to reinforce his larger-than-life picture of the teacher whom he had experienced as God's prophet. These comparisons with biblical figures ascribed to Luther the authority of the prime interpreter of Scripture, authority which, Spangenberg was convinced, he exercised as a living voice of God's gospel.

Both Musculus and Spangenberg went beyond respecting Luther as a prophet whose actions and teachings had shaped and still guided the life of their churches. The Reformer's apostolic aura and his prophetic profile served as bases for a myth that took on new form after his death. The writings of this special servant of God joined the Augsburg Confession and other authoritative documents as a means for deciding disputes regarding the proper interpretation of Scripture. Since their authoritative prophet was dead, Luther's followers had to turn from the myth of the man to his writings. This move from the personal authority of a living voice to the authority of the written words which he had be-

40. Ibid., [Dviij]^{r}.

41. *Die vierde Predigt/Von dem grossen Propheten Gottes/Doctore Martino Luthero/Das er ein rechter Helias gewesen . . .* (Erfurt: Georg Baumann, 1564).

queathed to his church was obviously a necessity after 1546, and it happened quite naturally. Clearly, Musculus and Spangenberg made that move without giving much thought to the matter. Spangenberg frequently cited Luther to prove his own position, particularly in defending the view of Matthias Flacius that original sin is the substance of the fallen human creature. Others who shared his position did the same.[42] Musculus marshaled Luther's authority in similar fashion as he defended what he believed to be Luther's understanding of good works and of the two natures of Christ.[43]

In 1573 Musculus published his own compendium of Christian doctrine, which set forth biblical teaching on the basis of quotations from the Scripture, from Luther, and from the ancient fathers of the church. The work was patterned after similar works based solely on Scripture and patristic authors. Luther should be heard as the German prophet, Musculus claimed, because he had freed the church from the darkness of the papacy. His heroic action had demonstrated that he was God's prophet. Musculus noted that he daily meditated on the Word of God and joined to it a careful reading of Luther's writings, "so that I recall the pious words which once I heard from his mouth." At the same time Musculus read the ancient fathers, or at least those who had fewer errors in their writings, so that he might be armed by their consensus against corruptions of biblical teaching. Musculus found primary authority in the Bible itself. Interpretation was to be guided, he declared, by Luther's writings—without any mention of error—and by the ancient fathers insofar as they were free from error. This distinction may explain why Musculus used Luther's words but none of the patristic writings as a formal authority for the church of Brandenburg.[44]

Luther's Authority in Mid-Sixteenth-Century Confessions and Corpora Doctrinae

Luther, and therefore his writings, had unique secondary authority for Musculus, Spangenberg, and many of their contemporaries. A critical

42. See pp. 189–90.

43. *Von der vnzertrennlichen voreynigung in einer Person beider naturn vnsers Herrn Jesu Christi Gottes vnd Marien Son/Docto. Martini. Lutheri bekentnis/Glaub/vnd Leere/aus seinen bu[e]chern zusamen getragen/wieder den neulichen erregten Nestorischen vnd Eutichischen miesvorstandt vnd jrrthum* (Frankfurt/Oder: Johann Eichorn, 1553).

44. *Compendivm doctrinae Christianae collectvm, Ex S. Scriptura, S. Ecclesiae Patribvs, S. Luthero* (Frankfurt/Oder: Johann Eichorn, 1573), A2^{v}. See also Robert Kolb, "The Fathers in the Service of Lutheran Teaching: Andreas Musculus' Use of Patristic Sources," in *Auctoritas patrum,* ed. Leif Grane, Alfred Schindler, and Markus Wriedt (Wiesbaden: Steiner, 1998), 2:105–23.

occasion for the exercise of such authority arose in the individual confessions and collections of confessions—called *corpora doctrinae*—composed and assembled by German evangelical churches in the third quarter of the sixteenth century for the regulation of public teaching and ecclesiastical life. Beyond their individual efforts to employ Luther's writings as adjudicating interpretative authority, both Musculus and Spangenberg had opportunities to use Luther's works in similar fashion in confessions of the faith that were designed to regulate public teaching in evangelical lands.

Musculus had more success than did Spangenberg in this endeavor. In 1572, along with the elector's court preacher Georg Coelestin, Musculus guided the composition of a constitution which formalized Luther's authority for the church of electoral Brandenburg. Secondary doctrinal authority, authority for interpreting the Scriptures, in Brandenburg's churches was to be found first of all in the Augsburg Confession and Luther's Small Catechism, as understood in the light of Luther's postils and doctrinal writings. There Musculus and Coelestin found "clear, faithful teaching grounded in God's Word." As a part of the secondary authority to which all pastors in Brandenburg had to pledge themselves, Musculus and Coelestin added to these documents excerpts from Luther's works on the topics of original sin, the free will and natural human powers, the law, the gospel, the justification of the sinner in God's sight, true repentance, the fruits of faith and good works, baptism, and the Lord's Supper.[45] Apparently Musculus recognized that he could not appeal to the whole of Luther's corpus to resolve disputed doctrinal problems, so he selected sections that were critical to the situation of the church of Brandenburg in 1572.

Begun at Augsburg in 1530, the pattern of defining the public doctrine of the church through confessional documents continued during the quarter century after Luther's death.[46] After 1560 such documents were gathered into *Corpora doctrinae* which contained authoritative definitions to regulate public teaching, adjudicate disputes over proper biblical interpretation, and delineate the life of the church.

Above all, Gnesio-Lutheran theologians went beyond Luther's catechisms and his Smalcald Articles to formally place the whole corpus of

45. *Die Augspurgische Confession/aus dem Rechten Original . . . Der Kleine Catechismus Erklerung vnd kurtzer Ausszug aus den Postillen vnd Lehrschrifften des thewren Mans Gottes D. Lutheri/daraus zusehen/wie derselbe von fu[e]rnembsten Artickeln vnserer Christlichen Religion gelehret/Aus verordnunge . . . Johansen Georgen . . .* (Frankfurt/Oder: Johann Eichorn, 1572). See also Wolfgang Gericke, *Glaubenszeugnisse und Konfessionspolitik der Brandenburgischen Herrscher bis zur Preussischen Union, 1540 bis 1815* (Bielefeld: Luther, 1977), 20–21, and, in the present volume, pp. 216–17.

46. Kolb, *Confessing the Faith,* 119–30.

his writings among the documents which should guide the church's public teaching. However, Luther's writings did not find such a place in every public statement which Gnesio-Lutherans helped write on what the Lutheran churches taught and how they determined what was correct biblical teaching. In the first of their confessional documents, the birth certificate of their movement, the Magdeburg Confession of 1550, the group of antiadiaphoristic preachers gathered in that city claimed that their teaching was based simply on God's Word and that it conformed to the teaching of the Augsburg Confession.[47] The Augsburg Confession would not receive imperial approval as a legal expression of the Christian faith within the Holy Roman Empire until 1555, but it did have an aura of authority about it by virtue of its presentation at the imperial diet in 1530 and by virtue of its use in several Lutheran lands as a public expression of correct teaching. While stressing Scripture and the Augsburg Confession, the author of the Magdeburg Confession, Nikolaus Gallus, undoubtedly in concert with Nikolaus von Amsdorf and other pastors in the city, recognized Luther's key role in God's economy: God had raised him up, as he had raised up Daniel, Paul, and John to counter the forces which opposed God and to speak God's Word. At Augsburg Gallus's and Amsdorf's predecessors had presented "the confession of Luther's teaching, which is the teaching of Christ," to the entire Holy Roman Empire. Now the events of the period surrounding the Smalcald War and the promulgation of the Augsburg Interim were necessitating a reaffirmation of that teaching.

Two things are clear regarding Gallus's and Amsdorf's understanding of authority in the church of Magdeburg. First, they equated Luther's teaching with Christ's teaching. Luther had served—and continued to serve—as a faithful and accurate expositor of God's Word. Second, they found the authoritative form of Luther's teaching in the Augsburg Confession, not in the corpus of his writings itself, as would become the case for Musculus, Spangenberg, and others within the following decade. The text of the Magdeburg Confession states precisely that those who subscribed to this document pledged themselves to give public witness to the "teaching of the holy gospel, which was again revealed to us through Dr. Martin Luther, [the teaching] of the Augsburg Confession." Thus their confession was "a brief summary of our Christian teaching, . . . particularly the articles which Dr. Martin Luther had specially renewed and which had been comprehended in the Augsburg

47. *Bekentnis Vnterricht vnd vermanung der Pfarhern vnd Prediger der Christlichen Kirchen zu Magdeburgk* (Magdeburg, 1550), [A]v; the Latin version, *Confessio et apologia pastorum et reliquorum ministrorum ecclesiae Magdeburgensis* . . . (Magdeburg, 1550), [A]v. See Kolb, *Confessing the Faith,* 122–24, 129–30.

Confession."[48] The reader is further commended to "the writings of Dr. Martin Luther and other pure teachers of his kind, to gain further explanation and a certain basis for the articles and confession" contained in the Magdeburg document itself, which, its authors claimed, was drawn from the writings of the prophets and apostles and agreed with the writings of the early church.[49] Luther's writings are not prescribed, however, as an adjudicatory authority.

The heart of the Magdeburg Confession treats seven articles of faith: on God, creation and sin, the law and good works, the gospel and justification, the sacraments, the church and the servants of the church, and the hierarchies of temporal government and the home. The presentation is biblically based, with little express appeal to any authority apart from that implicit in the use of Scripture. It contains no citations or mention of Luther and his writings. Following these seven doctrinal sections comes the most extensive section of the Confession. It treats the right of lesser magistrates to use force in defending the gospel. In it the Magdeburg confessors continue their biblical argument, but—in contrast to the doctrinal sections—they here appeal to Luther's writings and letters which argued for the right to resist higher magistrates.[50] Following this defense of Lutheran resistance theory is an admonition to remain faithful in the face of papal threat; a marginal observation in this section refers the reader to Luther's *Warning to His Dear German People.*[51]

The Magdeburg Confession did not offer an analysis of its own system of authority or its view of the place of Luther's writings in that system. It is clear, however, that the Magdeburgers regarded Luther as a figure of critical importance for the history of God's revelation of his Word, a figure whose message was completely dependent on the prophetic and apostolic Word of Scripture and whose writings faithfully conveyed that Word. Nonetheless, the few references that the confession makes to Luther's writings do not ascribe to them the authority that the Magdeburgers ascribe to the Augsburg Confession as an apt summary of Luther's teaching, "which is the teaching of Christ."

As struggles over the proper interpretation of Luther's message engaged theologians in the decades following the Magdeburg Confession, Lutherans composed other public documents to confess their faith. Some of them, such as the Saxon Book of Confutation (1559) and the Mansfeld Confession of the same year, contained no discussion of ec-

48. Magdeburg *Bekentnis,* Aiij^{v}–Bij^{r}; *Confessio,* A2^{v}–A3^{v}.

49. Magdeburg *Bekentnis,* [Biiij]; *Confessio,* A4^{r}.

50. Magdeburg *Bekentnis,* Miij^{r}; *Confessio,* H.

51. Magdeburg *Bekentnis,* Oij^{v}; *Confessio,* I2^{r}, where the marginal note is omitted.

clesiastical authority; they presumed the primary authority of Scripture and the sufficiency of its authority.[52] Other such confessions did establish the secondary authorities which would be used to judge public teaching and guide biblical interpretation among their adherents.

Some confessions authored by Gnesio-Lutherans specifically included the whole corpus of Luther's writings as secondary sources of authority for judging doctrine and biblical interpretation. Joachim Mörlin drafted a declaration for the theologians of Lower Saxony who met in July 1561 to establish a common front against certain errors within contemporary Lutheranism. This Lüneburg Declaration clearly affirmed Luther's authoritative role in determining the teaching of the churches which bore his name. It accorded formal authority to "the catechisms and the other writings of Luther of blessed memory" along with the Scriptures and the ancient creeds, the Augsburg Confession, its Apology, and the Smalcald Articles. (All of these later documents were recognized as based on the Word of God, but a specific distinction between Scripture and them was not explicitly drawn.) Citations from Luther's writings do not appear in the brief text of the Lüneburg Declaration, but the general appeal to his authority reflects the subscribers' belief that the corpus of Luther's writings could be used as a basis for formally judging public teaching.[53]

In 1567 a series of disputes between pastors led the counts of Reuss (Greitz and Gerau) and Schönburg to commission another group of Gnesio-Lutherans with composing a confession of faith. The text of this Confessional Writing stated as part of its purpose the maintenance of Luther's teaching.[54] Simon Musaeus, Georg Autumnus, and Bartholomaeus Rosinus, prominent Gnesio-Lutherans and the leading authors of this document, stated explicitly their understanding of ecclesiastical authority: "We pledge ourselves to and recognize as the basis and guide [for teaching the faith] first the writing of the prophets,

52. . . . *solida & ex Verbo Dei sumpta Confutatio & condemnatio praecipuarum Corruptelarum* . . . (Jena: Rebart, 1559); in German, *Confutationes* . . . *etlicher* . . . *zu wider* . . . *Gottes wort* . . . *Corruptelen* . . . (Jena: Rebart, 1559); *Bekendtnis der Prediger in der Graffschafft Mansfelt/vnter den jungen Herren gesessen. Wider alle Secten/Rotten/vnd falsche Leren/wider Gottes wort/die reine Lere Luthers seligen/vnd der Augspurgischen Confession/ an etlichen o[e]rtern eingeschlichen/mit notwendigen widerlegungen derselbigen* (Eisleben, 1560, dated 20 Aug. 1559).

53. *Erklerung aus Gottes Wort/vnd kurtzer bericht/der Herren Theologen/auff dem Tag zu Lu[e]neburg/im Julio des 61. Jars gehalten* (Regensburg, 1562), Biij^{r}–[Biiij]^{r}, Ciij^{v}–[Ciij]^{r}, Dij^{r}, Diij^{v}.

54. *Confessionschrifft. Etlicher Predicanten in den Herrschafften/Graitz/Geraw/Schönburg/vnd anderer hernach vnterschriebenen* . . . (Eisleben, 1567), Biij^{v}. See also O. Meusel, "Die Reussische oder Reussisch-Schönburgische Konfession von 1567," *Beiträge zur sächsische Kirchengeschichte* 14 (1899): 149–87.

Christ, and the apostles according to their natural and uncoerced meaning, and thereafter we pledge ourselves to" the three catholic creeds, the Augsburg Confession of 1530 and its Apology, the Smalcald Articles, the Saxon Confutation of 1559, the Lüneburg Declaration of 1561, the Mansfeld Confession of 1564, the catechisms of Luther, and—in order to understand the catechisms—"we also hold, along with God's Word and the previously cited creeds . . . the writings of Doctor Martin Luther [as] certain, correct, and true, according to which we interpret and apply the holy catechisms. We pledge ourselves to these writings of Luther expressly with faithful mouth and heart, and we understand, interpret, and explain the Augsburg Confession and the catechisms according to them." Readers of this confession are reminded that Luther's writings come from the pen "of the prophet," while the writings of Melanchthon and others issue from the pens "of the prophet's children."[55]

In contrast to these two confessions, a number of others contained no explicit ascription of secondary authority to the entire corpus of Luther's writings. The Austrian Confession of 1567 recognized the Scriptures, and then the ancient creeds, the unaltered Augsburg Confession, the Smalcald Articles, and Luther's two catechisms as "a correct form and rule for explaining and understanding all articles of faith and the most important parts of the entire Christian religion."[56] No distinction was made between scriptural authority and the documents which claimed to be based on the word and authority of the Bible. The Austrian confessors endorsed Luther's translation of the Bible, but they did not otherwise mention the Reformer or the corpus of his writings. The reason for this omission was that Austria was still controlled by Roman Catholic princes and under the weighty influence of Roman Catholic clerics, so Luther's voice in and of itself carried little public authority there.

Lutheran confessors were in a similar situation as they drafted a statement of faith for the struggling Lutherans of Antwerp. This confession is of interest because Cyriakus Spangenberg was among its authors. It acknowledges as its "norm of truth" only the three ecumenical creeds and the Augsburg Confession, the Apology of the Augsburg Confession, and the Smalcald Articles. The Antwerp confession also states clearly that the contemporary standards arose out of the work of Luther, "the Elijah of the Last Age." But the corpus of Luther's writings is not given any normative status even though the confessors of Ant-

55. *Confessionschrifft,* Diij^{r}–F^{v}.

56. *Confessio. Christliche Bekentnis des Glaubens/etlicher Euangelischen Prediger in Oster-Reich* (Eisleben: Gaubisch, 1567), [Biij]^{v}.

werp do refer their readers to the Saxon Confutation of 1559 and "other writings of the churches [note, not of individuals] which agree with the Word of God." No normative status or authority is, however, accorded to these works.[57]

While we would expect Spangenberg's personal opinion on Luther's authority in the church to have played a role in shaping the Mansfeld Confessions of 1559 and 1564, neither document contains an explicit statement regarding authority within the church. However, the 1559 Confession occasionally cites not only a number of ancient church fathers, but also Luther's words when the issues involve disputes among Lutherans. His authority is not invoked wherever those outside the Lutheran churches are being condemned. Thus, against Servetus, the Anabaptists, Schwenckfeld, and Zwingli and the Sacramentarians, the ancient teachers are quoted but never Luther. But in regard to the antinomians, the Osiandrians, the synergists, and the Majorists, Luther is cited.[58] The 1559 Confession uses Luther's words in exactly the same way in which it uses the fathers of the ancient church, that is, as a reliable guide for proper teaching to which it can appeal in reinforcing its interpretation of Scripture—but only in those disputes in which the opponents are Lutherans and therefore presumably obliged to listen to Luther.

In the Confession of 1564 the Mansfeld theologians acclaimed Luther as God's chosen vessel who restored the light of Scripture to the present age, the Elijah of the last time, the true disciple and the straightforward interpreter of Saint Paul.[59] This Confession used rather extensive material from Luther's works to support its critiques of the view of the Lord's Supper held by the Philippist Wittenberg professor Paul Eber, of certain questions and answers in the Heidelberg Catechism, of the antinomianism of Johann Agricola, of Georg Major's assertion that good works are necessary for salvation, and of Viktorin Strigel's synergism. These citations from a variety of Luther's works occur along with limited use of ancient fathers—among them Ambrose, Augustine, Basil, Chrysostom, Cyril, Gregory, Cyprian, and Origen. The 1564 Confession also quoted Bernard, Lombard, and contemporary theologians, including Spangenberg and his Mansfeld colleague Christoph Irenaeus, the Braunschweig superintendent Joachim Mörlin, the Regensburg superintendent Nikolaus Gallus, the Freiberg rector Hieronymus Weller, and

57. *Confessio ministrorum Jesu Christi, in ecclesia Antwerpiensi, quae Augustanae Confessioni adsentitur* (n.p., 1567), Bij.

58. Mansfeld *Bekendtnis,* 97–98, 107ʳ, 110ᵛ, on the antinomians; 236ᵛ–37, 241ʳ, 251ᵛ–54, on the Osiandrians; 279ᵛ–80ʳ, on the synergists; and 287ᵛ–93, on the Majorists.

59. *Confessio et sententia ministrorum verbi in comitatu Mansfeldensi, de dogmatis quorundam proximo triennio publice editis* (Eisleben: Gaubisch, 1565), 1ʳ, 31ʳ, 200ᵛ.

the Swabian theologian Johannes Brenz.[60] Neither the 1559 nor the 1564 Mansfeld Confession spelled out presuppositions regarding authority in the church. Therefore it is uncertain whether the citations of Luther's corpus reveal a regard for him as a secondary authority or simply as a highly respected mentor. If Spangenberg's regard for Luther had been undisputed in the ministerium of the county, we would expect a more explicit statement regarding Luther's authority. Instead, the Mansfeld Confessions leave undefined the way in which his writings were to be used.

Some princely and municipal governments eventually gathered together the documents which stood as secondary authority in their churches. The first of this genre, the *Corpus doctrinae Philippicum* (or *Corpus doctrinae Misnicum*), contained only writings of Melanchthon,[61] but in the decade following its appearance in 1560 several other such collections appeared and contained materials from Luther, Melanchthon, and other contemporary authors. These collections were much alike in their treatment of Luther. For instance, that for ducal Saxony, the *Corpus doctrinae Thuringicum* of 1570, announced on its title page that it contained a summary of Christian teaching from the writings of the prophets and apostles as comprehended "by Doctor Martin Luther in particular and other teachers of these lands,"[62] but it did not include his writings in the list of documents by which public doctrine might be judged.

In 1576 Martin Chemnitz aided two principalities in codifying their doctrinal standards into collections—the *Corpus doctrinae Julium* for Braunschweig-Wolfenbüttel and the *Corpus doctrinae Wilhelminum* for Braunschweig-Lüneburg.[63] Although he had ascribed to Luther's writings in general a role in the public exercise of authority in the church when he fashioned a church constitution for Braunschweig-Wolfenbüttel in 1569, and although he had in 1571 based his ministerium's rejection of Crypto-Philippist[64] sacramental theology on Luther's writings (along with Scripture, the Augsburg Confession, and other confessional

60. Ibid., 37^r (Weller on Eber); 115^r (Irenaeus, Mörlin, and Gallus on Majorism); 155^r (Irenaeus and Spangenberg on synergism); 160^v (Brenz on synergism).

61. Dingel, "Melanchthon und die Normierung des Bekenntnisses," 195–211.

62. *Corpvs doctrinae Christianae. Das ist/Summa der Christlichen lere/aus den Schrifften der Propheten vnd Aposteln/fein kurtz/rundt vnd gru[e]ndtlich/durch D. Martinum Lutherum sonderlich/vnd andere dieser Lande Lerer zusamment gefasset . . .* (Jena: Christian Rödinger's heirs, 1570).

63. *Corpvs doctrinae. Das ist/Die Summa/Form vnd vorbilde der reinen Christlichen Lehre/welche aus der heiligen Go[e]ttlichen Schrift der Propheten vnd Apostel zusammen gezogen ist . . .* (Uelzen: Michael Kröner, 1576); and *Corpus Doctrinae . . .* (Wolfenbüttel: Conrad Horn, 1576).

64. On this term see p. 106.

documents),[65] he now omitted the corpus of Luther's writings from his list of secondary authorities. Chemnitz followed this pattern as he took a leading role in the composition of the Formula of Concord.

Luther's Authority in the Formula of Concord

Chemnitz and the other authors of the Formula of Concord (1577) worked out a formulation about authority somewhat similar to that of the two Braunschweig *corpora doctrinae* of 1576. They regarded Luther, in the words of Irene Dingel, as guarantor of the true understanding of the Scripture; his writings assumed the role of an authority which reinforces and explicates the truth of the biblical text.[66] The Formulators acknowledged that "by a special grace our merciful God has in these last days brought to light the truth of his Word amid the abominable darkness of the papacy through the faithful ministry of that illustrious man of God, Dr. Luther." Thus the eschatological nature of Luther's career remained as clear as it had been a half century earlier. But the corpus of Luther's writings was not to be found in the Formula's list of those documents which replaced popes, councils, and bishops as the secondary authority for determining biblical interpretation and the teaching of the church. He was no longer accorded adjudicatory authority. Items from just anywhere in the corpus of his writings could no longer be cited in a binding way as could his Smalcald Articles or catechisms, Melanchthon's Augsburg Confession and its Apology, the ancient creeds, and the Formula of Concord itself. The Formulators now placed exclusively in certain confessional documents the authority which had lain earlier in Luther's writings, for Luther's doctrine, "drawn from the Word of God, is summarized in the articles and chapters of the Augsburg Confession against the aberrations of the papacy and of other sects."[67]

The Formula of Concord makes it clear where primary authority lies: "the prophetic and apostolic writings of the Old and New Testaments" are to be regarded "as the pure and clear fountain of Israel, which is the only true norm according to which all teachers and teachings are to be

65. *Kirchenordnung Vnser/von Gottes Genaden/Julij Hertzogen zu Braunschweig . . .* (Wolfenbüttel: Conrad Horn, 1569), A^{v}–[Aiij]^{v}, where it is stated that the Augsburg Confession is to be understood as it is interpreted in its Apology, in the Smalcald Articles, in Luther's Catechisms, "and in other writings of Luther." See also *Vom Catechismo etlicher Wittenbergischen. Der Lerer im Land zu Braunschweig Bedencken* (Jena: Richtzenhan, 1571), [Aii]^{r}–[Aiiij]^{v}.

66. Irene Dingel, "Ablehnung und Aneignung: Die Bewertung der Autorität Martin Luthers in den Auseinandersetzungen um die Konkordienformel," *Zeitschrift für Kirchengeschichte* 105 (1994): 38.

67. "Die Konkordienformel," in *Die Bekenntnisschriften der evangelisch-lutherischen Kirche*, 5th ed. (Göttingen: Vandenhoeck & Ruprecht, 1963), 834 (Solid Declaration, Rule/Norm, 5).

judged and evaluated." The Formulators then enumerate the three ecumenical creeds, the Augsburg Confession, its Apology, the Smalcald Articles, and Luther's two catechisms as documents which represent "the sum and pattern of the doctrine which Dr. Luther of blessed memory clearly set forth in his writings on the basis of God's Word and conclusively established against the papacy and other sects."[68] These writings are to be regarded as "a single, universally accepted, certain, and common form of doctrine to which all our evangelical churches subscribe, and from which and according to which, because it is drawn from the Word of God, all other writings are to be approved and accepted, judged and regulated."[69]

Luther's teaching is here regarded as historically most significant because he brought the light of the gospel to a church darkened by papal oppression. He was a prophetic figure, a special servant, an instrument of God. He "understood the true intention of the Augsburg Confession better than did anyone else"; indeed, he could be regarded as "the chief teacher of the Augsburg Confession." The authors of the Formula even conceded that "since Dr. Luther is rightly to be regarded as the most eminent teacher of the churches which adhere to the Augsburg Confession and as the person whose entire doctrine in sum and content was comprehended in the articles of the aforementioned Augsburg Confession . . . , therefore, the true meaning and intention of the Augsburg Confession cannot be derived more correctly or better from any other source than from Dr. Luther's doctrinal and polemical writings."[70]

Nonetheless, apart from his catechisms and the Smalcald Articles, the Formula accorded Luther's writings no formal secondary authority in the church, as Spangenberg and Musculus and others had been doing. As a matter of fact, Arthur Carl Piepkorn's judgment regarding the entire Book of Concord is apt in regard to the Formula of Concord in specific: "the astonishing thing is not how frequently the Lutheran symbolical books quote Luther's non-symbolical works but how infrequently (speaking relatively) they do so, not how often they appeal to his great magisterial authority but how rarely."[71]

68. Ibid., 834–37 (Solid Declaration, Rule/Norm, 3–9).

69. Ibid., 837–38 (Solid Declaration, Rule/Norm, 10).

70. Ibid., 982–83, 984–85 (Solid Declaration, VII, 33, 34, 41). On the dispute over whether Luther is to be regarded as the (or an) author of the Augsburg Confession, see Kolb, *Confessing the Faith,* 57–59.

71. Arthur Carl Piepkorn, "The Lutheran Symbolical Books and Luther," in *Luther for an Ecumenical Age: Essays in Commemoration of the 450th Anniversary of the Reformation,* ed. Carl S. Meyer (St. Louis: Concordia, 1967), 258–59. See also Bengt Hägglund, "Die Rezeption Luthers in der Konkordienformel," in *Luther und die Bekenntnisschriften* (Erlangen: Martin Luther, 1981), 107–20.

In the course of arguments on the Formula's twelve topics, the Solid Declaration does use passages from Luther's writings to support and clarify its positions more than sixty times. There are seventeen citations in the article on the person of Christ (VIII) and eleven each in the articles on freedom of the will (II) and the Lord's Supper (VII). Except for Article XII, on factions and sects which had never accepted the Augsburg Confession, each article cites Luther at least once. In Article XII the Formulators seem to have followed the principle of the Mansfeld Confession of 1559: they avoided citing Luther against those who had no positive regard for him.

In constructing their basis for Lutheran harmony the Formulators used Luther's words in two different ways. First, in defining what it meant to be Lutheran, they cited his writings in defense of their own interpretation of the intent of his teaching on controverted issues within Lutheranism. In Articles I and II the authors of the Formula quoted Luther to assure their readers that their understanding of Luther's teaching on original sin and freedom of the will was correct, and that the interpretation of their Flacian opponents was not. In Articles VII and VIII the authors appealed to Luther's authority to demonstrate that he had rejected the errors which their Crypto-Philippist opponents had tried to foist on the doctrines of the Lord's Supper and the person of Christ.

Second, the Formulators cited Luther in a more general way, using his authoritative voice to support their interpretation of Scripture. In Articles III (on justification through faith, against Osiander and Rome) and IV (on good works, against Major), for example, Luther's works are cited merely to add support to the biblical argument of the authors, not to adjudicate the issues involved. (Perhaps because Osiandrism and Majorism seemed to have receded by 1577, their citations of Luther no longer required intensive clarification of what Luther had really said on the controverted topics.) Some of these citations in the Formula come not from Luther's writings in general, but from the Smalcald Articles and the catechisms, documents which had been accepted as sources of secondary authority by most Lutherans and by the Formulators themselves in their introductory remarks on authority which follow the description of the entire work as a "Rule and Norm." Nonetheless, some of the appeals to Luther's other works approach the use of his words as a secondary authority even though those works were not formally accepted as such in the introductory remarks.

The Decline of Luther's Prophetic Authority

Why were Luther's works as a whole not universally accepted as a secondary authority among his followers? The explanation for the absence of Luther's corpus of written work from the list of secondary authorities in the Formula of Concord probably rests on three interrelated reasons.

First, the corpus of Luther's writings was immense. The Latin and German series of the Wittenberg edition comprised nineteen volumes, and the Jena edition twelve. Such a mass of material was simply too bulky for expeditious use in monitoring public teaching in the church and adjudicating disputes over biblical interpretation. That indeed had been the experience of Spangenberg and others who had tried to use it.

Second, Luther could be cited against himself. Tolerating adiaphora as a means of avoiding persecution was both supported and rejected on the basis of quotations from Luther. The Osiandrians used Luther to defend their definition of justification by grace through faith, while both the Philippists and Gnesio-Lutherans refuted the Osiandrian position with Luther citations of their own.[72] When Spangenberg fell into disagreement with fellow Gnesio-Lutherans over the proper definition of original sin, both sides marshaled Luther in behalf of their respective positions.[73] In the midst of the controversy over synergism with Viktorin Strigel, Joachim Mörlin complained to Spangenberg and his Mansfeld colleague Hieronymus Menzel that Luther's words could be used and abused by both sides in the dispute.[74] Luther's corpus was simply unwieldy as a source of secondary authority for determining public teaching—not only because of its size, but also because of the diversity of issues and perspectives which determined his particular expression of doctrine in varying situations.

Finally, in the struggles to attain concord among warring Lutheran factions in the mid-1570s, political sensitivity warranted de-emphasizing Luther's authority in order to rehabilitate the partially discredited

72. Osiander issued *Etliche schon Spruche/von der Rechtfertigung des Glaubens/Des Ehrwirdigen Hochgelerten D. Martini Luther heiliger gedechtnis Welche aus den vornemisten vnd besten desselben Bu[e]chern zusamen gezogen . . . Hat Andreas Osiander . . .* (Königsberg: Hans Lufft, 1551); *Excerpta qvaedam dilvcide et perspicve dictorvm de ivstificatione fidei, in commentario, super Epistolam Pauli ad Galatas, reverendi patris, domini Martini Lvtheri,* ed. Andreas Osiander (Königsberg: Hans Lufft, 1551); and *Christlicher vnd Gru[e]ndtlicher bericht/Von der Rechtfertigung des Glaubens/Einwonung Gottes vnd Christi in vns . . . D. Martini Luthers . . . Johannis Brentzij . . . Vrbani Regij . . .* (Nuremberg: Johann Daubmann, c. 1550). Replies came from the Philippist professor Bernhard Ziegler, *Zwo Predigten des Ehrwirdigen herren Doctoris Martini Lutheri . . .* (Leipzig: Hantzsch, 1551); from Musculus or his circle, *Drei Sermon D. Martini Lutheri/darin man spu[e]ren kan wie ein Herlicher Prophetischer Geist in dem manne gewesen ist/das er das/was itzt vngo[e]tliche/vom Andrea Osiandro geleret wird/lengst zuuor/als wu[e]rd es bald geschehen gesehen hat* (Frankfurt/Oder: Johann Eichorn, 1552); and from Flacius's circle, *Tro[e]stliche Gegenspru[e]ch des Ernwirdigen Herren Doctoris Martini Lutheri/vnd Matthie Jllyrici/ wider des Rabe Osiandri Primarij spruch . . .* (Magdeburg: Rödinger, 1552).

73. See pp. 189–90.

74. *Briefwechsel des M. Cyriakus Spangenberg,* 1:6, a letter of 25 February 1563.

Melanchthon. As he campaigned for his Formula of Concord in electoral Saxony in 1577, Jakob Andreae was trying to woo the followers of Melanchthon who felt that the Formula had made too little of his authority. Andreae observed that it was not false humility which had caused Luther to express the wish that almost all of his works would perish, so that nothing but the Bible and his catechism would remain. For Luther had prophesied, Andreae recalled for his readers, that the devil would turn the church once again from the Scriptures to human glosses.[75] Nonetheless, Andreae remained mindful of Luther's informal authority in the popular mind. Three years later, defending the Book of Concord to a much tamed Saxon ministerium, Andreae delivered a five-sermon series that included a number of citations from Luther. As in the Formula itself, the citations in these sermons carried only a limited authority. Luther's words came from the mouth of the "prophet of the last times, God's hero, God's man, God's instrument."[76] They did not, however, command the acceptance which they would have if they had still been the legally authoritative basis for examining public teaching.

An example of the shift which took place in how theologians regarded Luther's works as a source of secondary authority within the church can be found in a series of treatises by Johannes Wigand, a Gnesio-Lutheran pastor and professor. In 1569, in the midst of the tensions over attempts to reconcile the Philippists and Gnesio-Lutherans through compromise, Wigand wrote from his study at the University of Jena on the necessity of confessing the faith without concession. In that treatise he set forth his understanding of the source of authoritative teaching in the church. The norm for confessing the faith was to be

> the Word of God comprehended in the prophetic and apostolic documents. . . . We testify freely and publicly before God and the whole world that we embrace with our whole heart and confess the Word of God as it is handed down and comprehended in the authentic books of the prophets and apostles, [and we further embrace and confess] the three creeds, Apostles', Nicene, and Athanasian; the Augsburg Confession, which was presented in 1530 to Charles V and the entire Holy Roman Empire; its Apology; the Smalcald Articles and the writings of Luther; and the Confutation of the illustrious dukes of Saxony.[77]

75. *Passional Bu[e]chlein/Das ist/Die Historia des bittern vnd thewren leiden vnd sterbens/auch der fro[e]lichen Aufferstehung vnsers Herrn Jhesu Christi* . . . (Wittenberg: Johann Krafft, 1577), 125–26.

76. *Fu[e]nff Predigten: Von dem Wercke der Concordien/Vnd endlichen Vergleichung der vorgefallenen streitigen Religions Artickeln* . . . (Dresden: Gimel Bergen, 1580); on Luther's authority, see B^{r}–Bij^{r}, [Biiij], Eij^{r}–Fij^{v}, T^{r}–[Tiiij]^{r}, [Yiiij] ^{r}–Ziij^{v}, gij^{r}–h^{v}, hiij^{v}–[hiiij]^{v}, i iiij$^{r–v}$.

77. *De confessione in doctrina divina, & necessarijs factis* (Jena: Rödinger, 1569), C5^{v}–[C6]^{r}.

Wigand's standards for public teaching were those held by many Lutherans of his day. The corpus of Luther's writings stood among other documents of secondary authority, as far as Wigand was concerned.

Two years later Wigand delivered an "oration on the teaching and chief battles of Luther" to the students at the University of Jena. Still embroiled in the conflict over defining Luther's legacy, Wigand focused on Luther's struggles. In that context he depicted Luther as hero. Wigand pointed out at the beginning of his oration that throughout history God had sent heroes to change the world. Abraham, Moses, Gideon, David, Judas Maccabeus, Constantine the Great, Charlemagne, and others within the people of God, and Cyrus, Alexander the Great, and Julius Caesar outside God's people had all served as his heroic instruments for guiding world history. Wigand accorded a greater dignity, however, to those who struggled against impious teaching and idolatry within the church. Nothing deserved more praise, nothing could be more useful for humankind, than teaching God's Word properly. Some praised the victories of Hercules, Hannibal, and Julius Caesar. Others praised the lives and miracles of the Fathers. But Luther deserved highest praise for struggling to restore the proper teaching of God's Word.

Wigand presented a typical list of Luther's heroic characteristics. He excelled in the study of the liberal arts, in his knowledge of languages, in his keen judgment and his ability to speak eloquently in sermons, lectures, disputations, and private conversation. He could write eloquently as well. He had a heroic spirit which enabled him to slay not only Goliath but the whole realm of the Antichrist. He had steadfastly and clearly taught heavenly doctrine and had lived a pious life on the basis of his understanding of the righteousness which God had given him. To all this God had added the ideal location, the university, and outstanding associates there, as well as pious and powerful rulers to aid his cause. As God had once used the high priest Hilkiah and King Josiah (2 Kings 22), so had he used Luther to pull Scripture from the darkness of the papal, scholastic labyrinth.[78]

Combining a humanistic sense of the heroic with a sense of the eschatological conflicts at hand, Wigand's oration then reviewed Luther's battles against papal foes, Anabaptists, Schwenckfeld, antinomians, Jews and Turks. Wigand concluded by reminding his hearers of the five most precious bequests which Luther had left them: his German Bible, his catechisms, his comments on the chief books of the Bible, his postils, and his polemical writings against all the enemies of the faith. Wigand urged his students to take seriously Luther's warning that after his death many

78. *Oratio de doctrina et praecipuis certaminibus Lutheri* (Jena: Günther Hüttich, 1571), esp. A3^{r}–B^{v}.

teachers of the church would no longer listen to him and would return to Pelagianism, antinomianism, and sacramentarianism. Against the likes of these Wigand appealed to the hero of the faith, Martin Luther. This appeal, issued in 1571, did not focus on Luther's authority in the church, but only on his example, both in fighting the foes of the faith and in confessing true doctrine.[79] Perhaps Wigand took Luther's authority for granted as he reviewed his hero's teaching on a number of doctrinal topics, but the oration did not explicitly define Wigand's understanding of ecclesiastical authority. The occasion gave no reason to do so.

In the same year, however, in trying to settle the controversy over original sin, Wigand specifically appealed to Luther's writings as authority for adjudicating the dispute and placed them on the same level as the new, legally binding *Corpus doctrinae Thuringicum*. In fact, Wigand explained certain passages from Luther's works which his Flacian opponents had used to support their position. The title of one of his tracts announced that he based his teaching on "God's Word, the *Corpus doctrinae Thuringicum*, and Doctor Luther's books." The opposing position was contrary to "God's Word and the writings of Luther and the confessions of our church."[80]

Wigand again employed Luther's authority directly some seven years later—in 1578—when as bishop of Pomesania (in Prussia) he was locked in a struggle over proper christological formulations with his former friend Tilemann Hesshus. Three criteria could be used to judge public teaching, Wigand argued: the Word of God (in the prophetic and apostolic Scriptures), Luther's writings, and the *Corpus doctrinae* of Prussia, a doctrinal standard formulated by Joachim Mörlin and Martin Chemnitz for the duchy of Prussia in 1567. In his critiques of Hesshus's position Wigand repeatedly appealed to Luther's teaching in general and in specific to a passage in his commentary on Isaiah 53.[81] Luther's teaching could be used to judge the public teaching of the church, Wigand was convinced.

79. Ibid., C2^{r}–[D4]^{v}.

80. *Von der Erbsu[e]nde/Lere aus Gottes Wort/aus dem Du[e]ringischen Corpore Doctrinae/vnd aus D. Luthers Bu[e]chern* . . . (Jena: Donatus Richtzenhan, 1571), Gij^{r}; see also Fiij^{r-v}, M^{v}, and Miij^{v}. The extended treatment of controversial passages in Luther's writings is found in Niiij^{r}–Qiiij^{v}.

81. Johannes Wigand, *1. De abstracto theologico Methodus. 2. Collatio de nova Controuersia. 3. Synodvs Prvtenica de hac re. 4. Cavsae, cvr Locvtiones & doctrinae &c. sint scandalosae & falsae per se* (Königsberg: Georg Osterberg, 1578), 62–65, suggests using a broader base to settle this controversy: the Word of God, the ancient fathers, Luther's writings, and recent expressions of Christian doctrine. But throughout his writings on this controversy Wigand adhered in fact and in practice to the rule set down in his *Wider den blawen dunst eines newen Propheten* (Königsberg: Georg Osterberg, 1578), 11: "Sie/die Kirche Christi/hat diese drey κριτήρια, das ist Regeln des vrteils/Nemlich: Gottes Wort: die schrifften Lutheri: vnd das Preussische Corpus doctrinae."

Four years later—in 1582—after the Book of Concord had been accepted as secondary authority in a majority of German Lutheran churches, including the Prussian church in which Wigand was serving as a bishop, he did address the matter of the teaching authority within the church. He published a personal confession of faith that he had composed several years earlier. In the preface he stated that this confession contained nothing new; its teaching was what he had taught and confessed for the thirty-five years of his public ministry, what he had "heard and learned from God's Word and from Saint Luther's mouth and writings." He was publishing the confession so that others could see how he thought and taught in terms of theses and antitheses, the manner of teaching which the Formula of Concord employed. He thanked God for letting him live long enough to see "such a magnificent, necessary and salutary book of unity [the Book of Concord] in such a form." He went on to defend it against attack by Sacramentarians and Manicheans, by the Crypto-Philippists and Flacians against whom parts of the Formula of Concord were specifically aimed, and by the adherents of the pope as well. In specifying the standard to which his teaching and confession conformed, Wigand then appealed to the Book of Concord, not to the list of documents which had served as his secondary authorities in 1569, 1571, and 1578 (most of which were included in the Book of Concord).[82] The corpus of Luther's writings had fallen by the wayside. Lutheran churches had formally adopted a new secondary authority, and Wigand was determined to teach in accord with it. He insisted that the Book of Concord contained nothing which he had not taught all along; that this was true, the works of Luther and other faithful Lutherans would demonstrate. Thus Luther remained for Wigand, as for the compilers of the Book of Concord, most significant as a source for determining the meaning of God's truth in Scripture. But secondary authority no longer rested in the corpus of his writings. The Book of Concord sufficed.

A similar development can be traced in selected writings of Nikolaus Selnecker of Leipzig. As he helped rebuild the Saxon church after the Crypto-Philippist collapse in 1574, Selnecker delivered a public oration on Luther, the Augsburg Confession, and the agreement between Luther and Melanchthon. He felt that it was imperative to preserve the concept of their agreement since the Saxon church had strongly leaned on Melanchthon's reputation and authority in the previous decades. The settlement for which Selnecker was working depended on winning those whose personal attachment to Melanchthon remained strong.

82. *Confession oder Bekentnis Gotlicher reiner/heilsamer Lere von den fu[e]rnemesten Artickeln des Glaubens/sampt etlicher widerwertigen Lere/Corruptelen vnd Irthum/kurtze vnd gegru[e]nte widerlegung* (Erfurt: Isaiah Melchler, 1582).

Refashioning material which he had gleaned from Johannes Sleidanus's history and Johannes Mathesius's sermons on Luther's life, Selnecker presented the new generation with the story of God's elect instrument, the last Elijah of the last days, one whom Melanchthon could call a hero.[83] As Selnecker reviewed Luther's career, he noted the conflicts with which Satan had afflicted Luther and Luther's bold confession of the faith against error. In discussing the indulgence controversy, Selnecker reviewed the prophecies which had foretold that someone would come in the last days to call the church back to the gospel. At the Wartburg Luther had written much, and what he had written was worthy of a prophet. To secure the Melanchthonian church for Elector August in the wake of the Crypto-Philippist collapse, Selnecker was anxious to show how Luther and Melanchthon had agreed throughout their careers. So he pointed to instances in which they had stood and worked together, in which Melanchthon had functioned as Aaron to Luther's Moses. Above all, Selnecker sought to demonstrate that both Melanchthon and Luther had opposed Zwingli and Calvin.[84] He also quoted Melanchthon's praise of Luther in his analysis of the Wittenberg faculty, which noted the strengths of Bugenhagen (the grammarian), Melanchthon himself (the dialectician), Jonas (the rhetorician), and Luther, "who is all things in everything, to whom none of us can compare."[85]

In 1575 Selnecker freely asserted that divine guidance had led Luther as he engaged in daily writing, preaching, lecturing, and consoling the people of God. However, Selnecker was concerned above all with where interpretive authority lay and how the Saxon church might sort out its doctrinal questions in the midst of the current crisis. He affirmed the authority of the ancient creeds, the Augsburg Confession and its Apology, Luther's Smalcald Articles and his catechisms. Then, in the German version of the oration, he wrote, "We judge Luther's writings not according to what others have written, but we understand what others have written according to Luther's writings, and that which does not agree with Luther we reject, whoever wrote it. For Luther faithfully leads us at all times to the Word, mouth, and foundation of Christ Jesus. Of that we are most certain."[86] Selnecker was directing his audience to read Melanch-

83. *Historica narratio et oratio de D. D. Martino Luthero, postremae aetatis Elia, & initijs, causis, & progressu Confessionis Augustanae, atque Lutheri ac Philippi omonoia sancta*... (Leipzig: Heirs of Jacob Baerwald, 1575), B3^{r}. This work was translated as *Historica Oratio. Vom Leben vnd Wandel des Ehrwirdigen Herrn/vnd thewren Mannes Gottes/ D. Martini Lutheri. Auch von einhelliger vnd bestendiger Eintrechtigkeit Herrn Lutheri vnd Philippi*... (Leipzig: Johannes Rhambau, 1576).

84. *Historica narratio,* [F8]^{r}–G5^{r}.

85. Ibid., G5.

86. *Historica Oratio,* 91^{v}.

thon in the light of Luther, to be sure, but he was revealing something of the same attitude toward Luther's authority which Wigand, Spangenberg, and Musculus had demonstrated. Luther's authority stood next to Scripture in judging the public teaching of the church. More than a respected teacher, more than a hero in the battle against papal error, Luther could also serve as an adjudicating authority for the church.

However, Selnecker himself was soon drawn into the efforts to construct a new secondary authority for Lutherans, efforts which culminated in the publication of the Book of Concord in 1580. His personal defense of the Lutheran position outlined in the Formula of Concord (which he had helped compose in 1577) was represented in a series of lectures published in 1581. One of them treated "the authority of Luther and Philip." Here Selnecker reiterated his belief that Luther's teaching would continue to be the "voice of Christ and the light of the gospel" as long as the earth should last. For God had sent Luther to restore and cleanse the teaching of the gospel, and the Holy Spirit had moved him to do what he had done as a teacher of the church. "We do not place our faith in Luther, as we place our faith in no other human being, but we love Luther because he leads us to Christ and because his writings are subject to the Word of Christ. He instructs us out of this Word."[87] Luther, then, serves the church as a faithful witness and proclaimer, but not as one whose writings can be used as a secondary authority in adjudicating disputes. By 1581 Selnecker had no need of Luther's writings as a replacement for popes, councils, and bishops. The church in Saxony and other Lutheran churches had accepted the Book of Concord as the secondary authority for interpreting the Scriptures and judging public teaching. Luther's writings conveyed God's teaching in a most valuable and perhaps even unique way, but they were no longer needed as secondary authority.[88]

87. *Recitationes aliqvot* . . . (Leipzig: Georg Defner, 1581), 263–74, esp. 263, 265, 268 (4. "De avtoritate Lvtheri et Philippi . . .").

88. In his observation on this point as formulated in Kolb, "Die Umgestaltung," Thomas Kaufmann ("Die Konfessionalisierung von Kirche und Gesellschaft: Sammelbericht über eine Forschungsdebatte," *Theologische Literaturzeitung* 121 [1996]: 1018) misunderstood the argument in suggesting that it does not accord with Johannes Wallmann's analysis of the use of the confessional writings in seventeenth-century Lutheran orthodoxy (e.g., in "Theologie und Frömmigkeit im Zeitalter des Barock," in *Gesammelte Aufsätze* [Tübingen: Mohr/Siebeck, 1995], 46–50). Wallmann noted that the confessional documents did not often function as authorities in the arguments of Lutheran theologians of that period. However, that they cited Luther more frequently than the confessions does not obviate the fact that they accorded the Reformer no formal authority. These citations generally functioned as support for argument based on the primary authority of Scripture rather than as a secondary authority themselves. Even if the orthodox theologians in general cited the Book of Concord relatively seldom as either a formal or functional authority, it remained their legal as well as theological standard.

By the 1590s this change became even more apparent when Selnecker once again used Luther's biography to define the nature of the Lutheran church and of Lutheran teaching. The Crypto-Philippist tendencies had not completely disappeared from the Saxon court; after Elector August's death his son Christian I and a coterie of advisors attempted an introduction of sacramentarian thought once again. This effort failed, but during its half decade in the ascendancy it elicited a storm of public critiques, Selnecker's among them. In the midst of this revival of sacramentarianism within the Saxon church, he reissued his Leipzig oration on Luther because he thought that people were forgetting what great blessings God had given his church in Luther and in the Augsburg Confession. In addition, the Lutheran message remained under threat from both Roman Catholics and Calvinists. Therefore, Selnecker believed it worthwhile to rework his fifteen-year-old oration extensively and make it available to the public once again. He depicted Luther as a unique hero in the history of the church, "the Moses of our age," "the prophet of our time, the last age of the church."[89] However, the notion of a unique authority for judging public teaching had vanished from Selnecker's view of Luther's role in the church.[90]

In the turbulent days of the early Reformation Luther's thunderous call for reform had commanded the attention of the populace and the intellectual elite of Germany. As his call for reform was institutionalized, and his church refused to concede interpretive authority to popes and councils, a new secondary level of authority had to be found. The church needed some means of interpreting passages of Scripture which did not self-evidently interpret themselves. In the midst of disagreements theologians had to find arbiters to guide them into the meaning

89. *Oratio historica de initiis, cavsis, et progressv confessionis Augustanae, et de vita ac laboribus D. D. Martini Lvtheri, postremae aetatis Eliae . . .* (Jena: Tobias Steinmann, 1592), 34ʳ, 55ᵛ, 60ᵛ.

90. In his "Die Lutherbiographie von Nikolaus Selnecker: Selneckers Berufung auf die Autorität Luthers im Normenstreit der Konfessionalisierung in Kursachsen," *Archiv für Reformationsgeschichte* 86 (1995): 91–123, Hans Peter Hasse disagrees with my interpretation that Selnecker's regard for Luther's authority shifted over the years following 1574 (see esp. 113–15). He is indeed correct in observing that after 1580 Luther remains for Selnecker a teacher with authority, and he is also correct in observing that in 1574 the Augsburg Confession, e.g., functioned alongside Luther as a secondary authority for Selnecker. I do not find in Hasse's discussion, however, evidence to contradict my contention that in 1574 Selnecker, identifying Luther's writings as a source for clear and correct teaching from the Master, used language that attributed to them adjudicatory authority that could be used to decide doctrinal disputes, whereas language ascribing such formal authority to the corpus of Luther's works cannot be found in the laudatory comments that Selnecker made in the 1580s and 1590s about the Reformer's usefulness as a guide and instructor for public teaching.

of the Bible. Indeed, every organized group of Christians has standards for regulating the teaching and life of the church, whether they be codified or uncodified. Luther himself loomed so large over the developing Lutheran Reformation that it was only natural for his followers to regard him as the voice of prophetic authority, the authoritative interpreter of God's Word for their day.

The humanist appreciation of the power of oral presentation helped make it possible for his contemporaries to view Luther's proclamation as authoritative. His own concept of "the living voice of the gospel [viva vox evangelii]" expressed the biblical idea that God's Word is an active force in the mouths of preachers. This belief that the Word, spoken or written, is performative as it encounters hearers or readers—combined with and supported by the humanists' emphasis on rhetoric and lively speech—made it natural to look to a contemporary proclaimer such as Luther, with his command of words and the Word, for authority.

Luther submitted his entire teaching to the authority of God's Word in the text of Scripture. The humanists also respected ancient texts. They attributed authority to texts composed by the wise, learned, and insightful. They were prepared to rely on such texts as standards for, as well as conveyors of, the truth. The Augsburg Confession served and sufficed for a time alongside the Wittenberg faculty, but after Luther's death disputes arose over the interpretation of the text of the Confession and the integrity of the faculty. A number of Lutheran principalities and municipalities assembled collections of doctrinal documents to which they ascribed interpretive authority. Some of Luther's followers turned to the corpus of his writings for authoritative pronouncement on disputed questions. When this corpus was found too cumbersome, too contradictory, too controverted, to serve as a secondary authority, Melanchthon's heirs found in the Book of Concord a new interpretive authority for the church.

3

The German Prophet

Luther as Hero of the People and the Nation against the Baalites of Rome

Luther's prophetic authority may have faded for the Lutheran churches, but Lutherans continued to regard him as a heroic figure, the advocate of God's gospel against its enemies, above all against the papacy. In the popular mind the German Hercules of the 1520s remained the champion of God's truth and God's people for generations. The image of Luther as defending church and nation by defying evil endured.

Depicting the Hero

Not only words but also pictures played a role in imprinting Luther's heroic image on the popular mind. Alongside the new medium of print the medium of the commemorative medallion brought Luther's visage and short summaries of his message to wider circles of the population, and particularly to the nobles and the burghers. "The Reformation coincided with the peak production of German medallions in the sixteenth century. . . . As products of their time [the commemorative coins and medallions] are able to offer a deep glimpse into the judgment of the people of that age and into the change of view which took place in the course of that time. While they reflect the currents of the age, they also set its accents in place and contribute to a deeper, more richly colored understanding of the Reformation."[1]

Both in artistic imagery and in the content of their inscriptions these medals echoed the tracts which presented the person and message of the Wittenberg monk to the public. Luther's portrait appeared on me-

1. Hugo Schnell, *Martin Luther und die Reformation auf Münzen und Medaillen* (Munich: Klinkhardt & Biermann, 1983), 13, 14–15.

dallions as early as 1517; more were issued in the 1520s. In 1521 Luther appeared in his doctoral hat and monk's cowl on the front of a coin; on the back was written in Latin that if Luther was guilty of the charge of heresy, Christ, too, had been a criminal.[2] A medallion produced in 1524 placed Luther in more modest company, depicting him as an apostle; another from 1537 affirmed that he was the prophet of Germany.[3] A number of these medallions appeared at the time of his death, some repeating the defiant cry of Johannes Bugenhagen and other Lutherans, "Doctor Martin Luther, the German prophet: I was your plague while I lived, Pope; as I die, I will be your death."[4] The practice continued. Luther medallions issued around the centennial observations of the posting of the Ninety-Five Theses proclaimed that "Luther's teaching is God's Word, and it will therefore never perish."[5] Most medallions commemorating the Reformer presented him as proclaimer and defender of the Word of God, and therefore as the pope's foremost enemy, a hero of the faith.

Luther as Portrayed by Cranach's Studio (1560) (Lutherhalle, Wittenberg)

Luther's message and person were celebrated in other visual forms as well. Pictures of him were mass-produced in artists' studios and printshops. If contemporary reports are to be believed, his friend Lukas Cranach the Elder supervised the production of literally thousands of portraits of Luther in several series and poses.[6] Probably many hung on walls in homes and shops. Some may have received adulation not unlike that given saints in the Middle Ages, but most undoubtedly were displayed out of an appreciation for Luther as a national hero or even as a religious prophet. His old friend, the Saxon elector's onetime physician Matthaeus Ratzeberger, had a picture of Luther on his wall. As he lay dying in 1558, he smiled at Luther's

2. Ibid., 115, #5.
3. Ibid., 116, #6; 117, #10.
4. Ibid., 118, #13.
5. For examples see *Luther mit dem Schwan, Tod und Verklärung: Katalog zur Ausstellung in der Lutherhalle Wittenberg anläßlich des 450. Todestages von Martin Luther* (Wittenberg: Lutherhalle and Schelzky & Jeep, 1996), 110–11.
6. *Lukas Cranach, Ein Maler-Unternehmer aus Franken: Katalog zur Landesausstellung* . . . , ed. Claus Grimm et al. (Augsburg: Haus der Bayerischen Geschichte, 1994), 352–54.

Wolfgang Stuber, "Luther as Jerome" (c. 1587) (Lutherhalle, Wittenberg)

image and said, "My dear Luther!" and then commented to those surrounding his deathbed, "If God wills, I will be with him soon, and then we will have a really good chat with each other and discuss the many strange and wondrous things that have happened since his death"[7]—not an invocation, but simply a warm, personal appreciation of a friend.

Throughout the sixteenth and into the early seventeenth century such portraits of Luther were being produced ever anew and distributed

7. Andreas Poach, *Vom Christlichen Abschied aus diesem sterblichen Leben des lieben thewren Mannes Matthei Ratzebergers der Artzney Doctors Bericht . . .* (Jena: Thomas Rebart, 1559), [Fiiij]$^{r-v}$.

widely. Painters and engravers inserted Luther into traditional settings, such as Saint Jerome's study. With the skull and lion conventional in portraits of Jerome, and the unconventional aphorism addressed to the papacy, "I was your plague while alive, and dying I will be your death," Wolfgang Stuber depicted Luther studying the Scriptures (c. 1587).[8]

More often artists of the period portrayed the Reformer in his university gown, standing firm with Bible in hand, sometimes closed, often open, a likeness from the Cranach workshop reproduced literally thousands of times. The figure of a swan—to signify Luther's fulfilling the prophecy of reform allegedly uttered by John Huss (see p. 34)—or the "Luther rose" (a white rose together with a red heart and black cross) often decorates such portraits. Words support the image of confessor and teacher that they convey. Such portraits also sometimes repeat the motto, "I was your plague while alive, and dying I will be your death." For example, a painting by Hamburg craftsman Jacob Jacobsen in 1603 inserts this message in the upper-right-hand corner. On the pages of the open Bible in this picture are the words of John 3:16, "For God so loved the world that he gave his only begotten Son, that all who believe in him may not be lost but have eternal life."[9] A decade later the artist Valentin Köser executed a similar picture, with swan and Luther rose. It acclaimed the "great man Martin Luther" as the greatest light which had come to earth "from Jaspis's blood and lineage." This motif was repeated in contemporary engravings which announced, "Luther, God's faithful hero against the devil, the pope, and the world, brought to light, pure and clear, what had been placed in darkness."[10] Such portrayals of both the positive and negative elements of Luther's heroic prophetic action—proclamation of the gospel of Christ and destruction of the realm of the Antichrist—reminded viewers of his courageous stance of confession against all the enemies of the truth.

Popular art in the form of broadsides reinforced this image of Luther. He appeared in a broadside that was produced by Pankratius Kempff around 1550 and that focused on the hymn "Lord, Keep Us Steadfast in Your Word," and prayers to Father, Son, and Holy Spirit. Luther is pointing an audience of princes to the heavens, where the three persons of the Trinity are depicted. Under the throne of Christ his wrath is bringing fiery judgment upon popes, monks, and other assorted Roman clerics.[11] A broadsheet from 1569 entitled "Luther Tri-

8. *Martin Luther, 1483 bis 1546: Katalog der Ausstellung in der Staatlichen Lutherhalle Wittenberg* (Wittenberg: Lutherhalle, 1983), 140–41.

9. *Luther mit dem Schwan,* 84–85.

10. Ibid., 85–88.

11. *Martin Luther, 1483 bis 1546,* 216 (and plate 46).

"Luther Triumphing" (1569) (Lutherhalle, Wittenberg)

umphing" depicts him holding the Bible against Pope Leo X; the accompanying text recalls his battle for Christ's truth and his confession of faith in the grace of the Son of God.[12]

12. Ibid., 88–89. See also Carl C. Christensen, *Princes and Propaganda: Electoral Saxon Art of the Reformation* (Kirksville, Mo.: Sixteenth Century Journal, 1992), 79–83, on similar antipapal polemic in picture form.

Sixteenth- and seventeenth-century artists portrayed Luther as more than the hero of the fight against papal darkness. In the 1530s Lukas Cranach the Elder depicted him and other Reformers together with members of the Saxon ducal family; thus the theologians were associated with the political leadership of Saxony, and the Wettin family was associated with the religious prophet and his colleagues.[13] In 1554 Peter Heymanns, artist at the court of the Pomeranian dukes in Stettin, created a large tapestry in which Luther proclaims to Saxon and Pomeranian princely families the words of John 1:29 and 3:15–16 as he points to Christ on the cross.[14] In 1556 Cranach's son, Lukas the Younger, created a painting of the baptism of Christ in the presence of members of the princely family of Anhalt; Luther is in their midst and the city of Dessau in the background. About the same time Jakob Lucius executed a similar picture of Christ's baptism in the Elbe at Wittenberg; Luther is in the company of the recently deceased Elector John Frederick and his family. This basic formula was often reproduced.[15] Luther and the princely families mutually reinforced each other's standing through such depictions; the verses recorded under the picture of the baptism in the Elbe make it clear that John Frederick provided his people with a model of confessing the faith which Luther had taught.

Such portrayals also enhanced the perception that Luther was among the primary witnesses to Christ, a gospel teacher of the first order. In an altar panel painted by Lukas Cranach the Younger for the parish church of Kemberg in 1565, the Reformer appeared in the company only of other Wittenberg theologians—and the artist's father—as observers of Christ's baptism.[16] In the same year the same group, including Melanchthon, Bugenhagen, and others, appeared with Christ in a Lord's Supper scene Cranach prepared for the village church in Mildensee near Dessau. In addition, an altarpiece Cranach prepared for Nordhausen's Church of Saint Blasius in 1558 depicted the same company of theologians as witnesses to Christ's raising Lazarus from the dead. And in an altarpiece made for the city church in Weimar

13. *Martin Luther und die Reformation in Deutschland: Ausstellung zum 500. Geburtstag Martin Luthers veranstaltet vom Germanischen Nationalmuseum Nürnberg* . . . (Frankfurt/Main: Insel, 1983), 324–25.

14. *Kunst der Reformationszeit, Staatliche Museen zu Berlin* . . . (Berlin: Elefanten, 1983), 368, 412–13. See also Christensen, *Princes and Propaganda,* 101–18, 136–38.

15. *Kunst der Reformationszeit,* 361–63. The theme was repeated in Nuremberg in the 1550s and 1560s, with the baptism taking place in the Pegnitz, and with different groups of evangelical theologians and princes (pp. 422–25).

16. On this and similar altarpieces see Carl C. Christensen, *Art and the Reformation in Germany* (Athens, Ohio: Ohio University Press, 1979), 136–54.

"Baptism of Christ, with the Electoral Family" (Lutherhalle, Wittenberg)

three years earlier Cranach had placed Luther and the elder Cranach alongside John the Baptist at the foot of the cross. This was part of a representation of law and gospel such as the Cranachs had produced in several artistic genres. Luther is pointing to the biblical text as he gives witness to Christ. Similarly, the predella of the altar that Lukas Cranach the Elder had made for the town church in Wittenberg about the time of the Reformer's death had portrayed Luther as the proclaimer of the Word. The center of an engraving by a Wittenberg artist of the following generation depicted Luther preaching in the pulpit. The engraving also represented the Reformer and John Huss distributing the Lord's Supper while assorted papalist figures are being consumed by the fiery jaws of hell.[17] The Cranachs and others repeatedly painted Luther, sometimes alone, sometimes in the midst of his colleagues. In this way artists reinforced the images promulgated by their literary comrades who used words to describe the teacher and hero who had returned the church to Christ's teaching and routed the papal tyrant.

It was not only on altarpieces that Luther was represented as teacher of the biblical truth. By the end of the sixteenth century he had begun to appear on pulpits as well. On a pulpit fashioned in 1565 for the Church of Saint John in Chemnitz, Luther along with John the Baptist pointed parishioners to the crucified Christ. The castle church of Altenburg received a pulpit in 1595 which featured Moses, Paul, Christ, John the Baptist, and Luther upon its panels. Adam and Eve, Moses, Christ,

17. *Kunst der Reformationszeit,* 421–22. On this motif see Christensen, *Princes and Propaganda,* 118–21.

Paul, and Luther appeared on a sandstone pulpit created in 1598 for the church in Mengeringhausen in northern Hesse.[18]

Other visual images served to impress Luther's person and message upon the minds of the people. His personal coat of arms, the Luther rose, became a powerful symbol of his ministry. In the 1570s a pastor in Illeben, Andreas Kreuch, could point above his pulpit to a painted representation of Luther's emblem. As he explained it to his hearers, Kreuch rejected the charge that Lutherans had made an idol out of Luther. They cited him instead because he had conveyed the teaching of Christ, Paul, and all the other prophets and apostles. After sketching Luther's biography, Kreuch explained the symbolism of the Luther rose: the white rose suggests the comforting promise of God's affirming his gracious aid against sin, death, the devil, and all the enemies of the believer; the red heart represents the confession which believers make from the heart; the cross recalls the suffering of the Christian life and points to Christ as the crusader who defeats all the enemies of his people. The cross's color, black, reminds Christians how bitter Christ's suffering was and how bitter theirs is.[19]

Moved by such symbolism and explanations, the Lutheran populace continued to celebrate the victory of the man and his message over the papal enemy. Luther's followers continued to cast him in the role of the prophet Elijah opposing the prophets of Baal. Among the populace, which had been aroused by tract writers and preachers and had greeted Luther as an Elijah and a Daniel in the 1520s, he remained that kind of prophetic figure. For supporters such as Kreuch at least, the heroic pastor was inseparable from his message. Luther's symbol not only recalled his heroic confession, but also conveyed the gospel of Christ, a prophetic message.

The Characteristics of the Prophetic Hero

To a singular extent Luther's message and his person became entwined with each other. The medium of the proclaimer's person became a significant part of the message in the case of this prophetic figure. Whether viewed and used as a secondary authority for adjudicating disputes and determining the truth, or as a learned and insightful teacher

18. These and other examples are discussed in *Luther mit dem Schwan,* 44–50. He also joined the four Evangelists on pulpits made in the nineteenth century and in the United States, e.g., at (Old) Trinity Lutheran Church in St. Louis.

19. Andreas Kreuch, *Sigillum Lutheri. Eine Christliche vnd einfeltige Predigt/Vom Sigill vnd Merckzeichen/des Hocherleuchten vnd Gottseligen Mannes Gottes/D. Martini Lutheri, welches gewesen Ein Rot Hertz/mit einem schwartzen Creutze/in einer Weissen Rosen: Darinnen vnser gantz Christenthumb abgebildet . . .* (n.p., 1579).

of the church, or as a hero whose overthrow of papal error and tyranny symbolized the hopes and aspirations of the people of his nation—or as a combination of two or three of these paradigms—Martin Luther remained an important tool for Lutheran theologians and for other public leaders. They continued to interpret his unique role in God's economy for church and culture. In the public square these efforts at defining his significance took form in several ways.

As noted above, medieval expectations of heroic and saintly figures influenced popular conceptions of Luther's person and role. Saints, for example, were expected to reveal divine presence and power with their predictive abilities. Thus some contemporaries regarded Luther as a prophet who had not only proclaimed God's Word, but also predicted God's intervention in the course of human history. Luther's predictions regarding the judgment of God which would fall over Germany after his death were fulfilled, the people believed, in the Smalcald War and in the distress which followed it.[20]

According to popular tales, Luther himself fulfilled several prophecies. The astronomer Johannes Lichtenberger had prophesied that a "small prophet" would be born in 1484, and some believed that Luther was indeed that prophet even though Luther had dismissed Lichtenberger's claim as fantasy.[21] Much more popular was the prophecy constructed out of utterances of Jerome of Prague and John Huss as they were condemned to the stake at the Council of Constance in 1415. Huss predicted that although his goose (in Czech "Huss") would be cooked, eagles and falcons with greater power and insight than he had would arise to complete his work of reform. His colleague, Jerome of Prague, expressed his wish to see what the church would be like a century later. From these two statements came the popular belief that Huss had predicted that a swan would come to grace Christendom a hundred years after his burning (see p. 34). Robert Scribner has traced the evolution of this prophecy from Luther's own designation of himself as a swan singing the "clear, sweet song of the evangelical message," through Bugenhagen's phrasing of Huss's prophecy in the words "You may burn a goose, but in a hundred years will come a swan you will not be able to burn," to the assertion in 1556 that this sentence was uttered by Huss as he was taken to his execution. Both populace and theologians took

20. Robert W. Scribner, "Incombustible Luther: The Image of the Reformer in Early Modern Germany," *Past & Present* 110 (Feb. 1986): 63–64. Regarding collections of such prophecies, see pp. 178–83.

21. Robert W. Scribner, "Luther-Legenden des 16. Jahrhunderts," in *Martin Luther, Leben, Werk, Wirkung,* ed. Günter Vogler et al. (Berlin: Akademie, 1986), 383–84; see also Will Erich Peuckert, *Die Grosse Wende, Geistesgeschichte und Volkskunde* (Darmstadt: Wissenschaftliche Buchgesellschaft, 1966), 613–19.

this prophecy very seriously as a confirmation that Luther was indeed a special agent and hero whom God had commissioned against the papacy for the reform of his church.[22]

Johannes Mathesius listed two other predictions which he regarded as certain indications of Luther's role as a divine prophet. As Luther lay deathly ill at some time during his youth, an old man had prophesied that he would not die but become an important man. And while imprisoned in Eisenach in 1483, a Franciscan heretic, Johann Hilten, predicted that another reforming monk would be sent to the church in 1516. In the popular imagination Luther clearly fit into God's plan.[23]

New legends of prophecies concerning Luther sprang up during the course of the century following his career. At the time of the centennial anniversary of the posting of the Ninety-Five Theses a report was published concerning a prophetic dream which Elector Frederick the Wise allegedly had on the eve of Luther's challenge to his colleagues to address the issue of indulgences. The report claimed to be based on an account which a contemporary had heard from Luther's student and friend, Anton Musa, who had allegedly received it directly from Georg Spalatin, who was Frederick's secretary at the time as well as Luther's early and close associate.

Awakened in the middle of the night, Frederick prayed for the souls in purgatory and for God's grace that he might lead his electorate to the truth and salvation. He slept again and dreamt that God had sent a monk to him, the son of Saint Paul, and this monk wanted to write something on the castle church in Wittenberg. Saints from throughout Christian history testified in the monk's behalf, so in his dream Frederick granted the monk permission. He proceeded to write his message both in very large print, so that it could be seen from a long way off, and with a quill pen so large that it reached to Rome, pierced through the ears of a lion there, and struck and shook the crown of the pope. Frederick awoke at that point, fell asleep again, and the dream repeated itself, this time revealing the fury of the lion against the monk. In a third installment Frederick tried to help break the quill of the monk, but it would not crack. Frederick asked the monk where he had gotten such a feather quill, and he replied that it had come from a hundred-year-old Bohemian goose (John Huss). Suddenly, before Frederick's wondering eyes appeared a host of similar quills in Wittenberg, reinforcing the

22. Scribner, "Incombustible Luther," 42–43.

23. Johannes Mathesius, *Historien/Von des Ehrwirdigen in Gott Seligen thewren Manns Gottes, Doctoris Martini Luthers/anfang/lehr/leben vnd sterben . . .* (Nuremberg: Johann vom Berg's heirs and Ulrich Neuber, 1566), IIII^{r-v}.

monk's mission.[24] This report served to confirm for its readers the divine origin of Luther's calling from the outset of his public career. It affirmed Luther's place in the sequence of those who testified to God's truth throughout the history of the church, including John Huss, and it called attention to Luther's use of the printed word in shaking papal power.

In the popular mind Luther's status as a prophetic hero was reinforced not only by prophecies about him, but also by a touch of the supernatural which surrounded his own utterances and actions. Some stories spread among the people regarded Luther as something of a miracle worker—in some cases approaching the kind of miracle ascribed to the medieval saints. Stories of his incombustibility, for example, seemed to prove his special status. Fueling such stories was a report from Bavaria according to which Luther, in the form of a paper image, proved to be quite combustible but nonetheless brought fire—and thus God's wrath—down upon his Jesuit opponents. The occasion was a Jesuit-arranged disputation in the presence of Bavarian princes and the common people between a Jesuit clad as a Roman Catholic bishop and a life-sized picture of Luther, set alongside a pile of his books. Although the author of the report was certain that Luther would have won had he been there in person, the Jesuit cast as a bishop was deemed to have triumphed. Following this trumped-up debate the princes forced the citizenry to take an oath "against God and the Christian religion" and then ordered a search of homes for Lutheran books to add to the pile. The picture of Luther and the books were burned. The author of the pamphlet commented that the Jesuits could not, however, burn Christ, and that one word from Luther's catechism was stronger than all of theirs. The comedy turned to tragedy, the report continued, when a spark from the fire landed in the ducal castle, destroying several buildings and, with them, food supplies and weaponry.[25] Luther had claimed his recompense; even in the form of a paper replica, he could deliver God's word of judgment.

24. The report of the dream is reproduced and analyzed in Ernst Benz, "Der Traum Kurfürst Friedrichs des Weisen," in *Humanitas-Christianitas: Walther v. Loewenich zum 65. Geburtstag,* ed. Karlmann Beyschlag, Gottfried Maron, and Eberhard Wolfel (Witten: Luther, 1968), 134–49. The dream became the subject of artistic broadsides in 1617; see Hans Volz, "Der Traum Friedrichs des Weisen vom 30./31. Oktober 1517: Eine bibliographisch-ikonographische Untersuchung," *Gutenberg-Jahrbuch* 45 (1970): 174–211. See p. 128 of this volume for a depiction of the dream in a broadside from 1617.

25. *Newe Zeitung. Eine warhafftige Geschicht/welche sich zugetragen hat zu Mu[e]nchen im Beyerland/von der Jesuuitischen Rotte/wie sie Doctor Luthern sein Ebenbild: welcher in Gott seligen lengest vorschieden ist/mit seinem Bu[e]chern vorbrendt haben. Was aber fu[e]r vnglu[e]ck daraus entstanden ist/werdet jhr in dieser Geschicht lesen . . .* (Lübeck[?]: Johann Balhorn der Jüngere[?], 1580).

Later accounts of Luther's incombustibility described portraits of Luther which did not burn in house fires and ascribed this phenomenon to divine intervention. Such accounts reflect a story circulated already in 1521 that a picture of Luther did not burn when a set of his books was set aflame. That story did not purport to be historical but allegorical. However, seventeenth- and eighteenth-century accounts of Luther's pictures or personal effects refusing to burn were reported as true.[26]

A careful review of the legends gathered in the nineteenth century concerning Luther's alleged miraculous powers shows that his miracles were for the most part of a different type from those of the medieval saints. For every example of something genuinely inexplicable or extraordinary there were several miracles from the realm of spiritual warfare or spiritual heroics. In the catalog of 139 Luther legends assembled by Heidemarie Gruppe from nineteenth-century sources,[27] the largest single group falls into the category of "Luther slept here" stories, explaining why a local tree or spring was named for Luther. Certain stories celebrated his common touch as a man of the people. For instance, he turned to the local butcher for aid in determining the right words for translating animal parts in Leviticus, and he used his lathe in his spare time. Some stories attributed to his message or his career, or even his prayers, a special power. While this power came through this particular holy representative of God, it became clear, as the stories were retold, that the power involved was the power of the gospel—not of the man. Other stories recounted his struggles against the devil, including ordinary accounts of resisting temptation as well as reports of exorcism and of his hurling his inkpot at Satan. To be sure, some stories attributed to Luther the magical powers of medieval saints to stop fire and to cause the rain to fall or not to fall, but these were relatively rare in comparison to those of his spiritual power exercised through the Word of God. In the popular imagination Luther took on larger-than-life proportions, though those proportions usually remained at the edge of normal human expectations.

Writing the Life of the Hero

Many of the popular attitudes toward Luther as hero and prophet were reflected in and were fed by the biographical literature produced by Luther's students and followers. Luther's own reflective thoughts on his career as they are found in the Wittenberg edition of his works and the

26. Scribner, "Incombustible Luther," 38–68.

27. Heidemarie Gruppe, "Katalog der Luther- und Reformationssagen des 19. Jahrhunderts," in *Volkserzählung und Reformation,* ed. Wolfgang Brückner (Berlin: Schmidt, 1974), 295–311. See also Scribner, "Incombustible Luther," 42–43; and Wolfgang Brückner, "Luther als Gestalt der Sage," in *Volkserzählung und Reformation,* 261–94 (a survey of literature regarding Luther as prophet and hero).

several descriptions of his life issued by his colleague Philip Melanchthon around the time of his death gave impetus to students and followers who wanted to record the details of Luther's life for a variety of reasons and purposes. Most prominent among them was his former student, Johannes Mathesius, pastor in Joachimsthal in Bohemia. His homiletical life of the Reformer, first published in 1566, shaped and influenced subsequent Luther biography in all its forms for more than two centuries to come.

Mathesius was not the first to attempt a comprehensive overview of Luther's life. That effort was made by Johannes Cochlaeus, a canon at Breslau and one of Luther's most strident Roman Catholic critics. Cochlaeus constructed a piece of polemic in the form of biography which appeared in 1549.[28] Nor was Mathesius the first among Luther's students to attempt to sketch his life. While compiling the first Lutheran martyrology, Ludwig Rabus, pastor in Strassburg and Ulm, produced a survey of Luther's life with a focus on his confession of the faith as evidenced in his writings.[29] Rabus called Luther "our dear father and the prophet of the German nation" and regarded his mentor as a key figure in the course of the history of the church and the world. Although the contemporary era of martyrdom had begun with John Huss and Jerome of Prague, Luther stood clearly at the center of the last age of the church with his proclamation of the gospel. His eschatological importance was made clear to Rabus's readers.[30]

But Rabus's work appeared in only two editions, the first of them in two printings. Mathesius's sermons on Luther's life were reprinted eleven times before the end of the century and many times thereafter. Whether the assertion that his work is "the only German biography of the sixteenth century which can lay claim to a higher significance" is true or not,[31] Mathesius did determine to a large extent the way in

28. Cochlaeus, *Commentaria Ioannis Cochlaei, de actis et scriptis Martini Lvtheri Saxonis . . .* (Mainz: Franz Behem, 1549). See also Remigius Bäumer, *Johannes Cochlaeus (1479–1552): Leben und Werk im Dienst der katholischen Reform* (Münster: Aschendorff, 1980), 101–12; A. Herte, *Die Lutherkommentare des Johannes Cochläus* (Münster: Aschendorff, 1935); and Martin Spahn, *Johannes Cochläus: Ein Lebensbild aus der Zeit der Kirchenspaltung* (Berlin: Dames, 1898), 237–45.

29. See Robert Kolb, *For All the Saints: Changing Perceptions of Martyrdom and Sainthood in the Lutheran Reformation* (Macon, Ga.: Mercer University Press, 1987), 41–83 (on Rabus) and 108–15 (on Rabus's treatment of Luther).

30. *Der Heyligen ausserwo[e]hlten Gottes Zeugen, Bekennern vnd Martyrern . . . Historien . . .* (Strassburg: Samuel Emmel, 1556), 4:j[r]–cccxliiij[v]; in the second edition, *Historien der Martyrer* (Strassburg: Josias Rihel, 1572), 2:110[r]–211[v].

31. E. Fueter, *Geschichte der neueren Historiographie,* 3d ed. (Munich/Berlin, 1936), cited by Eike Wolgast, "Biographie als Autoritätsstiftung: Die ersten evangelischen Lutherbiographien," in *Biographie zwischen Renaissance und Barock: Zwölf Studien,* ed. Walter Berschin (Heidelberg: Mattes, 1993), 63.

which Luther's life was viewed by many of his contemporaries and by most Lutherans in succeeding generations. Fourteen of his sermons chronicled Luther's career; the concluding three memorialized him as a mentor, praised the University of Wittenberg, and tied Luther's life to the mining activities of Mathesius's parishioners in Joachimsthal.

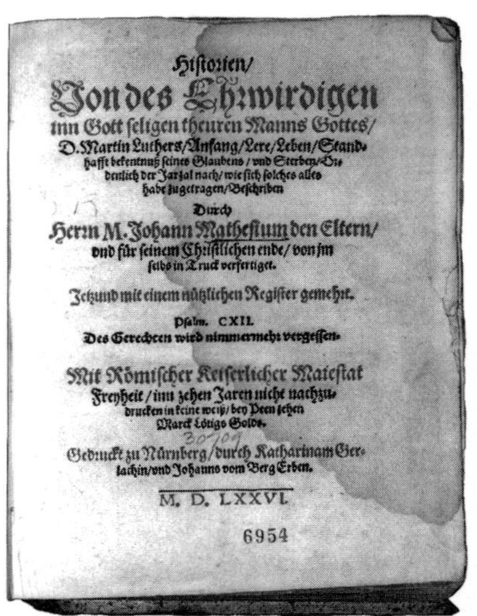

Historien/
Von des Ehrwirdigen
inn Gott seligen theuren Manns Gottes/
D. Martin Luthers/Anfang/Lere/Leben/Standhafft bekentnuß seines Glaubens/vnd Sterben/Ordenlich der Jarzal nach/wie sich solches alles habe zugetragen/Beschriben
Durch
Herrn M. Johann Mathesium den Eltern/
vnd für seinem Christlichen ende/von im selbs in Truck verfertiget.
Jetzund mit einem nützlichen Register gemehrt.
Psalm. CXII.
Des Gerechten wird nimmermehr vergessen.
Mit Römischer Keiserlicher Maiestat Freyheit/inn zehen Jaren nicht nachzudrucken in keine weiß/bey Peen zehen Marck Lötigs Golds.
Gedruckt zu Nürnberg/durch Katharinam Gerlachin/vnd Johanns vom Berg Erben.
M. D. LXXVI.
6954

Johann Mathesius, *Historien/Von . . . Martini Luthers anfang/lehr/leben vnd sterben . . .* (edition of 1576) (Concordia Seminary Library, St. Louis)

Ernst Walter Zeeden has summarized the Luther whom Mathesius depicts as, above all, curate of souls, and that he certainly is. But in Mathesius's own words Luther appears more often as one who conveys the Word of God, as doctor of the church, and as "the worthy German prophet."[32] (Because this was an era of loose allegiance to the emperor and empire, "German" here is not technically a national designation; rather, it had a strong confessional component in Joachimsthal, where the term for German-speaking people linked them with their adherence to the Wittenberg Reformation.) Luther's exercise of the office to which God called him, doctor of the church and prophet for the Germans, reflected the positive and negative elements of contemporaries' interpretation of the Reformer's mission. Luther brought the light of the gospel to shine again—in the midst of papal darkness. He preached and taught the pure Word of God—against all the impurities introduced by the pope's followers and the sects.[33] As Eike Wolgast notes, Mathesius's picture of Luther is psychologically static. He did not trace any development of Luther's personality.[34] He presented to his reader the man of heroic and prophetic proportions whom he had encountered for the first time as an awestruck student in 1529. Without benefit of modern psychological presuppositions, Mathesius needed no further analysis of his mentor's personality. He knew a prophet when he experienced one.

By calling him Elijah, Mathesius made it clear to his readers that Luther occupied a unique role in the history of the church. To this he

32. Ernst Walter Zeeden, *Martin Luther und die Reformation im Urteil des deutschen Luthertums,* 2 vols. (Freiburg/B: Herder, 1952), 1:37; Kolb, *For All the Saints,* 115–20.

33. Hans Volz, *Die Lutherpredigten des Johannes Mathesius: Kritische Untersuchung zur Geschichtsschreibung im Zeitalter der Reformation* (Halle: Waisenhaus, 1929), 46–52.

34. Wolgast, "Biographie," 64.

joined Jonas's and Melanchthon's phrase "the horseman and chariot of Israel."[35] Mathesius did not argue explicitly, however, that Luther had secondary authority in the church, nor did he use him in efforts to settle controversies, as did Musculus and Spangenberg. Mathesius's latter-day Elijah battled the Roman priests of Baal. His Luther proclaimed the prophetic and apostolic word with fresh clarity and insight. He gave his hearers and readers the gospel of Jesus Christ with strength and sweetness. He struggled against God's foes, Satan and his minions within the papalist and sectarian groups of his day. He was a heroic man of God in the line of succession which included Moses and David, as well as Paul and Athanasius and finally John Huss and Girolamo Savonarola.[36] Mathesius regarded Luther also as the German prophet, and in the fashion of earlier northern humanists reflected national consciousness shaped largely in opposition to Italian and Roman tyranny.[37] But above all, even as Mathesius recognized the historic chain of witnesses to God's truth of which his prophet was a part, he emphasized the eschatological struggle in which Luther had engaged.

Although Hans Volz has concluded that Mathesius's description of his mentor reveals the influence of humanistic biography, not of medieval hagiography,[38] the sermons on Luther do contain elements which reinforced his heroic, if not superhuman, status as a specially chosen instrument of God. Undoubtedly, Mathesius believed that he was recounting a crucial—and indeed the beginning of the concluding—chapter in the history of salvation as he set forth Luther's presentation and defense of the gospel of Christ. There was certainly proof for that, Mathesius believed. He reminded his readers of the prophecies which had pointed to Luther's coming, such as those of Huss and Hilten, and he also recalled Luther's own predictions which reinforced the impression of his prophetic call. For instance, he had predicted that the Peasants' Revolt would end in a bloodbath, that Zwingli and Oecolampadius would die in unfortunate ways, that the papacy would fall, and that war

35. Mathesius, *Historien,* Aij^{v}, Aiij^{r}, X^{v}, XIII^{v}, XXXIII^{r}, XXXVI^{r}, CXXV^{v}, CXLIIII^{r}, CXCVIII^{v}, CC^{v}, CCXXX^{r}, CCXXXVII^{r}. See also Volz, *Lutherpredigten,* 63–68, 72–76.

36. Mathesius, *Historien,* CXCVIII^{v}, CC^{v} (comparison with Elijah); LIX^{r} (comparison with Moses, David, Paul, and Athanasius); L^{v}–LVI^{r}, LXV^{r}, XCII^{v} (Moses); I^{r}–II^{r}, XX^{v}–XXI^{v}, LXXXIX$^{r–v}$ (battle against the papacy); C^{v} (comparison to John the Baptist); CXCIX$^{r–v}$ (comparison to John Huss); LXXVIII^{v} (comparison to Savonarola). See also Volz, *Lutherpredigten,* 68–72.

37. Mathesius, *Historien,* XIII^{v}–XIIII^{r}, XL$^{r–v}$, CCXIIII^{r}.

38. Volz, *Lutherpredigten,* 31–35; see also Robert Kolb, "Die Umgestaltung und theologische Bedeutung des Lutherbildes im späten 16. Jahrhundert," in *Die lutherische Konfessionalisierung in Deutschland: Wissenschaftliches Symposion des Vereins für Reformationsgeschichte 1988,* ed. Hans-Christoph Rublack (Gütersloh: Mohn, 1992), 202–31.

and sectarianism would engulf the church after his death.[39] Mathesius's Luther was indeed a unique prophet, a hero of the Word of God like none other in the divine plan for the conclusion of the church's history. His sketch of Luther differed only in details from that portrayed in Cyriakus Spangenberg's *Luther, Man of God,* even if Mathesius's Luther did not fulfil the function of secondary authority.

Without doubt Spangenberg—the passionate defender of Matthias Flacius's view of original sin and thus a radical Gnesio-Lutheran—and Mathesius—a disciple of Melanchthon who remained largely on the sidelines in the strife between Philippist and Gnesio-Lutheran—differed on some questions regarding the proper interpretation of Luther's legacy. They did not disagree on their estimate of the man, however. Though Mathesius did not go as far as Spangenberg in employing Luther's writings to settle disputes within the church, they both had experienced and later reflected his unique impact on their lives.

The two did use different forms in preaching about their prophet and hero. Those who would later try to retell elements of Luther's life in defense of his message and cause could not easily adapt Spangenberg's biblical images and metaphors to their own purposes. Mathesius, on the other hand, provided not only an interpretation of Luther's significance as doctor of the church and prophet of God. He also provided the facts, the essential elements, in chronological order and narrative form. From a variety of sources he had gathered what was known about the man's career and set it forth for all to read and borrow. He had read Luther's works carefully; he cited them largely from the Wittenberg edition, but also demonstrated familiarity with products of Luther's pen which were not included in it. He also referred to works by other contemporaries who gave special insight into Luther's ministry and person. These sources extended from Philip Melanchthon and Paul Eber to Martin Bucer and Johannes Sleidanus. Mathesius also had access to manuscript materials, letters, lecture notes, and others' recollections of the talk at Luther's table. He incorporated oral reports which he had heard from acquaintances. Finally, his own recollections from his three periods of study in Wittenberg, between 1529 and 1545, enriched his account.[40] No other source could match Mathesius as a resource for those who wanted to tell Luther's story again for their own purposes.

39. Mathesius, *Historien,* IIII^{r-v}, CXCIX^{r-v} (prophecies regarding Luther); CCI^{r}–CCIII^{r} (prophecies by Luther). See also Volz, *Lutherpredigten,* 71–78.

40. For analysis of Mathesius's sources see Volz, *Lutherpredigten,* 101–28, 134–58; and for analysis of his own eyewitness accounts, 168–212. The appendix gives a tabular overview of Mathesius's use of his sources (215–86).

Among those purposes was certainly the defense of Luther against papalist attack. Volz notes that Mathesius's biography itself occasioned more attacks on Luther because of its depiction of him as a prophet of God. A convert to Catholicism from the evangelical faith, Johannes Nas, challenged both Spangenberg's and Mathesius's conclusions regarding Luther, and the Jesuit Conrad Vetter took on a pseudonym to attack a number of later biographies of the Wittenberg Reformers.[41] Although, as Volz observes, Mathesius did not explicitly react to the biography by Johannes Cochlaeus (itself an attack on Luther's person and thus on his message), he must have been aware of its publication more than fifteen years before his own work, and he must have been concerned about its influence.[42] Even if Mathesius wrote first of all for the people of his own church because of—as he alleged—their ignorance regarding Luther's ministry and their ingratitude for it,[43] it seems likely that at least one reason for his setting himself to the biographer's task was to counter the misimpressions and falsehoods found in Cochlaeus's work.

In the following decades many of those who attempted to sketch Luther's life were responding to Roman Catholic polemic. In 1582 Ingolstadt professor Albert Hunger made a somewhat scurrilous comparison of Luther's thought with that of Epicurus.[44] Three Lutherans came forward to defend the Wittenberg prophet. One of them, Marburg professor Otto Waltper (Gualtperius), waited seven years and then used Hunger's opprobrious attack as an occasion for a baccalaureate address without much reference to Luther himself.[45]

Using Hunger's quite undistinguished oration as the occasion for an academic address of his own, Zacharias Schilter, a professor of theology at Leipzig, responded more quickly.[46] His carefully crafted reply countered each of Hunger's points with the facts. Hunger had stated that Luther, like Epicurus, was an atheist; Schilter produced evidence of his heroic zeal for God's glory and his firm faith in Jesus as his mediator. Hunger had asserted that Luther, like Epicurus, was hostile to true

41. Ibid., 22–28.

42. Ibid., 57–58.

43. Mathesius, *Historien,* preface, Aij^{v}.

44. Hunger, *Orationes dvae, vna, de fide ac religione magni illius Athanasii Alexandrini . . . , altera, de homologia sive consensv concentvqve theologiae Lutheri cum Philosophia Epicvri . . .* (Ingolstadt: Weissenhorn, 1582).

45. *Oratio pro defensione Lvtheri Lvtheranorumque doctrina: opposita orationi Albert Hvngeri Iesviticae sectae professoris et procancellari & Academiae Ingolstadiensis, in qua malitiose conatus est Theologiam Lutheri, Caluini, aliquorumque, vt ipse ait, Nouatorum, cum Philosophia Epicuri comparare . . .* (Marburg: Paul Egenolff, 1590).

46. *Orationes dvae . . . Altera. Continens apologiam . . . patris DD. Martini Lutheri, repurgatoris doctrinae Co[e]lestis celeberrimi, praeclarissimique de Republica Christiana meriti . . .* (Leipzig: Johann Steinmann, 1583).

learning, philosophy, and theology; Schilter argued that Luther had promoted learning, especially the study of God's Word. Hunger's charge that Luther, like Epicurus, had confused the order of society prompted Schilter to accuse the Antichrist of doing precisely that and to show that Luther promoted public order in all his writings, which themselves were models of clarity and order. Schilter defended Luther against Hunger's charges that he had resurrected all of the ancient heresies and, like Epicurus, had played to the rabble, currying the favor of the common people by preaching the security of the flesh and moral license. Luther, according to Schilter, not only remained faithful to catholic teaching, but also displayed moderation in dealing with the emperor on all occasions. Even in his *Warning to His Dear German People* of 1531 Luther had reacted to the threats against his movement without breathing murder, blood, and sedition.[47] Finally, by clarifying the Reformer's understanding of marriage and celibacy Schilter rebutted Hunger's charge that Luther cultivated the Epicurean pleasure principle. Schilter's regard for Luther as a hero and God's chosen instrument permeated his oration and fostered that same regard in his students. Luther had restored the gospel at God's bidding, and he remained for Schilter a "father among the saints."[48] Thus refuting the papalist criticism of his heroic prophet, Schilter defended the integrity of Luther's church and his theology.

The pastor at the church of Saint Nikolaus in Luther's birthplace, Eisleben, Anton Probus, also came to his defense against Hunger's charges. Though unable at first to secure a copy of Hunger's harangue, Probus did obtain Schilter's reprinting of it, along with Schilter's declamation. In the first of two dedications for the printed version of his own "oration on the call and teaching of Martin Luther, great teacher and the last prophet of Germany," Probus likened Hunger's attack on Luther to the barbs of other enemies, including Johann Eck, Friedrich Staphylus, and Johannes Cochlaeus.[49] Because Luther had attacked the papal crown and monks' bellies, these men had had to defend their own cause.

Probus focused his defense of Luther on the validity of his call to be an authoritative spokesman for God. Probus was not alone in doing so. Although he did not argue that Luther should continue to be used as

47. It is ironic that Schilter singles out this particular work of Luther (*WA* 30.3:276–310), for Mark U. Edwards Jr., *Luther's Last Battles, Politics and Polemics 1531–1546* (Ithaca: Cornell University Press, 1983), 29, concludes that "the polemical force of this treatise . . . favored resistance. In fact, it was an incitement to resistance."

48. Schilter, *Orationes dvae,* C^{v}–C3^{r}.

49. *Oratio de vocatione et doctrina Martini Lvtheri doctoris magni & Prophetae Germaniae vltimi, co[e]lesti & divina recitata publice Islebij in patria S. Lutheri: & opposita Epicureae orationi Alberti Hungeri . . . de homologia, sive consensu doctrinae Lutheri cum Philosophia Epicuri* (Leipzig: Heirs of Jacob Baerwald, 1583), A2^{r}–A3^{r}.

secondary authority, he echoed Mathesius's approach to the question of whether the church should listen to Luther at all. From the earliest days of the Reformation Roman Catholic opponents had accused Luther and his followers of fomenting disorder in church and society. Above all, they contested Luther's right to challenge popes and councils. Mathesius had emphasized that the church had given Luther a proper call to be a teacher and interpreter of the Holy Scripture and thus a "faithful witness of the Lord Jesus Christ and a true prophet." Mathesius lived in an era when Lutheran theologians were combating sectarians who did not depend on official calls to begin a preaching career; hence his emphasis on Luther's orderly entrance into public ministry. As Volz points out, this same emphasis is also found in Luther's description and defense of himself as early as 1524. Although many of his followers believed that God had spoken directly to Luther's heart when he called him to the task of restoring the gospel to the church, Mathesius echoed Luther in focusing on his indirect call through the established human means of an ecclesiastical order.[50]

In his second dedication, to Dukes Frederick William and John of Saxony, Probus cast light on what he saw as the significance of Luther's career. The Reformer had revealed biblical teaching, especially the chief articles of faith, the work and the benefits of Christ the Mediator, the justification of the sinner, repentance, the sacraments. Those who confess the truth have always encountered opposition, as can be seen from Eusebius's and Nicephorus's histories of the church. Probus placed Luther in the great chain of conflict which had been a necessary part of proclaiming Christ's gospel.[51]

Probus's account of Luther's career followed the lines laid down by Mathesius and other predecessors. He specifically named as his sources Philip Melanchthon, Ludwig Rabus, Johannes Mathesius, David Chytraeus, Nikolaus Selnecker, Conrad Porta (on Luther's writings), and Christoph Stauffenbuel.[52] Thus Probus's purpose was not to break

50. Volz, *Lutherpredigten,* 52–56.

51. Probus, *Oratio,* A3^{v}–B3^{r}.

52. Ibid., C^{v}–C3^{v}. For Probus's sources see in the present volume p. 36 nn. 60–61 (Melanchthon), p. 71 n. 83 (Selnecker), p. 84 n. 23 (Mathesius), p. 87 n. 30 (Rabus), and David Chytraeus, *Historia der Augspurgischen Confession* (Rostock: Lucius, 1576); see also Rudolf Keller, *Die Confessio Augustana im theologischen Wirken des Rostocker Professors David Chyträus (1530–1600)* (Göttingen: Vandenhoeck & Ruprecht, 1994). Probus also gave credit to lectures given by Conrad Porta (see p. 192 n. 123) and Christoph Stauffenbuel, the latter of which seems not to be extant. Delivered in 1580, it was entitled "Oratio de beneficijs Lutheri & ingratitudine mundi." A native of Mansfeld, Stauffenbuel matriculated at the University of Wittenberg in 1575 and may have delivered the oration as a university exercise. See *Album Academiae Vitebergensis ab A. Ch. MDII usque ad A. MDCII* (Halle: Niemeyer, 1894), 2:255.

new ground as a biographer but to defend Luther against Roman slander. He was writing popular biography for the benefit of the people of Eisleben and Mansfeld.

According to Probus, God had called Luther to restore true Christian teaching before Christ's return. In carrying out that call Luther served as "God's chosen instrument, the great prophet of Germany, the last Elijah of the last days." By placing his propositions on the door of the castle church in Wittenberg in October 1517 Luther had fulfilled God's special calling to restore the gospel against the lies of the Roman Antichrist. Probus cited the Lutheran catena of biblical passages regarding the Antichrist (2 Thess. 2, Dan. 7, Ezek. 38–39, Rev. 20, and others) to demonstrate that the Antichrist would come to afflict the church with his tyranny. Probus then reviewed the Roman persecution of Huss and Luther, carefully rehearsing the events of the indulgence controversy as recorded in Luther's *Against Hanswurst.*[53] He concluded that Luther fulfilled John's prophecy of an angel who would come bearing the everlasting gospel (Rev. 14:6). Six decades after they had first been formulated, Probus was reproducing the elements of the earliest assessments of Luther's significance.

Largely on the basis of material gleaned from Matthias Flacius's *Catalog of Witnesses to the Truth,* Probus further argued that Luther's call to heroic prophetic action against the Antichrist had been predicted throughout church history. Citing theologians from Ambrose and Augustine through Catharine of Siena and Theodore of Croatia to the recent critics of Rome, such as Huss, Mechthild, John of Wessel, John Ostendorp, Johann Hilten, and Andreas Proles, Probus compiled a battery of prophecies regarding apostasy and the inevitability of the restoration of the gospel in the church. The citation from Ambrose and Augustine consisted of the numerological interpretation of their antiphon, "tIbI CherVbIn & SerephIn, In CessabILI VoCe pro CLaMant," which contained Roman numerals adding up to 1517, thus disclosing the year in which the Antichrist would be revealed. This interpretation of the antiphon had circulated in Lutheran circles for some time, appearing in the sermons of both Spangenberg and Mathesius.[54] To this Probus added arguments regarding the advantages which Luther's reform had brought and its necessity. He cited again criticism of Rome from a number of recent historians and offered on the basis of the catechism, a common Lutheran device for organizing theological arguments in

53. Probus, *Oratio,* C3^{v}–[F4]^{v}; Luther, *Wider Hanswurst, WA* 51:469–572.

54. Probus, *Oratio,* [F4]^{v}–G3^{r}; Flacius, *Catalogus testium veritatis, qui ante nostram aetatem reclamarunt Papae . . .* (Basel: Oporinus, 1556). On Mathesius's use of the numerical interpretation see Volz, *Lutherpredigten,* 77–78.

this era,[55] an analysis of papal error. The Ten Commandments reveal the sins of the papacy; particularly, commandments one and two reveal its idolatry. The Creed shows how far the papacy had strayed from preaching God's truth. The Lord's Prayer reminds all Christians of the false prayers to the saints and the false forms of worship which the papacy had promoted. The Catechism's treatment of the sacraments reveals the abuses of the sacraments which were rampant in the papacy. To these arguments Probus added Luther's *Papal Ass,* which he had found in the Jena edition. He also reproduced Melanchthon's interpretation of the beastly sculpture reportedly dragged out of the Tiber in 1496, so horrible in appearance that no human could have created it—Melanchthon saw it as God's sign of his wrath against the papacy.[56]

Probus continued to prove the validity of Luther's call by examining "the infallible signs of the presence and efficacy of the Holy Spirit" in Luther's work. They included his lively, burning faith, his ardent prayer, and his steadfast perseverance in confessing the faith, which he displayed, for instance, in his confrontation with Cardinal Cajetan at Augsburg in 1518. Other such signs included his skill at consoling distressed consciences and his singular gift of interpreting the Scriptures and explaining all parts of Christian teaching, for instance, in his catechisms and his postils. Probus viewed Luther above all as a man of God's Word. In his view Luther had also performed miracles and made predictive prophecies. He had shown boldness and zeal in attacking sin and had displayed a host of virtues which revealed the presence of God's Spirit in his heart. Finally, Probus urged his readers to test Luther's message and the validity of his call by Gamaliel's standard (Acts 5:33–39): "If [they are] of God, you will not be able to overthrow them." Luther's message had spread into many nations. The efforts of his papal foes to stop his message had not been successful. Indeed, many of his enemies had died tragic deaths, but Luther had experienced a peaceful, tranquil demise.[57]

Further proofs were unnecessary. Hunger's attack proved nothing. Luther's message and actions clearly demonstrated that God had called him as his prophet to oppose the papacy and to reveal the gospel. But Probus's argument for the validity of Luther's call went significantly beyond the ordered calling to the ranks of teachers of the church, which Luther and Mathesius had emphasized. Probus also

55. See Robert Kolb, "Jakob Andreae's Concern for the Laity," *Concordia Journal* 4 (1978): 58–67.

56. Probus, *Oratio,* [G4]^{v}–I3^{r}; see also Luther, *Deutung der zwei graulichen Figuren, Papstesels zu Rom und Monchkalbs zu Freiburg in Meissen gefunden, WA* 11:369–85.

57. Probus, *Oratio,* I3^{r}–[P4]^{r}.

demonstrated the validity of that call through a variety of proofs confirming that this doctor of the church had indeed been God's special instrument and spokesman.

That Probus regarded Luther as prophetic hero more than prophetic authority became clear some six years later when he published the first of what apparently was intended to be a series of sermons on Luther's renewal of the gospel. Having moved to Weimar as general superintendent of the churches in that area of ducal Saxony, Probus had again encountered the rising pressure of an ever-more-virulent Counter-Reformation. Roman Catholic theologians were issuing increasingly bitter and abusive polemic against his hero, this time in the writings of Andreas Fabricius Leodus and Conrad Vetter, who used the pseudonym Andreae (claiming to be Jakob Andreae's brother) in his anti-Lutheran polemic.[58] Probus's "first sermon" dealt chiefly with the indulgence controversy. It boasted of Luther's heroic rehabilitation and renewal "of the primal, prophetic, apostolic, and catholic teaching, which had been snuffed out and obscured in terrible and miserable fashion by the pope's terrible idolatry, false teaching, lies, and human opinions." Here Probus compared Luther to the Maccabees as they did away with the Syrian abuses and restored the proper worship of God among the Jews. Luther, as the third Elijah, had taken similar action against the idolatry of the Roman Antiochus. His heroic stature cast its protective shadow over the church and the people of Germany.

Probus's Latin oration of 1583 had provided the pastors of Mansfeld and beyond with material for their own defense of Luther, but others thought that the story should be made available again in German. That was the reason which Georg Gloccer, a pastor in Strassburg, gave for publishing his *Reliable History and Thorough Summary Report* on Luther's teaching, career, call, and death, four major evidences of Luther's crucial significance for the church. Gloccer noted that Melanchthon, Caspar Cruciger, Johannes Bugenhagen, Mathesius, and "from our times . . . Nikolaus Selnecker, Jacob Heerbrand, Ludwig Rabus, and most recently Anton Probus" had defended Luther. They had proven false the slanders against him in works by a train of Roman Catholic critics, Lorenz Surius, Peter Canisius, Martin Eisengrein,

58. Probus, *Renovalia Lvtheri. Von der Gnadenreichen Offenbarung des Heiligen Evangelij/Vnd der grewlichen Abgo[e]tterey des Bapsthumbs/aus den Schrifften des thewren vnd seligen Mannes Gottes/D. Martini Lvtheri/vnd andern Scribenten zusamengebracht. Die erste Predigt* . . . (Jena: Tobias Steinman, 1590), esp. Aij^{r}–B^{r}. Probus was probably referring to Fabricius, *Harmonia Confessionis Augustanae, doctrinae evangelicae consensvm declarans* (Cologne: Maternus Cholinus, 1573). It is more difficult to identify which of Vetter's works was in view since in 1590 Vetter stood at the beginning of his publishing career, having issued only a few pieces of polemic, against Jakob Andreae and Philip Heilbrunner, that year.

Jacob Rabus, Gregorius de Valentia, Albert Hunger, Georg Schere, and Jodocus Lorich, all of whom followed in the train of earlier critics such as Johann Eck, Johannes Cochlaeus, and Friedrich Staphylus. Gloccer's little book, however, was designed for those who could not buy the big, expensive books which his fellow Lutherans had published.[59]

Gloccer introduced his retelling of the story with Erasmus's remarks that Luther had committed two sins: attacking the pope's three-tiered crown and poking the monks' bellies. After a brief chronological summary of the chief events in Luther's career, which included the years of his birth, attainment of his master's and doctoral degrees, the indulgence controversy, the confrontation with Cajetan, his marriage and the Peasants' Revolt, the Augsburg Confession, and his death,[60] Gloccer launched into his presentation of the contribution which Luther had made to the life of the church. He sketched the situation to which Luther came: consciences were suffering miserably because of the false teaching of the papacy. The Holy Spirit had guided and channeled Luther in orderly fashion to the office of teacher of the church, so that he might be used to restore the sound teaching of the gospel in the face of Satan's enmity and the whole world's opposition. Gloccer then continued with an outline based on Probus's work and with much of Probus's material reproduced quite closely, though with occasional elaboration. He summarized Luther's teaching and showed that his call to destroy the papacy was based on Scripture and fulfilled the prophecies of many throughout church history. Gloccer reviewed the benefits which Luther's message had brought the church and the gifts which God had bestowed upon him. He concluded with an overview of the spread of Luther's message and the story of his blessed death, which Probus had also presented. Gloccer's digest of the current interpretation of Luther's life and significance brought to the common people the message which Probus and others had designed for the clergy, and which Spangenberg and Mathesius had presented in too much detail, pricing their writings beyond the means of the average person. Now Gloccer had enlisted the prophetic hero to serve in the battle for the allegiance of the common people.

Similar defenses of Luther's prophetic action and teaching arose out of specific polemical situations in the last two decades of the sixteenth century. In south Germany members of the Württemberg min-

59. *Warhafftige Historia/Vnd gru[e]ndlicher Summarischer Bericht/von der Lehr/Leben/ Beruff/vnd seligen Abschiedt des thewren Gottes Manns Doctoris Martini Lutheri/fu[e]r einfeltige Christen/auss bewerten vnd glaubwu[e]rdigen Scribenten auff das ku[e]rtzest zusammen gezogen* (Strassburg: Anton Bertram, 1586), B5^{r}–[B6]^{v}.

60. Ibid., Aij^{v}–[Aviij]^{v}.

isterium took the lead in occasionally using Luther's biography to aid in the defense of his cause, particularly against Jesuit attacks. Sebastian Flasch, who was a native of Mansfeld, a convert from the evangelical faith to Roman Catholicism, and a Jesuit professor at Ingolstadt, used citations from Luther to prove that "he was no holy prophet of Germany but pure filth." Flasch's treatise, issued in 1577, was followed seven years later by an explanation of why he converted "from the Lutheran heresy in which he had been born," repeating citations from Luther's works against the Reformer. This latter piece was refuted by the court preacher in Stuttgart, Anton Varnbuller, and by a pseudonymous author.[61]

In connection with defending the integrity of Luther's person, Lutheran theologians also moved to protect the integrity of his writings. Certain Jesuits had issued an "improved" version of Luther's Small Catechism in 1587, and Jacob Heerbrand rushed to rescue Luther's text. In the introduction to his analysis of Luther's catechism, which he found to be thoroughly in accord with Scripture, Heerbrand also discussed Luther's earliest writings. The opponents had charged that these writings contradicted themselves, and Heerbrand agreed. Until 1520, he judged, Luther still was stuck in papal error on a number of points. Though Heerbrand did not go into detail regarding the basis for this dating, he did cite a few examples, including remarks from 1519 which treated penance as a sacrament. At some point thereafter God had marvelously and in fatherly fashion enlightened Luther and led him away from the errors of the papacy.[62]

61. Flasch wrote *Augenscheinliche Erweisung auss D. Martin Luthers aigenen Bu[e]chern vnd worten/dass er kain heiliger Prophet Teutschlands/sondern ein rechter Vnflat gewesen. Jederma[e]nigklich/so wol Lutherischen als Catholischen/zu guter erinnerung vnd ernstlichem nachdencken zusamen getragen* (Ingolstadt: David Sartorius, 1577), and *Zwey vnd zwaintzig Vrsachen/Des . . . Sebastiani Flaschij von Manssfeldt Warumb er die Lutherisch Ketzerey/darinn er geboren/vnd von Jugend aufferzogen/verlassen hab. Daneben auss D. Martini Luthers aigenen Bu[e]chern vnd Worten augenscheinlich erweisung/dass er kein heiliger Prophet Teutschlandts/sondern ein rechter Vnflat gewesen* (Munich: Adam Berg, 1584). Varnbuller replied with his *Auff M. Sebastiani Flaschen von Mansfeldt/vnd anderer seines gleichen Bapstischen Scribenten/verklerungen vnd lo[e]sterungen: da sie auss D. Luthers seeligen Schrifften (wie die gifftigen spinnen) etwas heraus saugen/vnd daraus beweisen wo[e]llen/das D. Martin Luther/kein heyliger Prophet dess Teutschlandts/ sonder ein rechter vnflat gewesen sein soll* (Tübingen: Alexander Hock, 1585). Six years later the pseudonymous tract appeared under a false imprint from the press of Bernard Jobin in Strassburg: Caspar Gobler, *Wieder die lesterliche Calumnia des vngelerten Esels M. Flachens/eines Manßfeldischen Jesuiters/von D. Martino Luthero. Bericht/Daraus zu sehen/das Gott durch D. Lutherum der gantzer Christenheit wunderbarlich aus Papistischer Finsternis geholffen . . .* ("Christlingen," 1591).

62. *Rettung Des kleinen Catechismi D. Luthers/Vnd Bericht Auff vnnd wider der Jesuiter zu Gratz/bosshafftige/du[e]ckische verbo[e]serung/verfa[e]lschung vnnd verstu[e]mplung desselbigen* (Tübingen: Georg Gruppenbach, 1587).

A colleague in the Württemberg ministerium, Lucas Osiander, took up Heerbrand's cause more than a decade later by reissuing both the Large and the Small Catechisms and by defending their teaching. His preface placed Luther's ministry in the context of the struggle against the Roman Antichrist. He acknowledged that the hefty price of the weighty tomes in which Luther's works were contained made it difficult for most people to evaluate the Jesuits' quotations from Luther. Osiander offered a hermeneutical correction. Sometimes the papalist writers misrepresented the mature Luther by citing comments he had uttered while still under the influence of medieval papal theology. Or they took his irony and interpreted it literally. Or they attributed to him the errors of the old-style heretics, such as Schwenckfeld, Karlstadt, and the Anabaptists, or the anti-Trinitarians, such as Servetus and Blandrata, or the Sacramentarians, such as Zwingli, Calvin, Oecolampadius, and Beza. Osiander praised Luther's teaching but paid little attention to his person. His Luther was a teacher of the church but not a prophet or a hero.[63] A similar defense of Luther's teaching and career came in the same year from another Württemberg theologian, Philip Heilbrunner. It attacked Conrad Vetter above all.[64]

As Roman Catholics continued to impugn Luther's reputation and his teaching, or his translation of the Scriptures, Lutherans rose to his defense with further theological and biographical arguments that increasingly fell into certain typical forms.[65] One Jesuit, Nikolaus Sera-

63. *Der kleine vnd der grosse Catechismus/Herrn D. Martini Luthers/seliger geda[e]chtnus. Aus welchen ein Christ fein kurtz vnd gru[e]ndlicht erlernen kan/was D. Luther seliger von allen vnd jeden Articuln vnd Stucken der Christlichen Religion Geglaubt vnd gelehret . . . Sampt Einer aussfu[e]rlichen Vorred D. Lucas Osianders/in denen gru[e]ndtlich angezeigt wu[e]rdt/wie vnbillich die Jesuiter/vnd jhres gleichen Papistische Scribenten/die reine Christliche Lehr/vnd die Person D. Luthers/mutwillig calumnieren/ verkehren/vnd verla[e]stern . . .* (Tübingen: Georg Gruppenbach, 1599).

64. *Der Vnschuldige Luther/Das ist/Augenscheinliche Beweisung/Das alles das jenige/so die Iesuiter, in jhren jungst aussgesprengten Lesterschrifften/wider weyland D. Martin Luthers Person/aus seinen eignen Schrifften (die reine Lehre dess H. Euangelij dadurch verda[e]chtig zu machen) auffbringen/von jhnen vbel angezogen/bosshafftig verkehrt/vnd lauter Betrug sey . . .* (Lauingen: Leonhart Reinmichel, 1599).

65. To Melchior Zanger's *Examen versionis Lutheri in Biblia . . .* (Mainz: Johann Weiss, 1605), Tübingen law professor Michael Beringer replied with his *Rettung der Teutscher Biblischen Dolmetschung D. Martin Luthers: Wider die offenbar vnua[e]rschampte Vnwarheit des Melchior Zangers . . . damit er gedachte D. Luthers Biblische Translation/allerley beschwerlicher fa[e]hrlicher Irrthumben ohne Grund beschuldiget . . .* (Tübingen: Dietrich Werlin, 1613). The work by Zanger, a priest in Ehingen am Neckar, was published posthumously by his cousin Georg Zanger, a canon in Horb. To Sixtus Sartorius's *Causae motiuae . . . conuersionis rationes . . .* (Ingolstadt: Andreas Angermann, 1602) Lorenz Laelius replied with his *Rettung D. Martin Luthers/seeligen/Lehr/ehr/vnd guten Namens: Wider D. Sixti Sartorii . . . in den Causis Motivis seines Abfals/angehefften Schmachreden . . .* (Onaltzbach: Paul Bohem, 1614).

rius, provided the occasion for a burst of biographical detail in interconfessional polemic around the turn of the century. From his position as professor of theology at the new Roman Catholic university in Würzburg, Serarius wrote a series of attacks on Luther. Presupposing that Luther was the devil's disciple, Serarius in the scurrilous fashion of the time called into question both his behavior and his teaching. He was answered in kind by several Lutheran professors. They used citations from Luther's works to demonstrate his faithfulness to the Scriptures. As they repeated his fierce critiques of the medieval papacy against which God had called him to stand, they wove in biographical details which could strengthen their argument. Serarius's *Luther-Turkish Orations,* published originally in 1594, elicited criticism from Johann Simon, professor of poetry and eloquence at the University of Rostock. The Jesuit's *On Luther's Master* of 1604 provoked analysis by Friedrich Balduin, professor of theology at the University of Wittenberg. Serarius replied to both in the middle of the seventeenth century's first decade, and Simon replied to Serarius in his own and Luther's defense. Balduin's colleague Johann Forster also joined the fray about the time of Serarius's death.[66] To further their polemical goals, all these works em-

66. Serarius's *Lvtherotvrcicae orationes qvarvm, post praefationem, indicvlvs* (1594; Mainz: Balthasar Lipp, 1604 reprint) was answered by Johann Simon, *Lvthervs Theosdotos. Oratio, Mendacijs Papisto-Turcici cujusdam Jesuitae, origenem doctrinae co[e]lestis, cujus ὑποφήτης interpres & doctor diuinibus excitatus fuit MARTINUS LUTHERUS, Diabolo blaspheme ascribentis* (Rostock: Stephen Myliander, 1606; Rostock: Christoph Reussner, 1608 reprint). Serarius's *De Lutheri magistro, vt digito possit monstrari et diceri hic est ad Lutheranos praedicantes non belli sed pacis ergo, in vnius ex eorum numero, Frid Balduini . . .* (Mainz: Balthasar Lipp, 1604) was critiqued by Balduin, *De disputatione Lvtheri cum Diabolo: in controversia de privata Missa, Tractatio theologica et Scholastica Apologetici loco . . .* (Eisleben: Jacob Gubisius, 1605). Earlier orations by both Balduin and Simon commemorating anniversaries of Luther's death had praised him and also used some biographical details: Balduin's *Parentatio Anniversaria pro D. Martino Lvthero P.M. qva ostenditur Beatissim. illum Patrem Verum fuisse Episcopum & Evangelistam Germaniae . . .* (Wittenberg: Zacharias Lehmann, 1599), and Simon's *Parentatio Lvtheri oratio de Beneficijs, quae Deus per electissimum Spiritus Sancti organum Martinvm Lvthervm generi humano exhibuit . . .* (Rostock: Stephan Myliander, 1596). Parts of Serarius's polemic were translated into German as *Dass Luthers Nachtliecht/das ist/Kurtzer Warhafftiger/besta[e]ndiger vnd gru[e]ndlicher Bericht/von der grossen vnd ersten/vornembsten vnd wunderbarlichen Erleuchtung/durch welche dem thewren vnd hochgelehrten Mann D. Martin Luther seine Lehr im anfang offenbaret worden . . .* (Ingolstadt: Andreas Angermayer, 1603). Serarius defended his position against Balduin in *Apologiae pro discipvlo et magistro, Lvthero et diabolo . . .* (Mainz: Balthasar Lipp, 1605), and against Simon in *Lvthervs theosdotos Rostochiensi rhetori revissvs, Cum Discipulo suo Calvino . . .* (Mainz: Balthasar Lipp, 1607). Simon responded with *Apologeticvs, in quo Nicolai Serarii S. J. presbyteri tum theosdoto remisso, tum Orationi de Disputatione Diaboli cum Luthero, respondetur* (Rostock: Stephen Myliander, 1608). Forster's work was entitled *Vindiciae Lutheri: id est, Orationes dvae, pro Luthero Theologorum omnium, ab Apostolorum aetate, Phosphoro aduersus conuitia & calumnias Jesuitarum, Nicolae Serarii imprimis . . .* (Wittenberg: Johann Gormann, 1609).

ployed biographical detail incidentally. The Lutherans also used historical analysis to demonstrate the necessity of God's calling and sending Luther to reform the medieval papacy. Balduin concluded, "Luther remains indeed our man of God and hero, sainted and godly, holy and blessed: these Theones [satirists] may grind their teeth at him and chew on him now that he is dead. May they break their teeth before they damage the good name of our man of God."[67]

In tracing how various accounts of Luther were put to use against Roman opponents in the closing decades of the sixteenth century, it is clear that most Lutherans still regarded him as a prophet even though they did not attribute to him prophetic authority in determining public teaching. As a teacher of the church and preacher of the gospel he had taken a heroic prophetic role in bringing the gospel's light into the darkened world of the papacy. The Wittenberg school had taken as a fundamental interpretive principle the continuing conflict between God and Satan, particularly within the church.[68] This principle made it clear that papal—demonic—opposition to the truth would always challenge people like Luther, and that those who wanted to serve God would be caught up in that battle. Luther's fearless confession of the biblical faith against the Roman Antichrist provided the model for his followers, and for that they praised him and the God who had called him. They supported and defended his teaching with thorough biblical argumentation. Luther the prophetic hero served the purpose of rallying his latter-day followers to the cause of Protestant or evangelical independence from Roman control. His teaching and his authority meant less than his power as a symbol of political and religious forces which had brought truth and freedom to the German people. For Martin Luther incorporated in his person the reformation of the church's teaching and life. He had served during his lifetime as a living logo for his movement and his theology. In death he continued to embody for his followers the renewed revelation of the gospel which God had given the world at the end of time.

67. Balduin, *De disputatione,* 383.

68. John M. Headley, *Luther's View of Church History* (New Haven: Yale University Press, 1963), 19–41, 59–69.

4

The Teaching Prophet

Luther as Instructor of Pure Teaching in Conflict with the Sacramentarians

Although circumstances changed and thereby diminished Luther's usefulness as a secondary authority in the church, his writings continued to be a highly respected and often cited source of instruction among the Lutherans. The voices of the wise have echoed throughout human history and taken their place in discourse long after departing this life. Both through oral tradition and through written records the respected teachers of every culture have continued to exercise their instructional role among their followers in succeeding generations, conveying the content of their insights and the inspiration of their enthusiasm to their spiritual posterity. This was indeed true for Luther. His teaching served as a model and as a rallying point for his followers, both as they comforted distressed sinners and as they fought against others who denied Luther's pattern of sound teaching.

But dead teachers are at the mercy of their living teaching assistants. Times changed; the political situation in the empire continued to be fraught with confessional tension. Dogmatic and organizational strains affected the church. Societal developments brought stress to the economic and moral dimensions of believers' lives. Luther's thought did not fit exactly into the discussions of a new era, even in the lifetime of his own students. The succeeding generations found different uses for Luther's ideas and applied them in different contexts and in different modes. In each generation, to the beginning of the twenty-first century, debates have simmered and raged among adherents of his thought regarding the proper interpretation and use of his theology and his person.

Luther's Teaching Office through the Republication of His Works

In the century following his death Luther functioned as an instructor of Lutheran laity and pastors in a variety of ways. In the context of controversy over the definition of his legacy, and particularly as those who had sat at his feet in Wittenberg began to fear that their younger colleagues did not know Luther, an urgency developed in the 1550s and 1560s to make some of his works available as a remedy for the often voiced complaint that even those who boasted of the label "Lutheran" were ignoring his teaching.[1]

During Luther's lifetime his colleagues began efforts to assure that complete editions of their mentor's writings would be available to the reading public. After his death they continued the production of such editions, and they also assembled collections of his correspondence and even of his conversation at table (see ch. 6).

For those who could not afford the costly complete editions, many of Luther's works were published individually or together with other treatises or excerpts on a common theme. The market was not flooded with Luther's individual writings after his death, but from time to time in the succeeding generations some of his works were available in anthologies or reprints. From such treatises his later disciples gained access to Luther's teaching on biblical books or portions thereof, as well as to his polemical and pastoral treatment of a variety of doctrinal and social issues. The most significant republication of his works, Luther's postils, found a steady market because of their importance for the practice of the pastoral ministry and the instruction of parishioners. The postils guided the preaching of a new generation of pastors, and the catechisms carried Luther's teaching to a new generation of laypeople. Books of prayers and collections of prophecies met the pastor's professional needs and the parishioner's spiritual needs alike. Pastors called upon and used Luther's teaching as they brought consolation to their people and taught them how to pray and sing in praise. An overview of these publications will suggest which aspects of Luther's thought his followers found most helpful in their own situations (see ch. 7).

1. See, for example, Johannes Corvinus, *Loci commvnes Doct: Mart: Lutheri totius Doctrinae Christianae. Das ist/Heubtartikel Vnsers Christlichen Glaubens/vnd rechtschaffener Lere/aus D. Mart. Luthers Schrifften/mit seinen eigenen worten/Einfeltiglich vnd trewliche zusamen getragen* . . . (Ursel: Nicolaus Henricus, 1564),)(r–A3v; Johannes Mathesius, *Historien/Von des Ehrwirdigen in Gott Seligen thewren Manns Gottes, Doctoris Martini Luthers/anfang/lehr/leben vnd sterben* . . . (Nuremberg: Johann vom Berg's heirs and Ulrich Neuber, 1566), Aijv.

At the same time, less than twenty years after the Reformer's death some began to excerpt a broad range of Luther's works by doctrinal topic. They did so by fitting his teaching into their own schema. Melanchthon's method of organizing theology by loci had so determined his and Luther's students' way of thinking that they felt compelled to force Luther into the Melanchthonian forms. In such forms pastors and laity had at hand, in one or a few volumes, a broad—even if predigested—sampling of Luther's teaching and a guide to his thought. These *Loci communes Lutheri* provided readers with biblical doctrine for use in teaching and preaching and pastoral care (see ch. 8).

Luther's instruction was used for pastoral and edificatory purposes, but he also remained the foremost teacher of Lutheran churches in the public struggle over the proper definition of the biblical message, even in situations where his prophetic or adjudicatory authority could not be asserted and claimed. Perhaps the best examples of his continued role of teaching the church in the midst of public controversy can be found in the debates in Saxony in the mid-1570s and around 1590 over the Lord's Supper.

Luther's Teaching in the Crypto-Philippist Controversy

Since the 1550s Lutherans had engaged questions of sacramental doctrine, particularly in conflict over the real presence of Christ's body and blood in the Lord's Supper. These confrontations took place above all with the church in Geneva and its Reformed cousins from Zurich, and then from Heidelberg, France, and the Netherlands. But the tenor of the dispute became even more strident when those who claimed to adhere to Luther's view most strictly (members of the Swabian and Gnesio-Lutheran parties) accused the Wittenberg faculty of teaching a form of Melanchthon's sacramental doctrine which diverged from Luther's in what seemed to be a Calvinist direction. The strife involving the Philippist theologians of Wittenberg was perhaps more bitter than that against the Reformed parties because the strictest Lutherans felt themselves betrayed by fellow adherents of the Augsburg Confession. Furthermore, the image of Luther and faithfulness to his viewpoint became a more critical consideration as the Philippist theologians battled other Lutherans on issues made more difficult by twenty years of ever intensifying accusations of betrayal and bad faith on the part of both sides.[2]

Since their doctrine derived from Melanchthon's teaching rather than directly from exposure to Calvin's system, it is misleading to continue to label the electoral Saxon theologians of the 1560s and early

2. See pp. 40–45.

1570s Crypto-Calvinists (as did their foes from Württemberg, Jena, Hamburg, and other Lutheran centers of the time). They may better be designated Crypto-Philippists. "Crypto-" they were, for they did indeed operate in a way designed to conceal their doctrinal agenda, which they seemed to know departed from Luther's position, and asserted another. This different doctrinal agenda developed, however, far less under Calvinist influence than through continuing adaptation of insights gained from Melanchthon's Christology and sacramental theology. The Wittenberg faculty was elaborating what they had learned from Melanchthon, even though they formulated a more spiritualized view of the sacrament than the positions of some of Philip's disciples, Martin Chemnitz and Tilemann Hesshus—or even of other Philippists such as Nikolaus Selnecker and Paul Krell. Thus the Wittenberg faculty members were faithful Philippists; they were not technically Calvinist, even though their contemporaries saw the similarities clearly.

In propagating their views, the Wittenberg professors did take care to anchor their positions with citations from both Luther and Melanchthon and to assert the equality of the authority of the two Wittenberg mentors.[3] For instance, a position paper issued in 1571 buttressed its christological doctrine with lengthy citations from Luther.[4] But those who criticized the Wittenbergers' published efforts to infiltrate their positions into the public teaching of Saxony rejected their claim to be followers of Luther.

Also in 1571 the Wittenberg theologians produced a new catechism for use in electoral Saxon schools. Its treatment of certain critical issues

3. E.g., in *De praecipvis horvm temporvm controversiis propositiones, orationes et qvaestiones, continentes svmmam confessionis ac Academiae Vvitebergensis, congruentem cum perpetua sententia purioris & orthodoxae antiquitatis. Scriptae et propositae publice Vvitebergae, Anno Christi 1570* (Wittenberg: Johannes Schwertel, 1571), A4^{r-v} (see also Ernst Koch, "Auseinandersetzungen um die Autorität von Philipp Melanchthon und Martin Luther in Kursachsen im Vorfeld der Konkordienformel von 1577," *Lutherjahrbuch* 59 [1992]: 130), and above all in *Endlicher Bericht vnd Erklerung der Theologen beider Vniuersiteten/Leipzig vnd Wittemberg Auch der Superintendenten der Kirchen in des Churfu[e]rsten zu Sachsen Landen/belangend die Lere/so gemelte Vniuersiteten vnd Kirchen von anfang der Augspurgischen Confession bis auff diese zeit/laut vnd vermu[e]ge derselben/zu allen Artikkeln gleichfo[e]rmig/eintrechtig vnd bestendig gefu[e]ret haben/vber der sie auch durch hu[e]lff des allmechtigen Gottes gedencken fest zu halten* (Wittenberg: Hans Lufft, 1570).

4. *Von der person vnd Menschwerdung vnsers HERRN Jhesu Christi/Der waren Christlichen Kirchen Grundfest/Wider die newen Marcioniten/Samosatener/Sabellianer/Arianer/Nestorianer/Eutychianer vnd Monotheleten/vnter dem Flacianischen hauffen. Durch die Theologen zu Wittemberg/aus der heiligen Schrifft/aus den Symbolis/aus den fu[e]rnemesten Concilijs vnd einhelligem Consenss aller bewerten Lerer. Widerholet vnd Gestellet/zu trewer lere vnd ernster verwarnung an alle frome vnd Gottselige Christen. Neben warhaffter vorantwortung/auff die gifftigen vnd boshaftigen verleumbdungen/so von den Propositionibus vnd Catechismo zu Wittemberg ausgangen/von vielen dieser zeit ausgesprenget werden* . . . (Wittenberg: Hans Lufft, 1571), 66^{v}–75^{r}.

promoted the faculty's spiritualizing views of the complex of questions surrounding the Lord's Supper. The Lüneburg ministerium's critique of this catechism expressly stated that the new textbook departed from "the form and purity of the salutary teaching of the Holy Scripture . . . and from the reliable norm for salutary teaching, as Saint Luther presented it to God's church in written and oral form."[5] Luther, then, was a source not only of proper teaching but also of adjudicatory authority in 1571. The Braunschweig ministerium asserted that the catechism contained doctrine inimical to God's Word and the confession of "our church, as contained in Luther's writings, the Augsburg Confession, the Apology, the Catechism, the Smalcald Articles, and other similar writings," as well as Melanchthon's own collection of doctrinal writings, the *Corpus doctrinae Philippicum.*[6]

Both Gnesio-Lutherans in Jena and the Württemberg theologians voiced suspicions of the same sort in criticizing other documents from the Wittenbergers: Luther's name and writings were being used to cover errors, actual departures from his teaching.[7] The Wittenbergers rejected these accusations. They employed Luther to plead for peace as the storm of controversy over the Lord's Supper approached.[8] In exile they cited Luther's works to defend themselves and to define specifically where differences lay between their views and Luther's, particularly on the reception of Christ's body and blood by the unbeliever.[9] They also attempted to reinforce their position by defending Melanchthon with praises accorded him by Luther.[10]

By this time the Crypto-Philippists had lost their control over the electoral Saxon church. In 1574 Elector August came to the conviction that his theologians had been revising the Lutheran theology with which he had grown up. He arrested those who he believed had secretly

5. *Bedencken oder Censura der Theologen im Fu[e]rstenthumb Lu[e]neburg/von dem Newen Wittenbergischen Catechismo* (Jena: Richtzenhan, 1571), Aij^{v}–Aiij^{r}.

6. *Vom Catechismo etlicher Wittenbergischen. Der Lerer im Land zu Braunschweig Bedencken* (Jena: Richtzenhan, 1571), [Aii]^{r}–[Aiiij]^{v}.

7. Koch, "Auseinandersetzungen," 132–33.

8. *Reuerendi Viri D. Martini Lvteri missa ad theologos Norimbergenses (orta quadam inter ipsos dissensione) pia et vere Apostolica Epistola: qvemadmodvm tvm ad exemplum illius tempore, Vir dignitate & autoritate & studio pietatis excellens ascripsit . . .* (Leipzig: Voegelin, 1572).

9. *Kurtze vnd gru[e]ndliche Erkla[e]rung/in welchen Puncten D. Luther/vnd die so man Caluinische nennet/in der Lehr vom H. Abendmal/einig vnd auch strittig sein/Auss Herrn Lutheri eigen Schrifften aussgezogen . . .* (n.p., 1577; Bremen: Bernhardt Peters, 1592).

10. *Epistolae aliquot D. Martini Lutheri cum alijs testimonijs illius de Philippo Melanthone & eius scriptis . . .* (Görlitz: Ambrose Fritsch, 1579); *Testimonia D. Martini Lvteri de socio laborvm et pericvlorvm svorvm Philippo Melanchthone . . .* (Görlitz: Ambrose Fritsch, 1580); *Propositiones disputatae, Wittembergae pro doctoratu eximiorum D. Hieronymi Weller, & M. Nicolai Medler . . .* (Eisleben: Urban Gaubisch, 1585).

pursued this subversive plan. In their trials they appealed to Luther, arguing only that they had kept his thought abreast of new developments.[11] Their opponents worked on returning electoral Saxony to its earlier position regarding the Lord's Supper. Aiming at a more careful presentation of Luther's sacramental teaching, they republished his classic works on the theology of the Lord's Supper.

At a diet of the electoral Saxon estates held at Torgau in September 1574 the theologians whom August had appointed to begin the rebuilding of his church in the wake of the fall of the Crypto-Philippists produced a confession on the Lord's Supper. They too wished to believe that Luther and Melanchthon had taught the same doctrine. At this point such a belief remained a political as well as an emotional necessity in electoral Saxony. The idea that the two had agreed was of particular importance since the leaders of the Saxon church had strongly leaned on Melanchthon's reputation and authority in the previous decades. Even with the Crypto-Philippists removed from high office in the Saxon church, Melanchthon's reputation and authority remained. If the ideas of the Crypto-Philippists were to be defeated, August had to demonstrate that Melanchthon's teaching did not differ from Luther's.

Therefore, those who were charged with returning the Saxon church to its moorings in Luther's teaching appealed to the authority of both Luther and Melanchthon, "Elijah and Elisha," who had "lived together in agreement, . . . faithfully serving in the Lord's house, and thus we want to recognize and retain their writings and proper interpretation of these writings . . . with the appropriate gratitude." The confession insisted that use of the *Corpus doctrinae Philippicum,* which included none of Luther's writings,[12] should in no way be therefore understood as a rejection of his teaching. Though Scripture remained the only "form and norm" for the teaching of the Saxon church, it also submitted itself to the books of both "dear fathers and preceptors."[13] Under the direction of August's court, Saxon theologians also worked on the republication of these writings, so that the reading public might recognize their unanimity. To that end the court preacher Peter Glaser was commissioned to supervise the reissuing of those works of Melanchthon which would most readily support the argument that his understanding of the Lord's Supper coincided with Luther's.[14]

11. Koch, "Auseinandersetzung," 139–40.

12. See Irene Dingel, "Melanchthon und die Normierung des Bekenntnisses," in *Der Theologe Melanchthon,* ed. Heinz Scheible (Sigmaringen: Thorbecke, 1999).

13. *Kurtz Bekentnis vnd Artickel vom heiligen Abendmahl des Leibs vnd Bluts Christi* . . . (Wittenberg: Hans Lufft, 1574), [Biiij]^{v}–C^{v}, cited in part in Koch, "Auseinandersetzungen," 141.

14. Koch, "Auseinandersetzungen," 141–44.

Glaser and his fellow theologians also set out to combat "sacramentarian errors" through the best refutation that could be offered, the instruction contained in the writings of "the dear and blessed instrument of God, Doctor Martin Luther." Because they felt that the Smalcald Articles had been neglected in the Crypto-Philippists' emphasis on Melanchthon's works, they reissued this confessional document.[15] They also prepared a new edition of Luther's writings on the sacraments: *Three Sermons on Holy Baptism* (1535); the sermon on the baptism of Christ from the House Postil; sermons on the Lord's Supper (1526, 1534); the second part of *That These Words of Christ, "This Is My Body," Still Stand Firm against the Fanatics;* the Brief and Large Confessions on the Lord's Supper; and his *Open Letter to the Christians in Frankfurt am Main.*[16] As Glaser participated in the visitation of parishes which Elector August arranged for his theologians to conduct, he found that many pastors had not read these works. But, he conceded, many of them would not have been able to follow Luther's line of argumentation, so Glaser put together digests of Luther's writings in understandable form.[17] He was aiming at bringing the pastors of his own church into line with Lutheran standards. He was not engaging Calvinist opponents but instructing his own flock. Therefore, appealing to Luther could determine the point at issue: was the Saxon church's teaching faithful to its father's teaching?

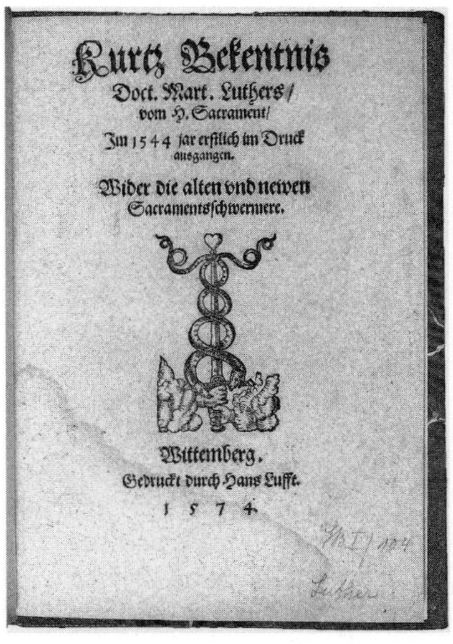

Republication of Luther's *Kurtz Bekentnis . . . vom H. Sacrament* (1574) (Concordia Seminary Library, St. Louis)

Outside electoral Saxony the criticism of the Crypto-Philippist party and its teachings did not cease even with its overthrow. As bishop of Pomesania, Johannes Wigand was the leading churchman in the duchy

15. Ibid., 144–49.

16. *Die fu[e]rnemsten vnd besten Schrifften des Hocherleuchten vnd Geistreichen Mannes Gottes/Herrn Doctoris Martini Lutheri/Von den beiden Sacramenten des Newen Testaments . . .* (Wittenberg: Hans Lufft, 1575).

17. *Wie der thewre Man D. Martinus Lutherus/wider die Sacramentirer gelehret/geprediget vnd geschrieben/ausserhalben derer Bu[e]cher/darinnen er insonderheit vnd durchaus wider sie handelt . . .* (Leipzig: Jacob Berwald's heirs, 1577); *Argvmenta Vnd Gru[e]nde/der Sacramentirer/damit sie jhre meinunge zubeweisen gedencken/Vnd kurtze Widerlegung derselbigen. Aus den Streitbu[e]chern Lutheri . . .* (Dresden: Gimel Bergen, 1578, 1579; Dresden: Matthes Stoeckel, 1598).

of Prussia. In a critique which specifically examined the question of whose position was to be taught at Wittenberg, he reviewed the advance of sacramentarian thinking. He considered whether Luther's and Melanchthon's writings were completely in agreement with one another. His spotlight fell first on Luther, whom "God raised up according to his divine counsel on the basis of his immeasurable mercy" to bring the pure teaching of God's Word out of papal darkness. God appointed Melanchthon to assist him and to set forth the riches of the liberal arts. "And these two truly great 'Wundermenner' were in the world, without peer in any other nation, and with their writings and confessions they did great things through God's governance, and the writings of both are to be regarded and read as a great treasure."[18] However, Wigand noted, Melanchthon had succumbed to the old Adam—his sinful inclinations—and had not always faithfully confessed the truth. In his writings readers could find incorrect teaching which disagreed with God's Word and Luther's teaching, confession, and writings. The errors had to be rejected, Wigand insisted, but that did not mean that the good in Melanchthon's writings should be thrown away.[19] Nonetheless, Luther remained the utterly reliable instructor in the faith and tutor of biblical teaching.

Wigand also compared Luther and Melanchthon as he reviewed the content of the controverted articles of faith. Luther had remained faithful to Christ's words in treating the Lord's Supper, but Melanchthon "had not remained faithful to his initial position." He had "deviated from Luther's position," and had failed to condemn those who erred on the sacrament. Instead, he had agreed with Reformed theologians such as Heinrich Bullinger. The bishop continued by showing how Melanchthon and Luther disagreed in one respect or another on the freedom of the will, the distinction of law and gospel, justification through faith, and papal ceremonies—the core of the controversial issues which had divided Gnesio-Lutherans and Philippists.[20] Wigand had studied under both professors, and he knew to whom he must turn for proper instruction in the biblical message whenever his own understanding of Luther deviated from Melanchthon's.

Wigand's regard for Luther's authority displayed itself in other polemical exchanges. In the disputes which followed the composition of the Formula of Concord, criticism was heard from outside Germany as well as inside the estates bound to the Augsburg Confession. Among the

18. *Ob Die Newen Wittenberger/stets bis daher/einig mit den alten geleret: Vnd ob Lutheri vnd Philippi schriften/durch aus gantz einig vnd einhellig . . . Christliche Vnd Notwendige Erinnerung vnd bericht* (Königsberg: Bonifacius Daubman, 1575), 8ʳ.

19. Ibid., 8ʳ⁻ᵛ.

20. Ibid., 10ʳ–18ᵛ.

volleys in these debates was one which Wigand fired against the criticism of Pierre Loyseleur de Villiers, court preacher for Prince William of Orange.[21] Here Wigand again defended the propriety of using Luther as a teacher, but he sharply rejected the charge that the adherents of the Formula of Concord placed Luther's views and writings above Scripture. For in controversy with those outside the Lutheran tradition, Luther's prophetic authority could not be employed.[22] Thus the content of his teaching and its faithfulness to Scripture had become the issue instead of the means of resolving the issue.

The team charged with drawing up the Formula of Concord had struggled with the question of secondary authority in the church. It finally agreed to cite only Luther among the contemporary teachers of the church. But within electoral Saxony the campaign in behalf of the Formula of Concord could not avoid addressing the question of the authority of Luther and Melanchthon and the relationship between the two. Among those whom Elector August had engaged to complete the "relutheranization" program of his government was Jakob Andreae. In his sermons preached and printed to help pastors and people understand Luther's theology better, Andreae addressed the question of the authority of the two Wittenbergers with utmost care. He downplayed Luther's authority in relationship to Scripture,[23] but in his defense of the Formula of Concord he skillfully used Luther's teaching against Melanchthon's views when he believed that the latter deviated from the biblical truth.[24]

Others who helped defend the Formula of Concord to the people similarly affirmed Luther's continued teaching activity. The popular defense offered by the Saxon court preacher Caspar Fuger made relatively little of Luther's position and person.[25] It was different with a

21. Loyseleur's *Ratio ineundae Concordiae inter Ecclesias Reformatas* . . . (n.p., 1579) was answered by Wigand's *Commonefactio de fravdibvs qvorvndam sacramentariorum* . . . (n.p., n.d.). See also Irene Dingel, *Concordia controversa: Die öffentlichen Diskussionen um das lutherische Konkordienwerk am Ende des 16. Jahrhunderts* (Gütersloh: Gütersloher Verlagshaus, 1996), 176–83.

22. Wigand, *Commonefactio,* 9. Wigand's appraisal of Luther's authority shifted in this period (see pp. 67–70).

23. E.g., in his Lenten sermons, *Passional Bu[e]chlein/Das ist/Die Historia des bittern vnd thewren leiden vnd sterbens/auch der fro[e]lichen Aufferstehung vnsers Herrn Jhesu Christi* . . . (Wittenberg: Johann Krafft, 1577), 125^{v}–26^{r}. See also p. 67 in the present volume.

24. *Fu[e]nff Predigten: Von dem Wercke der Concordien/Vnd endlicher Vergleichung der vorgefallenen streitigen Religions Artickeln* . . . (Dresden: Gimel Berger, 1580), B^{r}–Bij^{r}, Eiij^{r}–G^{v}, Y^{r}–[Yiiij]^{r}, biij^{v}–ciij^{v}.

25. Irene Dingel, "The Echo of Controversy: Caspar Fuger's Attempt to Propagate the Formula of Concord among the Common People," *Sixteenth Century Journal* 26 (1995): 515–31.

popular tract prepared in 1582 by Fuger's fellow Saxon Paul Seidel, who made a case for the Formula of Concord as a proper exposition of Luther's teaching. Seidel had matriculated at the University of Wittenberg in 1573. Thus he had experienced the disruption of the following year, when Crypto-Philippists battled those who would a few years later establish the Formula of Concord as the Saxon standard of faith and the proper interpretation of Luther's legacy. He had earned his master of arts degree and was continuing his studies when he wrote his tract. It reflects the mood in Saxony following the adoption of the Formula as a new standard for determining public teaching. In addition to appreciation of the Formula that mood carried with it a strong anti-Calvinist edge in the early 1580s. Seidel wrote out of gratitude to God for his Word and for Martin Luther, the "worthy instrument" who brought it to his land in his time. Seidel had studied Luther's writings diligently and had found them second only to the Holy Scriptures in value. In view of the needs of his time, he wanted to make Luther's teaching better known to the laity and to demonstrate that the Formula of Concord indeed agreed with all that Luther had taught. To achieve these purposes Seidel included a biographical overview of Luther's career and cited the testimony of others.[26] Without sharp polemic against any particular individuals, Seidel's essay provided a basis for casting aside the objections of those of a sacramentarian bent who believed that the Formula would lead the church backward, away from the proper course which reform should take. He instructed the laity through a summary exposition of Luther's teaching. Thus, like others at the time, Seidel found Luther an apt teacher of biblical truth for the people in the pew.

The Apology of the Book of Concord

The Formula of Concord had had this very goal: to bring those who claimed to be Lutheran into accord on basic Lutheran teaching and to promote the proper instruction of parishioners in that teaching. But be-

26. *Historia vnd Geschicht Des Ehrwirdigen vnsers in Gott lieben Vaters/Herrn Doctoris Martini Lutheri, seliger gedechtnuss/wie durch Gottes Geist getrieben/vnd sich anfenglich aus sonderlicher schickung des Allmechtigen zwischen jm vnd dem Bapst der Streit erhoben/domit das selige Liecht des heiligen Euangelij in diesen letzten zeiten wider an tag gegeben/Vnd wie es bis auff diese stund/nach vielen vnd mancherley eingeschlichenen Corruptelen/heimlichen vnd offentlichen Verfelschungen/wunderbarer weis erhalten/vnd jtzt in die new auffgerichte Formulam Concordiae rein vnd vnverfelscht ist gebracht worden. Aus seinen eigenen Schrifften vnd andern Historien vmb gemeiner Leute besserer nachrichtung willen/zu Trost Warnung vnd Vermanung . . .* (Wittenberg: Heirs of Hans Krafft, 1582), esp. [Aij]^{r}–C2^{v}.

cause one of its chief concerns was its rejection of the Saxon Crypto-Philippists' sacramentarian positions on the Lord's Supper, the Formula necessarily attracted attention from the German Calvinist or Reformed party, whose views resembled the Crypto-Philippist interpretation of Melanchthon's teaching on the real presence of Christ's body and blood in the Lord's Supper and on the person of Christ. Like the Saxon Crypto-Philippists, German Calvinists had striven to assert their faithfulness to the Augsburg Confession—albeit in its variant form—so that they might find protection under the Peace of Augsburg (1555). In addition, the Calvinists had attempted to use Luther in their own behalf—perhaps to reinforce their claim to this legal status. In 1581, the year following the publication of the Book of Concord, Christopher Grandmundt published a rebuttal of the Lutheran "ubiquitists'" citations of Luther in their own behalf. He charged that they took Luther's wildest statements, uttered in the heat of controversy, to cover their own error. God permits all great people to fall into such weakness, and those, such as Jakob Andreae, who were alleging that Luther's teaching opposed the Reformed had fallen into error themselves.[27]

Other representatives of the Reformed party avowed their profound respect for Luther and their deep gratitude to God for sending him to battle the papacy at a critical point in the church's history. The Palatine court preacher Daniel Tossanus and Christoph Herdesianus, a former student of Melanchthon and now a municipal attorney in Nuremberg, sought to salvage something of Luther's authority for their own positions as they criticized the Formulators' interpretation of Luther's the-

27. *D. Martini Lutheri Seeligen Lehr vnd Meinung/Von der Person Christi. Von seiner Himmelfahrt. Vom Sitzen zur Rechten Gottes. Auss welchem der christliche Leser/so Frieden vnd Wahrheit liebet/zusehen/dass Doctor Jacobe Andreae (genant Schmidlin) vnnd seiner mithelffer/Newe Lehr von Obgesetzten puncten/mit der Heiligen vnd Allgemeinen Christlichen Kirchenlehre/auch Doctor Luthero/wie sie des die Leut zübereden gedencken/mit nichten vbereinstimmet. Alles auss den schrifften D. Martini Lutheri vnd zum theil Johan Brentij/zusammengetragen/vnd in 100 Propositiones gefasset* . . . (Neustadt/Hardt: Matthaeus Harnisch, 1581). The Calvinists had earlier employed Luther's writings as they called for a second Reformation in evangelical Germany. The Heidelberg theologians reprinted his *On the Abuse of the Mass* (1522) in *Verantwortung Wider die vngegrundten auflagen vnd verkerung/mit welchen der Catechismus Christlicher lere zu Heidelberg jm Jar M.D.LXIII. aussgangen / . . . beschweret ist . . . Item/D. Martini Luthers meinung vom Brotbrechen im H. Abendmal* . . . (Heidelberg: Johann Maier, 1564), which was later republished with Zacharias Ursinus, *Catechismus Oder Kurtzer vnterricht Christlicher Lehr* . . . (Neustadt/Hardt: Matthaeus Harnisch, 1592, 1595). In addition, seemingly reconciliatory correspondence between Luther and the Swiss from 1537 and 1538 was published by the Heidelberg theologians in *Acta Concordiae. Das ist/Was sich in Dem Tractat vnd handel der Concordien . . . vber dem stritt desz heiligen Nachtmals Christi . . . verloffen* (Heidelberg, 1572), and was republished under the title *Antwort vnd Widerantwort/Herrn Doctor Martin Luthers/Vnd Herrn Philippi Melanchthonis . . . Auff der Schweitzerischen Reformirten Evangelischen Sta[e]tten* . . . (Marburg: Paul Egenolff, 1614).

ology of the Lord's Supper.[28] However, the Heidelberg professor Zacharias Ursinus, like Calvin earlier in the century, sharply rejected the claims that Luther had exercised a prophetic or apostolic office.[29] The Heidelberg theologian did not believe that Luther should be regarded as having been specially illumined or taught directly by God. Ursinus also rejected the claims that Luther had demonstrated predictive powers or had performed miracles.[30] In the early seventeenth century similar statements were made by Calvinist theologians in Brandenburg who, under the direction of the electoral court, sought to ease the church there toward the Reformed position.[31] Thus polemic over Luther's person entered into the polemic over his theology in the continuing disputes between Reformed and Lutheran theologians in the wake of the Formula of Concord. How worthy, how complete, a teacher of the church was he to be? Advocates of the Formula were called upon to give an answer.

This question and a variety of attacks against the Formula of Concord prompted Martin Chemnitz, Timotheus Kirchner, and Nikolaus Selnecker to compose an Apology in its defense in 1583. It dealt particularly with the Lord's Supper, the person of Christ, and original sin. But it also addressed the polemic aimed at Lutheran sacramental doctrine through attacks on Luther's person and the authority of the Augsburg Confession. A chapter "on the authority of Doctor Luther and the regard with which he should be held" was directed above all against the work of Herdesianus.[32]

The Apology avoided appeals to Luther's adjudicatory authority. Instead it emphasized that Luther had not arrogated the office of the biblical prophets to himself, but had instead purged the papal idolatry, error, and filth from the teaching of the church. The Apologists insisted that they and their fellow believers did not count Luther among the prophets and apostles who had received their teaching directly from

28. Irene Dingel, "Ablehnung und Aneignung: Die Bewertung der Autorität Martin Luthers in den Auseinandersetzungen um die Konkordienformel," *Zeitschrift für Kirchengeschichte* 105 (1994): 50–55.

29. See B. A. Gerrish, "John Calvin on Luther," in *Interpreters of Luther: Essays in Honor of Wilhelm Pauck,* ed. Jaroslav Pelikan (Philadelphia: Fortress, 1968), 67–96.

30. Dingel, *Concordia controversa,* 141–48; Robert Kolb, "Luther, Augsburg, and the Late Reformation Concept of Confession," in *Controversy and Conciliation: The Reformation and the Palatinate 1559–1583,* ed. Derk Visser (Allison Park, Pa.: Pickwick, 1986), 33–49.

31. See Bodo Nischan, "Reformation or Deformation? Lutheran and Reformed Views of Martin Luther in Brandenburg's 'Second Reformation,'" in *Pietas et Societas: New Trends in Reformation Social History: Essays in Memory of Harold J. Grimm,* ed. Kyle C. Sessions and Phillip N. Bebb (Kirksville, Mo.: Sixteenth Century Journal, 1985), 203–15.

32. Dingel, *Concordia controversa,* 207–79.

God and therefore could not err. Everyone knows the difference between the prophets and apostles on the one hand, and bishops, doctors, and authors on the other. Luther could err, of course, the Apology conceded, but its authors nonetheless found in his writings "the unchangeable truth repeated, demonstrated, and set forth on the basis of the prophetic and apostolic writings; therefore we regard them as a witness to the pure, sound teaching" of Scripture. Luther's works contain this teaching in unadulterated form, but they are witnesses to the truth only because—and insofar as—their doctrine follows God's infallible Word found in the writings of the prophets and apostles.[33]

The Apologists continued with a careful examination of seven further charges made by the Reformed opponents against Luther or his sacramental teaching.[34] When dealing with the question of whether Luther's understanding of the real presence was correct, the Apologists were, of course, driven to argue the issue on the basis of Scripture. In no case would Luther's authority have sufficed for that particular dispute. For the Calvinists accorded Luther no special place of formal authority in God's economy. He had taught the truth of Scripture and therefore commanded a faithful following. But his voice could not compel Calvinist consciences, for it exercised no authority over them. Recognizing that fact, the authors of the Apology did not attempt to use Luther as a secondary authority.

Luther as Prophetic Teacher in the Crypto-Calvinist Controversy of the 1590s

It had not always been so among the heirs of Luther. Nikolaus Selnecker had affirmed Luther's role as a secondary authority in the church a decade earlier.[35] By the 1580s, however, the Book of Concord

33. *Apologia, Oder Verantwortung dess Christlichen Concordien Buchs/In welchen die ware Christliche Lehre/so im Concordi Buch verfasset/mit gutem Grunde heiliger Go[e]ttlichen Schrifft vertheydiget . . .* (Dresden: Matthes Stoeckel, 1584), 182ᵛ–84ᵛ. See also Dingel, *Concordia controversa,* 607–19.

34. *Apologia,* 184ᵛ–92ᵛ. Gathering materials from the Apology, Zacharias Faber continued the presentation of Luther's teaching against Reformed views; he issued two defenses of Luther's doctrinal integrity: *100 Vnwarheiten. Welche die Caluinisten begehen an der H. Schrifft/der H. Va[e]tern/der Augspurgischen Confession, Christlichen Concordienbuch/vnd dem theuren Manne Luthero/etc. Colligirt aus der Apologia des Christlichen Concordienbuchs* (Wittenberg: Johann Krafft, 1598); and *Verzeichnis mehr denn Vierhundert Offendlicher vnd Schendlicher Lu[e]gen/welche die Calvinsten in jhren/in offenen Druck Publicirten, Bu[e]chern/in die gantze Christenheit fu[e]r die reine Seligmachende warheit Go[e]ttliches Worts/gantz Vnuerschempt spargirn vnd ausstrewen/vnnd darmit Vnsa[e]glichen Seelen schaden stifften* (Wittenberg: Johann Krafft d. Jungere, 1600).

35. See pp. 70–73.

had become his authority, and it served as his instrument for orienting the teaching of the church at the end of his life, which was embroiled in the second round of struggle over Crypto-Calvinism within electoral Saxony.[36] When Elector August's son Christian I assumed the throne in 1586, he began to introduce Calvinist teaching into his church. From his pastorate in Hildesheim in 1590 Selnecker joined the campaign against this second attempt to substitute a spiritualized doctrine of the Lord's Supper for Luther's. Recalled to Leipzig after Christian's death, Selnecker died hours after his return. Others did carry on his tasks in the reconstruction of the Saxon church. Among them was Georg Mueller, or Mylius, a professor at the University of Jena who was dispatched to Wittenberg to complete the rout of the Crypto-Calvinist party.

Mylius fought his battle with many weapons, one a sermon on Luther as God's chosen instrument. In observance of the forty-sixth anniversary of Luther's death, Mylius justified his praise of Luther by pointing to the Scriptures' praise of kings, prophets, judges, and others whom God used to accomplish great things. God's "Wundermann" and instrument deserved such praise.[37] These accolades were to serve as the basis for affirming the truth of Luther's instruction on the Lord's Supper.

Mylius proceeded to repeat biblical prophecies and those of later theologians of the church, such as Huss, Savonarola, and Hilten, which pointed to Luther's special role in the history of the proclamation of the gospel. He repeated the comparisons of Luther with Hercules and Samson, which highlighted Luther's heroic role in overthrowing "the abominable beast, the terrifying dragon, the many-headed snake" of the papacy, even as John had prophesied in Revelation. And Luther had accomplished this with the pen alone. Luther appeared as hero not only

36. In this period the Wittenberg faculty, as reconstructed by Christian I's government, associated with Reformed churches and lands. Hence the use of the term "Crypto-Calvinist" for the religious policy of electoral Saxony at this time is justified.

37. *Parentatio Lvtheri. Eine Christliche Predigt Vom Herrn Martino Luther/Was Gott durch diesen seligen thewren Mann/vnd ausserwehlten Ru[e]stzeug ausgerichtet/vnd gemeiner Christenheit fu[e]r Edele Wolthat erzeigt habe* . . . (Wittenberg: Matthes Welack, 1592), Aij^{r}–Aiij^{r}. In the previous year Mylius had used his own analysis of four of Luther's most important writings on the Lord's Supper as a tool against the Crypto-Calvinist party in Saxony: *ΤΕΤΡΑΒΙΒΛΟΣ ΑΝΤΙΔΕΙΠΝΟΣΟ-φισικη Martini Lvtheri: continens librorvm 1. Secundi, qui αὐτιπροφήλικοι inscribitur. 2. Cui titulus est περὶ τοῦ ῥητοῦ in verbis Co[e]nae. 3. Maioris Homologetici. 4. Minoris Homologetici. Analysin* (Jena: Tobias Steinmann, 1591). On Mylius, see Thomas Klein, *Der Kampf um die zweite Reformation in Kursachsen, 1586–1591* (Cologne: Böhlau, 1962), 37, 82, 93, 186. Mylius was not the only defender of the theology of the Formula of Concord. Joining the fray against the Crypto-Calvinist attack was the pastor in Halle, Samuel Cuno, *Lvthervs Rediuiuus. Das ist D. Martini Lutheri Sententz vnd Bedencken/von der formula Concordiae, vnd aller hierzu geho[e]rigen handel/welche sich in diesen viertzig Jahren in den Kirchen der Augspurgischen Confession zugetragen* . . . (Mühlhausen: Andreas Hantzsch, 1595).

in confronting the emperor at Worms, but also in returning to Wittenberg some months later to oppose Karlstadt. He later showed no fear in opposing antinomians, Anabaptists, Schwenckfeld, and even Jews and Muhammadans. Mylius argued that Luther did not need miracles to confirm that he was a special saint of God, for miracles are needed only to confirm new doctrine. Luther simply returned the church to the teaching of Christ and the apostles. Nonetheless, Luther did not lack marvelous signs and miracles. He took on the great Goliath of Rome, the Antichrist, and neither emperor nor king could prevail against him and his pen. He had even predicted the future himself, in foreseeing the deaths of Zwingli and Oecolampadius and the outbreak of war after his death.[38]

Mylius did relatively little in the way of citing Luther's arguments to attack Calvinist teaching. Instead, he taught Luther's doctrine against the background of his lifetime of teaching God's Word faithfully and accurately. Mylius surveyed Luther's heroic career and then cited three great benefits which God had bestowed through Luther's life. First, he delivered the church from the Roman Pharaoh's prison in the anti-Christian Babel of the papacy. He did for the Germans something akin to what Moses and Aaron had done in leading Israel out of Egypt, what Joshua had done in leading the Israelites into the Promised Land, what Ezra, Nehemiah, and Zerubbabel had done in bringing the Jews out of the Babylonian captivity. Second, Luther had restored to their proper place "the holy ordinances of God in the three hierarchies or estates [home, church, and secular government]." Mylius noted not only Luther's assertion of the proper place of secular government vis-à-vis the papacy, but also his defense of good order at the time of the Peasants' Revolt of 1525. If it had not been for Luther, Mylius asked, what prince would have been left in the land? Mylius also lauded Luther's views on marriage, particularly as they had been made clear on visits to congregations and in his postils. Finally, Mylius praised Luther's translation of the Scriptures and his catechism.[39]

Mylius's direct counterattack on the Sacramentarians was limited in this sermon to urging his hearers to follow and to treasure "this holy father and most worthy preceptor" because he had taught God's Word purely. Not as a prophetic authority, but as a heroic and faithful teacher Luther should command attention and respect. Mylius marveled at those who wanted to be regarded as orthodox and enlightened, yet refused to accept Luther's teaching on the Lord's Supper. On the one hand, sacramentarian preachers had boldly criticized the Re-

38. *Parentatio,* Aiij^{r}–Cij^{v}.
39. Ibid., Ciij^{r}–[Ciiij]^{v}.

former; a chaplain had even thrown his beer glass at Luther's picture. On the other hand, the Sacramentarians tried to cite him to confirm their own error. Lutherans are not ashamed of bearing Luther's name, Mylius declared, but the Sacramentarians refuse to claim the names of their patriarchs and grandfathers, Calvin and Zwingli.[40] By contrast, Mylius defended the Lutheran doctrine by hailing Luther as hero and pointing to his accomplishments. It is clear that Luther functioned for him as a symbol of that doctrine. Accordingly, Mylius did not employ Luther's own words or arguments and certainly did not rest his case on Luther's prophetic authority. He needed only a teacher par excellence for his task.

The defense of Luther's status as teacher took new forms as the battle between Lutherans and Reformed theologians continued; and on this field of conflict, as on that with Roman Catholics, biographical sketches of the great teacher of the church continued to be of use. In 1598 Matthaeus Dresser, professor at Leipzig, heard a rumor that Luther had confessed to Melanchthon that he had been in error on the doctrine of the Lord's Supper. It was also being said that Luther agreed with Calvin's *Institutes* on this teaching. Dresser took these "fables" as the occasion to publish a number of documents which illustrated Luther's steadfastness in his belief in the real presence of Christ's body and blood. Dresser cited documentary evidence from the weeks immediately preceding Luther's death to prove that at the very end he was firmly opposed to sacramentarian teaching.[41]

Among the several documents which Dresser republished were two essays of his own, which he had earlier published separately. The first came from his work on Christian and pagan festivals. It praised Luther for his boldness in opposing error and for virtues of temperance, chastity, and modesty in regard to riches, honors, and pleasures. The Re-

40. Ibid., D^{r}–[Dij]^{v}.

41. *Martini Lvtheri historia* . . . (Leipzig: Franz Schnelbatz, 1598), a3^{r}–A^{v}. Lutherans had repudiated such rumors since Joachim Mörlin had read them in the Palatine report on the Maulbronn Colloquy of 1564; see his *Wider die Landlu[e]gen der Heidelbergischen Theologen* (Eisleben: Andreas Petri, 1565), Aij^{r}.

The struggle to describe properly the relationship between Luther as teacher and the Preceptor Melanchthon continued in the aftermath of the Crypto-Calvinist collapse. Selnecker had attempted to place Luther and his Elisha, Philip Melanchthon, on the same side, but in the years after the Wittenberg Crypto-Calvinists had claimed Melanchthon as their own, many Lutherans objected. A sermon on Luther composed for Saint Martin's Day by Conrad Schlüsselburg, the ecclesiastical superintendent in Stralsund and a theologian of distinctively Gnesio-Lutheran disposition, contained a fierce attack on Melanchthon for abandoning Luther's teaching on justification, on good works, and above all on the Lord's Supper (*Postilla, Das ist: Ausslegung der Episteln vnd Evangelien* . . . [Frankfurt/Main: Johann Saur, 1604], 588–94).

former's writings displayed eloquence, clarity, fervor of spirit, and power of persuasion—the characteristics of a good teacher. Dresser's Luther was a great man of words, but he was not a unique Man of the Word, not an authoritative prophet.

Dresser's second essay, from his *Historical Introductions*, emphasized Luther's virtues and his learning. Dresser singled out the Reformer's knowledge and understanding of Scripture and of the patristic and scholastic commentators, but he praised particularly Luther's ability to apply the biblical word to those struggling with the trials of faith. Dresser further lauded Luther's transformation of the method of theological study, bringing it away from its scholastic mode to biblical foundations, and particularly the proper distinction between law and gospel. He also commended Luther's ability to fight against the enemies of the faith and yet to seek peace and tranquility, as he had in dealing with Karlstadt and in the Peasants' Revolt.[42]

Dresser understood Luther's theological method, and he could summarize his biography as well as it could be retold from the sources available. He revered Luther, it is clear, but did not accord him either prophetic authority or heroic status. Those images were fading. Dresser praised Luther to reinforce his value as instructor in the biblical faith. Luther was his teacher, the teacher of the doctrine codified in the Formula of Concord.

A similar perspective can be seen in two early-seventeenth-century efforts to use Luther's writings against the Reformed position. Theophilus Glaser, superintendent of the churches of Dresden, published a collection of Luther's statements on the Lord's Supper from works other than his polemical writings on the subject. These citations, which had been assembled by Glaser's father Peter, showed that Luther never departed from the teaching contained in his polemical pieces. Thus they could be used in combating the Sacramentarians.[43] A different collection of such quotations, which was attributed to Philip Glaser by its editor Caspar Finck, professor at Giessen, appeared in 1614. Theophilus Glaser reviewed thirteen charges which the Sacramentarians had made

42. *Martini Lvtheri historia,* [L8]^{r}–M5^{r}, the first essay, and M5^{v}–[M8]^{v}, the second essay. The first is from *De festis & praecipvis anni partibvs Liber . . .* (Wittenberg: Simon Gronenberg, 1584), 140–48; the second from *Millenarius Sextus Isagoges historicae . . .* (Jena: Tobias Steinmann, 1591), 180–87, where Dresser placed Luther among the "teachers of the church."

43. *Wie der thewre Mann D. Martin Luther/Wider die Sacramentirer gelehrt/geprediget/ vnd geschrieben/ausserhalb derer Bu[e]cher/darinnen er insonderheit vnd durchauss wider sie handelt. Daraus kla[e]rlich zu befinden/das er in seinen Lehrschrifften eben diss biss an sein ende gelehrt vnd bekent habe/Was er in seinen Streitbu[e]chern wider die Sacramentirer erstritten . . .* (Leipzig: Abraham Lamberg, 1603).

against Luther's doctrine of the real presence and refuted them to his own satisfaction. He defended Luther's teaching without any particular praise for his person. Finck expressed his regard for Luther's "heroic courage, comparable to Elijah's," but he, too, concentrated on presenting Luther's teaching, apparently presuming that his readers understood the significance of the fact that it was Luther who had taught it.[44]

When Luther's authority was first employed as a device to eliminate the Crypto-Philippist problem of electoral Saxony in the 1570s, it clearly carried much weight, for instance with Nikolaus Selnecker, because his prophet of God could be used to determine public teaching and the church's interpretation of Scripture. Much earlier Luther had taken his place among the teachers of the Lutheran churches—at the head of the line—in many areas other than sacramental doctrine. By the eve of the Thirty Years' War Luther's teaching was still cited as significant, if not determinative, but his followers no longer argued that he should be heard because of his prophetic status or as an adjudicatory authority. They had found another substitute for the authority once exercised by bishops, councils, and popes: the Book of Concord was now the secondary norm and rule for public teaching. Nonetheless, Luther remained for his followers a most valuable and trusted instructor.

The polemic over the nature of Christ's presence in the Lord's Supper had led to a certain neglect of the topic of the sacrament's effects, and thus Luther's teaching regarding the power of the Lord's Supper for daily life lost some of its punch. Indeed, his teaching formulated in and for the early sixteenth century needed to be reshaped and readdressed to changing patterns of church life and new issues as well as old. In the course of that inevitable process the vigor and vitality of the prophetic teacher was tamed even as the content of his teaching was preserved within the forms which his followers found useful in their generations for conveying his message. They organized his teaching into specific categories which fit the needs of the contemporary Lutheran church, above all its polemical needs in battles not only with the Calvinists but also with the Roman Catholics. Luther the teacher had found a specific place in the public argumentation of the Lutheran position.

44. *Lvthervs redivivus, Das ist/Widerlegung aller Argumenten/welche die Calvinisten vnsere Stieffbru[e]der heutiges tages vom H. Abendemal fu[e]hren/auss den Schrifften vnd Bu[e]chern dess seligen H. D. Martini Lutheri. Auch Beweiss Dass heutiges tages die gedachte Calvinisten vnd Zwinglianer nichts auff die bahn bringen/welches nicht zuvor gru[e]ndlich vom Herrn Luthero widerleget sey . . .* (Frankfurt/Main, 1614).

5

The Hero of the Reformation

Popular Presentations of Luther in Maturing Lutheranism

The Book of Concord did not settle all disputes and tensions within the Lutheran churches, but it did establish a normative framework for Lutheran church life in (and even in some instances beyond) the lands which accepted it as a *corpus doctrinae.* The battles against external enemies—above all Roman Catholicism and Calvinism—did not cease, and these battles continued to shape the Lutheran understanding of Luther's teaching and biography. Toward the end of the sixteenth century few new doctrinal issues were raised, but Luther remained the founding figure of his movement and the churches which bore his name. His followers continued to celebrate his accomplishments as special gifts from God.

Martin Luther on Stage

The polemical treatises continued to appear, but Luther's image was also cultivated in the popular mind through other literary genres. At the turn of the century latter-day humanists were still using traditional genres, including poetry, to praise Luther,[1] yet for the first time another literary form was now being employed for the same purpose.

The Crypto-Calvinist controversy of the 1590s in Saxony elicited a defense of the "Lutheran" Luther in the form of drama. Zacharias Rivander, a popular author and superintendent in Bischofswerda, issued his "Luther Reborn" in 1593 as an attack on the recently displaced Crypto-Calvinists. With some sense of the dramatic, but with weighty

1. E.g., Heinrich Bolschenius, *Cvrrvs et avriga Lvtheri, denuo recognitus* (Magdeburg: Meisner, 1600).

didactic purpose and a sharply disputative presentation, Rivander carefully set before his audience the whole history of the sacramentarian controversies. He began in 1524 with Luther's confrontation with Karlstadt. Zwingli and Oecolampadius appeared, their arguments countered by Luther and Johannes Brenz. Rivander's Martin Bucer affirmed his full agreement with Luther on the doctrine of the Lord's Supper. Calvin, Bullinger, and other Reformed theologians were shown wrong on the basis of testimonies offered to the audience by Andreae, Hesshus, Selnecker, and a series of other Lutherans who had battled sacramentarian doctrine during the disputes of the late 1580s and 1590s in Saxony. Luther refuted claims often heard from late-sixteenth-century Calvinists that he had abandoned his own teaching on the Lord's Supper.[2] Rivander's dramatized polemic taught the basis of Lutheran sacramental doctrine in summary form.

The genre of drama was quickly employed as a didactic tool for refreshing the popular memory regarding the great Reformer. In 1600 Andreas Hartmann recast for the stage what he had learned above all from Johannes Mathesius's homiletical biography. Composed in German, the play was probably meant to be performed by upper-level schoolchildren. As Hartmann had read Mathesius's sermons on Luther's life, he recognized in Luther's career "a most wondrous work of the Highest." Furthermore, he realized that most of his contemporaries were ignorant about and ungrateful for this chosen instrument of God. So he studied the accounts by Sleidanus and Melanchthon, Luther's own works, and biographical pieces by others to prepare himself for writing a series of plays. Only the first was published, a fairly straightforward recounting of Luther's career through the Diet of Worms.[3]

2. *Lvthervs redivivvs. Eine newe Comoedia Von der langen vnd ergerlichen Disputation bey der Lehre vom Abendmal/derer so man Lutherisch vnd Calvinisch/So wol der andern/die man Philippisch vnd Flacianisch heisst. Darinnen Historischer Bericht/wenn/ von wem/vnd wie solch erbermlich wesen Anno 24. angefangen/vnd gefu[e]ret worden biss zum ende des 92. Jahres. Aus denen daruon ausgegangenen mehr als drey hundert Streitschrifften mit fleis colligiret/vnd menniglichen zur Lehr/Trost/Warnung vnd Vermahnung/ keinen Theil weder zu lieb noch zu leid/auffs aller glimpflichst fu[e]r augen gestellet* (n.p., 1593).

3. *Erster Theil/des cvrricvli vitae Lvtheri. Das ist: Warhafftige vnd kurtze Historische Beschreibung/der Geburt vnd Ankunfft/Auch Lehr/Lebens/Wandels/Beru[e]ffs/Standes vnd Ampts/Vnd sonderlich der beharlichen vnd standhafftigen Glaubens Bekendtnis/bey reiner Euangelischer Warheit/vnd in Summa/der gantze Laufft/beydes Lebens vnd Sterbens/Des Ehrwurdigen/Hocherleuchten/Gottseligen vnd Tewren Mannes Gottes/Herrn D. Martini Lutheri/etc. Heiliger Geda[e]chtnuss* . . . (n.p., 1601), Aiij^{r}, [Avj]^{r}. This work was reprinted under the title *Luther redivivvs* . . . (Halle: Peter Schmied, 1624). On Hartmann's work, see Amalie Zabel, *Lutherdramen des beginnenden 17. Jahrhunderts* (Ph.D. diss., University of Munich, 1911), 5–10.

Hartmann's drama followed the historical data quite closely, and yet, in spite of its occasionally primitive dramatic technique, it managed some "suspenseful, dramatic action," for instance as it presented Luther's confrontation with Cajetan at Augsburg in 1518 and his appearance before the estates at Worms in 1521.[4] The playwright made it clear at the very beginning that Luther was a "prophet selected by God to shine God's Word far and wide, and bring the pope to naught."[5] His Luther was above all a Christian knight and *Wundermann.* Hartmann played the heroic elements of Luther's life for all they were worth. At the same time he recognized Luther as a man of the Word and a man of faith, a heroic prophet who could serve as a model for other Christian lives.[6] While the play does not present Luther as a prophetic authority, those who saw it would have had little doubt that they were witnessing the career of a heroic man of God.

Thirteen years later a clergyman in the vicinity of Luther's native Eisleben, Martin Rinckhart, made much the same point as he tried his hand at casting Luther's story into dramatic form. More famous as hymnwriter than as dramatist, Rinckhart published what he projected as the first of a series of plays in 1613. In contrast to Hartmann, he went on to produce two more of his projected series, in 1618 and 1625.[7] Rinckhart's first effort took the form of a fable, an allegory of the Reformation, in line with the Baroque conventions of his time. Its truth was awkwardly expressed in the form of a myth, a secular story in which three sons fight over the legacy of their father Immanuel, who represents Christ. The three sons, Pseudo-Petrus (the pope), Sir Martin (Luther), and Sir John (Calvin), decide to resolve their dispute by a contest of shooting at the corpse's heart. Sir John's shot comes closer than

4. Zabel, *Lutherdramen,* 6–7.

5. *Erster Theil,* Aij^{r}.

6. Ibid., [Bvj]^{v}, Ciij^{r}–Cv^{r}, F^{r}.

7. *Der Eisslebische Christliche Ritter/Eine newe vnd schone/Geistliche Comoedia/darinnen nicht allein die Lehr/Leben vnd wandel des letzten deutschen Wundermans Luther/ sonder auch seiner/vnd zu forderst des Herrn Christi zweyer vornemsten Hauptfeinden/ Papst vnd Calvinisten . . . abegemahlet vnd auffgefuhret* (Eisleben, 1613); *Indulgentiarius Confusus/oder Eislebische Mansfeldische Jubel-Comoedia Von der offentliche/Wundermachtigen Beschamung des grossen vnd grewlichen Gottslesterers Johann Tezels: Sampt der vnverschambten/Bapstischen Ablass-Crahmerey: Wie noch des gantzen Romischen vnd Anti Christlichen Bapstthumbs: So Gott/die hohe Majestat/durch die hellklingende/Evangelische Jubel Posaun seines hierzu auserwehlten/hochfliegenden Posaun Engels/des Deutschen/ Mansfeldischen Wunder-Propheten/D. Martini Lutheri/nunmehr vor hundert Jahren glucklich anfahen . . .* (Eisleben: Heirs of Jakob Gaubisch, 1618); *Monetarius Seditiosus sive Incendia Rusticorum Bellica/& reliqua ejus lustri memorabilia . . . Der Müntzerische Bawren Krieg . . . Vnd was Gott die Hohe Maj. durch jhren dazu sonders auserwehlten Rustzeug Doct. Martinum Lutherum dabey gethan vnd verrichtet . . .* (Leipzig: Elias Rehfeld and Johann Gross, 1625).

Pseudo-Petrus's, but Sir Martin turns away in tears. Immanuel pronounces him the winner. Rinckhart's fable clothes historical events in allegorical garb.

Amalie Zabel finds Rinckhart's attempt at allegorizing the Reformation only partially successful. She points out that many details are introduced without sufficient historical clarification.[8] The figures of Emperor Charles V (Pentonomus) and Albrecht of Mainz (Astyages) appear without any doubt about who is being represented. Yet at some points the true intention of the fable would have been obscure to anyone unacquainted with the historical roots. Rinckhart's embodiment of all the nonpapal and non-Calvinist opposition to Luther, that is, of the sects, in the figure of Vertumnus produces a scene which has no other function than "to bring a little more noise to the stage" if the historical context of Luther's strife with the antinomians and Anabaptists is not understood.[9]

Embodying truth in fable or mythical form, Rinckhart's presentation of the Reformation moved beyond mere historical reporting, even of an eschatological kind. Baroque convention took command, although Rinckhart did struggle to maintain the historical grounding of his fable with marginal notes and historical introductions for each act. Furthermore, Rinckhart's chosen vehicle did not permit him to deal with the message of the Reformation, but only with its conflicts, first of all with the papacy, but also with Calvinists and sectarians. Thus Rinckhart presented to his audience neither an authoritative prophet nor a heroic prophet, but simply a symbol of heroic action.

When Rinckhart returned to his thespian activity in 1618, he was assisting in Eisleben's celebration of the hundredth anniversary of the posting of the Ninety-Five Theses. He turned to history and produced an account of the beginning of the Reformation. Luther was portrayed as a chosen "miraculous prophet" who had fulfilled the prophecy of Revelation 14 about the angel with the eternal gospel to proclaim. Relying on Hartmann and on Heinrich Kielmann's dramatic treatment of the same subject, Rinckhart offered four acts that surveyed with some dramatic skill and flair Luther's conflicts with the adherents of Rome in the indulgence controversy, at Augsburg in 1518, and at Worms in 1521. The fifth act followed the dramatic convention of the time in lifting the historical events to a superhistorical stage: Peter and Christ confront the pope at the gates of heaven in what Zabel deems a "fresh and lively scene." Luther, Frederick the Wise, Tetzel, and other assorted figures also appear in the final act, which is designed to glorify Luther.

8. Zabel, *Lutherdramen,* 32.
9. Ibid., 33–34.

Tying all the historical detail of the earlier scenes together, it celebrates Luther's career and his gifts to the church.[10]

The centennial of the Peasants' Revolt in 1625 occasioned Rinckhart's third drama, in which he presented Luther's message overpowering the errors of Andreas Karlstadt, Thomas Müntzer, and the peasants. The element of conflict again made the dramatic task easy: Satan confronted the angel of the apocalypse. But the complexity of the historical events, which Rinckhart tried to represent faithfully, made the presentation difficult. Nonetheless, Zabel finds his synthesis of the various strands of Luther's relationship with Müntzer filled with skillful characterization: Luther passionately resists his foe's raving and raging.[11] In this third and last piece in Rinckhart's cycle the historical ground on which the events took place is clearly presented, and Luther appears quite distinctly as a human figure in conflict, in a difficult and delicate situation, even as he is portrayed as the angel with the eternal gospel in his mouth.

Rinckhart's effort of 1618 was but one of several attempts to present Luther's story on the stage as part of the celebrations of the centennial of the posting of the Ninety-Five Theses. Another of these pieces was Heinrich Kielmann's "Tetzel Peddling." Kielmann's focus on Tetzel highlighted Luther's conflict with the Roman party. He used an allegorical framework, ranging Religion and her daughter Truth against Truth's siblings, Hypocrisy and Gnathester (the Parasite). Kielmann's satire mocked the corruption of the medieval church, exhibited above all in the greed which drove the indulgence trade. Reflecting a domesticated version of the early apocalyptic appraisal of Luther as the angel of Revelation 14, the hero of Kielmann's tale is a man with angel's wings who returns Scripture to its proper place and proclaims better times.[12] Kielmann celebrated Luther's triumph over the papacy in a manner suitable for centennial observances. Like Rinckhart he had followed the Baroque convention of abstracting ideals from history. In doing so, he sacrificed some of the personal and the eschatological edge of earlier tributes to Luther.

Similarly, Balthasar Voigt also extended the historical account of Hartmann into another level of theatrical presentation. His play is set in 1617; Luther has returned for the anniversary of the posting of the Ninety-Five Theses. Designed specifically for the centennial observa-

10. Ibid., 42–44.

11. Ibid., 55–57.

12. *Tetzelocramia, dass ist, Eine lustige Comoedie von Johan Tetzels AblassKram. Wie Gott der Herr denselben/Jtzo fu[e]r Hundert Jahren durch sein erwehltes Ru[e]stzeug, D. Martinum Lutherum in krafft des Heiligen Evangelii/vmbestossen vnnd aussgetrieben . . .* (Wittenberg: Johann Mathaeus, 1617). See also Zabel, *Lutherdramen,* 11–21.

tions, this piece uses comic overtones to emphasize the evil of the papacy and the heroic nature of Luther's efforts against it.[13]

In contrast, one of the plays prepared for the centennial observation in 1617 did present the historical events without allegory. Heinrich Hirtzwig, a school rector in Frankfurt am Main, produced a Latin script which traced Luther's career from his call to Wittenberg until his death. Based upon Mathesius, Sleidanus, Melanchthon, Luther's own works, Hartmann, and other sources, Hirtzwig's drama presented the chief elements of Luther's story with some apt sketching of the individuals and the psychological forces involved.[14] He also made the most of the opportunities for good dramatic conflict. His Luther had the characteristics of a heroic prophet.

These plays were intended as pedagogical devices for the schools. But instead of teaching doctrinal lessons (Luther's understanding of justification through faith was not ignored, but it was not emphasized either) they aimed primarily at cultivating an appreciation of Luther's contributions to German freedom from papal oppression. Even at that, their popular appeal was limited. They shaped, but perhaps much more reflected, the image of Luther one hundred years after his Reformation had begun. These theatrical representations of the Reformer were controlled to a significant extent by the literary conventions of the time. They exemplified the normal processing of history into mythical abstractions. Where they did not resort to mythical abstraction, they revealed that in the early 1600s Lutherans held on to a few good themes from the rich historical and doctrinal story of Luther's career. What remained was the heroic struggle which Luther had waged against the papacy, a topic of use at the beginning of the seventeenth century, and an argument for the authority of Scripture. These themes fit the needs of the new generation of Lutherans as they fought to maintain doctrinal and institutional identity against new forms of old threats.

The Reformation Jubilee and Luther's Image

Lutherans had observed anniversaries of the Reformation for some time before the centennial which occasioned the theatrical pieces composed by Rinckhart, Kielmann, Voigt, and Hirtzwig. Some governments celebrated the date of the initial publication of an evangelical constitu-

13. *Echo Jubilaei Lutherani. Das ist Ein Christlich Gedicht vnd Widerschall vom Lutherischen Jubelfest/so des abgewichenen 1617. Jahrs in der Christlichen Catholischen vralten vnd Lutherischen Kirchen Celebriert worden* . . . (n.p., 1618). See also Zabel, *Lutherdramen,* 22–26.

14. *Lutherus Drama* . . . (Frankfurt/Main: Sigismund Latomus, 1617). See also Zabel, *Lutherdramen,* 58–68; and Ruth Kastner, *Geistlicher Rauffhandel: Illustrierte Flugblätter zum Reformationsjubiläum,* Mikrokosmos 11 (Frankfurt/Main: Peter Lang, 1982), 205–8.

tion for their territory. Others selected the date on which the local Reformation had been introduced. Hamburg, Frankfurt an der Oder, and Pomerania-Stettin celebrated Luther's baptismal day each year, and Eisleben the day of his death. Hamburg and Lübeck also observed a special celebration of the Reformation around the beginning of November, near the anniversary of the posting of the Ninety-Five Theses.[15]

Lutherans by and large had not planned special observations of the centennial anniversary of the Ninety-Five Theses. Apart from the University of Wittenberg, little planning had gone into celebrating the jubilee of the outbreak of the indulgence controversy. Initial impetus for such observations came from Reformed political leaders, particularly Elector Frederick V of the Palatinate and his fellow princes in the Protestant Union, the league which he headed. The political maneuvering of the previous decade was casting a heavy shadow. Roman Catholic pressure on both Lutherans and Reformed churches having mounted since the turn of the century, Protestant leaders in both groups recognized the usefulness of an anniversary to heighten the consciousness of their people to the rising Roman threat. Therefore, Lutherans joined the efforts at the local level, and by October 31, 1617, festive commemorations had been organized in most Lutheran cities and principalities as well as those affiliated with the Union.[16] Within a year Frederick would lead the Union into war against the Habsburg emperor, Matthias.

Popular literature warmed the hearts of the people for the celebrations. Wolfgang Franz, a professor at Wittenberg, prepared a study replete with catalogs and documents regarding the indulgence collections at Wittenberg and Halle during Luther's time.[17] Pamphlets and broadsheets with brief surveys of Luther's life and often with illustrations reiterated the fundamental motifs of contemporary Lutheran dramas.

15. Hans-Jürgen Schönstädt, "Das Reformationsjubiläum 1617, Geschichtliche Herkunft und geistige Prägung," *Zeitschrift für Kirchengeschichte* 92 (1982): 5–6.

16. Ibid., 6–20. See also Hans-Jürgen Schönstädt, *Antichrist, Weltheilsgeschehen und Gottes Werkzeug, Römische Kirche, Reformation und Luther im Spiegel des Reformationsjubiläums 1617* (Wiesbaden: Steiner, 1978), 10–85. On the political situation leading up to the Thirty Years' War, see R. J. W. Evans, *Rudolf II and His World: A Study in Intellectual History, 1576–1612* (Oxford: Clarendon, 1973), esp. 43–115; J. V. Polisensky, *The Thirty Years War*, trans. Robert Evans (Berkeley: University of California Press, 1971), 1–97.

17. *Historische Erzehlung Der Beyden Heiligthu[e]men/nemblich eines/So in der Schlosskirchen zu Wittenberg im anfang der Reformation Herrn D. Lutheri vorhanden gewesen. Das Ander/So zu Hall in Sachsen nach der angefangenen Reformation Herrn D. Lutheri vollkommentlicher gemacht worden. Aus Welcher Historischen Erzehlung alle fromme Christen . . . anfingen zu greiffen/Auch jhren Nachkommen hinderlegen/vnd demselben also zu wiessen machen ko[e]nnen/mit was fu[e]r grossen Betrug vnsere liebe Vorfahren/vnter dem dicken Babstumb geplaget worden/dakegen was der Ewige Gott durch die Reformation Herrn D. Lutheri fu[e]r grosse Barmhertzigkeit allen Menschen erzeiget habe* (Wittenberg: Paul Helwig, 1618).

Göttlicher Schrifftmessiger / woldenckwürdiger Traum / welchen der Hochlöbliche / Gottselige Churfürst Friederich zu Sachsen / ꝛc. der Weise genant / aus sonderer Offenbarung Gottes / gleich jtzo für hundert Jahren / nemlich die Nacht für aller Heiligen Abend / 1517. zur Schweinitz dreymal nach einander gehabt / Als folgenden Tages D. Martin Luther seine Sprüche wider Johann Tetzels Ablaßkrämerey / an der Schloßkirchenthür zu Wittenberg angeschlagen. Allen jetzo jubilierenden Christen nützlich zu wissen / in dieser Figur eigentlich fürgebildet.

GLeICh aM ersten reChten eVangeLIsChen LVtherIsChen IVbeLfest

JCh habe offt in den Ländern / als ich ein Kind war / eine Propheceyung gehöret / Keyser Friedrich würde das heilige Grab erlösen / vnd / wie dann der Propheten Art vnd Natur ist / daß sie ehe erfüllet als verstanden werden / setzen sie allezeit anders wohin / denn die Wort für der Welt lauten: Also deucht mich auch / daß diese Propheceyung in diesem vnserm Churfürsten Hertzog Friedrichen zu Sachsen erfüllet sey. Denn was können wir für ein ander heilig Grab verstehen / denn die heilige Schrifft / darinn die Warheit Christi durch die Papisten getödtet / ist begraben gelegen / welches die Büttel / das ist / die bettel Orden vnd Ketzermeister behütet vnd bewahret haben / daß kein Jünger Christi käme vnd stele sie? Nun kan niemand leugnen / daß vnter Hertzog Friedrich / dem Churfürsten zu Sachsen / die lebendige Warheit des Evangelij ist herfür kommen / etc.

Somnium Friderici sapientis Electoris Saxoniæ.

DEr Ehrwürdige Herr Georgius Spalatinus hat mir Antonio Musæ glaubwürdig erzehlet einen Trawm / welchen Hertzog Friedrich Churfürst zu Sachsen gehabt hat zur Schweinitz / die Nacht zuvor / ehe Doctor Martin Luther seine erste propositiones wider den Bapst / vnd beyde Johan Tetzels Predigten von der Römischen Gnade vnd Ablaß / zu Wittenberg öffentlich zu vertheidigen / hat angeschlagen / welchen Trawm auch seine Churfürstl. Gn. bald frühe morgens jhme zum Gedächtniß hat auffgezeichnet / auch denselben jhrem Herrn Bruder / Hertzogen Hansen zu Sachsen / in beyseyn des Cantzlers / referiret vnd gesaget hat: Herr Bruder / Ewer Liebe muß ich erzehlen / was mich diese Nacht getrawmet hat / möchte gerne seine Bedeutung wissen / ich habe jhn so eigentlich vnd wol gemercket / vnd ist mir so tieff eingebildet / daß mich düncket / ich könte jhn nicht vergessen / wenn ich tausend Jahr leben solte / denn er mir dreymal nach einander vorkommen / doch jmmer verbessert. Hertzog Johan hat gefraget: War es dann ein guter oder böser Trawm? Wir wissen es nicht / Gott weis es / saget der Churfürst: Hertzog Johannes fraget weiter: Herr Bruder / E. L. setze nicht viel darauff / wenn mir etwas träwmet / so bitte ich allwege vnsern HErrn GOtt / er wolle es zum besten wenden / oder schlage mir jhn aus dem Sinne / wiewol ich auch diß bekennen muß / daß mir viel Träwme / beyde gut vnd böse / sind vorkommen / welche ich hernach erst verstanden habe / aber gemeiniglich in schlechten sachen. Es sage E. L. was war denn der Trawm? Churfürst Friedrich saget: Ich wils E. L. sagen: Als ich mich auff den Abend zu Bette legte / ziemlich matt vnd müde / war ich bald vber dem Gebet eingeschlaffen / vnd hätte bey drittehalb Stunden fein sanffte geruhet / als ich nun erwachte / vnd ziemlich munter worden / lag ich / vnd hätte allerley Gedancken biß nach 12. in Mitternacht / gedacht vnter andern / wie ich allen lieben Heiligen / vnd neben mir mein Hofgesinde / zu Ehren bringen wolte / betet auch für die liebe Seelen im Fegfewer / vnd beschloß bey mir / jhnen auch zu hülff in jhrer Glut zu kommen / bat den lieben Gott vmb seine Gnade / daß er doch mich vnd meine Räthe / vnd Landschafft / in rechter Warheit wolte leiten / vnd zur Seligkeit verhelffen / auch allen bösen Buben / die vns vnser Regiment sawer machen / nach seiner Allmacht wehren: nach Mitternacht war ich bald nach solchen Gedancken wieder eingeschlaffen / da träwmet mir / wie der allmächtige Gott einen Münch eines feinen erbarn Angesichts zu mir schicket / der war S. Pauli des lieben Apostels natürlicher Sohn / der hatte bey sich zu Gefehrten aus Gottes Befehl alle liebe Heiligen / die solten dem Münch vor mir Zeugniß geben / daß es kein Betrug mit jhm were / sondern er sey warhafftig ein Gesandter Gottes / vnd ließ mir Gott gebieten / ich solte dem Münch gestatten / daß er mir etwas an meine Schloß Capell zu Wittenberg schreiben dürffte / es würde mich nicht gerewen / ich ließ jhm durch den Cantzler sagen / weil mich Gott solches heist / vnd er auch sein gewaltig Zeugniß hat / so möchte er schreiben / was jhm geboten wer. Darauff fehet der Münch an zu schreiben / vnd macht so grobe Schrifft / daß ich sie hie zur Schweinitz erkennen konte / er führet auch so eine lange Feder / daß sie auch biß gen Rom mit dem Hindertheil reichte / vnd einem Lewen / der zu Rom lag / mit dem Sturtz in ein Ohr stach / daß der Sturtz zum andern Ohr wieder heraus gieng / vnd streckte sich die Feder ferner / biß an der Bäpstlichen Heiligkeit dreyfache Krone / vnd stieß so harte daran / daß sie begunte zu wackeln / vnd wolte jhrer Heiligkeit vom Häupte fallen. Wie sie nun also im Fall ist / deucht mich / Ich vnd E. L. stunden nicht weit davon / streckte auch meine Hand aus / vnd wolte sie helffen halten / in denselben geschwinden zugreiffen erwachte ich / vnd hielt meinen Arm in die höhe / war gantz erschrocken / vnd auch zornig mit auff den Münch / daß er seine Feder im schreiben nicht bescheidener führet. Als ich mich aber recht besann / da war es ein Trawm / ich aber war noch voll Schlaffes / giengen mir die Augen bald wieder zu / vnd war wieder fest eingeschlaffen / ehe ich es recht gewar worden / daß mir dieser Trawm wieder vorkommen / denn ich hatte wieder mit dem Münch zu thun / vnd sahe jhm zu / wie er jmmer fortschriebe / vnd mit dem Sturtz der Feder stach er jmmer weiter auff den Lewen zu Rom / vnd durch den Lewen auff den Bapst / darüber der Lew so grewlich brüllete / daß die gantze Stadt Rom / vnd alle Stände des heiligen Reichs zulieffen / zu erfahren / was da were / vnd da begehrte Bäpstliche Heiligkeit an die Stände / man solte doch dem Münch wehren / vnd sonderlich mich dieses Frevels berichten / darüber erwachte ich zum andern mal / verwundert mich / daß der Trawm wieder kommen war: ließ mich doch so gar nichts anfechten / bat aber / Gott wolte Bäpstliche Heiligkeit für allem Vbel behüten / vnd schlieff also zum drittenmal wieder ein / da kam der Münch mir zum dritten mal für / vnd bemüheten vns sehr / dieses Münchs Feder zu zerbrechen / vnd den Bapst hinweg zu leiten / aber je mehr wir vns an der Feder versuchten / je mehr sie starrete vnd knarrete / daß mir es in den Ohren wehe thet / wir denn endlich alle so verdrossen vnd müde darüber / daß wir ablieffen / verlohre sich einer nach dem andern vnd besorgeten vns / der Münch möchte mehr Feder können / als Brodt essen / er möchte vns jrgend einen Schaden zufügen / Nichts desto weniger aber ließ ich den Münch fragen / denn jetzt war ich zu Rom / bald zu Wittenberg / wo er doch zu solcher Feder kommen were? vnd wie es zugehe / daß sie so zehe vnd fest sey? Er mir sagen / sie were von einer alten Böhmischen hundertjährigen Gans / einer seiner alten Schulmeister hette jhn damit verehret / vnd gebeten / weil sie sehr gut were / er wolte sie zu seinem Gedächtniß behalten / vnd brauchen / er hat sie auch selbst temperiret / daß sie aber so lange währet / vnd so feste were / käme daher / daß man jhr den Geist nicht nemen / noch die Seele / wie mit andern Federn geschichet / heraus ziehen könte. Darüber er sich auch selbst nicht gnug verwundern könte. Bald darnach kömpt ein ander Geschrey aus / es weren aus der langen Münchs Feder vnzehlich viel andere Schreibfedern hier zu Wittenberg gewachsen / vnd es sey mit lust anzusehen / wie sich viel gelehrte Leute darumb reissen / vnd meynten eins theils / diese newe junge Federn würden mittler zeit auch so groß vnd lang werde / wie dieses Münchs Feder / vnd es werde gewißlich etwas sonderlichs auff diesen Münch vnd auff seine lange Feder erfolgen. Da ich nu gäntzlich im Trawm bey mir beschloß / nicht ehe je besser mit dem Münch in eigner Person zu vnterreden / da wachte ich endlich zum dritten mal auff / vnd war jetzo Morgen worden / wundert mich sehr vber dem Trawm / gedacht jhm nach / vnd bildet mir jhn wol ein / wie er nach einander mir war vorkommen / vnd zeichnete mir bald die vornembste stück zum Gedechtniß auff / bin gäntzlicher meynung / dieser Trawm sey nicht ohne Bedeutung / weil er mir so offt ist vorkommen / vnd bin bald willens / ich wil jhn meinem Beichtvater offenbaren / doch habe ich E. L. vorhin auch etwas wissen lassen / E. L. vnd Cantzler sagen mir jhr gutdüncken davon. Hertzog Johan saget: Herr Cantzler / was düncket euch / von trawmen ist nicht viel allemal zu halten / doch sind sie auch nit gäntzlich zu verwerffen / wenn wir hier einen verstendigen frommen Joseph oder Danielem hetten / der könte es treffen. Der Cantzler spricht: E. Churf. Gn. wissen / daß man pflegt zu sagen: Jungfrawen / gelehrter Leute / vnd grosser Herrn Trawme haben gemeiniglich etwas hinder sich / allein was es sey / wird man allererst / wenn sie nach etlicher Zeit / wenn sich etwa Händel zutragen / darauß man alßdenn vermutung nimmet / vnd spricht: Sihe / darauff hat gewißlich jener Trawm gewiesen / wie E. Churf. Gn. viel solcher Exempel werden bekant seyn. Sonst spricht Joseph: Trawme außzulegen / stehet Gott alleine zu: Vnd Daniel saget: Gott im Himmel allein kan verborgene ding offenbaren / darumb befehlen E. L. vnd E. Churf. Gn. nur diesen Trawm dem lieben Gott / die Münche haben offt bey grossen Herrn viel Vnglück gestifftet / an diesem Trawm vom Münche ist diß das beste / daß er von Gott gesand ist / zu schreiben Befehl hat / vnd daß alle Heiligen seine Zeugen sind / es were denn / daß der Teuffel vnter einem guten Schein sein Spiel haben wolte / E. Churf. Gn. wird am besten wissen den Sachen / neben andächtigen Gebet / Christlich nachzudencken. Hertzog Johan spricht: Ich halte es mit euch / Herr Cantzler / denn daß wir vns lange darüber grämen vnd martern sollen / ist nicht zu achten / Gott wird alles / so dieser Trawm von jhm herkömmet / wissen zum besten zu wenden / vnd vns zu seiner zeit die rechte Bedeutung mitzutheilen / oder so es ein böses bedeut / abzuschaffen. Hertzog Friedrich Churfürst spricht: das thue der getrewe Gott / allein daß ich des Trawms in deß nicht vergesse / ich habe auch wol bey mir meine Gedancken vnd Außlegung / aber die behalte ich noch zur zeit bey mir alleine / doch wil ich sie auffzeichnen / es wird vielleicht die Zeit hernach geben / ob ich es recht getroffen haben / vnd wir wollen vns diese Tage wieder miteinander vnterreden / etc.

HOc Somnium Illustrissimi Electoris Saxoniæ, ego D. K. ex Autographo M. Antonij Musæ Superintendentis Rochlicensis descripsi, Anno 91. die omnium Sanctorum Cal. Novembris, cùm in valle Ioachimica exul viverem, quod Autographum tùm temporis penes se habebat Reverendus Vir D. M. Bartholomæus Schönbach Rochlicensis, verbi divini in vallibus minister. Assignârat autem Dominus Musa hoc Somnium ex ore vel recitatione D. Georgij Spalatini, &c.

"The Dream of Frederick the Wise" (1617) (Lutherhalle, Wittenberg)

This popular literature repeated the old themes of earlier writers and viewed Luther as the angel of Revelation 14, the prophet of the German nation and the new Elijah, a hero who withstood powerful tyranny from ecclesiastical and political leaders, and the teacher of God's Word who brought the light of the gospel into the darkness imposed on Christendom by the papacy. Often these broadsheets depicted Luther in his doctoral robes and with a Bible in his hand—the teacher par excellence. They noted that he had freed family life and secular government from the oppression of the papal system. They reported his peaceful and blessed death. The goal of these broadsheets and pamphlets was to teach and edify pious Lutherans and reinforce the bonds which held them together in the community of their church.[18]

Some of these propaganda pieces mentioned the miracles which Luther had worked in overthrowing the papacy, his predictive powers, and the prophecies which had pointed to his ministry of reformation. Among the prophecies which had become popular in the years leading up to 1617 was the dream which Elector Frederick the Wise allegedly had on the night before Luther posted the Ninety-Five Theses. Whatever historical roots this report actually had,[19] it supported the belief that supernatural direction had set Luther on his course of conflict with Rome.

The standard themes associated with the heroic Luther appear also in sermons related to the jubilee. One of the most prominent Lutheran leaders of the time, the electoral Saxon councilor and court preacher Matthias Höe von Höenegg, had already preached sermons and written a treatise on Luther's significance for God's economy of the world and for his own time. In 1611 he had countered the "horrendous lies, accusations, blasphemies [!], and the coarsest falsehoods" lodged against Luther through the pen of a Reformed pastor from Bremen, Johannes Lampadius, formerly professor in Heidelberg. Höe's biographical and theological review of the significance of Luther and the Augsburg Confession for the proclamation of the gospel echoed earlier judgments that Luther had been God's chosen instrument and the third Elijah. At the end of his extensive historical and theological analysis of the issues which Lampadius and others had raised, Höe argued that Luther's "holy authority" still stood.[20]

18. Kastner, *Geistlicher Rauffhandel,* 167–202, 218–25.

19. The text is reprinted in *Deutsche Luthersagen,* ed. J. A. Benkert (Berlin: Eckart, 1937), 50ff.; see also pp. 84–85 in the present volume.

20. *Pro beato Luthero, Avgvstana Confessione, et veritate historica, Adversus Iohannis Lampadii . . . horrendas calumnias, criminationes, blasphemias, & crassissima mendacia . . . Apologia maxime necessaria . . .* (Leipzig: Abraham Lamberg, 1611), esp. 91, 115–16. Höe was attacking Lampadius's *Mellifici historici pars tertia . . .* (Marburg: Paul Egenolph, 1611), 425–64, which treated Luther and related matters.

As a preacher in Dresden, Höe had begun the task of presenting Luther a decade earlier. He collected his sermons on the German prophet for publication in 1617. His preface set these ten sermons in the context of the Book of Revelation. Revelation 11 speaks of the witnesses who will prophesy and then be slain by the beast. Luther's coming had been prophesied by witnesses such as Huss, Jerome of Prague, and Savonarola, who predicted the third Elijah even as they suffered death at the papacy's hand. Such witnesses repudiate all the accusations that their opponents, who in Höe's time were the Jesuits, lodge against God's anointed, the holy and precious instrument of the Highest. Yet the court preacher had not only common papal calumnies in view; his preface also defended "our German apostle and third Elijah" against charges lodged by Calvinists.[21]

Höe's Luther was a "spiritual knight and warrior . . . who turned the Roman Goliath on its head." As had many of his predecessors, Höe compared the Reformer's exploits against the pope with the exploits of Samson and David. The court preacher also repeated the Protestant commonplaces regarding the darkness and ignorance to which Satan had brought the church under the papacy. Throughout his sermonic biography Höe wove Luther's career into the warp and woof of salvation history as set forth in the biblical text, above all in the Book of Revelation. As he rehearsed the course of Luther's career, Höe reminded his readers that Luther was "doctor over all doctors" in the study of both Scripture and the liberal arts. He ascribed to the Reformer all imaginable virtues: Luther had been a genuine German prophet, a teacher sent from God, mighty in the Word, well versed in the Scriptures (Acts 18:24), well read in the Fathers, an eloquent man, well trained in the biblical languages, ardent in his love, zealous for the faith, steadfast in hope, patient under the cross and in distress, Christian and godly in life and conduct, resolute in tackling difficult questions, and prepared to give salutary and proper counsel. In summary, the spirit of Elijah was upon him twofold.[22]

Indeed, the spirit of Elijah flowed from Luther's harp when God sent him to comfort God's people in the Babylonian exile of Roman domina-

21. *Sanctus Thaumasiander et Triumphator Lutherus. Das ist/Bericht von dem heiligen Wundermanne/vnd wieder das Bapsthumb/auch andere Rotten vnd Secten/Triumphierenden Ru[e]stzeug Gottes/Herrn D. Martini Luthero . . . Wie hoch er von Gott vnd den Menschen geehret: Welche reine heilige vnu[e]berwindliche Lehr er gefu[e]hret: Vnd in Summa/ wie er sich als einen trewen Evangelisten vnd hochgewu[e]nschten dritten Eliam erzeiget habe* . . . (Leipzig: Abraham Lamberg and Caspar Closemann, 1617), aij[r]–[eij][r]. See also Höe's *Martinalia Sacra Pragensis. Das ist: D. Hoe unvermeidenliche Rettung/Der Ehr/Person/Lehr vnd Gaben des heiligen Thewren hocherleuchten Mannes Gottes/Herren Doctoris Lutheri seligen/wider allerley Jesuitische Lu[e]gen vnd Lesterungen* . . . (Leipzig: Abraham Lamberg, 1613).

22. Höe, *Sanctus Thaumasiander,* 1–41; see also 114–35.

tion. Luther's new song of the slaughtered Lamb, Jesus Christ, repeated what Moses, David, and Isaiah had taught, what Abraham had believed, what Elijah had proclaimed. Höe's contemporary, Sebastian Schwan, pastor in Lübeck, had reproduced Andreas Musculus's comparison of Luther and Elijah, and Höe may also have had the work of Musculus—and perhaps of Spangenberg as well—before him as he expanded the list of parallels. Both Elijah and Luther had had true friends among the princes. Both had been irreproachable in their lives and their teaching. Both had suffered fierce attacks even though they were innocent in their conduct, and both had endured false charges that they were causing trouble and division within God's people. Both had challenged their opponents in public debate, and both had triumphed over God's enemies. Elijah had had to flee Jezebel, Luther had retreated to his Patmos at the Wartburg, yet both of them returned to pronounce judgment upon the enemies of God.[23] In all of this no allusion to Luther's function as a secondary authority for the determination of public teaching is to be found. He functioned simply as the heroic prophet who had effected God's liberation of his people from papal oppression. Accordingly, his public image served as an appeal to preserve the freedom which God had bestowed a century earlier through him.

In the final sermon of his collection Höe reviewed Luther's contributions to the welfare of Christendom. This angel of the apocalypse had indeed preached the eternal gospel purely and clearly, according to God's will. He had driven away the wolves and protected the gospel from sectarian spirits. He had brought the Scriptures into the German tongue and had given his people the catechism, the hymnal, the Augsburg Confession, and a host of other writings, especially his polemical pieces and his biblical commentaries, of which those on Galatians and Genesis stood out. Finally, he had restored the proper understanding of the relationships between the three estates of society—church, home, and secular government.[24]

Hans-Jürgen Schönstädt's extensive studies of similar sermons and treatises written by Höe's contemporaries in 1617 and 1618 reveal much the same picture. The threat of a renewal of armed papal persecution as posed by the political manipulations in which some members of the Habsburg family, as well as other forces within the empire, and the Roman church had engaged in the preceding years, obviously

23. Ibid., 61–113; see also Sebastian Schwan, *De megalandro D. Martino Lvthero, sincerae religionis instauratore, eiusque praeclare gesto officio, ac piae obitu Oratio ad recolendam et praesertim hoc anno jubilaeo evangelico celebrandam operum Dei magnificentiam, ac beneficiorum Germaniae . . .* (Hamburg: Heinrich Carstens, 1618), 23.

24. Höe, *Sanctus Thaumasiander,* 191–99.

shaped the agenda from which the theologians took their cues for their celebration of the centennial. No new themes emerged, but the old themes epitomizing Luther's life were marshaled to rally Lutherans to the defense of their faith against the papal menace. The Lutheran preachers of 1617 shared the fundamental conviction that the history of God's people is always marked by conflict, mortal combat between Satan and the Word of God, between Satan's minions and God's faithful. That combat had broken out again when God raised Luther up as the heroic warrior and prophet called to reveal the nature of the Roman Antichrist.[25]

Luther's faith had spread beyond the borders of the German empire, of course, so the centennial anniversary of the initiation of his reform gave cause for celebration elsewhere. In an oration delivered in 1617 and published four years later, a Bergen-born professor of theology in Copenhagen, Konrad Aslaksen, wove Luther's story together with that of his Reformation as it spread to Denmark-Norway and to Sweden. For Aslaksen, Luther was God's chosen instrument for freeing Christendom from servitude under the papacy. The momentous events of 1517 had taken place when "that second Joshua, Martin Luther, with his godly and heroic spirit, was raised up to tear down and break down the walls of papist Jericho through the trumpet of the divine Word."[26] Similarly, most of the other literature of the jubilee celebrations accorded Luther a heroic role. Thus he was cast as Elijah the conqueror of the priests of Baal to a far greater extent than he was cast as Elijah the proclaimer of God's Word—although the two obviously could not be completely separated.

Schönstädt points out in detail that the preachers of 1617 and 1618 called attention to (1) the renewal of the church and its teaching, and (2) the restoration of family life and secular government to their proper place in society, as the most important results of Luther's reform efforts. They emphasized that the renewal of God's original plan for life in the church and in society had been made possible by Luther's return to the Scriptures and his cleansing of both teaching and worship by removing the accretions of papal error. They clearly pointed to Luther as God's chosen instrument who had been given tasks comparable to those of the prophets and apostles.[27] However, they elaborated his teaching relatively little—and his role as authoritative teacher not at all. Schönstädt notes:

25. Schönstädt, *Antichrist,* 247–53.

26. *Oratio theologico-historica. De religionis per D. Martinum Lutherum reformatae origine & progressu in Germania; & ejusdem in hisce Regnis Danicae & Norvegiae, elapso hac centenario, videlicet ab Anno 1517. ad Annum 1617. . . .* (Copenhagen: Heinrich Waldkirch, 1621).

27. Schönstädt, *Antichrist,* 200–303; idem, "Reformationsjubiläum," 37–45.

> The positive presentation of the foundation, accomplishments, and effect of the Reformation moved into the background in relation to the apology motivated by theological controversy. Convinced of the absolute truth of their point of view, the preachers were concerned much more to prove the continuity of Reformation teaching with that of the Bible and the early church, and they sought to demonstrate again and again the legitimacy of the Reformation which Catholic controversialists were always disputing.[28]

One hundred years after his career began, Luther was still being celebrated as a hero who had overcome the priests of Baal at Rome in the fashion of Elijah. The well-worn images were put to special use for the centennial anniversary taking place in troubled times. Like Moses, Luther had led the people of God out of captivity under papal tyranny.[29] But his contribution to the teaching of the church, to its dogmatic tradition, was a historical datum, not an ongoing function by which he through his writings would continue to exercise authority within the church. The battle to determine which secondary expression or codification of interpretative and adjudicatory authority would hold sway among the followers of the Reformer was over. By 1617 a generation of Lutherans had agreed that the Book of Concord would be the primary adjudicator of disputes over public teaching and the proper interpretation of the Scriptures. The Catholics, on the other hand, looked on the teaching of the pope as a primary authority. That is to say, they accorded the papacy the same level of authority which Lutherans accorded to the Scriptures themselves. So in disputes with Rome the Lutheran argument centered less on how to interpret Scripture than on whether papal interpretation of the Scriptures had primary authority within Christendom.[30]

The battle with the Calvinists took different forms, but Luther's prophetic authority counted for little among them too. Although most Reformed theologians at least begrudgingly—and often more enthusiastically—embraced Luther as a most significant hero of the faith, they could not concede special status to him as a teacher, for they feared that in doing so they would be surrendering too much in regard to the doctrinal issues under dispute with the Lutherans. Against the Calvinists Luther's teaching could only be repeated and used as a model of what Lutherans believed to be the biblical faith.

Luther's prophetic authority served little or no purpose within the Lutheran churches once the Book of Concord had achieved the status

28. Schönstädt, "Reformationsjubiläum," 37.
29. Schönstädt, *Antichrist,* 261–67; idem, "Reformationsjubiläum," 34–37.
30. Schönstädt, *Antichrist,* 169–79; idem, "Reformationsjubiläum," 47–50.

of secondary authority for Lutheran theologians. They regarded him as a great teacher, a prophetic doctor of the church, and they made extensive use of his published teachings (see chs. 6–8). Yet above all Luther remained for his followers a critical figure in the march of church history, the one chosen by God to introduce the Reformation and thus end the papal darkness. That marked a domestication of the eschatological excitement which first began to label Luther the angel of the apocalypse and the third Elijah just a little less than a hundred years earlier. Michael Stiefel, Cyriakus Spangenberg, and Andreas Musculus would never have thought of limiting Luther's significance to the terms which Konrad Dietrich, superintendent in Ulm, used in 1618 to describe him: Luther was "not the one who instituted our evangelical teaching but the one who reinstituted it, not the one who introduced it but the one who reintroduced it, not the one who authored it but the one who restored it, not its promulgator, but the one who purged it, not its innovator but its renovator."[31] Luther's memory lived, and his voice was heard, but its authority had been tamed.

31. Konrad Dietrich, in *Vlmisches Evangelisches Jubelfest . . . durch das Ministerium oder Predigampt daselbsten* (Ulm: Johann Medern, 1618), Giij^{v}.

Part Two

Opera Omnia Reverendi Domini Martini Lutheri

The Reprinting of Luther's Works in the Half Century after His Death

6

The Complete Luther

The Initial Editions of Luther's Published Teaching

"Be devout. Hold to God's Word. Stick with your catechism as you learned it. Read [Luther's] House Postil. Be obedient to your mother. Beware of bad company and of the evils of this world." With this parting advice to his son Christoph, Matthaeus Ratzeberger departed this life. As physician to the counts of Mansfeld, the elector of Saxony, and the people of the towns of Brandenburg and Erfurt over a period of more than thirty years, Ratzeberger had actively promoted and supported Luther's Reformation. He believed that continued reading of the works of Martin Luther was vital for the sustenance of the church. For reading Luther nourished piety and edified the faithful.[1]

Whether followers of Luther believed that Luther was the most authoritative teacher of the faith since the apostles or that the Reformer was only a very worthy teacher of God's Word, they continued to receive his instruction even after his death. For much of his teaching could be found in works which he himself had published or in lectures and sermons which his students subsequently edited. Thus a large body of teaching from Germany's prophet for these last times was available to his followers in 1546, and they continued to make the most of his printed legacy as they brought their message to their contemporaries and descendants throughout the second half of the century. Luther continued to teach his church.

Doctor Ratzeberger had practiced what he was urging his son to do. In an account of Ratzeberger's death his pastor, Andreas Poach, described the regimen of Luther readings which the physician had im-

1. Andreas Poach, *Vom Christlichen Abschied aus diesem sterblichen Leben des lieben thewren Mannes Matthei Ratzenbergers der Artzney Doctors Bericht* . . . (Jena: Thomas Rebart, 1559), F^{r-v}.

posed upon himself. Every morning he began his day by reading a half or whole chapter of the Bible, Luther's interpretation thereof, and something from Hippocrates and Galen. He had read through Luther's printed commentaries on Genesis, Joel and the other Minor Prophets, Galatians ("several times"), and the first two volumes of the Wittenberg edition of Luther's works. Then, after he had helped create the Jena edition in his role as advisor to Duke John Frederick the Elder of Saxony, he read its first two German volumes and its first Latin volume. He was reading the second Latin volume at the time of his death. After mealtime, both midday and evenings, he read to his family a passage from the Bible and the appropriate sermon in Luther's House or Church Postil or another German work of Luther. He had, for example, read Luther's comments on Matthew 5–7 and John 14–17 as well as the Church and the House Postil sermons on those texts. On Saturday afternoon he read passages from the Large Catechism to his children and servants and heard their recitation of the Small Catechism. Sunday mornings he read to his oldest sons the Latin Bible or Luther's commentary on Genesis.[2] Ratzeberger was not a typical German of his day in this regard. In keeping such a schedule, he was perhaps not even typical of the most ardent among Luther's followers. But he does illustrate that Luther's contemporaries regarded his writings highly. They used his written legacy in their own devotional life for inspiration and edification.

Cyriakus Spangenberg tried to cultivate among the laypeople an appreciation for the Reformer's works: "the common people among us diligently read Luther's writings," he reported to Hartmann Beyer.[3] To whatever extent this pious wish may have been true, it was a real possibility because Luther had been born a generation after the invention of movable type. Inadvertently, and quite innocently, the Wittenberg professor had launched the first modern media event when he penned his Ninety-Five Theses on indulgences in 1517. His writing career took off with the dramatic spread of these theses, and people throughout Germany as well as scholars across western Europe devoured his ideas immediately. Their hunger for his thought continued through succeeding decades.

This hunger could be satisfied in part because early on in his career Luther had begun entrusting the editing of his words and works to students. They brought a mass of material into print alongside those treatises which Luther himself prepared for publication. In the twentieth century a debate arose over the quality of their work. By and large, how-

2. Ibid., Aij^{v}–Aiij^{v}.

3. *Der Briefwechsel des M. Cyriacus Spangenberg,* ed. Heinrich Rembe, 2 vols. (Dresden: Naumann, 1887–88), 2:101, a letter of 27 February 1573.

ever, the Reformer's contemporaries, though they had different political and theological perspectives, found the work of these editors, such as Luther's one-time amanuensis Veit Dietrich and Andreas Poach, above reproach.[4] Their texts were, with few exceptions, broadly accepted as genuine Luther when they were published in the mid-sixteenth century.

Luther's followers recognized the key role of the printing press in extending his proclamation of God's Word. In writing on problems of censorship, Matthaeus Judex (1528–64), Wigand's close friend, credited the invention of printing by "hardworking Germans" to the "special blessing of God," so that several thousand copies of a work could be made at once for a relatively small cost. God had bestowed such a blessing, Judex asserted, so that "in these last times the truth of the gospel might be propagated, many kinds of errors might be refuted, and the church might be edified."[5] Given the theological point of view they had learned from the Reformer, Luther's students inevitably regarded the invention of the printing press as a providential gift of God, a part of the divine plan to use Martin Luther as his special prophet for the latter days and for the German nation.

The First Collected Works

Published nearly fifty years after the indulgence controversy, Judex's opinion had been shared by those who were the first to read Luther's printed works. That audience had wanted more. Within three years of his posting of the Ninety-Five Theses, Martin Luther became the first

4. Some twentieth-century scholarship was negative regarding Dietrich's work as editor of the Genesis lectures; see particularly the studies of Erich Seeberg, *Studien zu Luthers Genesisvorlesung* (Gütersloh: Bertelsmann, 1932), and Peter Meinhold, *Die Genesisvorlesung Luthers und ihre Herausgeber* (Stuttgart: Kohlhammer, 1936). A more reasonable perspective is presented by, among a number of more-recent scholars, Bernhard Klaus, "Die Lutherüberlieferung Veit Dietrichs und ihre Problematik," *Zeitschrift für bayerische Kirchengeschichte* 53 (1988): 33–47, who concludes that Dietrich's editorial work found approval from Luther himself as well as other contemporaries.

5. Matthaeus Judex, *De typographiae inventione et de praelorvm legitima inspectione, libellvs brevis et vtilis* (Copenhagen: Johannes Zimmermann, 1566), 12–13, 4–5; see also Robert Kolb, "Matthaeus Judex's Condemnation of Princely Censorship of Theologians' Publications," *Church History* 50 (1981): 401–14, esp. 405–6 (= *Luther's Heirs Define His Legacy: Studies on Lutheran Confessionalization* [Aldershot, Eng.: Variorum, 1996], 14). Judex's Gnesio-Lutheran comrade, Johann Friedrich Coelestin, viewed the relationship between the Reformation and the printing press in exactly the same way in his *Von Buchhendlern/Buchdruckern vnd Buchfu[e]rern: Ob auch one su[e]nde/vnd gefahr jrer Seligkeit/Vnchristliche/Ketzerische/Bepstische/Vnzu[e]chtige/oder sonst bo[e]se Bu[e]cher drucken/vnd offentlich feil haben/oder von andern kauffen/vnnd widerumb/one vnterscheidt/menniglich verkauffen mo[e]gen. Auch Allen andern Christen/sonderlich Kremern/ Kauff/Handels vnd Handwerckleuten/zu diesen gefehrlichen zeitten nu[e]tzlich zulesen* (n.p., 1569).

author whose works were assembled into a collected edition at the outset of his career—something that three years later Desiderius Erasmus dreamt of for his own works as only a posthumous possibility.[6] The Basel printer Johannes Froben recognized the market for Luther's writings and obtained a number of them at the Frankfurt book fair in 1518. Within a few weeks Wolfgang Capito, cathedral preacher and a professor of theology at Basel, had edited these publications, and Froben had produced the first *opera omnia* of Martin Luther.[7] Its five hundred pages included every Latin treatise, set of theses, and sermon which Luther had published to that time. Froben not only sold copies to German bookdealers, but also sent them to France, Spain, Italy, the Netherlands, and England.

R. P. DOCT.
MARTINI LV
THERII AVGVSTINIANI THEO
LOGI SYNCERI LVCVBRA
TIONVM PARS VNA,
quas ædidit usq; in annum præ
sentem XX. Catalogum carũ
uersa tibi pagina indicabit.
ALIO TOMO, DOMINO VO
lente, post hac meliora trademus, ut ab
soluta fuerint eodẽ autore, nempe
in Psalmos & Paulum.
BASILEAE APVD ADAM PE
TRI, ANNO DOMINI M. D.
XX. MENSE IVLIO.

R. P. Doct. Martini Lvtherii . . . lvcvbrationvm pars vna . . . (1520) (Concordia Seminary Library, St. Louis)

Froben's edition sold out quickly, but he did not issue a second since his close friend Erasmus was angered by the printer's publication of Luther's works. The Dutch humanist threatened to break off their friendship because of it. In Strassburg the printer Matthias Schürer used the Froben edition as a model for his own, and Froben's fellow Basler, Andreas Cratander, did the same in 1519.[8] By 1520 another printer in Basel, Adam Petri, had engaged a local Franciscan theologian, Konrad Pellikan, to revise the texts and prepare them for his own edition.[9] In early 1520 Cratander also produced an edition of Luther's German works, and Schürer followed suit in Strassburg.[10]

6. *Opus epistolarum Des. Erasmi Roterodami,* ed. P. S. Allen (Oxford: Clarendon, 1906), 1:38.

7. *Ad Leonem X. pontificem maximvm, Resolutiones . . .* (Basel: Johann Froben, 1518).

8. *Ad Leonem X. pontificem maximvm, Resolutiones . . .* (Strassburg: Matthias Schürer, 1519); *Prima [Secvnda . . .] pars opervm Reverendi patris, ac sacrae theologiae Doctoris Martini Lvtheri . . .* (Basel: Andreas Cratander, 1519).

9. *R. P. Doct. Martini Lvtherii . . . lvcvbrationvm pars vna . . .* (Basel: Adam Petri, 1520).

10. *Martini Luthers der waren go[e]ttlichen schrifft Doctors/Augustiner zu Wittenbergk/ mancherley bu[e]chlin vnd tractetlin . . .* (Basel: Andreas Cratander, 1520); *Martini Luthers . . . mancherley bu[e]chlin vnnd tractetlin . . .* (Strassburg: Matthias Schürer, 1520). On these first *opera omnia,* see Eike Wolgast, "Geschichte der Luther-Ausgaben vom 16. bis zum 19. Jahrhundert," in *WA* 60:431–60. For fuller details see idem, "Die Wittenberger Luther-Ausgabe: Zur Überlieferungsgeschichte der Werke Luthers im 16. Jahrhundert," *Archiv für Geschichte des Buchwesens* 11.1–2:1–336.

With the imperial edict issued at the Diet of Worms in mid-1521 forbidding publication of Luther's works, and with the growing number of individual publications which issued from his pen, printers ceased to attempt to produce volumes of his collected works. They were more expensive—and thus risky—to print than were his individual treatises.

The Wittenberg Edition

Friends and supporters of Luther continued to believe that publication of his collected works would benefit the church. Plans for such a project came from Luther's former student and amanuensis, Stephan Roth; from a prince, Count Ludwig XV of Öttingen; and from the Strassburg printer Wendelin Rihel, who was working with the original editor of Luther's collected works, Wolfgang Capito. None of these plans of the 1520s and early 1530s came to fruition.[11] In the late 1530s, however, the rumors of Rihel's plan seem to have aroused the Wittenberg printer Hans Lufft and a consortium of investors who had already financed the publication of Luther's translation of the Bible. In autumn 1538 they formed plans for the publication of Luther's works, by this time a massive project. Within a year the first volume had appeared in German under the editorship of Luther's amanuensis Georg Rörer and Caspar Cruciger, his colleague on the Wittenberg theological faculty.[12] Eleven more German volumes followed, the last appearing in 1559. The first of seven Latin volumes was printed in 1545, the last in 1557. Cruciger died in 1548; Rörer continued to work on the project until 1551 when another Wittenberg theologian, Georg Major, assumed the editorship. Eike Wolgast summarizes the goals of the enterprise: to fix the historical significance of Luther's work; to aid in systematizing his theology; and to canonize his writings as the recorded deposit of the words which he had uttered while alive.[13] This evaluation reflects the convictions of many of Luther's followers.

One of the goals of the Wittenberg project was to make Luther's proclamation of the gospel as widely available as possible. For the sake of the common people the German volumes contained translations of material which originally appeared in Latin. And to enable foreign scholars to read material which originally appeared in German, many such

11. Wolgast, "Geschichte," 460–64.

12. Ibid., 464–65, 488.

13. Eike Wolgast, "Biographie als Autoritätsstiftung: Die ersten evangelischen Lutherbiographien," in *Biographie zwischen Renaissance und Barock: Zwölf Studien,* ed. Walter Berschin (Heidelberg: Mattes, 1993), 42–43.

items were translated into Latin. Thus the editors were responsible for assembling both originals and translations.

To achieve the proper effect, Rörer in particular felt free to edit the material which lay before him. He seldom altered the substance of Luther's content, but he refined the language and occasionally even the order of sentences and paragraphs. His goal was to place before the reader a reliable expression of Luther's teaching in its final form, and so he took the liberty of clarifying certain earlier passages according to his own understanding of Luther's later intent. He also omitted some passages. Luther's attacks on princes such as Dukes Georg of Saxony and Heinrich of Braunschweig-Wolfenbüttel, on Archbishop Albrecht of Mainz, and on Elector Joachim of Brandenburg were not printed until they had appeared in the rival edition begun after the Smalcald War and published at Jena. The names of some of Luther's evangelical foes, such as Andreas Karlstadt and Johann Agricola, were suppressed at points, as were certain references to Landgrave Philip of Hesse and Emperor Charles V. From *That These Words of Christ, "This Is My Body," Still Stand Firm against the Fanatics* Rörer left out Luther's polemic against Martin Bucer; Luther's expression of toleration toward the medieval mass was dropped from the *Formula for the Mass,* as were some of his comments on marriage in *The Babylonian Captivity of the Church.* Rörer also altered the texts of *The Bondage of the Will* and of the *Defense and Explanation of All Articles* in regard to the concept of absolute necessity. When Georg Major assumed the editorship, the changes in Luther's texts ceased for the most part. It is not clear to what extent Luther gave his consent for such changes in the first volume of both the German and the Latin series. It is possible that he approved them since he was alive at the time the initial volumes appeared.[14]

The editors wanted to continue Luther's public teaching through his writings, and they wanted to provide a historical sourcebook for the Reformation. Therefore they included more than Luther's published works. Rörer also edited some manuscript materials, sermons, and letters (although initially the Wittenberg edition contained few letters). As the Jena edition moved ahead of the Wittenberg in its publishing schedule, Georg Major found it most convenient simply to reprint certain materials found there, just as the Jena editors had previously borrowed from the Wittenberg edition. To aid the reader in understanding the historical context in which Luther's thought unfolded, the Wittenberg editors also included a number of documents written by others. Correspondence from the Saxon court, accounts of negotiations at the Diets of Augsburg and Worms, and imperial, princely, and papal mandates

14. Wolgast, "Geschichte," 465–66, 471–75.

can all be found in the Wittenberg edition, along with some writings by Luther's colleagues, especially Melanchthon. All this material was organized by topic or theme, as the Preceptor would have it; within the volumes a chronological scheme was used in some cases, but often not.[15]

In spite of Luther's rather negative appraisal of efforts to republish his writings, he was persuaded to address the readers of the first volume in a preface. When the first of the German series appeared in 1539, he provided a guide to the study of God's Word and his own disclaimer regarding the usefulness of theologians' books in general and his own in particular: "It was also our intention and hope, when we ourselves began to translate the Bible into German, that there should be less writing, and instead more studying and reading of the Scriptures. . . . I cannot, however, prevent them from wanting to collect and publish my works through the press (small honor to me), although it is not my will. I have no choice but to let them risk the labor and the expense of this project. My consolation is that, in time, my books will lie forgotten in the dust anyhow." Luther asked his readers not to let his own works keep them from studying the Scriptures. For him the Scriptures sufficed as the source of God's truth. He included in the preface his guideline for studying the Bible: prayer, meditation, and spiritual struggle *(Oratio, Meditatio, Tentatio)*.[16] This preface, soon after its appearance in the Wittenberg edition, was published separately as a guide for reading the Scripture.[17]

Der Erste
Teil: der Bücher vber etliche Epistel der Aposteln.
D. Mart. Luth.
Wittemberg.
Gedruckt durch
Hans Krafft.
1556.

The First Volume of the Wittenberg German Edition (reprinting of 1556) (Concordia Seminary Library, St. Louis)

Luther lived long enough to write the preface for the second volume in the Wittenberg edition, which was the first in the Latin series. There he recommended to his readers "a great many systematic books . . . , among which the *Loci communes* of Philip [Melanchthon] excel." Not-

15. Ibid., 468–77.

16. *Der Erste Teil der Bucher D. Mart. Luth. vber etliche Epistel der Aposteln* (Wittenberg: Hans Lufft, 1539) (henceforth *Witt A*, German), (ij^{r}–(iij^{v}; *LW* 34:283–88.

17. *Ein Christlich Vrtheyl D. Martin Luthers von seinem eigen Buchern. Sampt einer Vnterricht/was darzu geho[e]re/wenn man jnn der heiligen Schrifft recht studirn/vnd darnach gutte Bucher schreiben will* (Nuremberg: Leonhart Milchthaler, 1539; Augsburg: Philip Ulhart, 1540).

ing the "crude and disordered chaos" that made it necessary to arrange his own works in some systematic order, he repeated his wish that they be "buried in perpetual oblivion." Following this introduction was a brief memoir of the early days of the Reformation from the indulgence controversy through his discovery in 1519 of the true meaning of the "righteousness of God."[18]

Each of the succeeding volumes of the Wittenberg edition was graced with a preface dedicating it to a patron or orienting the reader to its contents. Rörer fashioned a preface for volume 2 of the German series from Luther's own words about the "ravers," that is, the antinomians, Anabaptists, spiritualists, and Sacramentarians who are Luther's targets in many of the writings that follow.[19] Melanchthon composed a biography of Luther for the second Latin volume. In it he used the devices of humanist biography to praise Luther and defend him against his foes. In so doing he placed Luther in the humanist tradition and strove to associate him with the heritage of Erasmus.[20]

Melanchthon continued to write prefaces. Most of them discussed the course which the Word of God had taken throughout human history; few of them did more than mention Luther in cursory fashion. In the preface to volume 3 of the German series, Luther's commentary on the Psalms, Melanchthon furnished observations on the value of the study of the Psalms.[21] In volume 4 Melanchthon emphasized Luther's cleansing of Christendom from papal darkness. He placed Luther's criticism of the papacy in the line of heroic actions taken by the spokesmen of God: Elijah's and Elisha's castigation of the priests of Baal, John the Baptist's polemic against the Pharisees, John the Evangelist's censure of "Ebion" and Cerinthus, Athanasius's condemnation of Arius, Augustine's attacks against Pelagius. Melanchthon then invited his readers to compare Luther's teaching and that of the papacy in the light of the Scriptures.[22] For his contemporaries, Luther's office as teacher could not be separated from his role as the heroic prophet who had battled the error, tyranny, and oppression of Rome (see ch. 3).

When Georg Major had assumed the editorship of the project, he relieved Melanchthon of the duty of composing the preface for volume 5. At the time Major was in the midst of a losing battle to maintain his

18. *Tomvs primvs omnivm opervm Reverendi Domini Martini Lutheri . . .* (Wittenberg: Hans Lufft, 1545) (henceforth *Witt A*, Latin), +ij^{r}–+v^{r}; *LW* 34:327–38.

19. *Witt A*, German, 2: ij^{r}–[xij]^{r}.

20. *CR* 6:155–70. On this biography see James Michael Weiss, "Erasmus at Luther's Funeral: Melanchthon's Commemorations of Luther in 1546," *Sixteenth Century Journal* 16.1 (1985): 91–114.

21. *Witt A*, German, 3: aij^{r}–[aiiij]^{r}.

22. *Witt A*, German, 4: ()ij^{r}–)(iij^{v}.

hold on the office of ecclesiastical superintendent in Mansfeld. Associating himself with Luther in the midst of that battle could only help his cause, as did the list of the evils of the papacy which Major showed that Luther had fought. Major, too, believed that Luther stood in a line of God's representatives although he, like Melanchthon, avoided the labels of prophet, apostle, and angel of the apocalypse. Accordingly, he did not place Luther in the company of apostles, prophets, or the fathers of the early church, among whom others often placed him. Instead, Major's list began with Anselm and included Bernard of Clairvaux, Hugo of Saint Cher, Abbot Joachim of Fiore, Bonaventura, Nicholas of Lyra, Johann Tauler, John Huss, Jean Gerson, Johann Geiler von Kaisersberg, and John of Wessel. Luther had been assigned a place among the modern teachers of the church.[23]

The Reformer belonged to a longer tradition, however, according to Melanchthon. When he resumed writing the prefaces for the German series, Melanchthon urged the readers of volume 6 to study Luther for the strengthening of their faith because he had presented God's unchangeable truth and the simple beliefs of the true and catholic church. His writings in his battles against the papacy contained nothing but what the prophets and apostles had taught, as it had been repeated by Irenaeus, Gregory Nazianzus, and Athanasius. Melanchthon then provided a list of those teachings of Scripture which Luther had taught with particular clarity, a list which was repeated in later volumes: the proper distinction of law and gospel, true repentance, grace, faith, true invocation of God, the distinction between genuine worship of God and human traditions, the use of the sacraments, and separation of the ministry of the gospel from political power.[24]

Melanchthon's other prefaces made only brief mention of Luther, praising his teaching without ascribing to him any prophetic role. The prophetic theme returned when Basilius Faber, one of the authors of the *Magdeburg Centuries* (a comprehensive church history), and Johannes Guden, a pastor in Braunschweig, composed prefaces for their translation of Luther's Genesis lectures of 1535–45. In volume 10 Faber hailed Luther as "father and prophet," and he praised the clarity of the Reformer's teaching, particularly on the forgiveness of sins and justification through faith. So Faber wanted to make the Genesis commentary, a digest of all of Luther's teaching, available as a source of comfort and edification for heads of households and the common people.[25] In volume 11 Guden repeated standard lines in describing what Luther

23. *Witt A,* German, 5:)(ij^{r}–)(iiij^{v}.
24. *Witt A,* German, 6: (ij^{v}–(iij^{v}; see also *Witt A,* Latin, 5: +iij^{v}.
25. *Witt A,* German, 10: *ij^{r}–[*iij]^{r}.

had accomplished: God had raised him up to sweep away the old leaven of the false teachings of men. God had chosen him as his own agent, "the Germans' final prophet," for revealing true divine teaching once again.[26] The Wittenberg prefaces reiterated and reinforced Melanchthon's interpretation of Luther: he was not a prophetic authority, but he remained a teacher and a hero for the church.

What did the Germans have in the Wittenberg edition? "The writings and exegesis of Luther are to be found in the Wittenberg edition almost without omission," states Eike Wolgast.[27] When pastors purchased Luther's works in the Wittenberg edition, they were provided with more than a sampling of what he had written. They had in the nineteen volumes almost everything which might have been available to the most assiduous collector of Luther's individual publications. Apart from the postils, this edition offered whatever of the Reformer's works had become available in print.

The Jena Edition

However, the Wittenberg edition did not reproduce Luther's works in their correct form or assemble them in proper fashion—according to the charge lodged by Luther's friend for more than thirty-five years, Nikolaus von Amsdorf. Amsdorf became the grandfather of the Gnesio-Lutheran movement in the years immediately following Luther's death, and in the wake of the Smalcald War he became particularly sensitive to hints that the Wittenbergers in the employ of Elector Moritz might betray Luther's legacy. Therefore, when he spotted the omission of Luther's criticism of Martin Bucer from *That These Words of Christ, "This Is My Body," Still Stand Firm,* he issued a sharp critique of the entire Wittenberg project. Luther had attacked Bucer for making alterations when he reprinted works written by Luther and Bugenhagen, as well as for stating that Melanchthon had denied the real presence of Christ's body and blood in the Lord's Supper. Rörer had also omitted from the Wittenberg edition one of Luther's warnings against the Sacramentarians.[28] Amsdorf was probably unaware that Luther had, in all likelihood, been consulted about these omissions before his death. Luther and Bucer had come to something of a reconciliation in 1536, and in the 1540s the Wittenbergers had no desire to offend an ally in the important city of Strassburg, a man whose influence extended far beyond his own city.

26. *Witt A*, German, 11: ()ij^{r-v}.
27. Wolgast, "Geschichte," 469.
28. *Das die zu Wittenberg im andern teil der bucher Doctoris Martini im buch das diese wort Christi (Das ist mein Leib etc.) noch fest stehen mehr denn ein blat vier ganzter Paragraphos vorsetzlich aussgelassen haben wie folget* (Magdeburg, 1549).

Amsdorf's critique fed into plans being made at the ducal court of John Frederick the Elder. He had launched the Wittenberg edition as elector of Saxony, but he had lost the electoral title, the University of Wittenberg, and supervision of that edition when Emperor Charles V conquered his forces in the Smalcald War. When Charles released John Frederick from prison in 1552, the duke began to plan a supplementary edition of Luther's works. A proposal for a new complete edition developed at the urging of Amsdorf and the duke's court preacher, Johann Aurifaber, who had come to Wittenberg in 1537 and spent more than half of Luther's final eight years there, approximately two as his last amanuensis. In 1553 John Frederick recalled Georg Rörer, who had left Wittenberg for Denmark in 1551, to work on the new project. To have a fine press at hand, the duke also subsidized the move of the Magdeburg printer Christian Rödinger to his university town, Jena.

John Frederick died on March 3, 1554, but his three sons, led by the oldest brother, John Frederick the Middler, continued the project with an expanded view of its possibilities. Aurifaber and his colleague as court preacher, Johann Stolz, worked on plans for a new compilation which would offer what the rival edition offered and more. Stolz drafted a plan for the project, which included a new principle for arranging the material. Amsdorf had expressed the fear that when readers turned to Luther's works in the Wittenberg edition, which were grouped by topic, they would not easily be able to tell when he was still under the influence of medieval theology and when he had come to his mature evangelical thought. Therefore Stolz suggested that the new edition, which was to be printed at Jena, be arranged chronologically. Those who were planning the Jena edition also decided in principle not to do any translating of Luther's works (though in fact they did so in a number of instances). Stolz had determined as well that there would be no changes in content or words from the original texts, although warnings to the reader might be given in marginal notes when the sense of Luther's original was hard to follow. The Jena editors were prepared to print passages which might give offense to supporters of the deceased Bucer or to Roman Catholic princely families whose members Luther had attacked. They hoped to print only what Luther himself had written, but they did not maintain this principle. They recognized that certain other documents were necessary to supply historical context.[29]

Rörer returned to Germany to manage the Jena edition, but he had to endure the suspicions of colleagues at the ducal Saxon court. They had not forgotten that he had been in charge when the offending parts

29. Wolgast, "Geschichte," 495–506.

of the Wittenberg edition had been planned and produced. In failing health and under direction from the ducal court and its chaplains, he did little more than supervise the technical assembling of the volumes. He followed Stolz's guidelines in something less than the strictest fashion, however. Often he simply reproduced his earlier work on the Wittenberg edition, omitting, for instance, the names of Karlstadt and Agricola where he had done so earlier in Wittenberg. Like the Wittenberg edition, the Jena edition did not reprint the postils of Luther; unlike the Wittenberg edition, it omitted the Genesis commentary of 1535–45. With the exception of letters in the German volumes, few unpublished materials were gathered into the Jena edition.[30]

Apart from the first volumes in both Latin and German, there were no prefaces written by those responsible for production of the Jena edition. In the second volume of each series Amsdorf advised the readers that he found it unnecessary to compose prefaces for each volume. He did not think he was so skillful a writer that he could issue something worthy of each succeeding volume, so he had decided to abide by the edition's principle of not including other materials. That was an indirect snub of Melanchthon and Major, who had composed the prefaces for the Wittenberg volumes.[31]

For the first volume of each series, however, Amsdorf wrote a preface in German and Latin respectively. In it he listed various objections to certain principles and practices of the Wittenberg edition. These objections, which Stolz had outlined in his plans for the Jena edition, included alterations in the text, the reprinting of books of other learned men alongside Luther's, the use of translations, and the use of a topical rather than chronological scheme for ordering the material. The prefaces also had warm words of praise for Georg Rörer, ignoring his role in the Wittenberg edition.

Amsdorf warned the reader that Luther's works are not to be regarded equally. "In the beginning, as a faithful, pious papist he had conceded much to the Roman Antichrist, and he later changed such things as he recognized them as untrue in the course of his great struggle, distress, and temptation." Amsdorf reviewed Luther's internal and external battles with medieval theology and the papacy. While conceding that Luther had wanted his books to disappear so that everyone would be moved to read the living source and fountain of the Holy Scriptures, Amsdorf also believed that no one since Saint Paul had interpreted the Scripture so clearly. No one had so decisively rejected false teachings

30. Ibid., 501–16.

31. *Der Ander Teil aller Bu[e]cher vnd Schrifften des thewren/seligen Mans Doct. Mart. Lutheri* . . . (Jena: Christian Rödinger, 1555), *ij^r.

and heresies. No one had explained salvation by grace through faith in Christ nor elucidated the sacraments as Luther had. He had exposed the papacy as the Antichrist. Because Amsdorf believed that the Christian faith had not been explained so well by any teacher of the church nor by any council, he wanted Luther's works available without any changes.[32]

There are two reasons why the specific items contained in the Jena edition differ relatively little from those in the Wittenberg edition. First, the parallel goals of providing readers with all that Luther had written imposed upon both editions their basic table of contents, however it might be ordered. In addition, the editors of both series borrowed from the other. The Jena edition took the Wittenberg edition as one of its sources, and the Wittenberg edition added two volumes to its German series and some material to its Latin series because these items had appeared in the Jena edition.

Amsdorf's initial attack on the Wittenberg edition turned out to be the first salvo of one of the skirmishes fought between Gnesio-Lutherans and Philippists in the wars between the Wittenberg brethren during the 1550s, 1560s, and 1570s. In Melanchthon's preface to the third German volume of the Wittenberg edition (1550) and in Amsdorf's prefaces to the first volumes of each series in the Jena edition charges were exchanged and defenses erected. In eight separate tracts between 1558 and 1571 Christoph Walther, the Wittenberg copy editor, attacked the Jena edition and Aurifaber's subsequent work of producing Luther material for the public. The Gnesio-Lutherans answered from time to time with general and specific complaints about the work of Walther and his Wittenberg colleagues.[33]

Both editions found a waiting market. The Jena edition was more popular than the Wittenberg edition, both German series more popular than the Latin. By ducal command the entire set of the first printing of the Jena edition cost sixteen gulden if purchased in Jena, not more than seventeen gulden if purchased in Leipzig, Frankfurt am Main, or Naumburg.[34] That price was beyond the means of many

32. *Der Erste Teil aller Bu[e]cher vnd Schrifften des thewren/seligen Mans Doct: Mart: Lutheri/vom XVII. jar an/bis auff das XXII.* (Jena: Christian Rödinger, 1555), ⁺iij^{v}–*ij^{v}; *Tomvs primvs omnivm opervm Reuerendi Patris D. M. L. quae vir Dei ab Anno XVII. vsque ad Anni vicesimi aliquam partem scripsit & edidit . . .* (Jena: Christian Rödinger, 1556), *iij^{v}–)(^{v}.

33. For a detailed analysis of the controversy over the two editions, see Eike Wolgast, "Der Streit um die Werke Luthers im 16. Jahrhundert," *Archiv für Reformationsgeschichte* 59 (1968): 177–202; and Wolgast's summaries, "Geschichte," 490–95; and "Die Wittenberger Luther-Ausgabe," 199–204.

34. Wolgast, "Geschichte," 539.

theological students and pastors,[35] but many did purchase one or more of the volumes. Sixteenth-century Lutherans wanted to read Luther!

The Eisleben Edition

There was, of course, always more from Luther's pen to be found. Johann Aurifaber had urged further publication of some of Luther's manuscripts, and his employer, Duke John Frederick the Middler, was supportive. However, their relationship soured as Aurifaber and his Gnesio-Lutheran colleagues sharply criticized the duke's efforts to control the church in his lands and to diminish the role of the clergy in church government.[36] After the duke had sent him into exile, Aurifaber successfully pleaded with his former prince to send him the editorial work already completed on the Luther manuscripts. As a pastor in Eisleben Aurifaber also appealed to the counts of Mansfeld to sponsor his new supplement.

In 1564 and 1565 two volumes of German material from 1516–29 and from 1530–37 were published. The projected third volume did not appear, probably because the printer had difficulty selling his stock of the first two volumes. Sermons, some from the Church Postil, filled a good part of the first volume, alongside many letters, some of which had already been published in Latin and were translated for this edition. Aurifaber also included some documents from other authors to aid the reader's understanding of the context. Volume 2 contained some tracts and some documents which pertained to material Luther had written. Among these documents was a report from the southern German delegation which negotiated the Wittenberg Concord (1536). Without financial support and without much encouragement from the market to continue, Aurifaber could not complete his supplementary work.[37] Perhaps readers felt that Luther's sermons and letters were not so important as his larger treatises. Their interest was directed more toward his teaching than toward the details of his biography, it would appear.

35. In this period a grown pig cost one gulden, a cow three. In 1512 books in the electoral library cost an average of one-and-a-half gulden apiece. Instructors at the arts faculty in Wittenberg in 1535 earned between forty and sixty gulden per year; most pastors' salaries, in part paid in kind, were lower. See Ernest G. Schwiebert, *The Reformation* (Minneapolis: Fortress, 1996), 317, 376, 334.

36. See Martin Kruse, *Speners Kritik am Landesherrlichen Kirchenregiment und ihre Vorgeschichte* (Witten: Luther, 1971), 57–63; and Kolb, "Matthaeus Judex's Condemnation," 401–4.

37. Wolgast, "Geschichte," 544–58.

Luther's Correspondence

Aurifaber had practiced for editing his supplement by assembling and publishing two volumes of Luther's Latin letters. As his colleagues were producing the Jena edition, he was preparing a collection of letters on which he had been working for the previous decade. Other smaller, occasional collections of Luther's letters had appeared earlier. One prepared by Matthias Flacius in 1549 provided the reading public with Luther's letters urging no compromise with the papacy at the time of the Diet of Augsburg (1530).[38] In 1547 Aurifaber himself had published eleven letters of Luther which were designed to offer comfort to the pastors of Weimar as John Frederick the Elder lay in imperial prison in Brussels.[39]

Aurifaber incorporated these letters with some other Latin letters which had already appeared in print and some manuscript material at his disposal. A majority of the items in the first volume came from Luther's correspondence with Georg Spalatin and Johann Lang. Aurifaber introduced his readers to Luther's letters with a historical overview of the beginnings of the Reformation. Here he depicted Luther as the last in a line of patriarchs, prophets, apostles, and teachers of the church who had opposed the enemies of the faith. Aurifaber intended with this overview to help his readers put Luther's letters into context. He wanted them to understand the horrible state in which the church had existed before Luther and his role in cleansing its teaching and leading it out from Egyptian and Babylonian captivity.[40]

This first volume did not sell well, and only support from the counts of Mansfeld enabled Aurifaber to get the second volume of Latin correspondence published in 1565. It contained letters from 1522 to 1528, and provided readers with an overview of Luther's correspondence with Spalatin, Nikolaus Hausmann, Wenzeslaus Linck, Amsdorf, and Lang.[41] It, too, did not command a large market, and thus Aurifaber's publishing of Luther's correspondence came to an end except for his attempt in the mid-1560s to carry out this plan through the more broadly conceived supplementary Eisleben edition. As we noted, it also failed to

38. Hans Volz and Eike Wolgast, "Geschichte der Lutherbriefeditionen des 16. bis 20. Jahrhunderts," *WA Br* 14:400–408. See p. 42 in the present volume.

39. Ibid., 367–69; *Etliche scho[e]ne Trostschriffte/des Ehrwirdigen Herrn Doctoris Martini Lutheri/So er an den Durchleuchtigsten Fu[e]rsten vnd Herrn/Hertzog Joannes/ Churfu[e]rsten zu Sachsen/Gottseliger gedechtnis/Vnd an andere seine Herrn vnd gute Freunde gethan* . . . (Erfurt: Wolfgang Sturmer, 1547).

40. *Epistolarvm Reverendi patris Domini D. Martini Lutheri, Tomus primus continens scripta viri Dei, ab anno millesimo quingentesimo septima, vsqve ad annum vicesimum secundum* (Jena: Christian Rödinger, 1556), Aij^{r}–* [=*v]^{r}.

41. *Secundvs Tomvs epistolarvm Reuerendi patris Domini Doctoris Martini Lvtheri* . . . (Eisleben: Andreas Petri, 1565).

sell.[42] Reprints of the correspondence did appear, however, in 1579 and 1597/1598.[43] In the latter half of the century, other editors worked on some of Luther's letters, but no one other than Aurifaber attempted a complete edition of the correspondence.[44] Luther's daily life, as reflected in his letters, was far less interesting for the next generation than were his preaching and his theological treatises.

Table Talk

Members of the next generation were eager, however, to learn about Luther's chats as he sat at table. Aurifaber was also responsible for the first attempt to gather what students could remember from conversations over supper in the Black Cloister. Yet even in this case memories of Luther's discourses were shaped by the myth of the proclaimer and prophet. For Aurifaber felt compelled to organize his material by topic. By placing these tidbits from the table in the form of *loci communes,* Aurifaber predigested them for his readers. Thus his Table Talk presented Luther in a form which provided a useful reference work for preaching and teaching. The verbal crumbs from Luther's table found a ready market and became a major form in which his thought, processed by his students, spread to the succeeding generations.[45]

As Luther's last amanuensis, Aurifaber himself had sat at supper with Luther on many an evening, feasting on his mentor's wisdom as well as the fare at his table. In 1566 he gathered for publication the written recollections of several others who had frequented Luther's table. He included the notes of Veit Dietrich, Hieronymus Besold, Johann Schlaginhaufen, Johannes Mathesius, Georg Rörer, and others; and he made use of collections already compiled by Johann Stolz, his former colleague at the ducal Saxon court, and Jacob Weber.[46] He also incorporated material from Luther in other forms: letters, memoranda, ser-

42. Volz and Wolgast, "Geschichte," 363–400.

43. The two volumes of letters were reissued by Michael Heutzlein in Berlin in 1579 and by Friedrich Hartmann in Frankfurt/Main in 1597; Hartmann also reissued the first volume by itself in 1598.

44. Volz and Wolgast, "Geschichte," 400–450.

45. Not only the *Tischreden,* of course, comes to us in a form edited by Luther's students. Much of his postils and academic lectures was edited by students, though to a large extent with Luther looking over their shoulder. Therefore it is important to remember that student refinements may be present in many of the Luther texts which we possess. On the *Tischreden* see Ernst Heinrich Rehermann, "Die Protestantischen Exempelsammlungen des 16. und 17. Jahrhunderts," in *Volkserzählung und Reformation,* ed. Wolfgang Brückner (Berlin: Schmidt, 1974), 588–95.

46. *Tischreden Oder Colloquia Doct. Mart: Luthers/So er in vielen Jaren/gegen gelarten Leuten/auch frembden Gesten/vnd seinen Tischgesellen gefuret/Nach den Heuptstucken vnserer Christlichen Lere/Zusammen getragen . . .* (Eisleben: Urban Gaubisch, 1566), iiij^{r-v}.

mons, and lectures. Aurifaber organized the material topically under eighty loci, beginning with "God's Word or the Holy Scripture," and treating doctrinal and ethical topics as well as matters of concern at the university. He rendered all the material into German so that his collection would find the widest possible circulation.[47]

It did. At least one printer rushed to duplicate Aurifaber's work and occasioned thereby a public battle over publishing rights.[48] In addition, several editors revised Aurifaber's work for still other publishers, and they thus expanded the availability of Luther's utterances. In 1571 Andreas Stangewald, a recent student at the University of Jena and one of the team which had produced the *Magdeburg Centuries,* recast Aurifaber's material for the publishing firm of the Rebart family. He reduced Aurifaber's topics from eighty to forty-three, and he grouped them under nine chief headings, "Scripture, the Word of God," "God," "Creation," "The Human Creature and the Communion of the Human Creature with God," "The Church," "The Household," "The School," "The State," and "The End of All Things." Stangewald's version of the Table Talk, which was produced anonymously, had become a textbook. The preface criticized Aurifaber for using some material which did not originate from Luther and for failing to organize the work properly. Topical organization had assumed critical importance for Melanchthon's intellectual heirs. Stangewald had employed, he claimed, Joachim Mörlin's personal copy of Aurifaber and its marginal notes to aid him in the task of improving the Table Talk.[49]

Six years later, in 1577, Nikolaus Selnecker made minor refinements in Stangewald's work, including the addition of indices of Bible texts and topics, and his own biography of Luther, which had been separately published.[50] The Table Talk also appeared in Latin translation in 1571. Produced by a pastor, Heinrich Peter Rebenstock, it was intended to provide Aurifaber's text to those in Italy, France, and other nations who could not read German. The market apparently failed to develop, and it was not reprinted.[51]

By 1621 some twenty-three editions of the Table Talk, including the Latin translation, had appeared in print.[52] Much of the popular impres-

47. Johannes Schilling, "Bibliographie der Tischreden-Ausgaben," *WA* 59:748–49.

48. Ibid., 751–53.

49. Ibid., 753–56.

50. Ibid., 757–58. For Selnecker's biography see pp. 70–73 in the present volume.

51. Ibid., 759–60.

52. Fifteen (both authorized and pirated) were of the Aurifaber text (1566, 1567 [3], 1568 [2], 1569 [2], 1570, 1571, 1573, 1574, 1576, 1577, 1593); four of the Stangewald text (1571, 1591, 1603, 1621); and three of the Selnecker version (1577, 1580, 1581). See the bibliography, *WA* 59:761–80.

sion of Luther's teaching came through this text. It gave the prophet's voice a particularly attractive and living quality. Although theologians used the Table Talk relatively seldom in formal arguments, they undoubtedly found its pages profitable for leisure reading and homiletical anecdotes.

Luther continued to teach after his death. His students worked hard to enable him to influence a new generation of Lutheran pastors and people. They provided access to almost all that he had published—and in some cases even more, that is, the manuscript form of letters, sermon notes, and expositions of biblical texts. The cost of these collected works put them beyond the reach of many. Nonetheless, demand was sufficient to justify reprintings of the Jena and Wittenberg editions a number of times.[53]

Complete works provide material for those who wish to engage in broad study of the subject or to have at hand for occasional reference everything Luther wrote. These collected works did not digest Luther for easy use. They gave each reader the opportunity to pursue his or her own employment of the Luther texts. Thus they did not shape or channel the way in which Luther influenced the readers. In these collected works readers confronted him directly as they used his teaching and preaching to formulate their own. Those who used these works were undoubtedly influenced by what they read, particularly if they read Luther often. Nonetheless, as is the case with readers of every age, they placed his thought into their own conceptual framework, which was being shaped by new events and circumstances as well as by the dogmatic tradition expressed in Melanchthon's *Loci communes theologici* and its successors.

53. See the appendix, pp. 231–32.

7

Blossoms and Bouquets from Luther's Thought

Topical Collections and Individual Reprints of Luther's Publications

Joachim Mörlin, a onetime student of Luther and then superintendent of the church in Braunschweig, seized upon an ancient motif to picture Luther as a "godly little bee who had drawn forth noble saving honey from all the roses and lovely flowers of God's paradise" and then poured this sweetness of God's Word into the catechism.[1] Without drawing such elaborate analogies many of Luther's followers did view his writings as blossoms. They continued the medieval tradition of florilegia, the gathering together of bouquets of the thoughts of the wise on a specific topic for handy use by the pious.[2] Others republished individual works by Luther, pastoral, devotional, edificatory, and polemical.[3] Luther's thoughts were put to use as readers studied Scripture, prepared to give pastoral care, engaged in personal meditation, and sought consolation in times of trouble. Thus Luther's role as a teacher of the church made as great an impact on the lives of people as did his image as prophet or hero.

For the Comfort and Instruction of God's People

Above all, Luther had been a pastor. He had often endeavored to provide consolation for the people of God and support for their pastors. His

1. *Enchiridion. Der Kleine Catechismus Doc. Martini Lutheri/Sampt der Haustafel/in mehr Fragestu[e]ck vorfasset* (1554; Leipzig: Heirs of Valentin Babst, 1560).

2. Ernst Koch, "Lutherflorilegien zwischen 1550 und 1600: Zum Lutherbild der ersten nachreformatorischen Generation," *Theologische Versuche* 16 (1986): 105–17; see also the article on florilegia by Ekkehard Mühlenberg and Franz Brunhölzl in *Theologische Realenzyklopädie* (Berlin: de Gruyter, 1983), 9:215–21.

3. Robert Kolb, *For All the Saints: Changing Perceptions of Martyrdom and Sainthood in the Lutheran Reformation* (Macon, Ga.: Mercer University Press, 1987), 127–32.

successors found that a wide variety of materials from his pen could continue to offer such consolation and support. Two powerful tools for promoting Luther's understanding of the Christian faith had been frequently published before his death: his postils and his catechisms. They were accompanied by anthologies of prayer, prophecy, and missives of comfort, all of which conveyed Luther's theology and continued to edify the people.

The Postils

Inaugurated with his first postil in 1521, Luther's program for improving parish preaching made a significant impact upon his followers during his lifetime. Republication of the postils proceeded apace in the latter half of the sixteenth century. The Church Postil provided pastors with guidance for preaching on the pericopes. Newly graduated Lutheran pastors could quite easily obtain the Church Postil for their libraries.

Luther had turned his hand toward preparation of printed sermons for pastors while he was at the Wartburg; he completed his Latin postil for Advent in early 1522. Then he turned to German postils for the first half of the church year. By the late 1520s students were assisting him in preparing such model sermons for the reading public. These postils not only supplied sermons to be used directly, but, as models of Luther's exegetical method and of his distinguishing between law and gospel, also provided a program for the continuing education of parish pastors.

Edited by Luther's student Stephan Roth and his colleague Caspar Cruciger, the Church Postil of 1527 was issued in whole or in part in twenty-two editions.[4] The House Postil provided Christian households with material for family devotions. The first edition of this work was assembled by Veit Dietrich for publication in 1544. It was revised in 1559 by Andreas Poach, the Gnesio-Lutheran pastor who worked hard to preserve Luther's legacy through his own personal program of editing previously published as well as unpublished writings of his mentor. Poach, in the spirit of the Jena edition of Luther's works, wanted to make certain that the widely used House Postil truly reflected Luther's own thought. Poach's edition appeared seven times before the end of the century, all from presses in Jena.[5] The original Dietrich edition was printed in a number of centers twenty-eight times in the half century following

4. The Church Postil was often printed in two volumes, one or both of which appeared from Wittenberg presses in 1547, 1550, 1554, 1555, 1557, 1562, 1563, 1567, 1568, 1575, and 1584. Both the Cruciger and the Roth versions were published in 1560 in Nuremberg by Johann von Berg and Ulrich von Neuber. See *WA* 10.1.2:ix–lxxv; 17.2:ix–xxiv; 21:ix–xxv; 22:ix–lxxxix.

5. In 1559, 1561, 1562, 1568, 1570, 1572, 1591. The final printing was called the Jena House Postil and republished three times (Jena, 1596, 1597; Leipzig, 1598).

Luther's death.[6] Clearly it was not only the Ratzeberger family that used the House Postil as a source of edification.

Many other postils were composed by Luther's followers, more than thirty in all in the period between Luther's death and the end of the century. Some of them were republished a number of times. None equaled Luther's in popularity. His postils appealed to those who wanted to continue to proclaim his message; in them they found help for carrying out their calling as preacher.

Luther's *Hauspostil* (Edition of 1545)
(Concordia Seminary Library, St. Louis)

The Catechism

In addition to the postils Luther's catechisms guided the teaching of the Lutheran pastors. His Large and Small Catechisms would soon supersede his catechetical sermons and meditations almost completely, although two exceptions can be mentioned. In 1579 Sigismund Feierabend, the Frankfurt printer, published Luther's treatment of the Creed together with his review of biblical history.[7] Earlier, in 1562, Franz Scharschmidt had published Luther's 1537 sermon on the Creed. Scharschmidt was certain that this explanation of Christian teaching by "Germany's last prophet" would be particularly helpful for the heads of households as they instructed their children.[8]

The Large Catechism appeared some twenty-nine times in the years before Luther's death, and in the half century after his death twenty-five

6. In Nuremberg, 1546, 1548, 1549, 1553, 1554 (2), 1555, 1557, 1560, 1562, 1564, 1566, 1568, 1569, 1571; Augsburg, 1547; Frankfurt/Oder, 1548; Wittenberg, 1548, 1549, 1552 (2), 1591 (2), 1598; Pforzheim, 1560; Frankfurt/Main, 1564, 1574; and Torgau, 1597. In addition a Low German translation of the postil, first published in 1545, was reprinted in the years immediately following Luther's death (Magdeburg, 1546, 1550, 1552; Wittenberg, 1550, 1551), as was a Latin translation also first published in 1545 (Frankfurt/Oder, 1552, 1553; Wittenberg, 1553). On both the Poach and the Dietrich editions, see *WA* 52:vii–xxxv.

7. *Passio/Vnsers Herrn Jhesu Christi/Auss den vier Euangelisten gezogen. Mit scho[e]nen Figuren gezieret . . . Item/Das Symbolum der heiligen Aposteln . . . aussgelegt* (Frankfurt/Main: Sigismund Feierabend, 1579).

8. *Auslegung des Glaubens/Gepredigt durch D. Martinum Lutherum/zu Schmalkalden/ Anno 1537. Itzund zum ersten mal im Druck ausgangen* (Eisleben: Urban Gaubisch, 1562), A2^{r}.

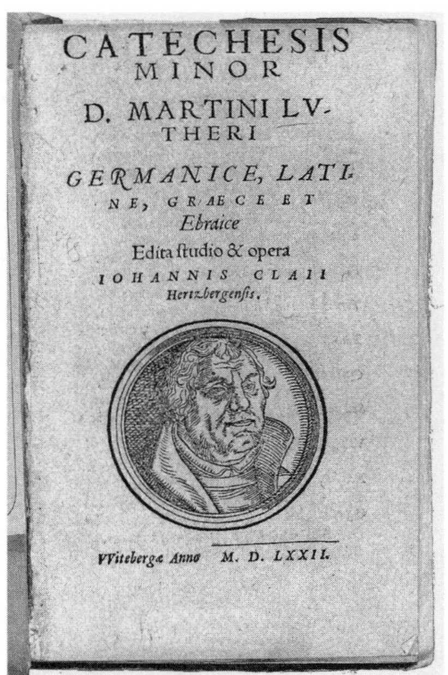

Luther's *Catechesis Minor* in German, Latin, Greek, and Hebrew (1572) (Concordia Seminary Library, St. Louis)

new editions were issued in German, five in Low German, and three in Latin. Not all of these editions of the Large Catechism were exact reproductions of Luther's text, however. His devoted friend and Reformer in Nordhausen and Mansfeld, Johannes Spangenberg, prepared a student edition of the Large Catechism in 1541.[9] In question-and-answer form Spangenberg's recasting of the text followed Luther's words closely at some points, reproducing his text almost exactly in answering certain questions. At other points Spangenberg paraphrased Luther, and at still others he forged questions of his own, with answers of his own, that ventured far afield from the original text even as Spangenberg endeavored to reflect Luther's theology faithfully. Particularly in the section on the Creed, where Luther passed over certain topics quickly or ignored them altogether, Spangenberg expanded Luther's text so that it could serve as a textbook at the secondary level. Eleven of the twenty-five German editions and all three Latin editions of the Large Catechism issued in the period between 1546 and 1593 were the Spangenberg version. The Large Catechism was, of course, available in other forms, particularly in the *corpora doctrinae* of the 1560s and 1570s. It is significant, however, that the Large Catechism, though conceived of as the instructor's manual for teaching the life of faith, did not appear more frequently in print in this period.

The Small Catechism certainly did appear often. It was issued in thirty editions in German before 1546; by the end of the century at least 125 more had been published in one form or another. In addition, thirty Latin editions were printed for use in teaching the language as well as the faith. One Greek translation and several Greek/Latin translations were produced by seven individual scholars and issued in a total of fifteen editions. Six German/Latin and one German/Latin/Greek edition also made their way to the market between 1550 and 1600. A polyglot

9. On Luther's catechisms see *WA* 30.1:426–829. Spangenberg's version appeared under the title *Der Gros Catechismus vnd Kinder Lehre D. Mart. Luth. Fu[e]r die jungen Christen/in Fragestu[e]cke verfasset* . . . (Frankfurt/Main: Johann Wolf, 1565).

publication in German, Latin, Greek, and Hebrew appeared in 1572 and went through twelve editions by 1599. Two dozen Low German printings of the Small Catechism also were issued, along with thirteen Low German/Latin editions prepared by the Wittenberg professor Georg Major.[10] Thus the Small Catechism was used for instruction in both the Christian life and the languages.

The Small Catechism often appeared in its unvarnished form as it had developed during Luther's lifetime. But the parents whom Luther had wanted to be the primary instructors of their children and servants needed aid for their task,[11] and pastors, too, found a need for expanded catechetical helps. After the handbook prepared by Johannes Spangenberg in 1542,[12] the earliest and most popular edition was that prepared by the superintendent in Braunschweig and later Prussia, Joachim Mörlin. His preface, dedicated to Electress Elisabeth of Brandenburg, employed the metaphor mentioned at the beginning of this chapter, a metaphor often used by Mörlin's contemporaries when speaking of Luther's Small Catechism. Like a busy bee Luther, God's fine, holy tool, had gathered the noble and salutary honey of the Scriptures' rose blossoms and had placed it in the jar of the Small Catechism. It summarizes the Scripture for children and simple folk so that they can grasp and retain the eternal treasure found there. Mörlin ventured the opinion that the Holy Spirit must have guided Luther's hand and pen as he composed the Small Catechism, "for there is not a word, indeed, not even a syllable or letter in it, which does not point to such lofty thought that I must daily learn it anew, and I still remain a poor, simple, young pupil of the catechism." Mörlin expressed the wish to be never more than a simple preacher of the Catechism, that is, of God's law and gospel, as Luther had also wished to be.[13] In introducing the

10. These statistics are taken from the *Verzeichnis der im deutschen Sprachbereich erschienen Drucke des XVI. Jahrhunderts,* ed. Bayerische Staatsbibliothek (Munich) and the Herzog August Bibliothek (Wolfenbüttel), part 1, vol. 12 (Stuttgart: Hiersemann, 1988), 241–77, #5020–49. It is almost certain that other editions not yet incorporated into the *Verzeichnis* can be found in libraries. It is not beyond the realm of possibility (though less than likely) that some editions were totally consumed by use and are not extant.

11. Few such helps were aimed specifically at parents; an exception was the work of Andreas Fabricius, pastor in Nordhausen: *Die Hauskirche. Das ist: Wie ein Hausvater neben dem o[e]ffentlichen Predigtampt auch daheime sein Heufflein zu Gottes Wort vnd dem lieben Catechismo reitzen soll* (Eisleben: Andreas Petri, 1572).

12. *Des kleinen Catechismi kurtzer begrieff und der Haustaffel/wie man sie in aller gemeine zu Halle/für die Kinder handelt . . .* (Halle: Hans Frischmut, 1542).

13. *Enchiridion,* Aiij^{r-v}. On Mörlin's and other catechisms of this period, see Robert Kolb, "The Layman's Bible: The Use of Luther's Catechisms in the German Late Reformation," in *Luther's Catechisms—450 Years: Essays Commemorating the Small and Large Catechisms of Dr. Martin Luther,* ed. David P. Scaer and Robert D. Preus (Fort Wayne, Ind.: Concordia Theological Seminary Press, 1979), 16–26.

text Mörlin oriented the reader to its content; he then provided questions which expanded on those of Luther and added Bible texts as well. All those who prepared similar supplementary primers followed much the same format.

Almost as popular as Mörlin's *Enchiridion* was the *Golden Jewel* of Johann Tettelbach, a Gnesio-Lutheran pastor in Albertine Saxony and the Palatinate. Tilemann Hesshus's preface for this catechetical work appraised the Small Catechism as a divine miracle. Warning against catechisms filled with sacramentarian poison (a reference above all to the Heidelberg Catechism), he urged the use of Luther's Catechism, for in it "there are more of the Holy Spirit, more lofty teaching, richer comfort, more correct explanation, and a stronger basis laid for the articles of the Christian faith than in many hundred big books and tomes of all the teachers of the church who are called the Fathers."[14] Hesshus could commend this exposition of Luther's Catechism because Tettelbach was Luther's faithful student, following in his footsteps.

The adaptations of Luther's Small Catechism classified its essential elements in different ways. Peter Praetorius, a Philippist pastor in Albertine Saxony, divided the catechism into four parts, the law, the Creed, prayer, and the sacraments, omitting Luther's categories of family prayers and the table of responsibilities.[15] Mörlin divided the catechism into three parts, law, gospel, and the table of responsibilities.[16]

14. *Das Gu[e]lden Kleinod. D. Mart. Lutheri Catechismus/In kurtze Frage vnd antwort gefasset/Vnd der lieben Jugend einfeltigklich aussgelegt* (1568; Frankfurt/Main: Catherina Rebart and Kilian Han, 1571),)(ij^{r}–)(v^{r}. In an impressive gathering of material from this period Hans-Jürgen Fraas (*Katechismustradition: Luthers kleiner Katechismus in Kirche und Schule* [Göttingen: Vandenhoeck & Ruprecht, 1971]) ignores the rhetorical nature and force of such praise. He also fails to understand that these authors held a dynamic doctrine of the Word of God which presumed that the Word in Scripture could be repeated with the same effect in catechetical writings (or preaching) derived from Scripture; as a result, he registers an inappropriate indignation that the "equation of Luther's catechism with God's Word" is actually a "forsaking of the ground of the Lutheran confession of the faith" (p. 58). Similarly, his misinterpretation of the title of Joshua Opitz's *Kinder-Bibel/Der Kleine Catechismus D. Martini Lutheri mit scho[e]nen Spru[e]chlein heiliger Schrifft erklert* . . . (Büdingen, 1583) to mean that "the catechism is no longer an aid for the engagement of the laity with the Bible and an introduction to Scripture, but the Bible is in fact degraded to the status of a source of help for understanding the catechism" (p. 57), disregards that Luther himself called the catechism "the Bible of the laity." Opitz, like Luther, viewed the catechism as a digest of and a pathway into Scripture; his pedagogical method begins with the catechism's texts and then takes his readers a few steps further into Scripture.

15. *Der Kleine Catechismus Doctoris Martini Lutheri Fu[e]r die Jugent vnd Einfeltigen der Christlichen Gemeine/in Ko[e]nigsbergk/zu derselben jerlichen vnterweisung die Fasten* . . . (Wittenberg: Heirs of Georg Rhau, 1563), C^{r}–Cij^{r}.

16. Mörlin, *Enchiridion*, Biiij^{v}.

Tettelbach taught that the catechism had the five chief parts of Christian teaching that Luther had originally proposed—the Ten Commandments, the Creed, the Lord's Prayer, baptism, and the Lord's Supper—along with four additional parts: confession and absolution, morning and evening blessings, the table prayer, and the table of responsibilities.[17] Most expanded versions of the Small Catechism offered comparable classifications.

As faithful students or followers of Luther, those who amplified his catechism for parish use undoubtedly did wish to convey his teachings purely and simply. Yet the formulations of their expanded interrogatory on the faith also often revealed their debt to Melanchthon. Praetorius straightforwardly admitted this;[18] others did not. All of them claimed in their introductions to have used the distinction between law and gospel to discipline their presentation of God's Word even though their conception of this distinction was sometimes wooden and shallow. Some effectively reinforced the sense of law and gospel with questions similar to Mörlin's first: "What is above all else in the world your comfort?" The child was to answer: "Though I am by nature a child of wrath (Eph. 2), I have indeed become another person and a Christian since I have been baptized into Jesus Christ . . . and place all my hope and confidence, with genuine trust and faith, in him."[19]

This clear orientation around the proper distinction between law and gospel is expressed less well in other guides for catechetical instruction that were issued in the period. Praetorius distinguished the Christian faith from other religions, "such as the pagan and the Muhammadan," by noting that those religions taught only the law. This rather simplistic and wooden explanation is not dissimilar to the muddling of law and gospel presented by Conrad Porta, pastor at the Church of Saints Peter and Paul in Eisleben. In 1578 he prepared a handbook for parents and pastors who were charged with instructing young people in the faith. In his dedication of the book to the elders of his congregation, he reviewed the goals he had in mind when he was composing his guide: It would summarize his own confession of the

17. Tettelbach, *Das Gu[e]lden Kleinod,* Aiij^{r}. Bartholomaeus Wolffhart (superintendent in Hildesheim), *Der Kleine Catechismus Lutheri: durch etliche Kurtze vnd Kindische Fragestu[e]ck erkleret/damit jhn die Jugent desto besser verstehen mo[e]ge* (Ursel: Nicolaus Henricus, 1566), [Avij]^{r}, divided the entire catechism simply into law and gospel. Opitz, *Kinder-Bibel,* D^{r}, used Luther's six chief parts of Christian doctrine as the divisions of his catechism.

18. Praetorius, *Der Kleine Catechismus,* Biiij^{r}.

19. Mörlin, *Enchiridion,* Biij^{v}; for almost identical expressions see Wolffhart, *Der Kleine Catechismus,* [Avij]$^{r-v}$, and Opitz, *Kinder-Bibel,* [C8]$^{r-v}$.

faith; it would move the leaders of his congregation to set examples for their children by learning and putting into practice Luther's catechisms; it would entice them into buying Luther's other works and reading them. Through a series of Luther citations Porta's answers to ten questions defined the catechism, its use and usefulness, and the obligations of pastors, parents, and schoolteachers to teach it. Warning against showing contempt for the catechism, against taking the task of instruction lightly, he cited others on the particular value of Luther's catechism. The concluding section of Porta's work contained warnings against new catechisms, among them the Heidelberg Catechism.[20] Porta's popular introduction to the art of catechetical instruction served both to motivate pastors, schoolteachers, and parents to use Luther's text and also to acquaint them with Luther's understanding of the faith. Nonetheless, Porta did not work within Luther's distinct conceptual framework and thereby failed to help the catechist to convey Luther's careful distinction between law and gospel. Thus his guide reveals a change in Lutheran theology and practice.[21]

Luther's catechism did not by itself suffice as a text for basic instruction in the Christian faith. Sixteenth-century Lutheran theologians produced a significant number of other catechisms or textbooks to be used in place of or alongside Luther's catechisms in teaching young people the biblical message.[22] Even when Luther's text provided no more than

20. *Des Heiligenn Catechismi: oder Leyen Bibel/Nutz vnd hoheit. Aus den geistreichen Bu[e]chern D. Martini Lutheri des Mans Gottes/Vnd anderer Furtrefflicher Theologen bedencken . . . in Frage vnd Antwort verfasset. Allen trewen Predigern/vleissigen Schulmeistern/vnd frommen Hausuetern/gehorsamen Kindern vnd Gesinde/nu[e]tzlich zu wissen vnd zu lesen* (Halle: Urban Gaubisch, 1578).

21. One must avoid, however, an oversimplified theory of the decline and fall of Lutheran catechetical instruction, such as is suggested by Fraas, *Katechismustradition,* 58–102. He notes, for example, that Matthias Flacius protested against mechanical memorization and limited learning of biblical content (pp. 64–65). Luther, on the other hand, was concerned that simple standard texts be memorized, as he advised in the preface to the Small Catechism. Rather than seeing a decay or decline, we must keep in mind that catechists of the late sixteenth century fought the same battle that all catechists fight as they try to find the balance between learning the material and understanding and applying it. We must also keep in mind the pedagogical methods of the time and the use of the catechism as a textbook in schools. But the placement of the Catechisms in the Book of Concord did not, as Fraas contends (p. 63), introduce a "certain stiffening" in their use. Our evaluation of seventeenth-century catechetics must be based on a much broader and deeper look at the ways in which the Christian faith was taught than Fraas takes (pp. 97–102). That the catechism took on a textbook quality when it was employed as a textbook may be regrettable, but it reflects the practice which church and society found necessary for instruction in the faith.

22. See Johann Michael Reu, *Quellen zur Geschichte des kirchlichen Unterrichts in der evangelischen Kirche Deutschlands zwischen 1530 und 1600,* 9 vols. in 3 (Gütersloh: Bertelsmann, 1902–24). While not all the works cited by Reu were Lutheran, many were.

the basic skeleton for instruction in the faith, his name sometimes had to remain on the title page, as the rector of Lemgo, Johannes Gisen, demonstrated in 1611.[23] "Catechism" and "Luther" had become to a large extent synonymous. Despite the reprocessing and repackaging of his instructional base, Lutherans did grow up breathing Luther's simple summary of the faith into their lives. Perhaps no other piece from his pen so broadly and deeply shaped the lives of those who bore his name in succeeding generations.

The Hymns

Luther also continued to shape the faith of his followers through the legacy of his hymns. Zacharias Praetorius, a Gnesio-Lutheran pastor in Eisleben, composed Latin paraphrases of hymns which Luther had written and of older hymns which Luther had recast.[24] Such translations aided the development of both the language skills and the piety of secondary-school pupils.

Hymnals in the period often gave Luther high billing; for example, that issued in Brandenburg in 1575 was entitled *Hymns of Dr. Martin Luther and Other Pious Christians*.[25] Two generations later the people of Braunschweig-Wolfenbüttel were singing from a hymnal called *Divine Music, That Is, the German Hymns of Doctor Martin Luther and Others*, even though many of the hymns were not Luther's and his contributions to hymnody and to German church life went unmentioned in the preface.[26]

Only rarely were individual hymns of Luther reprinted,[27] but they did become texts for pious interpretation and instruction. At the turn of the century Michael Julius, pastor in Gotha, published three volumes which contained sermons on individual hymns by Luther, "Lord, Keep Us Steadfast in Thy Word," "Now We All Implore the Holy Spirit," and

23. *Catechismus B. Lutheri est parva Biblia, Idque ostenditvr praecipuis Scripturae Sacrae dictis Doctrinae Christianae sedem, & fundamentum continentibus* (1611; Strassburg: Paul Ledertz, 1620).

24. *Libellvs cantionvm Lutheri* (Eisleben: Andreas Petri, 1571).

25. *Geistliche Lieder/D. Mart. Luth. vnd anderer frommen Christen/nach Ordnung der Jarzeit mit Collecten vnd Gebeten* (Frankfurt/Oder: Johann Eichorn, 1575).

26. *MVSICA DIVINA, Das ist/Die Geistreichen Doctoris Martini Lutheri, vnd etlicher anderer Christlichen Lehrer/Teutsche/fu[e]rnembste Gesa[e]nge/So in der christlichen Versamlung durchs gantze Jahr gesungen werden . . .* (Wolfenbüttel: Elias Holwein, 1620).

27. There were reprints of *Christliche Geseng Lateinisch vnd Deudsch zum Begrebnis. D. Martinus Luther* (Leipzig: Jacob Berwaldt, 1552; also Nuremberg, 1560, 1563) and two editions of *Ein geistlich Lied Von vnser heiligen Tauff Darin fein Kurtz gefasset Was sie sey? Wer sie gestifftet habe? Was sie nutze? . . .* (Regensburg: Hans Kohl, c. 1554). In addition, Hieronymus Weller published a line-by-line comment on Luther's "God the Father, Be Our Stay": *Der Christliche vnd gemein Kirchen Gesang. Gott der Vatter wohn vns bey/ec . . .* (Nuremberg: Johann von Berg and Ulrich Neüber, c. 1555).

"Christ Jesus Lay in Death's Strong Bands."[28] Earlier, at least two Lutheran pastors had provided interpretations of a number of Luther's hymns for the edification of pious families.

The four thick quarto volumes of Cyriakus Spangenberg's *Luther's Cithara* contained sermons on twenty-four of Luther's hymns and psalm paraphrases. Just as in his sermons on Luther Spangenberg had drawn parallels between biblical models and the Reformer's activities,[29] so in these homilies on hymns he compared the power of Luther's hymns to David's psalms. The Holy Spirit used both in combating Satan and comforting the troubled. Spangenberg also regarded Luther as a master of poetic composition.[30]

Magdeburg pastor Simon Pauli also commented line by line on Luther's hymns (as well as the hymns of others, including Elisabeth Cruciger and Hermann Bonnus). Pauli shared the widespread view of Luther as the third Elijah. He marveled that Luther had not only preached, taught, translated the Bible, and written many fine books, but had also captured in rhyme and song the articles of the Christian faith and the foremost works, benefits, and actions of God. He had adorned his hymns with beautiful melodies so that God's Word could be grasped and retained much more easily. These hymns awakened true understanding of God, faith, thankfulness, and other God-pleasing virtues in those who sang them. Thus Luther followed in a long line of hymn writers from Moses, David, and other biblical figures through Ambrose, Augustine, Sedulius Fortunatus, and Lactantius. Pauli dedicated his work to two abbots of Riddagshausen as an aid for pastors and cantors as they introduced the Reformation by teaching their parish-

28. *Sechs kurtze Predigten: In welchen das herrliche scho[e]ne Kinderliedt: Erhalt vns Herr bey deinem Wort/etc. erkleret vnd ausgelegt ist/allen Christen/in diesen fehrlichen vnd betru[e]bten Jharen/nu[e]tzlich vnd tro[e]stlich zu lesen* (Erfurt: Esaias Mechler, 1589); *Das scho[e]ne Pfingst vnd Trostliedt Nun bitten wir den heyligen Geyst/ec. Welches der theure Mann Gottes D. Martinus Lutherus auss dem lateinischen Sequentz vnd Prosa genommen/vnnd in deutsche Reimen verfasset . . .* (Erfurt: Zacharias Zimmer, 1595), reprinted under the title *Pfingst Sequentz oder Prosa* (Erfurt: Johann Beck, 1603); also *Christus redivivvs. Das ist: Der Ostergesang/Christ lag in Todesbanden/von der Passion vnd Aufferstehung Jesu Christi/Aus dem 4. Capit. der Epistel an die Ro[e]mer/vnd dem Oster sequentz/Victimae Paschali laudes, in deutsche Reimen gebracht durch D. Martin. Luth. P. M.* (Erfurt: Johann Beck, 1602).

29. See pp. 48–50.

30. *Cythara Lvtheri. Die scho[e]nen/Christlichen/trostreichen Psalmen vnd Geistlichen Lieder/des Hochwirdigen thewren Lerers vnd Diener Gottes/D. Martini Luthers. Der Erste [-Vierder] Theil* (Erfurt: Georg Bawmann, 1570), Aiij. See also Kolb, *For All the Saints,* 123–24. Spangenberg's work is undoubtedly that referred to by Jirí Pesek, "Protestant Literature in Bohemian Private Libraries *circa* 1600," in *The Reformation in Eastern and Central Europe,* ed. Karin Maag (Aldershot, Eng.: Scolar, 1997), 44, as found "fairly frequently" in Prague private libraries in the late sixteenth century.

ioners Luther's hymns.[31] Luther sang his theology into the hearts of succeeding generations.

Pastoral Theology

For the pastors who preached the postils, taught the catechism, and led the worship in which Luther's hymns were sung, Conrad Porta also provided a handbook of pastoral care taken largely from Luther's writings, including the Wittenberg, Jena, and Eisleben editions, both postils, the Table Talk, and Aurifaber's edition of Luther's correspondence. Porta acknowledged that textbooks of pastoral theology were available from the pens of Martin Bucer, Erasmus Sarcerius, and Niels Hemmingsen. But Porta believed that Luther had said it better. In addition, those many pastors too poor to purchase their own set of Luther's works needed to have at hand his exact words on topics of pastoral concern and practice. For Luther had explained all the articles of the faith well, particularly justification through faith, the proper distinction of law and gospel, and true repentance and conversion.

When presenting his citations from Luther, however, Porta often failed to practice the proper distinction of law and gospel. These citations he gathered under twenty-four topics. Among them were the worthiness of the office of the ministry, the pastor's calling, pastoral conduct, the condemnation of sin, the comfort of the sinner, the admonition of Christians, prayer, marriage, the sacraments, care for the poor, the melancholy and possessed, the sick, and the imprisoned. He shared with his readers Luther's thoughts on Christian burial, on the salary and support of pastors, and on the persecution which pastors must often endure. Luther's pastoral counsel, as Porta had organized it, proved valuable to parish pastors. The work was republished in 1586, 1591, and 1615.[32] Though Porta assembled a wealth of citations, he put together a rather mechanical and superficial view of the pastoral office. His manual answered how-to questions, but provided at best only a partial understanding of how Luther perceived the Holy Spirit's work through those whom he had called into the pastoral office.

31. *Avsslegung der Deutschen Geistlichen Lieder/so von Herrn Doctore Martino Luthero vnd anderen Gottseligen Christen gemacht/oder aus dem Latein ins Deutsche vbersetzet vnd gebracht sind . . . ordentlich nach dem gantzen text erkleret* (Magdeburg: Ambrosius Kirchner, 1588), Aij^{r}–[biiij]^{v}.

32. *Pastorale Lvtheri. Das ist/Nvtzlicher vnnd no[e]tiger Vnterricht/von den fu[e]rnembsten Stu[e]cken zum heiligen Ministerio geho[e]rig/Vnd richtige Antwort auff mancherley wichtige Fragen/von schweren vnd gefehrlichen Casibus, so in demselbigen fu[e]rfallen mo[e]gen. Fu[e]r anfahende Prediger vnd Kirchendiener zusamen bracht . . .* (Eisleben: Andreas Petri, 1582; later editions include Petri, 1586; n.p., 1591; and Leipzig: Henning Gros, 1615). See also Robert Kolb, "Luther, the Master Pastor: Conrad Porta's *Pastorale Lutheri,* Handbook for Generations," *Concordia Journal* 9 (1983): 179–87.

Devotional Materials

Even before Luther's death his followers began to organize other kinds of edificatory material for special use by the general public. Caspar Cruciger assembled *Several Writings of Comfort and Sermons for Those in Death and Other Distress and Temptation* in 1544. With this collection drawn from the pages of Luther's works Cruciger intended to provide simple folk with comfort for every kind of affliction. He included Luther's letters to his parents as they lay ill and to others in the midst of various kinds of spiritual struggles. In addition, Cruciger reprinted several of Luther's sermons which gave comfort to the dying.[33]

Georg Rörer's revision of this collection was issued by presses in Jena (1554, 1558) and Leipzig (1559).[34] Rörer omitted the sermonic material and added some twenty of Luther's letters of spiritual counsel. It is clear that the comfort of the gospel rather than preservation of Luther's own words was Rörer's chief concern, for he also included material by Friedrich Myconius, Caspar Cruciger, and others. That had also been the case with a collection of comments on Bible passages which Rörer had issued in 1547. In his dedication of this work to Albert of Brandenburg, the disciple praised Luther as a schoolmaster with a special lesson for his people, who were not behaving properly and were ungrateful for his instruction. Rörer here anticipated the complaints of his colleagues in Jena and a rising number of Luther's students as they grew older and frequently expressed their deep regret that no one was listening to Luther in their day. Rörer used material from Melanchthon, Cruciger, Johannes Bugenhagen, and Nikolaus von Amsdorf as well as from Luther in this summary of the biblical message. The majority of the comments did, however, come from Luther's illumination of passages in Deuteronomy, Psalms, Proverbs, several of the prophets, the four Gospels (mostly John), several of Paul's letters, and 1 and 2 Peter.

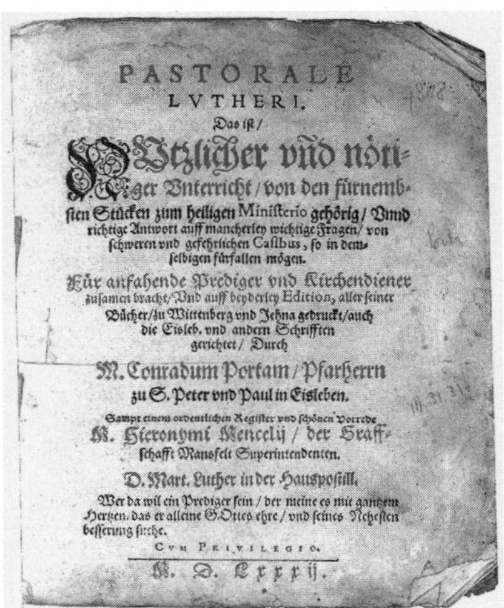

PASTORALE
LVTHERI.
Das ist/
Nützlicher vnd nötiger Vnterricht/ von den fürnembsten Stücken zum heiligen Ministerio gehörig/ Vnnd richtige Antwort auff mancherley wichtige Fragen/ von schweren vnd gefehrlichen Casibus, so in demselbigen fürfallen mögen.
Für anfahende Prediger vnd Kirchendiener zusamen bracht/ Vnd auff beyderley Edition, aller seiner Bücher/ zu Wittenberg vnd Jehna gedruckt/ auch die Eisleb. vnd andern Schrifften gerichtet/ Durch
M. Conradum Portam/ Pfarherrn zu S. Peter vnd Paul in Eisleben.
Sampt einem ordentlichen Register vnd schönen Vorrede M. Hieronymi Mencelij/ der Graffschafft Mansfelt Superintendenten.
D. Mart. Luther in der Hauspostill.
Wer da wil ein Prediger sein/ der meine es mit gantzem Hertzen/ das er alleine GOttes ehre/ vnd seines Nehesten besserung suche.
CVM PRIVILEGIO.
M. D. LXXXij.

Conrad Porta, *Pastorale Lvtheri* (1582)
(Concordia Seminary Library, St. Louis)

33. *Etliche Trostschrifften vnd predigten/für die so in tods vnd ander not vnd anfechtung sind. Doct. Mar. Luth.* (Wittenberg: Hans Lufft, 1544; Veit Creutzer, 1546, 1548).

34. *Etliche Trostschrifften vnd Predigten des Ehrwird. Herrn Doct. Mart. Luth. fu[e]r die so in Todes/vnd ander not vnd anfechtung sind/. . . von newen zugericht/vnd . . . gemeret . . .* (Jena: Christian Rödinger, 1554).

Cruciger's work was but the first of several such collections for those who needed the comfort of Luther's gospel. Johann Aurifaber may have taken his cue from Cruciger when he began assembling inscriptions that Luther had written in Bibles and postils that he presented to various nobles and friends. These comments on various Scripture passages were offered as a source of comfort for the reader.[35] In the half century following Luther's death a number of his former students and other followers prepared such collections of his words for the comfort of believers. Among them were the Leipzig pastor Nikolaus Selnecker,[36] the pastor in Weissenfels Johannes Policarius,[37] the deacon in Halle Georg Walther,[38] Andreas Musculus, professor in Frankfurt an der Oder,[39] Caspar Melissander, Gnesio-Lutheran professor at Jena,[40] and an official at the University of Wittenberg, Johannes Schütz.

In his *Shield of Faith* Schütz used copious quotations from Luther to address a number of spiritual problems. The intended audience was readers who did not have time to survey the corpus of the Reformer's

35. *Auslegung/etzlicher Trostspruche/so der Ehrwirdige Herr/Doctor Martinus Luther/ jnn seiner lieben Herrn/vnd guten Freunden Biblien vnd Postillen/mit eigner handt . . . geschrieben* (Erfurt: Wolfgang Sturmer, 1547; Nuremberg: Johann Petreius, 1547).

36. *Sententiae consolatoriae, collectae ex scriptura coelesti, quibus utimur, cum ad sacram communionem accedimus, quibus etiam D. Doctor Martinus Lutherus usus est* (Nuremberg: Johann Daubmann, 1553; reissued in 1556), translated as *Tro[e]stliche scho[e]ne Spru[e]che aus heiliger Schrifft gezogen/ausgelegt/vnd von newem vbersehen vnd gebessert/Allen Christen zu dieser elenden zeit/sonderlich den betru[e]bten gewissen zu gut/ mit vielen Gebetlin zugerichtet vnd verfertiget* (Dresden: Matthes Stoeckel, 1565), reissued as *Sehr scho[e]ne Trostspru[e]che/auss Heiliger Go[e]ttlicher Schrifft gezogen/Fu[e]r die angstigen gewissen. Durch Veit Dietrich* (Nuremberg: Ludwig Lochner, 1618).

37. *Trostspiegel der armen Sunder. Das ist/Vom warhafftigen Erkendtnus vnsers Herrn Jheus Christi/vnd vom seligen Trost/Fried vnd Freud desselbigen/wider die verzweifflung/ angst/trawrigkeit/vnd anfechtung des hertzens vnd Gewissens . . . Aus den Buchern . . . Martini seligers zusammen gezogen* (Leipzig: Jacob Berwald, 1556). Noteworthy is the length of Policarius's citations, which include entire sermons and long sections of biblical lectures.

38. *Trostbuchlein Auss der heiligen Schrifft/vnd D. Martini Lutheri Bu[e]chern von Wort zu Wort gestellet* (Nuremberg: Ulrich Neüber, 1560), [Avij]$^{r-v}$, reissued as *Das Erste [Ander . . .] Theil der Trostspruche D. Martini Lutheri. Angefochtenen vnd Betrubten Christen zum Trost verordnet . . .* (Bautzen: Johann Wolrab, 1571); *Beicht vnd Bettbu[e]chlein/Darin scho[e]ne vnd Kurtze erklerung/in Frag vnd antwort/auss dem Catechismo Lutheri vnd andern Schrifften gezogen/so vormals nie getruckt/jetzund erst aussgangen . . .* (Frankfurt/ Main: Sigismund Feyerabent, 1581).

39. *Das Guldene Kleinod. Wie ein Christ in Geistlicher anfechtung/sonderlich aber im Todtbett/sich von der Sund/Gesetz/Gottes zorn vnd gericht . . . entbrechen . . .* (Erfurt: Georg Baumann, 1561, 1562, 1570; volume 1 reissued by Baumann, 1566; Berlin: Michael Hentzsken, 1578 reprint [all four vols.]). A revised edition appeared under the title *Thesavrvs, Hochnutzlicher tewrer Schatz vnd gulden Kleinot . . .* (Frankfurt/Oder: Johann Eichorn, 1577; Frankfurt/Oder: Friedrich Hartmann, 1595 reprint).

40. Melissander, "Viel schoner Trostbrieffe vnd geistriche Rathschlege . . . Mart: Lutheri begriffen . . . zusamen geordnet," in Hesshus's and Musaeus's *Trostbuchlein Jn hohen geistlichen Anfechtungen/vnd schwermutiger Trawrigkeit . . .* (Jena: Ernst von Gera, 1572).

writings. The eight topics of this work included how to resist temptations to doubt and despair, how to find comfort when Satan cites Scripture against itself, how to fend off both the presumption and the despair which might come from struggling with the doctrine of predestination, how to deal with people who have cursed themselves, how to assess and deal with claims from erring spirits and miracle workers of the day, and how to deal with those who claim special knowledge or special revelation concerning the end of the world. Schütz gathered material from a number of sources, above all the Church and House Postils, but also Luther's comments on Genesis, Deuteronomy, Zechariah, and John.[41]

Such material from Luther's pen continued to appear into the period of the Thirty Years' War.[42] One example is the "sacred Lutheran bouquet" of the Saxon pastor Johann Lysthenius, which was published in 1630. It contains over seven hundred pages of devotional comments on selected Scripture passages. These comments from the "last prophet and third Elijah" are supplemented by excerpts from ancient fathers, medieval commentators, and sixteenth- and seventeenth-century Lutheran preachers.[43]

More sophisticated in content and form of argumentation is the six-hundred-page treatment of faith and works drawn from Luther's writings by Martin Statius, pastor in Danzig, in 1626. Set in a question-and-answer format which aided lay use of the volume, this protopietistic combination of devotional and catechetical material presented Luther's thought with a sensitive balance of law and gospel. "Did Luther continue to hold that position?" or "Can that be explained more clearly?" and similar questions moved the reader along through the extensive

41. *Schilt des Glaubens/Wider die Sicherheit vnd verzweiffelung/auch wider die Anfechtung von der Versehung/Vnd ob Gesichten vnd Offenbarung in diesen/letzten zeiten zu trawen sey . . . Aus D. Mart. Lutheri Schrifften/kurtzliche zusamen gebracht* (Wittenberg: Simon Gronenberg, 1583).

42. E.g., the Hamburg printer Heinrich Binder dedicated to Burgermeister Joachim von Kampen and his wife Rachel a series of Luther's letters of spiritual counsel including in Low German translation his correspondence to his parents as they lay dying and other letters of comfort: *Etlike Sehr scho[e]ne Trostschrifften vnd Predigeden D. Mart. Luth. an sinen leuen Vader Johan Luther in syner kranckheit/Anno 1535. geschreuen. Insunderheit sehr nu[e]tte vnd tro[e]stlick vor de/so in dodes vnd ander nodt vnd anfechtinge sint . . .* (Hamburg: Heinrich Binder, 1590). Also, Luther's sermons on John 14–17 were published in 1624 under the rubric of a treasure of treasures or wellsprings of consolation: *Thesaurus thesaurorum sive Fontes consolationvm. Die überaus scho[e]ne vnd herrliche Valet Predigt des Sohns Gottes wie dieselbe von dem heiligen Evangelisten Johanne in seinem XIV. XV. XVI. vnd XVII. Cap. beschrieben vnd von Martino Luthero . . . ausgelegt* (Leipzig: Lamberg, 1624).

43. *Florilegium sacrolutheranum, Das ist, Lutherisch Paradiessga[e]rtlein/Darinnen die furnemsten Spru[e]chlein Altes vnd Neues Testaments/sampt derselbigen Auslegungen von den H. Va[e]tern/wie dieselben im Register verzeichnet. Insonderheit aber/Des thewren Mannes/letzten Propheten/vnd dritten Eliae D. Martini Lutheri zu finden* (Leipzig: Gregor Risch, 1630).

quotations from the postils, Luther's biblical materials, and other works. Statius clearly wrote out of concern over the failure of many Christians to live the Christian life. His fifteen chapters on faith covered topics from "dead faith" to "true faith," from "saving faith" to the effects of faith. Faith, Statius showed through his citations, makes sinners into God's children who master sin, death, and the devil, and it unites them with Christ; it serves as a fountain of every kind of truly good work (which are treated in sixteen chapters on love and good works).[44]

Even when Luther citations were not used, it seemed good to mention his works as the source of the author's own meditations, as did Peter Columben in his *Christian Report from Holy Scripture and Luther's Books: How We Should Conduct Ourselves in Times of Pestilential Punishment. . . .*[45] In all such works interest in Luther's person retreated behind the pastoral concern to comfort, encourage, and admonish laypeople caught in the struggles of daily Christian life. They reflect a certain eschatological conviction regarding the tentativeness of life and regarding the devil and his power. Such works brought Luther's theology of repentance and consolation to bear on the lives of readers.

Individual tracts of Luther were also republished to cultivate the life of prayer and devotion among his followers.[46] Such devotional pieces

44. *Lutherus redivivus. Das ist: Lutheri Christenthumb Darinn der wahre lebendige Glaube/sein Vrsprung/Natur/Krafft vnd Wirckung/der waren Christen Majestaet/Herrligkeit/ Heiligkeit vnd Vereinigung mit Christo/wie auch jhr ungeferbte Liebe/vnd Christlichs leben/ mit Lutheri gantz herrlichen vnd geistrichen worten fu[e]r augen gestellet wird . . .* (Thorn: Franciscus Schnellboltz, 1626).

45. *No[e]tiger vnd Christlicher Bericht aus heiliger Go[e]ttlicher Schrifft vnd Lutheri Bu[e]chern zusammen gezogen/wie wir uns in Pestilentzischer Straffe/vnd geferlicher Todeszeit gegen unsern Frommen getrewen Gott/vnsern Nehesten/auch vnsere Seele vnd Leib (auff das Gott nicht ferner mu[e]ge erzu[e]rnet werden) verhalten sollen* (Magdeburg: Paul Donat, 1598).

46. E.g., *Ein einfeltige weise zu beten fu[e]r einen guten freund* had been issued in twenty-nine editions before Luther's death; thereafter in ten (Leipzig: Jacob Berwald, 1546; Nuremberg: Christoff Gutknecht, 1546; Leipzig: Valentin Babst, 1547, 1549, 1551, and Ernst Voegelin, 1561, 1565, 1568; Berlin: Michael Hentzer, 1579; n.p., 1569 [it was included in other works as well]). This tract was also reprinted by the superintendent of Coburg, Johannes Dinckel, along with three other tracts by Luther which set forth his interpretation of the Lord's Prayer, *Heiliges lehr vnd trostreiches Bett bu[e]chlein D. Martini Lutheri . . .* (Erfurt: Zacharias Zimmer, 1592).

Ob man fu[e]r dem sterben fliehen mu[e]ge. Martin Luther. Geschriben im Jar M.D. XXVII . . . appeared in at least twelve editions (Königsberg: Hans Lufft, 1549, as edited by Andreas Osiander; the edition of Hermann Butticher was more frequently reprinted: Leipzig: Georg Hantzsch, 1552, 1558; Nuremberg: Christoph Hessler, 1553; Wittenberg: Hans Lufft, 1564, and Johann Krafft, 1577, 1582; Dresden: Gimel Berger, 1581, 1582; Rostock: Christof Reussner, 1597; Goslar: Johan Vogt, 1609). It appeared also in Gervasius Marsteller's *Kurtzer vnd einfeltiger Bericht Wie man/so viel Gott gefellig/sich fu[e]r der grawsamen vnd schrecklicher Pestilentz bewaren . . .* (Uelzen: Michael Kroener, 1577), and Johann Eichmann's *Von dem ytzigen Sterben oder Pestilentz . . .* (Marburg: Andreas Collien, 1554). That also appeared in more refined forms and for instructional purposes. For example, in 1572 Rostock professor Johann Possel (1528–91) translated into Latin and Greek a sermon on prayer and another on preparing to die.[47] A variety of Luther's followers reproduced as tracts or portions of other works more-general aids for devotion, particularly biblical materials.[48] Thus Luther continued to provide many forms of meditational material for his followers.

Prayers

Alongside these collections of words of admonition and comfort from Luther stood collections of his prayers. Luther himself had recognized the need for an evangelical guide for prayer already in 1522; in fact, his Prayer Book, which has been called "not a formulary of prayer but a school of prayer," was republished (with revisions) some thirty times during his life, and in eight editions between his death and 1592, chiefly between 1553 and 1566.[49]

---

the republication of this tract was sometimes occasioned by specific need is suggested by the comment on the title page of Johann Krafft's 1577 edition, *Jtzo aber wegen der gegenwertigen beschwerlichen Leufften nachgedruckt.* Krafft included no other new comments nor a new preface.

To comfort those who faced death, Mansfeld pastor Stephan Agricola turned to Luther's Genesis Lectures and translated into German the comments on Abraham's death: *Christliche/tro[e]stliche Auslegung/D. Mart. Luthers/u[e]ber die Wort Genesis am 15. Capit. Vom Tode Abrahe. Aus der newen letzten Auslegung/u[e]ber dasselbige Buch/durch Vitum Dietrich/seligen/ausgangen* . . . (Leipzig: Wolf Guenter, 1551).

In 1547 the twenty-two-year-old son of the Wittenberg printer Georg Rhau died. To his dying son Rhau had read from the House Postil Luther's words on John 3:16. For his daughters he then edited a brief tract that included this excerpt: *Der Spruch Jhesu Christi Johan. am iij. Cap. Also hat Gott die Welt geliebet etc. Ausgelegt/durch D. Mart. Luther.* . . . It was reprinted several times (Wittenberg: Georg Rhau, 1546, 1547 [twice]; Nuremberg: Johann von Berg and Ulrich Neüber, 1548, 1566; Valentin Neüber, 1572; Leipzig: Ernst Voegelin, 1562, 1567, 1568; Hans Rhambau, 1565; Andreas Richter, 1566; Abraham Lamberg, 1597).

47. *LOGOI DUO . . . Dvae orationes Martini Lvtheri, vna de precatione: altera de praeparatione ad mortem pie obeundam: lectu dignissimae, Latine & Graece redditae* (Magdeburg: Matthaeus Giseken, 1572).

48. Brief comments from Luther's treatment of John 12:35a, 8:12a, 10:7, and 14:6 appeared shortly before his death, and were reprinted ten times by 1587: *Der Weg zum Ewigen Leben. Johannis am xiiij . . . D. Mart. Luther* (Leipzig: Nikolaus Berwald, c. 1550, 1570; Valentin Babst, c. 1555; Ernst Voegelin, 1561; n.p., 1569; Johann Beyer, 1577, 1582; Bautzen: Hans Wolrab, 1568; Nuremberg: Valentin Neüber, 1568; and in Low German, Hamburg: Jochin Loewe, 1587). For a similar, less popular publication of Luther's treatment of a single verse, see *Der Spruch Christi Matthei am xx. Capitel. Viel sind beruffen: aber wenig sind auserwelt* (Augsburg: Hans Zimmerman, 1548; Wittenberg: Georg Rhau, 1548; Leipzig: Valentin Babst, 1548).

49. "Ein Betbuchlein der 10. Gebote, des Glaubens, des Vaterunsers und des Ave Maria," *WA* 10.2:376–501. The description is that of Frieder Schulz, *Die Gebete Luthers: Edition, Bibliographie und Wirkungsgeschichte* (Gütersloh: Mohn, 1976), 17.

Luther had of course recorded many more prayers in his various writings than had been included in this collection; his followers recognized the value of assembling these other prayers for pious use. In 1565 Anton Otto, the Gnesio-Lutheran pastor in Nordhausen, decided to compile a collection of the Reformer's prayers based upon the Prayer Book of 1522. Otto culled sermons, the Table Talk, lectures on biblical books, and other writings for his collection. It also included material from others, including Amsdorf and Stolz. Ten editions of Otto's collection appeared before 1600.[50]

Another Gnesio-Lutheran, Peter Treuer, recognized the need to expand Otto's work. While in exile in Strassburg, where he had fled with Cyriakus Spangenberg when the counts of Mansfeld ousted the supporters of Matthias Flacius's view of original sin, Treuer composed his *Little Bell of Prayer of Doctor Martin Luther* (1579); it was reissued in 1580, 1591, and 1594, and revived through printings in 1600, 1610, 1621, and 1632. Treuer grouped into three chief parts the five hundred prayers and related materials which he had found scattered through the Jena edition. The first part, "preparation for prayers," included material from prayers based on each of the petitions of the Lord's Prayer, each of the Ten Commandments, and the Creed. The second section offered the reader prayers from Luther's pen, most brief, on a variety of subjects. Included were prayers for the effective working of God's Word, for an understanding of the Holy Spirit and God's grace, for protection for ourselves and our neighbors, for knowledge of ourselves and our sin, for the forgiveness of sins, true faith, and the grace to use the sacraments well, and for the preservation and spread of Christ's kingdom. Treuer also provided prayers against the devil, the godless world, our own flesh, the papacy, the Turk, and sects. He also gathered prayers on behalf of Christians being persecuted or engaged in spiritual struggles. He found prayers from Luther's pen for Christian obedience, brotherly love, redemption from every evil, and for all three estates. The third section offered prayers for the dying.[51]

Treuer's exhaustive compilation could not be matched. In 1582 his former colleague in Mansfeld, Caspar Melissander, abridged Treuer's work and published one hundred prayers by Luther. The two men had chosen different sides in the dispute over original sin which rent the Mansfeld ministerium in the 1570s, so Melissander did not give Treuer any credit for his work.[52] Anton Probus recognized a further need for a

50. Schulz, *Gebete,* 20–21, 84–87.

51. Ibid., 21–26, 87–90. See also Hans Volz, "Magister Peter Treuer aus Coburg, 'Exul Christi' und erster Sammler von Luthergebeten," *Zeitschrift für bayerische Kirchengeschichte* 39 (1970): 238–58.

52. Schulz, *Gebete,* 26–27, 91–97.

handbook of Luther's prayers a decade later and also used Treuer to construct his own guide to prayer.[53] Luther modeled prayer life for his followers, teaching them through these volumes how to pray their own prayers.

Biblical Comment

In the years immediately following Luther's death a flurry of excerpts from his briefer biblical comment appeared. The intent was to preserve his message and to give encouragement and inspiration to beleaguered Lutherans at the time of the Smalcald War and the Interims. Luther's interpretation of Psalm 118, the *Beautiful Confitemini* of 1530, had appeared in six printings before his death. Georg Rhau issued it again in 1546, 1548, and 1551, and other printers made it available five more times between 1550 and 1572.[54] Rhau also published Luther's sermons on John 14 and 15 at this time.[55] In 1551 Hieronymus Weller, Luther's student who spent his career as superintendent of schools in Freiberg in Saxony, edited Luther's comments on Psalms 22 and 23 from two decades earlier. Weller added his own suggestions for using the Psalms in times of spiritual struggle.[56] Under direction from Johann Aurifaber and others, the presses of Magdeburg produced a number of tracts which brought Luther's biblical interpretations to bear on this period of threat.[57] Translations of Luther's comments on the Minor Prophets seemed particularly helpful for Lutherans who felt the threats of the Counter-Reformation and Lutheran apostasy, for they viewed their sit-

53. Ibid., 28, 97–98.

54. *Das scho[e]ne Confitemini an der zal der CXVIII. Psalm . . .* (Wittenberg: Hans Lufft, 1546, 1548, 1551; Leipzig: Jacob Berwald, c. 1550; Valentin Babst, 1562; Ernst Voegelin, 1565; Nuremberg: Johann von Berg and Ulrich Neüber, 1558; Heinrichstadt: Conrad Horn, 1572).

55. *Das XIIII. vnd XV. Capitel S. Johannis: durch D. Mart. Luther Gepredigt vnd ausgelegt* (Wittenberg: Georg Rhau, 1548); see also *Das XVII. Capitel S. Johannis/Von dem Gebet Christi* (Magdeburg: Andreas Ghene, 1568).

56. *Brevis ac ervdita enarratio Psalmi XXII. et XXIII. a reverendo viro D. Doctore Martino Lvthero sanctae memoriae, conscripta anno xxxi. Nvnc primvm edita . . .* (Leipzig: Valentin Babst, 1551).

57. *Der ander Psalm Dauids . . .* (Magdeburg: Christian Rödinger, 1550); *D. Martini Luthers auslegung/vber den 129. Psalm Verdeutscht/zu diesen betru[e]bten zeiten fast nutzlich zu lesen . . .* (Magdeburg: Michael Lotter, 1550); *Der Spruch Esaie am XXXV. Ausgelegt aus den Schrifften D. Martini Luth. seliger gedechtnis* (Magdeburg: Michael Lotter, 1548); *Enarratio 53. Capitis Esaiae prophetae ex praelectionibus Reuerendi D. Martini Lutheri . . .*, ed. Georg Rörer and Stephen Tucher (Magdeburg: Lotther, 1550). Also coming from this period were *Etlicke scho[e]ne Predigen/Vth der ersten Epistel S. Johannis von der Leue. D. Mart. Luth.* (Lübeck: Johann Ballhorn, 1551 reprint [1533]); and *Das Gebet Mose/des Mans Gottes. Der XC. Psalm. Durch/D. Mart. Luther . . .*, trans. Johannes Spangenberg (Wittenberg: Rhau, 1546; Leipzig: Johann Martoff, 1572; Low German, trans. Paul Knufflock [Lübeck: Asser Kroeger, 1567]).

uation as parallel to that of the beleaguered Old Testament people of God.[58]

The most energetic of those students of Luther who in the decades immediately following his death continued to edit unpublished materials from his pen was Andreas Poach, pastor in Erfurt and later in Utenbach near Jena. When his close friend Georg Rörer was near death, he gave Poach his notes on Luther's interpretation of John 18–20, and Poach made his first attempt at editing. Johann Stolz, the Saxon court preacher who had been instrumental in shepherding the Jena edition to the press, approved Poach's work and had Nikolaus von Amsdorf write a preface for it. Believing that with practice his editorial skills had improved over the following decade, Poach reissued this work in 1565.[59] More practice he had indeed acquired, for in the intervening years he had reproduced from Rörer's notes a sermon of Luther on Titus 2 and four on 1 Corinthians 15. In the 1570s Poach went on to edit Luther's comments on Psalm 8 and on Colossians 1.[60]

58. Amsdorf brought two such volumes to press: *Der Prophet Joel durch Doct. Mart. L. in Latinischer sprach gelesen vnd ausgelegt Vnd newlich verdeudscht etc.* (Jena, 1553); *Eine Predigt aus dem Comment des heiligen vnd trewen Dieners Christi Lutheri vber das fu[e]nfft capitel Hosee gezogen in rechtschaffenen vnd falscher Busse* (Jena: Donatus Richtzenhan, 1562). Also of note is *Ein Predigt aus den Schrifften Lutheri vber die Propheten gezogen. Das Deudsche land wie Israel Judea vnd Jerusalem wird zersto[e]rt vnd verwu[e]stet werden vmb gleicher Su[e]nde willen* (Jena: Thomas Rebart, 1562). Stephan Reich, who had studied in Wittenberg in the early 1530s, translated the Micah lectures originally published by Veit Dietrich in Latin: *Ein Christliche/Tro[e]stliche/vnd sehr Nu[e]tzliche Ausslegung/ vber den Propheten Micham. Auss der Lectionibus des Ehrwirdigen Herrn vnd Vatters/Doctor Martini Luthers/seliger gedechtnus/zusammen ordentlich getragen vnd ins Latein gebracht/Erstlichen durch Herrn Veit Dieterich . . . Jetzt mit fleiss auss dem Latein verdeutscht* . . . (Königsberg: Johann Daubmann, 1555).

59. *Das XVIII. XIX. vnd XX. Capitel S. Johannis Vom Leiden/Sterben vnd Aufferstehung vnsers HERRN Jhesu Christi. Gepredigt vnd ausgelegt/durch D. Martin Lvther/Anno M.D. XXVIII. vnd XXIX. Auffs new vbersehen/vnd zusamen bracht* . . . (Erfurt: Georg Baumann, 1565), [*vij]^{v}–[*viij]^{r}. The first edition was published as *Das achtzehend vnd neunzehend Capitel/vnd ein Stu[e]k aus dem zwentzigsten S. Johannis von dem Leiden/Sterben/ vnd Aufferstehung vnsers Herrn Jhesu Christi. Gepredigt vnd ausgelegt durch Doc. Mart. Luther* . . . (Jena: Heirs of Christian Rödinger, 1557).

60. *Von unser seligen Hoffnung/Aus der Epistel S. Pauli/Tit. 2. Cap. Durch D. Martinum Luther/gepredigt zu Kemberg/xix. Augusti/Anno M.D. XXXI. Vnd jtzt allererst aus M. Georgen Ro[e]rers/seliger/geschriebenen Bu[e]cheren/zusamen bracht vnd zugericht/Vor nie im druck ausgangen* (Erfurt: Georg Baumann, 1561); *Vier Predigten/Von der Todten Aufferstehung/vnd letzten Posaunen Gottes/Aus dem 15. Cap. der 1. Epistel S. Pauli/an die Corinther/ Gepredigt von dem Ehrwirdigen Herrn vnd thewren Mann Gottes/D. Martin Luther zu Wittenberg/Anno 1544. vnd 45. . . . Vor nie im Druck ausgangen/Vnd jetzt newlich aus M. Georgen Ro[e]rers geschriebenen Bu[e]cher zusamen bracht* (Erfurt: Georg Baumann, 1564; Esaias Mechler, 1570 reprint; Hamburg: Elias Hutter, 1592 reprint); *Der Achte Psalm Davids/gepredigt vnd ausgelegt durch Martin Luther/Anno 1537. Vor nie in Druck ausgangen* . . . (Mühlhausen: Hantzsch, 1572); *Von Jhesu Christo/Warem Gott vnd Menschen/vnd von seinem Ampt vnd Reich/so er fu[e]hrt in der Christenheit. Zwo Predigten D. Martini*

Comparable fresh editing, this time from the notes of Veit Dietrich, brought Luther's comments on Psalms 1–25, and others, to the press in 1560. Basilius Faber, the Gnesio-Lutheran school rector who helped compile the *Magdeburg Centuries* and translated half of Luther's Genesis commentary into German for the Wittenberg edition, completed this work.[61] The occasional publication of similar biblical materials in the 1560s and 1570s is difficult to classify.[62] Individual theologians or printers thought they recognized a need, so they produced for their contemporaries materials from Luther's biblical comments. No greater market for such publications developed.

In the period before the Thirty Years' War at least two volumes of biblical helps were produced from Luther's exegesis. In 1561 Jacob Hertel, a deacon in Basel who worked with local printers, published, on the basis of Luther's interpretations of specific passages, a study of allegories, types, and examples from the Old and New Testaments.[63] In 1610 Abel Nezenius, formerly a pastor in Braunschweig, then a member of the arts faculty at Jena, turned to the commentaries which Luther had produced on the Pentateuch for little snippets of insight into individual passages.[64] Such books, along with the various kinds of biblical interpretation found in the collected works available to the public, continued to cultivate Luther's understanding of Scripture among his followers. Nonetheless, in time the commentaries of his students became more frequently used as guides for pastors' study of the biblical texts.

Lutheri/aus der Epistel S. Pauli/Colos: Cap. 1. Gepredigt zu Wittenberg/Anno Domini. 1537. Vor dem Munde Lutheri auffgefangen sind/zusammenbracht/vnd in Druck verfertigt (Mühlhausen: Georg Hantzsch, 1579).

61. *Vber die ersten fu[e]nff vnd zweintzig vnd etliche folgende Psalmen/kurtze vnd richtige Ausslegungen/des Ehrwirdigen Herrn/D. Mart. Luth. Mit Christlichem fleiss durch M. Vitem Dietrich . . . Vnd vormals nie in Truck aussgangen. Auss dem Latein trewliche verdeutscht* (Nuremberg: Johann von Berg and Ulrich Neüber, 1560).

62. E.g., in 1579 Georg Coelestin, court preacher in Berlin, supervised the printing of a number of "classics," including Luther's preface to Romans, which was published as *Praefatio methodica totius scripturae in epist: Pauli ad Romanos e vernacula Doct: Mart: Luth: 1523. in latinum . . .* (Berlin: Michael Hentzker, 1579). Franz Scharschmidt produced *Eine Predigt D. Martini Lutheri/Vber diese Wort/Jm Anfang war das Wort/etc. Johannis j. . . .* (Wittenberg, 1562). Other such publications include *Comment/Oder Ausslegung/ weiland des Ehrwirdigen Herren Doctor Martin Luthers/vber den CXXVII. Psalm . . .*, trans. Erhardt Krauss (Strassburg: Christian Mueller, 1563); *Das XVII. Capitel S. Johannis/Von dem Gebet Christi* (Magdeburg: Andreas Ghena, 1568); and *Ein Sermon D. Martini Luthers/Auff das Evangelium Marci am. letzten Da die Elff zu Tisch sassen/offenbart sich jn der HERR Christus/vnd schalt jren vnglauben vnd jres hertzen hertigkeit . . .* (Wittenberg: Clemens Schleich and Anton Schoen, 1574).

63. *Allegoriarum, Typarum, et exemplorvm veteris & noui Testamenti Libri duo: Nunc primum ex omnibus Latinis operibus reuerendi Patris D. Martini Lvtheri . . .* (Basel, 1561). See p. 198.

64. *D. Mart. Lutheri Operationum Biblicarum singularis exercitationis Pars Prima. Super quinque Mosis libros, legales . . .* (Jena: Christoph Lippold, 1610).

Social Thought

Luther's understanding of the Scriptures also guided the daily Christian life of his followers. They turned to certain of his writings to address critical societal issues as well. Occasionally it was thought worthwhile to have Luther speak out again on marriage and family.[65] At the end of the century a pastor in Württemberg, Thomas Buck, composed *A Mirror of Marriage,* "a very funny and instructive comedy" on raising children and conducting a household. His lines were largely drawn from Luther's works duly annotated in the margins.[66]

Luther's words could be used to address a number of societal problems, for example, greed, selfishness, usury, drunkenness, anger and revenge.[67] One of the most vexing social problems of the time, particularly for pastors in commercial centers, was that of usury. Luther had expressed himself decisively in his opposition to early forms of capitalist enterprise, and his thoughts on interest and related matters were brought to the public's awareness from time to time in the half century after his death.[68] Realization of the welfare of society demanded more

65. Stephan Agricola, pastor in Mansfeld, translated remarks about marriage from Luther's commentary on Psalm 128: *Der CXXVIII. Psalm . . . Vom heiligen Ehestande. Durch Doctor Mart. Luther ausgelegt . . .* (Leipzig: Wolfgang Guenter, 1552). Georg Buchholzer in Berlin published *Ein scho[e]ner Sermon oder predigt vonn dem Ehestande/durch den Ehrwirdigen Vater Doctorem Martinum Lutherum/heiliger vnd seliger gedechtnis/zu Wittenberg gepredigt/vormals desgleichen nie ausgangen oder gedruckt worden . . .* (1560). Johann Pfeil, pastor in Schwalbach, constructed *loci communes* on marriage from Luther citations, *Schatzkammer Vnd Heuratsteur dess heiligen Geistes Darinnen zu lehrnen alles was einem jeden Christen Menschen vom heiligen Ehestande zu wissen von no[e]ten ist/Auss den Operibus dess Ehrwirdigen Hochgelarten Herrn/Doctor Martini Lutheri . . . gezogen* (Frankfurt/Main: Paul Reffeler, 1565). Material from Luther and his colleague Johannes Bugenhagen appeared as *Von Ehesachen D. Mart. Luth. Jtem. Vom Ehebruch vnd Weglauffen D. Johan Bugenhagen . . .* (Wittenberg: Georg Muller, 1592). See also *Eine Christliche Hochzeit Predigt vber den Spruch zun Hebreern am dreyzehenden Capitel . . .* (Jena: Johann Weidner, 1608).

66. *Ehespiegel. Ein sehr lustige vnd lehrhaffte Comedi/darinnen angezeigt wu[e]rdt: Wie die Eltern jhre Kinder auffziehen vnd verheyraten: Vnd welcher massen das jung Gesind/ beides im ledigen Stand/vnd hernach in wehrenden Ehe sich verhalten solle. Aus dem lebendigen kra[e]fftigen Wort Gottes/den Schrifften Lutheri/vnd andern guten Bu[e]chern gezogen . . .* (Tübingen: Georg Gruppenbach, 1598).

67. E.g., *Eine Predigt D. Martini Luthers. Von Nu[e]chterkeit vnnd Messigkeit Widder vo[e]llerey vnd Trunckenheit. Aus der Epistel S. Petri . . .* (Erfurt: Barbara Sachsse, 1552). Amsdorf brought out *Fu[e]nff Predigten D. Martini Lutheri/von den fu[e]nff Heubtsu[e]nden . . . das vmb solcher Su[e]nde willen Gott jtziger zeit Deudschland billich straffe* (Jena: Christian Rödinger, 1554).

68. *Vom wucher vnd widerkeufflichen Zinsen. D. Martinus Luther* (Magdeburg: Michael Lotter, c. 1552); *De vsvra taxanda ad pastores ecclesiarum commonefactio D. Mart. Lutheri,* trans. Johann Freder (1540) (Frankfurt/Main: Peter Brubach, 1554); *Von Kauffhandlung vnd wucher Martinus Luther. Auff das Newe Gedruckt* (Hamburg: Hans Binder, 1579).

than the suppression of vice, however. It demanded the cultivation of virtue and learning. Nonetheless, Luther's support of schools was brought only seldom to the public's attention.[69]

Luther's writings on the Jews were of little interest to his followers in the years after his death. When tensions mounted between Christians and Jews in Leipzig, however, Nikolaus Selnecker was prepared to serve the cause of some parishioners. He announced his distress at the "secretive and tricky" way in which some citizens in commercial centers were trying to suppress Luther's strong criticism of the Jews, and so he reissued *On the Jews and Their Lies, On Shem-Hamphoras, and Against the Sabbatarians* in 1577.[70] That this was the only republication of Luther's diatribes against the Jews suggests that his followers almost never viewed Luther as a tool to be used to campaign against them. The Reformer's writings on the Turkish peril also found little resonance among his followers. However, three times in the 1590s, when Turkish forces again threatened German lands, Luther's perspective on the Turkish threat seemed useful to preachers, who used Luther's words to call their contemporaries to repentance.[71]

Luther's comments on the calling of the governing authorities were also put to use from time to time in varying ways in the years after his death. In 1559 comments from the House Postil were republished to help

69. "To the Councillors of All Cities in Germany That They Establish and Maintain Christian Schools," trans. Vincent Opsopaeus (1528), in Nikolaus Selnecker, *Notatio . . . De studio sacrae Theologiae* (Leipzig: Johann Rhamba, 1579; Strassburg: Jodocus Martin, 1591 reprint); *Ein Gu[e]lden Kleinod . . . Anno 1524 . . . den Bu[e]rgermeistern vnnd Ratherrn/allen Sta[e]dte Deutsches Landes insonderheit verehret hat . . .* (Nuremberg: Alexander Dietrich, c. 1590; Nuremberg, 1600 reprint); *Libellus Martini Lutheri, de constituendis scholis Latine redditus . . .* (Hildesheim: Gossel, 1620); *Trewhertzige Vermahnung/An die Bu[e]rgermeister vnd Rhatherrn aller Sta[e]dte Deutsches Landes/das sie Christliche Schulen auffrichten vnd halten sollen/Mart. Luth. Doct. . . . ,* ed. Christopher Helwig and Joachim Jung, professors from the University of Giessen (Magdeburg: Wendelin Pohl, 1621).

70. *Von den Ju[e]den vnd jren Lu[e]gen. Vom Schem-Hamphoras der Ju[e]den/vnd von Geschlecht Christi. Wider die Sabbather/vnd der Ju[e]den Lu[e]gen vnd betrug. Durch D. Martinum Lutherum . . .* (Leipzig: Heirs of Jacob Berwald, 1577).

71. *Heerpredigt D. Martin Luthers/wider den Tu[e]rcken . . .* (n.p., 1593), reprinted in *Weissagung Des heiligen Propheten Obadiae von dem endlichen vntergang der Edomiter . . . Desgleichen Eine Heerpredigt wider den Tu[e]rcken durch D. M. Luther beschrieben* (Ursel: Nicolaus Henricus, 1594); *Antiturcica Lutheri: Das ist/Vom Kriege vnd Gebet wider den Tu[e]rcken/vnd von desselben Alcoran: etliche Schrifften/dess thewren vnd werthen Mannes Gottes/Doctoris Martini Lutheri . . . Sampt angehengten etlichen dess Herren D. Lutheri Propheceyungen/von dem ku[e]nfftigen grossen Vnglu[e]ck vber Deutschland,* ed. Johannes Rosinus, pastor in Naumburg (Leipzig, 1595). This work contained similar material by other Lutheran theologians as well. Three decades earlier Georg Major, dean of the Wittenberg theologians at the time, had issued *Vom Kriege Wider den Turcken Doct. Mart. Luth. Anno XXVIII. Mit einer Vorrede Doct. Georg. Maior* (Wittenberg: Hans Lufft, 1566).

both temporal and ecclesiastical authorities understand their proper roles in adjudicating disputes within the church.[72] Far more significant, at the time of the Smalcald War immediately after Luther's death, the evangelical princes who led the Smalcald League called on his writings to play a significant part in their propaganda effort. The publication of his seventy propositions "on the three hierarchies" or estates helped explain why the pope should not be interfering in German affairs and making the emperor his lackey.[73] Along with a number of other pamphlets from Luther's pen, his *Warning to His Dear German People* appeared in print a number of times during the period of the war (1546–47). It was also reprinted in 1552 and 1553, at the time when the Protestant party's renewed military maneuvers against Emperor Charles V resulted in the Truce of Passau (1552) and the subsequent negotiations which led to the Peace of Augsburg (1555).[74]

The Thirty Years' War elicited at least two republications of Luther's *Warning to His Dear German People* against emperor and pope,[75] as well as a pseudonymous argument which relied on Luther for support of

72. *Was Geistliche vnd Weltliche Obrigkeit/wider die offentliche Laster/zu thun schuldig ist/mit vnterscheidt beider Obrigkeit Ampt/vnd straffen. Aus der Hausspostil D. Lutheri . . .* (Eisleben: Urban Gaubisch, 1559).

73. *Septvaginta propositiones dispvtandae. De tribus hierarchijs, Ecclesiastica, Politica, Oeconomica: & quod Papa sub nulla istarum sit, sed omnium publicus hostis. D. Martinus Lutherus.* (Basel, 1546; Frankfurt/Main: Hermann Guelfferich, 1546; Lübeck: Johann Balhorn, 1546; in German translation, Nuremberg: Georg Wachter, 1546; and Wittenberg: Georg Rhau, 1546).

74. *Warnunge D. Martini Luth. An seine lieben Deudschen* (Augsburg: Valentin Otmar, 1546; Nuremberg: Johann von Berg and Ulrich Neüber, 1546; Hans Daubmann, 1546; Strassburg: Wendelin Rihel, 1546; Tübingen: Ulrich Morhart, 1546; Wittenberg: Hans Lufft, 1546, 1547). In the 1550s it was reprinted several times (Rostock: Ludwig/Dietz, 1552; Nuremberg: Hermann Hamsing, 1553; Christoph Heussler, 1556, 1557). Among the other tracts which appeared at the time of the Smalcald War were *Ein Rhatschlag Doctoris Martini Luther/Ob dem Keiser/so er jemants mit gewalt/des Evangelij halben/vberziehen wolte/mit rechte widerstandt geschehen mo[e]ge . . .* (Berlin: Hans Weiss, 1546; Dresden: Matthes Stoeckel the Elder, 1546; Leipzig: Michael Blum, 1546; Nikolaus Wolrab, 1546; Nuremberg: Johann von Berg and Ulrich Neüber, 1546; Regensburg: Hans Kohl, 1546; and n.p., 1550); *Etliche Schlu[e]sse D. Mart. Luth. Das man dem Bapst vnd seinem Schutzherrn wider vnrechte gewalt vnd Kriege/widerstand thu[e]n sol* (Wittenberg: Georg Rhau, 1546); and *Erklerung D. Mart. Lutheri von der frage/die Notwehr belangend* (Magdeburg: Michael Lotther, 1547; Wittenberg: Hans Lufft, 1547). On the entire propaganda effort of the Smalcald League at this time, see Oskar Waldeck, "Die Publizistik des Schmalkaldischen Krieges," *Archiv für Reformationsgeschichte* 7 (1909–10): 1–55; 8 (1910–11): 44–133.

75. *Hertzenswuntsch vnd allergetreuste Warnung des hocherleuchten Manns Gottes . . . Martin Luthers an seine liebe Teutschen . . . aus bemelter Warnung vnd andern . . . Schrifften Martin Luthers extrahirt* (n.p., 1620); *Alter Deutsche Trew/Lautere Warheit/vnd Wahre Auffrichtigkeit. Allen Getrewen Patrioten der Deutschen Redligkeit/vnd hertzen Freunden der Go[e]ttlichen Warheit/bey jtzigen Kriegsu[e]chtigen Zeiten wiederumb zu gute herfu[e]r gerbracht . . .* (Wittenberg, 1627).

Lutheran self-defense.[76] But Lutherans in that period also called upon Luther to reinforce a more pacifist stance, which corresponded to the policy of leading Lutheran princes such as the electors of Saxony and Brandenburg. The Hessian pastor Hermann Schipper composed his *Luther in Exile* in 1623 because young men who were entering the pastoral ministry neither knew nor cared about Luther. They were seeking "new, deeper" theologians, and thus they were falling from one error into another and were following the wise of the world who wanted to save the church and the gospel through the sword. Citing Luther's criticism of lawyers and councilors at court, Schipper opposed taking military action against the emperor in defense of the Lutheran faith. He argued instead that Christians must be prepared to endure the cross and suffering on behalf of their faith. Schipper ignored Luther's later conversion to a position which justified resistance to the emperor by lesser magistrates, and so he republished only Luther's *Admonition to Peace,* his *On the Twelve Articles of the Peasants,* his *Against the Robbing, Murdering Hordes of Peasants,* and his *Whether Soldiers, Too, Can Be Saved.*[77] Perhaps Luther's voice on the issue of resistance contributed more to the popular mind in the seventy-five years after his death than did his comments on other societal issues. Nonetheless, his views did not determine the actions of those who bore his name in the critical years around 1620. Instead, Luther's views were merely cited in support of policies that had already been decided upon and implemented.

Prophetic Prediction

Throughout the period after Luther's death Lutherans had listened more closely to his prophetic warnings about the fate of the church and society under God's coming judgment. Such warnings were viewed by his followers above all as prophetic predictions of what was to come for those Germans who had heard the gospel from Luther and then turned away from it. God's judgment on Luther's foes provided his followers the encouragement of knowing that God was on his side. Thus in the second half of the sixteenth century, Lutherans not only relished the Reformer's writings of comfort and consolation, but also cherished his proclamation of divine wrath and judgment, for it helped them understand the trials which followed the Smalcald War, when the Lutheran faith seemed threatened with extinction at the hands of Charles V's troops. At the end of the war Luther's sermon on the destruction of Jerusalem, in which he

76. *Christi Jesu des HERRN aller Herrn/durch Doctorn Lutherum. Gewiss vnd vbergewiss Defension, Sieg vnd Triumph Werck . . . auss Christi vnd Lutheri Rustkammer vnd Schrifften colligirt vnd verfasset Durch Sicomorobanten Lomonymum siderea* (n.p., 1619).

77. *Lvthervs Exvlans. Der ins Elend vnschuldig vertriebene Luther . . .* (Strassburg: Christoph von der Heyden, 1623), Aij^r–22.

had warned Germany of a similar fate, was reprinted. First published in 1525, it had appeared thirteen times in the turbulent period at the end of the Peasants' Revolt, and was issued once again in 1540. It must have seemed particularly appropriate to those who read it in 1547. For it assured them that God was governing according to his own will and plan even when it seemed that his enemies had triumphed.[78]

About the same time Johannes Timann (or Amsterdam), pastor in Hamburg, gathered from Luther's comments on a number of biblical books, including Genesis, Psalms, Hosea, and Micah, many of his prophetic proclamations of judgment and comfort. Timann believed that the Holy Spirit had raised Luther up as the third Elijah and that he had spoken directly of the disasters befalling Germany in the wake of the Smalcald War.[79]

At the same time Anton Otto, pastor in Nordhausen, was also gathering Luther's prophecies. Like the prophet Micah, Luther had been called to prophesy nothing but evil for succeeding generations. But, Otto was certain, he had spoken only the truth. Otto grouped the prophecies under five topics: public teaching, sects, punishment for contempt of God's Word, the pope, and the papal council. He drew very brief prophetic citations from a large number of Luther's tracts and books.[80] In the same vein, in 1554 the printer Hermann Hamsing issued a brief admonition from Luther regarding the last times.[81] His little tract and the

78. *Ain scho[e]ne Christliche Prophetische Sermon vnd Predig/vor etlichen iaren von einem Gotsgelerten mann vnd Apostel der Teutschen gepredigt/von der zersto[e]rung Jerusalem. Das auch das Teutschland also zersto[e]rt werden solle/wo es die zeyt seiner heimsuchung nicht erkennet. Was der Tempel Gottes sei. D. M. L.* (n.p., 1547). On collections of Luther's prophecies and their usage in and impact on the second half of the sixteenth century, see Robin Bruce Barnes, *Prophecy and Gnosis: Apocalypticism in the Wake of the Lutheran Reformation* (Stanford: Stanford University Press, 1988), 36–53; and Wolfgang Sommer, "Luther—Prophet der Deutschen und der Endzeit: Zur Aufnahme der Prophezeiungen Luthers in der Theologie des älteren deutschen Luthertums," in *Zeitenwende—Zeitenende: Beiträge zur Apokalyptik und Eschatologie,* ed. Wolfgang Sommer (Stuttgart: Kohlhammer, 1997), 109–28.

79. *Prophetiae aliqvot verae: Et sententiae insignes reuerendi patris, Domini Doctoris Martini Lutheri, Tercij Helie: De calamitatibus, defectione, & Tenebris, Germaniae obuenturis, eo in Domino mortuo, & perpetuo viuente* (n.p., 1550; Magdeburg: Michael Lotter, 1552), A2^{r}–A4^{v}; *Etliche warhafftige weissagung/vnd fu[e]rneme spruche des Ehrwirdigen Vaters/Hern Doctor Martini Luthers . . .*, trans. Albert Christian (Magdeburg: Michael Lotter, 1552).

80. *Etliche Propheceyspru[e]che D. Martini Lutheri/Des dritten Elias* (Magdeburg: Michael Lotter, 1552), Aij^{r}. Otto drew his prophetic material above all from Luther's *Against Henry, King of England; Answer on the Alleged Imperial Edict; On the Councils and the Church; Against the Roman Papacy, Founded by the Devil;* the Church Postil; the House Postil; and comments on Psalms 110 and 118, John 17, Matthew 5, and 1 Corinthians 15.

81. *Ein erinnerung vnd ermanung D. Martini Luthers des Man Gottes/Von den letzten schweren zeyten geschryben* (Nuremberg, 1554; Schleusingen, 1555).

somewhat longer collections of Timann and Otto fed the apocalyptic hopes and fears of their readers and found a ready market because Luther's followers shared his belief that the eschaton was at hand.

In the late 1550s two other collections of Luther's prophetic warnings (both from outside Gnesio-Lutheran circles) superseded the florilegia of Timann and Otto. Peter Glaser, pastor in Dresden, gathered 120 prophecies from a wide variety of Luther's writings. Seventeen years later he reissued this work, having improved it with the addition of 80 more prophecies and an index of the punishments which Luther had predicted would fall upon Germany in part because of the derelictions of the prince.[82]

Even more popular was the collection of prophecies which Georg Walther, deacon in Halle, gathered with Melanchthon's help. In the preface of his collection, dedicated to Elector August of Saxony, Walther observed that God had given Germany its own great prophet to call the land to repentance. However, the Germans, like the ancient Ninevites after Jonah, had regressed into impenitence as the years had passed, and forgotten the teaching and warning of "our third Elijah, Dr. Martin Luther." Walther set about to correct that situation. He reminded his readers that Luther had been predicted by pious men from Ambrose and Augustine to Huss and Hilten, and that as a hero and prophet he had opposed both the Roman Antichrist and the sects. Therefore his prophecies deserved to be taken to heart, for they would guide the way to both temporal and especially eternal blessings. Failure to hear and heed these prophecies would bring God's judgment upon those who had contempt for this word of God.[83] Unlike Glaser, Walther followed Otto's example and arranged the prophecies by topic, including prophecies on God's Word, pious and faithful preachers, schools, false preachers, books, the papacy, temporal authority, Germany, the Turk, greed and usury, and pride and luxury. Walther's work was incorporated into later editions of the Table Talk and thus gained widespread use.

In 1563 Basilius Faber wrote his own words of prophecy and comfort for a friend, Andreas Gerhardt, on the death of his daughter. In addition

82. *Hundert vnd zwanzig Propheceyunge/oder Weissagung/des Ehrwirdigen Vaters Herrn Doctoris Martini Luthers/von allerley straffen/so nach seinem tod vber Deutschland von wegen desselbigen grossen/vnd vielfaltigen Su[e]nden kommen solten . . .* (Eisleben: Urban Gaubisch, 1557); revised as *Zwey Hundert Propheceyunge oder weissagunge/des thewren Mans D. Martini Lutheri/von allerley Straffen/welche Deutschland nach seinem Tode/von wegen desselbigen vielfaltigen vnd grossen Su[e]nden vberfallen sollen* (Bautzen: Michael Wolrab, 1574).

83. *Prophezeiungen D. Martini Lutheri. Zur erinnerung vnd anreitzung zur Christlichen Busse/ordentlich vnd mit vleis zusamen getragen* (Wittenberg: Lorentz Schwenck, 1559), aij[r]–[bviij][v].

to an "appendix of warnings and prophecies of Dr. Martin Luther concerning Germany," much of Faber's "Christian Instructions on the Final Happenings of the World" consisted of Luther's utterances regarding both the coming judgment and the solace which believers have in waiting for the Lord. Faber balanced his discussion of the last judgment and hell with words of advice on how to die and words of consolation regarding the resurrection of the dead and eternal joy in heaven. Faber's work differed from the previous collections in its inclusion of material from others and his own meditation. Its popularity, however, may well have been due to its rich presentation of Luther's words from a variety of sources, among them the postils, his comments on 1 Corinthians 15 and several verses in John's Gospel, his sermons delivered at Smalcald in 1537, other biblical comment, and a variety of treatises. Faber's work was reprinted at least fifteen times between 1565 and 1596,[84] a reflection of its usefulness in explaining to the pious how to find comfort in troubled times through hope in God's decisive intervention on their behalf.

In spite of the availability of Faber's work, Johann Lapaeus, a village pastor who in the early 1560s had studied in Jena under Flacius and his comrades, published a new collection of Luther's prophecies in order to bring his call for repentance and the comfort of the gospel to the people of Germany. In 1578, a time when the Formula of Concord was being disseminated and doctrinal controversies were plaguing Lapaeus and his church (his adherence to Flacius's teaching had cost him two pastoral positions), he brought the message of God's faithful watchman and prophet to print once again. He reviewed testimonies from Luther himself as well as from late medieval figures who were thought to have prophesied of Luther, namely John Huss and John Hilten. To these were added praise for Luther's prophetic gifts from his contemporaries—Friedrich Myconius, Johannes Bugenhagen, Nikolaus von Amsdorf, Johannes Brenz, Joachim Mörlin, Urbanus Rhegius, Hieronymus Weller, Erasmus Alber, Johannes Wigand, Tilemann Hesshus, Andreas Musculus, Johann Marbach, and Georg Fabricius—to prove that Luther had indeed been a prophet. Lapaeus then reprinted prophecies

84. *Allerley Christliche/no[e]tige vnd nu[e]tzliche vnterrichungen/von den letzten Hendeln der Welt/Als: Vom Ju[e]ngsten tage/vnd wie man sich darzu bereiten sol. Vom Sterben. Von aufferstehungen der Todten. Vom ju[e]ngsten Gericht. Vom Himel vnd ewigen leben. Vnd von der Helle. Mit angehenckten warnungen vnd Prophezeiungen D. Mart. Luthers/ Deutschland betreffende* (Eisleben: Urban Gaubisch, 1565). Except for a printing in Quedlinburg (1569) and a Low German translation (Hamburg: Jacob Wulff, 1591), all of the later editions were published in Leipzig (Ernst Vögelin, 1569, 1575; Hans Steinmann, 1574, 1575, 1578, 1579, 1582, 1587; Johann Rhambau, 1579; Johann Beyer, 1584; Zacharias Berwaldt, 1587, 1594, 1596; and Bartholomaeus Voigt, 1596).

from a wide variety of the Reformer's works.[85] In 1592 he reproduced this material, this time organized into six sections. The first dealt with Luther's prophetic call. The remaining five presented citations from his works regarding the ingratitude and sinfulness of the German people, the destruction of true religion, the temporal punishment which God was visiting upon Germany, the warnings to the Germans, and the last day.[86] In 1595 the Lübeck publisher Johann Balhorn issued a brief excerpt from Lapaeus's work, with the suggestion that readers then turn to Lapaeus's work itself.[87]

Apart from these collections Luther's prophetic utterances were put to use for various other purposes. For example, on the basis of the appearance of a comet in 1577/1578 Christoph Irenaeus issued a general warning against his opponents in the discussion of original sin and supported his call for repentance with prophecies from Luther.[88] Luther was also enlisted in the battle against the Gregorian calendar on the basis of his *On the Councils and the Church,* which included a critique of the papal use of the Nicene Council's decrees regarding the date on which Easter should be celebrated.[89] Nor did use of the Reformer's prophecies end with the passing of his students' generation. In 1632 and again in 1662 his prophetic utterances were employed as a call to repentance, a warning, and a means of providing comfort and edification.[90]

85. *Warhafftige Prophezeiungen des thewren Propheten/vnd Heiligen Manns Gottes/D. Martini Lutheri seliger Gedechtnis Darinnen er den jetzigen kleglichen Zustandt Deutscher Nation/die Zersto[e]runge der Kirchen/Verfelschunge der Lere/vielerley grewliche Straffen Gottes/den Ju[e]ngsten tag/vnd anders dergleichen mehr eygentlich zuuor verku[e]ndiget hat. Dem gantzen Deutschlandt zur Warnung/vnd allen betru[e]bten Christen zu Christlichem Vnterricht vnd Trost/aus allen seinen Schrifften vleissig zusamen gezogen* (Ursel: Nicolaus Henrici, 1578), c[r]–dij[r].

86. *Propheceiung Des Thewren Propheten vnd seligen Mannes Gottes D. Martini Lutheri/ Darinnen er vns Deutschen ernstlich erinnert/vnserer 1. Gnedigen Heimsuchung 2. Schrecklichen Vndancks 3. Kleglichen zustands der Religion 4. Grewlichen straffen Gottes/mit angehengter 5. Warnung zur buss/Vnd Verku[e]ndigung des Ju[e]ngsten tages . . .* (Eisleben: Urban Gaubisch, 1592).

87. *Practica vnd Prognosticon/Oder erschreckliche Propheceyhung Doct. Martini Luthers/des ausserwehleten Ru[e]stzeugs vnd Propheten des Deutschlands/Vnd der letzten Posaunen Gottes . . .* (Lübeck: Johann Balhorn, 1595).

88. *Prognosticon Aus Gottes Wort no[e]tige Erinnerung/Vnd Christliche Busspredigt zu dieser letzten bo[e]sen Zeit . . . Auf den Cometen/so von Martini des 1577. Jars/biss zum Eyngang des 1578. Jars gesehen . . .* (n.p., 1578). See Sommer, "Luther—Prophet," 120–22.

89. *Herrlich Bedencken/Des tewren Mannes Gottes Lutheri seligen/von dem jetzund newen Bepstischen Calender/Daraus grundlich zuuernemen/Das der Mann/als ein rechter Prophet/die aus jtzigen Bepstischen Calender entstehende zuru[e]ttunge/vnd verbitterunge der hertzen/zuuor im Geist geschehen . . .* (n.p., 1584); this work is cited in *WA* 50:508.

90. See Sommer, "Luther—Prophet," 122–27, for discussion of Johann Saubert's collection of Luther's prophecies (1632) and Johann Michael Dillher's use of them in a larger collection (1662).

These collections of Luther's prophecies probably did more to bring Luther's message of law and gospel to the people of the latter half of the century than did the reprinting of individual works. Glaser and Walther were members of the electoral Saxon ministerium, although not part of its Philippist leadership. The other editors of these prophetic collections were associated more or less closely with the Gnesio-Lutheran party and its high eschatological sensitivities. Eschatological expectations and apocalyptic tensions continued to run high among the German populace, and Luther's interpretation of God's will and plan offered much comfort. The collections of his prophetic utterances gave preachers a ready catalog of material both for condemning sins and for giving comfort to those who feared the forces which were changing the face of Europe in their time. This was the chief goal of bringing Luther's writings to the populace. His followers believed that if he was to continue to have an impact on the people, it had to come through application of his message to the situations of their daily life. Through reprinted works his ministry of teaching and preaching was able to continue.

Polemic

Luther's followers began to use his writings for polemical purposes immediately after his death. In 1546–47 his *Warning to His Dear German People* and other tracts were republished as part of the propaganda effort against Emperor Charles V and Pope Paul III. All in all, however, Luther's polemical writings were republished less than might be expected given the continuing polemic traded among Lutherans, Roman Catholics, Reformed, and radical theologians of the late sixteenth century. One reason is that the florilegia of his prophecies, although designed primarily for edification, contained a good deal of polemic, aimed particularly against the Roman Catholics. And, of course, Luther's attacks on the papacy, like his edificatory writings, were available in the complete works. Polemic reflecting Luther's views continued against the Roman Catholic party, to be sure,[91] but largely without benefit of his own words as found in tracts and books which he had composed. The nature of polemic at least in part determined this. Citing Luther would not have contributed to winning Roman Catholics to the Lutheran side. And at any rate the purpose of polemic lay more in solidifying the Lutherans' own mighty fortress than in persuading foes to convert. At the same time even such consolidation required new arguments, for the focus of the struggle between Roman Catholics and evangelicals continued to change during the late sixteenth century.

91. See pp. 91–101.

Nonetheless, on relatively rare occasions Lutherans did republish Luther in their efforts to preserve his message against the Roman threat. At the same time that Luther's writings on resistance to the pope and emperor reappeared, and his prophecies regarding apostasy and the might of the papacy were being collected, the Wittenberg printer Veit Creutzer released a booklet incorporating Luther's *Chief Articles of the Christian Faith, Against the Pope* (1543) and his brief commentary on the ancient creeds and other material which demonstrated the catholicity of the Lutheran teaching. This booklet was reissued at least seven times by 1563 and again in 1585.[92] Basilius Faber saw Justus Jonas's translation of Luther's *On the Councils and the Church* into print as a favor to the dying Jonas; it was also reissued in the original German in 1584.[93] Nikolaus Gallus used Luther's comments on Daniel 12 as part of the coordinated defense of the faith which he and Matthias Flacius Illyricus were waging in the 1550s and 1560s, and in 1565 Luther's *Against the Roman Papacy, Founded by the Devil* appeared, without comment and without the name of the printer.[94] Along with materials from the pens of Melanchthon and Brenz, Luther's 1530 attack on purgatory was reprinted in 1570 to counter arguments from the Jesuits and others in behalf of the medieval piety surrounding the mass.[95] Luther's response to the Sienese Roman Catholic polemicist Ambrose Catharinus, first published in 1524, was reprinted by the Gnesio-Lutheran printer Nicolaus Heinrich in 1574.[96] All such works supported Lutheran polemicists who were

92. *Die Heubtartikel des Christlichen glaubens/Wider den Bapst/vnd der Hellen pforten zu erhalten. Sampt dem Bekentnis des glaubens/D. Mart. Lu. . . . Die drey Symbola oder Bekentnis des Christliche glaubens* . . . (Wittenberg: Veit Creutzer, 1548, 1559; Peter Seitz [and heirs], 1550, 1554, 1559; Lorentz Schwentz, 1557; Wittenberg, 1585; Jena, 1559; Nuremberg: Johann von Berg and Ulrich Neüber, 1562).

93. *De Concilijs et ecclesia, liber. Germanice scriptus iam olim a Reverendo patro D. D. Martino Lutero* . . . (Basel: Johann Oporinus, 1557; in German, n.p., 1584).

94. *Das Zwelffte Capitel Danielis/mit der Auslegung D. Martini Lutheri/vom Antichrist vnd seinem Reich/zu den fehrlichen diesen zeiten sehr nutzlich vnd tro[e]stlich zu lesen* . . . (Regensburg: Heinrich Giessler, 1560); *Wider das Bapstum zu Rom/vom Teuffel gestifft/ein notwendige schrifft D.M. Lutheri* . . . (n.p., 1565). About this time Anton Otto wrote a letter of comfort for those persecuted by papal tyranny and appended a similar work by Luther: *Eine Einfeltige vnnd Christliche Trostschrifft . . . an die Christen/so hin vnd wider vmb der Reinen Religion Jesu Christi willen/von den Papisten verfolget werden. Item/Ein Trostschrifft D. M. Lutheri/an die verjagten Christen/ec.* (Eisleben: Andreas Petri, 1564); see *WA Br* 6:422–23 (#1995).

95. *Wider die alte/grobe/Heydnische Lu[e]gen der Papisten/vom Fegfewer . . . I. Doctor Martinus Luther seligen/von jm geschrieben Anno 1530. . . .* (Frankfurt/Main: Nikolaus Basse, 1570).

96. *Der Garaus Von dem Endchrist/seinem Reich vnd Regiment/aus dem Propheten Daniel gezogen vnd gestellet/wider das gantze Bapsthumb vnd seinem Anhang* (Ursel: Nicolaus Henricus, 1574).

composing their own critiques of contemporary Roman Catholicism. On both sides of this battle the salvos were legion.

As the Thirty Years' War began, citation of Luther was employed in an effort to defend his church,[97] but in general his own writings had given way to the more sharply focused defenses composed by others in the struggle against the papacy. Since Roman Catholics did not acknowledge Luther's authority in any case, recalling his words against them did not actually advance the argument with them. That argument had to be pursued in biblical and logical discussion of newly raised questions and attacks. Luther's followers were sufficiently armed against the papal enemy by other materials from his own pen and the pens of other theologians.

The Lutheran defense of Luther's understanding of the Lord's Supper presents a different picture, largely because that particular battle took place not only against the openly Reformed or Calvinists in other lands, but also against those who claimed to be Lutheran and lived in lands which officially adhered to the Augsburg Confession and other Lutheran statements of faith. Like the Roman Catholics, Calvinists rejected Luther's authority, even though they appreciated his revelation of the gospel against the papacy (see ch. 4). Therefore, in the 1550s, the first stage of Lutheran-Calvinist polemic, little from Luther's pen on the Lord's Supper was reprinted.[98] But as the south German Lutherans engaged the neighboring Swiss in discussion, they found it useful to have some of Luther's treatment of the real presence and related christological teaching at hand once again.[99] Johannes Brenz's treatment of the

97. E.g., *Christi Jesu des HERRN aller Herrn/durch Doctorn Lutherum. Gewiss vnd vbergewiss Defension, Sieg vnd Triumph Werck . . .* (n.p., 1619).

98. In the midst of his controversy with John Calvin, the Hamburg pastor Joachim Westphal translated excerpts from Luther's *That These Words of Christ . . . Still Stand* into Latin: *Vera et propria enarratio dicti Christi Ioannis VI. Caro non prodest quicquam &c. a Reverendo viro sanctae memoriae D. Martino Luthero scripta contra Sacramentarios . . .* (Frankfurt/Main: Peter Brubach, 1554); see *WA* 23:167–205 (pp. 17–52), 243–60 (53–76), 349–51 (77–79). Matthaeus Judex brought out *Defensio . . . verborum coenae: accipite, comeditae: hoc est corpus meum. Contra Phanaticos Sacramentiorum spiritus, aedita Germanice a Luthero . . .* (Nuremberg: Johann vom Berg and Ulrich Neüber, 1556). Another publication which made Luther's comment on the sacrament available at this time was *Van dem Hochwerdigen Sacrament des Liues vnd Blodes Jhesu Christi/Eine scho[e]ne Predige des Erwirdigen vnd Seligen D. Mart. Luther . . .* (Hamburg: Johann Wickrodt the Younger, 1557).

99. E.g., *Verzeichnus etliche/der fu[e]rnember Spru[e]ch/ausser den Bu[e]chern Doctor. Martini Lutheri seelig/darinnen der recht Verstandt/von der Gegenwu[e]rtigkeit des waren Leibs vnd Bluts Christi/in dem heiligen Abentmal/auch von der Himmelfart Christi . . . erkla[e]rt wu[e]rdt* (Tübingen: Ulrich Morhart's widow, 1560), which contained excerpts from *Against the Heavenly Prophets;* the *Sermon on the Sacrament; That These Words of Christ, "This Is My Body," Still Stand Firm against the Fanatics;* and both Confessions on the Lord's Supper; and *Etliche fu[e]rneme Schrifften/Doct. Martin Luth. Darin die reine Christliche lehr vnd bekandtnuss vom H. Abentmal vnsers Herrn Jesu Christi be-*

personal union of Christ's human and divine natures, which was published in 1561, included excerpts from the second part of Luther's *Against the Heavenly Prophets;* his *Sermon on the Sacrament of the Lord's Body and Blood; That These Words of Christ, "This Is My Body," Still Stand Firm against the Fanatics;* and both Confessions on the Lord's Supper.[100] And even as the Crypto-Philippist movement was increasing its influence in electoral Saxony in the 1560s, Luther's *Brief Confession* of 1544, a sharp critique of Reformed sacramental teaching, was published there by two printers.[101]

When debate over the Lord's Supper and the position of the electoral Saxon ministerium rose in the early 1570s, the dukes of Pomerania and their pastors pledged themselves to Luther's position by accepting six of his works as a part of their public doctrinal confession. In addition to their church constitution, agenda, the *Corpus doctrinae Philippicum,* and Luther's Large Catechism and Smalcald Articles, they declared their acceptance of his teaching as set forth in his *Sermon on the Sacrament; Against the Heavenly Prophets; That These Words of Christ, "This Is My Body," Still Stand Firm against the Fanatics; Confession concerning Christ's Supper; Brief Confession on the Lord's Supper;* and his *Open Letter to the Christians in Frankfurt am Main.*[102]

Actually, both sides in electoral Saxony enlisted Luther in the battle over the sacrament. His writings on the Lord's Supper were selectively cited by the Crypto-Philippists in Wittenberg before their fall from grace and power; and these same works, along with others on the sacraments, became key instruments for the reeducation and reform of the electoral Saxon church in the mid-1570s.[103] The battle for the minds of

---

griffen ist . . . (Nuremberg: Johann vom Berg and Ulrich Neüber, 1561; Kauffmann, 1597 reprint), which contained the same material (either excerpts or the entire work) as did the previous volume, and Luther's *Open Letter against Certain Raving Spirits,* his *Open Letter to the Christians in Frankfurt am Main,* his preface to the *Swabian Syngramma* of 1526, and his *Booklet to the Waldensians in Bohemia and Moravia.*

100. *De personali vnione dvarvm natvrarvm in Christo, et ascensv Christi in coelvm . . .* (Tübingen: Ulrich Morhardt's widow, 1561).

101. *Offentliche gemeine Bekentniss vom Abendmal des Herrn. D. Martini Lutheri vnd derer Kirchen . . . Letzte Bekentnis D. Martini Lutheri/von dem hochwirdigen Sacrament. Anno 1544.* (Leipzig: Ernst Voegelin, 1562); *Kurtz Bekentnis Doct. Mart. Luthers/vom heiligen Sacrament . . .* (Wittenberg: Hans Lufft, 1567, 1574 reprint). Nikolaus Heinrich had also issued an edition in Ursel in 1559. The work was later republished during the Crypto-Calvinist controversy in electoral Saxony at the end of the century (Lauingen: Leonhart Reinmichel, 1589; Magdeburg: Johann Franck, 1592); see pp. 115–20.

102. *Des Ehrwirdigen vnd Geistreichen Mans Gottes/Doctoris Martini Lutheri Schrifften/wider die Sacramentirer vnd falsche Lere vom heiligen Abendmal vnsers Herrn Jesu Christi. Zu welchen sich die Pomerischen Kirchen vnd Landen je vnd alle wege bekant vnd noch bekennen/vnd hinfuro bestendiglich dabey zu beharren/durch Gottes gnade vnd hu[e]lff bedacht sein* (Stettin: Andreas Kelner, 1573).

103. See pp. 105–12.

Saxon pastors continued into the 1580s, particularly as Calvinists and certain heirs of Melanchthon attacked the Formula of Concord. Among the weapons forged for that battle was a collection of brief citations from Luther on twenty-four topics, most prominent among them the Lord's Supper and Christology. Its editor was the Wittenberg University councilor, Johannes Schütz. He turned to the Church Postil, Luther's comments on John's Gospel, *On the Councils and the Church, On the Bondage of the Will,* the Galatians commentary of 1535, and a number of other works, including *Against the Heavenly Prophets,* the (Large) *Confession concerning Christ's Supper,* and similar treatments of the sacrament.[104] *That These Words of Christ, "This Is My Body," Still Stand* was also republished at this time.[105]

When sacramentarian teaching returned to electoral Saxony after the death of Elector August and the accession of his son Christian I to the throne, the texts which the theologians of Wittenberg had published in 1575 were reissued, as were three of Luther's standard treatments of the sacrament.[106] As the dispute over the Lord's Supper and Christology between Lutherans and Calvinists continued into the late sixteenth and early seventeenth century, Luther was occasionally called upon again to put his case before the public.[107] In 1593, for instance, the ministerium of Frankfurt am Main, in defending themselves against charges of sac-

104. *Christliche Einhellige Lehr vnd Bekentnis. Von der Person Jesu Christi vnsers Herrn/etc. Von seiner Himmelfart/vnd sitzen zur rechten Hand des Vaters. Vom Heiligen Hochwirdigen Abentmal des Herrn. Laut heiliger Go[e]ttlicher Schrifft, Aus den Streit/vnd Lehrschrifften D. Martini Lutheri . . .* (Wittenberg: Simon Groeneberg, 1583?).

105. *Das diese Wort Christi . . .* (Magdeburg: Paul Donat, 1582) was issued to combat the Bremen ministerium's *Warhaffte Vnd Christliche verantwortung/der Prediger zu Bremen/auff die jhnen zugemessene Artickel vnd Puncten . . . Als Nemlich: I. Von der Person Christi. II. Von der heyligen Tauff. III. Von dem H. Abendmal. IIII. Von der Go[e]ttlichen Wahl. V. Von der Ceremonien* (Bremen: Arend Wessel and Dietrich Gloichstein, 1581). See Irene Dingel, *Concordia controversa: Die öffentlichen Diskussionen um das lutherische Konkordienwerk am Ende des 16. Jahrhunderts* (Gütersloh: Gütersloher Verlagshaus, 1996), 369–92.

106. *Das diese wort Christi . . .* (Frankfurt/Main: Johann Spies, 1586; Lauingen: Leonhart Reinmickel, 1589), *Von Abendmal Christi Bekandtniss* (Lauingen: Leonhart Reinmickel, 1589), and *Warnungschrifft . . . an die Zu Franckfurt am Meyn* (Lauingen: Leonhart Reinmickel, 1589). To promote Luther's Christology, his comments on John 14:16a were excerpted in *Nu[e]tzliche vnd zu diesen gefehrlichen zeiten no[e]tige erklerung Der Lehre von der Person Christi/D. Martini Lutheri . . . vber auslegung der wort des 14. Cap. Joan. . . .* (Wittenberg: Zacharias Lehmann, 1591). This episode in Saxon political history is analyzed in Thomas Klein, *Der Kampf um die zweite Reformation in Kursachsen, 1586–1591* (Cologne: Böhlau, 1962), esp. 68–129. Further theological analysis of the controversy is still needed.

107. See, e.g., Caspar Finck (professor at Giessen), *Luther redivivvs, Das ist/Widerlegung aller Argumenten/welche die Calvinisten vnsere Stieffbru[e]der heutiges tages vom H. Abendmal fu[e]hren/auss den Schrifften vnd Bu[e]chern dess seligen H. D. Martini Lutheri. Auch Beweiss Dass heutiges tages die gedachte Calvinisten vnd Zwinglianer nichts auff die bahn bringen/ welches nicht zuuor gru[e]ndlich vom Herrn Luthero widerlegt sey . . .* (Frankfurt/Main, 1614).

ramentarianism, reissued Luther's *Open Letter to the Christians in Frankfurt am Main* of 1533, which had dealt with rejection of the Lutheran understanding of the Lord's Supper.[108] Such appeals to Luther's own arguments served chiefly to reinforce the belief of those who accepted his position. Those who wished to move beyond that position had already left the Lutheran churches of Germany. Into the early 1590s, however, Luther could be cited to call those who claimed to be members of the church of the Augsburg Confession back to its public teaching.

Citations from Luther had been used in similar fashion since 1548 in other disputes among his heirs. Those who disagreed over the proper definition of Luther's legacy tried to place the Reformer on their side. The Gnesio-Lutherans more often appealed to Luther and used his words in their own defense, but both sides tried to demonstrate that Luther taught what they were teaching. Apart from his letters to the theologians at Augsburg in 1530, no larger works of Luther were thrown into the battle over the Leipzig Interim and its adiaphoristic concessions. Nonetheless, in the early 1550s both Nikolaus von Amsdorf and Joachim Westphal gathered brief excerpts from Luther's writing to prove their Philippist foes had erred in constructing their own Interim.[109]

When the Gnesio-Lutherans and the Philippists turned against Andreas Osiander and his aberrant doctrine of justification, both sides collected citations from Luther to prove their interpretation was his. Neither republished more than sermonic material. Their weapons were simple proof passages; for the most part brief excerpts sufficed to support their positions.[110]

As the Gnesio-Lutherans and the Philippists debated the assertion of Wittenberg professor Georg Major that "good works are necessary for salvation," Luther was often quoted, but again the controversy led to relatively little republishing of more than excerpts and proof passages. Exceptions included the republication of his theses on the works of the law and grace (1537) by the Magdeburg pastor Albert Christian and in German translation by Matthias Flacius.[111] This controversy continued within the ministerium of electoral Brandenburg, where Andreas

108. *Warnungsschrifft Doct. Martin Luthers/an die zu Franckfurt am Mayn/Anno 1533. aussgangen* . . . (Frankfurt/Main: Johann Spiess, 1593).

109. See p. 43 nn. 10–11.

110. See p. 66 n. 72.

111. *Disputatio Reuerendi patris D. Martini Lutheri de operibus legis & gratiae* . . . , ed. Albert Christian (Magdeburg: Michael Lotther, 1553); *Eine Disputation des thewren Mann Gottes D. Mart. Luth. sa[e]liger gedechtnu[e]ss/von den guten Wercken/Darin der jrrthumb/ das die guten Werck zur Sa[e]ligkeyt no[e]tig sein/verworffen wirdt,* ed. Matthias Flacius (Strassburg: Jacob Frohlich, 1557).

Musculus and Abdias Praetorius traded shots with Luther's words as ammunition.[112]

In the controversy over synergism and the bondage of the will, one of the leading Gnesio-Lutherans, Nikolaus Gallus, published Luther's *On the Bondage of the Will* in German translation. In the preface he carefully contrasted the position of Melanchthon and his followers with Luther's teaching.[113] The Mansfeld pastor Georg Autumnus contributed to the campaign against synergism with a collection of proof passages from Luther's works.[114]

In these disputes among Lutherans citation of Luther served to reinforce claims to proper interpretation of the Lutheran position. In no dispute was this more important than in the battle over the definition of original sin. Here the controversy broke out within Gnesio-Lutheran ranks, and it pitted friend against friend. Explaining why he believed that original sin could be defined as the substance of the fallen human creature, Matthias Flacius appealed to Luther in his own defense. Johannes Wigand, Tilemann Hesshus, and others rushed to prove his interpretation of Luther's understanding of sin false.[115] Particularly in Mansfeld the ministerium was badly divided, and the followers of Matthias Flacius were eventually driven out by force. Led by Cyriakus Spangenberg, they had defended their definition of original sin as the sub-

112. The Gnesio-Lutheran Andreas Musculus, in *Von Guten Wercken/vnterrichtung. Aus des thewren vnd seliger Lehrers/D. Martin Lutheri Bu[e]chern/trewliche vnd fleissig zusamen getragen* (Erfurt: Georg Baumann, 1562), restricted himself to citations from Luther. His Philippist opponent, Abdias Praetorius, in *De bonorvm opervm et novae obedientiae necessitate testimonia Ex Sacris literis. Ex Luthero. Ex Melanthone. Ex Confessionibus. Ex Patribus. Ex Scriptoribus recentioribus . . .* (Frankfurt/Oder: Johann Eichorn, 1562), cited others alongside Luther to prove that his teaching was biblical.

113. *Das der freye Wille nichts sey. Antwort/D. Martini Lutheri/an Erasmum Roterodamum/Verdeudscht durch D. Justum Jonam/Zuuor niemals allein im Druck ausgangen . . .* (Regensburg: Heinrich Geissler, 1559).

114. *Vom Freien Willen vnd Bekerung des Menschen zu Gott. Warhafftige/bestendige/ vnd in Gottes wort wol gegrundte Lehr vnd meinung/der heiligen Schrifft/Autoritet der Va[e]ter/vnd anderen Einreden vnd gegenwu[e]rffe/so die Schutzherrn des nichtigen Freen willens pflegen zu gebrauchen . . .* (Eisleben: Andreas Petri, c. 1565). German Calvinists later enlisted Luther in their condemnation of synergism, e.g., in *Bestendige Lehr D. Martini Luthers/Vom Vrsprung dess Glaubens . . .* (Amberg: Michael Forster, 1598).

115. Flacius issued *Warhafftige vnd bestendige meinung vnd zeugnis/Von der Erbsu[e]nde vnd dem freien willen . . . D. Martin Luthers Aus allen seinen schrifften trewliche vnd mit vleis zusamen gezogen . . .* (Jena: Thomas Rebart, 1560, 1561) before his colleagues began to attack him. The controversy was well under way when he published *Etliche Klare vnd treffliche Zeugnussen/D. Martini Luthers/von dem bo[e]sen Wesen . . . oder Gestalt des jrdischen todten Adams . . .* (n.p., 1574). Here he was meeting the attacks of Johannes Wigand, *Von der Erbsu[e]nde/Lere aus Gottes Wort/aus dem Du[e]ringischen Corpore Doctrinae/vnd aus D. Luthers Bu[e]chern . . .* (Jena: Donatus Richtzenhan, 1571), and Tilemann Hesshus, *Klare vnd helle Zeugnissen Doctoris Martini Lutheri. Das Die Erbsu[e]nde nicht sey das wesen des Menschen . . .* (Jena, 1572).

stance of the fallen human creature with citations from Luther, which were met by countercollections of quotations from the Reformer.[116]

At the end of the sixteenth century Luther was once more called upon for testimony in a struggle among those who claimed his name. A dispute arose within the faculty of the University of Helmstedt concerning the relationship of theology and philosophy. To defend their position, those who wished to diminish the use of reason in theological analysis published a letter which Luther had written to Spalatin in 1518 and a florilegium of citations from various works, including the Church Postil, *On the Bondage of the Will,* and biblical commentaries.[117]

As debates grew sharper during the course of the decades following Luther's death, his works became obsolescent as polemical tools. New controversies were less likely to be solved through direct citation of long sections from Luther's works. Furthermore, Luther's works against those outside the Lutheran churches carried no authority to persuade the foe. Apter arguments for a new day had to be forged from his tradition; his own attacks on the foes of the Lutheran confession no longer sufficed.

Aids for Reading Luther

Those who wanted to read Luther were not left to their own devices by those who believed that reading his works would reap great benefits. A decade after his writings began to shake the Western church, lists of what he had published were made available to the public.[118] A quarter century later Christoph Walther, one of the editors of the Wittenberg

116. From Spangenberg's side came, e.g., *Warhafftige/gewisse/bestendige/der heiligen Schrifft gemesse/vnd in Gottes Wort gegru[e]ndte Lere/von der Erbsu[e]nde. Doctor Martini Luthers/Daraus klar zusehen/das dieselbige nicht sey ein Accidens* (Eisleben: Andreas Petri, 1572); and *Beweyss/Das Magister Cyriacus Spangenberg vnd seine Mitbekenner inn der Lehre von der Erbsu[e]nde/mit Luthero durchauss vbereinstimmen . . . ,* ed. Emericus Sylvius (n.p., 1579). The opposing camp published, e.g., Andreas Schoppe, *Rettung Des Heiligen Catechismi wider den Schwarm der newen Manicheer vnd Substantijsten* (Jena: Donatus Richtzenhan, 1572), which included quotes from the Fathers and other contemporaries as well as Luther; and Johann Hugo, *Gru[e]ndlicher vnd Klarer bericht von der Erbsu[e]nde/Was dieselbe eigendliche sey. Aus des tewren Mans Gottes D. Luthers Schrifften gezogen . . .* (Eisleben, 1573).

117. *Zeugniss Des Herrn D. Martini Lutheri/von der Vernunfft vnnd dero Meisterin Philosophia . . . Auss Lutheri Schrifften zusammen getragen* (Magdeburg: Andreas Duncker, 1600); *De logica Ex fidei regno excludenda epistola Reverendi patris Martini Lutheri ex primo tomo epistolarum anno 1556. Jhenae excusarum excerpta, qua Ostenditur non novvm neque temerarium esse certamen, quod Hofmanno cum Caelianis intercedit* (Lemgo: Conrad Grothe's heirs, 1600).

118. *Verzeichnung vnd Register aller Bu[e]cher vnd schrifften D. Mart. Luther/durch yn aussgelassen/vom Jar 1518. bis yns acht vnd zwentzigst.* (n.p., 1528?); *Catalogus oder Register aller Bu[e]cher vnd schrifften/D. Mart. Luth. durch jn ausgelassen/vom jar M.D. XVIII. bis jns XXXIII.* (Wittenberg: Hans Lufft, 1533).

edition, issued an index for its volumes. In it he refuted the charges against the Wittenberg edition that were made by the producers of the Jena edition.[119]

Five years later a pastor in Breslau, Sigismund Schwob, issued an alphabetical index listing all Luther titles and their locations in both the Wittenberg edition and the Jena edition.[120] Timotheus Kirchner prepared four indices for the eight German volumes of the Jena edition. They filled more than two hundred folio leaves. The first guided the reader to places where Luther commented on some 350 topics from *Abgötterey* (idolatry) to *Zweifeln* (doubt); short summaries were included. The second index referred the reader to historical material, the names of prophets, apostles, fathers, heretics as well as heresies. The third index cataloged Luther's explanations of Hebrew, Greek, and Latin words. The fourth listed references to Scripture passages.[121] Kirchner did not prepare a similar guide to the Latin volumes of the Jena edition, nor did such a handbook appear to aid those who wanted to use the Wittenberg edition. Kirchner's indices do indicate that Luther's works were viewed as a compendium for every theological task. But the guides which Kirchner, Schwob, and Walther prepared were of use only to those with access to the standard editions of Luther.

REGISTER
Deudsch vnd Latinisch/aller Bü
cher vnd Schrifften des Ehrnwirdigen Herrn
D. Martini Lutheri/ gerichtet zu gleich auff die XIX.
Wittenbergischen/ vnd XII. Jhenischen Tomos/
des Alten vnd Newen Drucks/allen Liebhabern
der Bücher Lutheri gantz nütz-
lich zugebrauchen.
Durch
Sigismundum Schwob von
der Freistad.
Des Luthers Bücher/ gros vnd klein/
Las dir allzeit befohlen sein.
Man findt darin gar grosses Gut/
Wie dieses Büchlin zeigen thut.
Wittenberg
Gedruckt durch Peter
Seitz.
1564.

Sigismund Schwob, *Register* of Luther's Works (1564) (Concordia Seminary Library, St. Louis)

Of help to those who owned but a few of Luther's works were the introductions to reading Luther prepared by Conrad Porta and Joachim Mörlin. Mörlin began by telling his readers what to expect when they

119. *Register aller Bu[e]cher vnd Schrifften des Ehrnwirdigen Herrn Doctoris Martini Lutheri seliger gedechtnis . . .* (Wittenberg: Hans Lufft, 1556, 1558). On the controversy, see p. 149 in the present volume.

120. *Register aller Schrifften des Ehrwirdigen Herrn D. Martini Lutheri/gerichtet zugleich auff die XIX. Wittembergischen/vnd XII. Jhenischen Tomos . . .* (Breslau: Crispin Scharffenberg, 1563; Wittenberg: Peter Seitz, 1564 reprint); *Index omnium scriptorvm Reverendi patris D. Martini Luther: accommodatus & ad 19. Tomos Vitebergenses & 12. Ihenenses . . .* (Breslau: Crispin Scharffenberg, 1563; Wittenberg: Peter Seitz, 1564 and 1573 reprints).

121. *Index oder Register der die Achte deutsche Tomos/Ersten vnd andern Drucks/aller Bu[e]cher vnd Schrifften des thewren vnd seligen Mans Gottes/Doctor Martini Lutheri . . .* (Jena: Donatus Richtzenhayn and Thomas Rebart, 1564, 1573; Rebart's heirs, 1583; Tobias Steinmann, 1592).

ventured into Luther's works. First, Luther would lead them into the heart of the Scriptures. No parading of logic here—Luther's works proceed to what the Holy Spirit has established as the nerve center of the Scriptures. Second, Luther's language sets forth the fundamental meaning of the Scripture clearly and skillfully. His words are so filled with meaning that a page or two might demand a half day to read and three or four weeks to digest. Third, Luther's writings commend themselves because he worked diligently to present all the articles of faith purely and thoroughly on the basis of God's Word. He avoided ambiguous definitions and stated what is true forthrightly and simply, while sharply refuting what is false.[122]

Conrad Porta offered two sets of reasons why Luther's writings should command attention: Porta repeated and then expanded Mörlin's list of their praiseworthy characteristics. Luther had been called by God and moved by the Holy Spirit to proclaim the biblical message. His writings present every topic of Christian teaching with singular skill, and they contain the most efficacious consolations for troubled consciences. Luther had always used the most appropriate words and organized his arguments in the most effective way. Of all the books of that era, Luther's were the best, most useful, and most authoritative. God had preserved them miraculously, as he had preserved Luther himself, in a time of persecution and suppression.[123] Porta was echoing the common convictions of his contemporaries.

Both authors suggested reading programs. Mörlin counseled beginning with the Small Catechism, for its three parts—law, gospel, and the table of responsibilities in the callings of daily life—summarize the entire Word of God. From the Small Catechism the reader should move to the Large Catechism and then to those works of Luther which summarize basic Christian teaching: the Schwabach Articles, the *Confession concerning Christ's Supper* (1528), the Smalcald Articles, the Instructions for Visitors (1528), and the Augsburg Confession and its Apology, which Mörlin, like many of his contemporaries, counted among Luther's works as well as Melanchthon's. For learning the proper distinction of law and gospel the reader should turn to the Galatians commentary of 1535. Mörlin commended *On the Last Words of David* for its treatment of the second article of the Creed, and *On the Councils and the Church* and *Against Hanswurst* for their treatment of the third arti-

122. *Wie die Bu[e]cher vnd Schrifften/des tewren vnd Seligen Manns Gottes D. Martini Luthers nu[e]tzlich zu lesen Fu[e]r einfeltige frome Pfarherrn vnd andere Christen Liebhaber vnd Leser/der Bu[e]cher D. Martini Lutheri . . .* (Eisleben: Adam Petri, [1565]), Aij^r–Aiij^r.

123. *Oratio continens adhorationem, ad assidvam Lectionem scriptorum Reverendi Patris & Praeceptoris nostri D. Martini Lvtheri vltimi Eliae & Prophetae Germaniae* (Jena: Donatus Richtzenhan, 1571), A5^r–C5^v.

cle. The Genesis commentary would summarize and complete the study of Luther's thought.[124]

Porta began by classifying Luther's works as Luther himself had done at Worms in 1521. Some works dealt with matters of faith and morals. Others were critiques of the papacy. Still others were private, personal works. Porta also divided Luther's writings into six categories: biblical commentary; catechetical works; sermons; works of teaching, consolation, or admonition; treatments of politics, marriage, and economic life; and responses to critical questions, controversies, and like matters. He particularly praised the catechisms, the *Confession concerning Christ's Supper* (1528), the Smalcald Articles and the Augsburg Confession, and the commentaries on Galatians and Genesis.[125]

Both Mörlin and Porta agreed on the value of continued study of Luther and on the reasons for doing so. They also agreed on the key works which those who wished to steep themselves in his thought should read. The works of the earlier Luther, particularly the great trilogy of 1520—*The Freedom of the Christian, The Babylonian Captivity of the Church,* and *The Open Letter to the German Nobility*—were not on the lists, although they do appear on most such lists today. Most of the readers of Mörlin's and Porta's guides, if they had experienced Luther at all, had sat at the feet of the more mature Luther, so the works of the later period of his life served their purposes well. The presence of the catechisms on the lists does not surprise us, nor do the commentaries on Galatians (1535) and Genesis.[126] The *Confession concerning Christ's*

124. *Wie die Bu[e]cher vnd Schrifften,* Aiiij^{r}–[Avj]^{r}.

125. *Oratio,* [C6]^{r}–D^{r}.

126. Even though Lutheran commentators in the next generation did not feel themselves bound to the approach and conclusions of these works, they praised them highly; see Robert Kolb, "The Influence of Luther's Galatians Commentary of 1535 on Later Sixteenth-Century Lutheran Commentaries on Galatians," *Archiv für Reformationsgeschichte* 84 (1993): 156–84 (= Robert Kolb, *Luther's Heirs Define His Legacy: Studies on Lutheran Confessionalization* [Aldershot, Eng.: Variorum, 1996], 12); and idem, "Sixteenth-Century Lutheran Commentary on Genesis and the Genesis Commentary of Martin Luther," in *Théorie et pratique de l'exégèse: Actes du troisième colloque international sur l'histoire de l'exégèse biblique au XVIe siècle,* ed. Irena Backus and Francis Higman (Geneva: Droz, 1990), 243–58 (= *Luther's Heirs,* 11). My analysis of selected texts concludes that where Luther's exegesis makes peculiar points, his disciples for the most part did not repeat those peculiar interpretations, even though their commentaries make clear in broad strokes that they were committed to Luther's theology and often had learned from his exegesis. Mickey L. Mattox, "Martin Luther's Interpretation of the Women of Genesis in the Context of the Christian Exegetical Tradition" (Ph.D. diss., Duke University, 1997), 307, concludes that Nikolaus Selnecker's exegesis of Genesis 31 "parallels that of Luther in such a way as further to suggest [Selnecker's] dependence on [Luther]." I believe that Mattox's judgment and mine may differ in perspective but not in substance, for he also notes that the commentaries of Selnecker, Peter Palladius, and David Chytraeus on Genesis 31 "did little more than pass on a truncated version of Luther's own exegesis,"

Supper (1528) and the trilogy from Luther's later years, *On the Councils and the Church, On the Last Words of David,* and *Against Hanswurst,* reflect more than the obvious polemical concerns. In each of these works subjects vital to Lutheran teaching and piety were clearly and effectively expressed, particularly the mercy of Christ and his delivery of forgiveness of sins through his Word. If Mörlin and Porta succeeded in directing the reading program of pastors, key elements of Luther's thought must have shaped the theology of much of the succeeding generation.

Luther continued to teach and to preach, to console his followers, and to battle his enemies even after his death. A survey of the republications of individual works and of the florilegia which gathered materials on specific topics reveals that the Lutherans of the late Reformation turned to his teaching far more for instruction and consolation than for polemical purposes. Much of the republication of individual items from Luther's pen was to provide German-language materials for pastors to use in caring for parishioners or for laypeople to read themselves, as they sought the comfort of the gospel or Luther's point of view on topics vital to daily Christian living. Certain tools for pastoral practice, such as the postils, proved to be of particular value.

After his death Luther's writings were not reprinted in anything approaching the quantities of output during his lifetime, particularly during his early years. His heroic stature as the German prophet and appreciation of his value as an instructor in the faith—the latter-day doctor ecclesiae—translated into a steady—though not overwhelming—demand for his published works in handy, easily used form. The amount of material from his pen which was made available again after his death reveals something of the respect which German Lutherans had for his teaching. He remained for them a teacher of prophetic stature, but the mythical element was waning.

and that in regard to texts on Sarah and Rachel "Luther's Lutheran contemporaries seem to have found it equally difficult to adopt wholesale Luther's paradoxical way of reading such texts" (pp. 308–9). A good deal more study is needed of the ways in which Lutheran exegesis developed in the late sixteenth and the seventeenth centuries.

8

The Loci Communes Lutheri

Luther Systematized for Teaching the Faith

It is not true, argued Johannes Corvinus, that Luther wrote in a confusing and disorderly fashion, with everything mixed together. Yet Corvinus was also convinced that the only way to demonstrate that the Reformer's writings did set forth Christian teaching in an orderly fashion was to present them in topical form as *loci communes* or in the form of a *corpus doctrinae*. With this in view Corvinus compiled the first topical organization of the whole of Luther's thought in words culled from a wide range of his published writings.[1]

Introduction of the Topical Approach

Before the end of the sixteenth century three other men (Timotheus Kirchner, Georg Walther, Theodosius Fabricius) and one ministerium (Brandenburg) would follow Corvinus in presenting a comprehensive overview of Luther's doctrine organized according to topic. They joined a number of other disciples of the Wittenberg Reformers in using the method of gathering material by topic, and they followed the example of Georg Rörer, Caspar Cruciger, Johann Pfeil, and others in excerpting Luther's writings in order to focus on his understanding of particular topics. The *Loci communes Lutheri* of Corvinus and his successors distinguished themselves from the works of these others in that they aimed at providing a complete survey of Luther's teaching, at supplying read-

1. *Loci commvnes Doct: Mart: Lutheri totius Doctrinae Christianae. Das ist/Heubtartikel Vnsers Christlichen Glaubens/vnd rechtschaffener Lere/aus D. Mart. Luthers Schrifften/mit seinen eigenen worten/Einfeltiglich vnd trewliche zusamen getragen* . . . (Ursel: Nicolaus Henricus, 1564),)(4^{v}–A^{r}. On the term "corpus doctrinae" or "body of doctrine" as a synonym for analogy of faith, see Irene Dingel, "Melanchthon und die Normierung des Bekenntnisses," in *Der Theologe Melanchthon*, ed. Heinz Scheible (Sigmaringen: Thorbecke, 1999), 195–211.

ers with a treatment of the whole of Christian doctrine as understood within the topical system devised by Melanchthon.

Students of Luther and Melanchthon tended to arrange all learning in terms of topics, or *loci communes,* for Melanchthon had developed topical organization into the fundamental building block of education at Wittenberg. Medieval teachers had collected material from the ancient philosophers and fathers of the church into topical florilegia, but among the biblical humanists of the northern Renaissance, organization by locus or topic became "a form of thinking."[2] Melanchthon refined both the theory and the use of loci and thus gave all the disciplines of the early modern university one of their most important tools. Melanchthon also shared the theory of learning which guided most humanists of his day: understanding follows eloquence as shadows follow the body. Eloquence was produced by the practice of a rhetorical theory which swayed the mind not only with logical argument, but above all with examples from history or from the imagination.[3]

When Melanchthon composed his overview of biblical teaching in the form of *loci communes* in 1521, he replaced the Scholastic method of teaching theology—a question *(quaestio)* followed by often conflicting citations drawn from older authorities, and then the answer—with the topical method. By developing his topics he gave his readers help in applying to their task of instruction, whether preaching or teaching, the examples and other material which he had gathered.[4]

The list of topics which Melanchthon formulated for the discipline of theology was influenced by Luther's theology, particularly by its focus on three topics: sin, law, and grace. Nonetheless, as he composed the second edition of his *Loci communes theologici,* Melanchthon integrated Luther's theology into the structure of Christian doctrine that was based on a tradition rooted in the Creed, set in place by Augustine and John of Damascus, and used by medieval Scholastics at least since Peter Lombard.[5] Furthermore, he strengthened the role which logical

2. Wolfgang Brückner, "Loci Communes als Denkform, Literarische Bildung vnd Volkstradition zwischen Humanismus und Historismus," *Daphnis* 4 (1975): 1–12. On Melanchthon's organization of the loci and his influence on later Lutheran loci, see Robert Kolb, "The Ordering of the *Loci Communes Theologici:* The Structuring of the Melanchthonian Dogmatic Tradition," *Concordia Journal* 23 (1997): 317–37.

3. Brückner, "Loci Communes," 3–4.

4. Wolfgang Brückner, "Historien und Historie: Erzählliteratur des 16. und 17. Jahrhunderts als Forschungsaufgabe," in *Volkserzählung und Reformation,* ed. Wolfgang Brückner (Berlin: Erich Schmidt, 1974), 54–60.

5. Wilhelm Maurer, *Der junge Melanchthon zwischen Humanismus und Reformation,* vol. 2, *Der Theologe* (Göttingen: Vandenhoeck & Ruprecht, 1969), 139–48. See also Karl Heim, *Das Gewissheitsproblem in der systematischen Theologie bis zu Schleiermacher* (Leipzig: Hinrich, 1911), 268–69.

analysis played. In so doing he took a long step back in the direction of the old *quaestio* form and practice.

Melanchthon's students found the topical method of use in many areas of learning. Johann Pfeil's treatment of marriage and Johannes Wigand's and Tilemann Hesshus's tracts on original sin, all collections of Luther citations, are but three examples of how Wittenberg students used *loci communes* to organize knowledge and instruct their readers or hearers.[6] Anthologies such as the Table Talk and most of the collections of prophecies or prayers gathered from Luther's writings were organized according to the loci method. In the 1550s and 1560s a number of Melanchthon's and Luther's students also used this method as they composed their own textbooks of Christian doctrine.[7] Having won Luther's endorsement,[8] Melanchthon's topical approach provided invaluable assistance for parish pastors who needed aid in organizing their understanding of the biblical message as they preached and taught. Therefore it is little wonder that in the 1560s Johannes Corvinus and Timotheus Kirchner gathered citations from Luther's works in order to pass on to a new generation the whole of his message as they understood it. This was the right project. It was the right time for the project. Twenty years after his demise Luther's students were worrying that knowledge about their mentor, their prophetic hero, was declining among members of the younger generation.[9] Therefore, a number of printed reminders of what he had proclaimed appeared in loci form, some serving rhetorical, others instructional purposes.

When Corvinus's *Loci communes Lutheri* was published in 1564, the reading public did have recourse to at least two superficially similar works. In 1558 Melanchthon himself had written a preface for

6. See p. 175 n. 65, p. 189 n. 115, and Robert Kolb, "Philipp's Foes but Followers Nonetheless: Late Humanism among the Gnesio-Lutherans," in *The Harvest of Humanism in Central Europe: Essays in Honor of Lewis W. Spitz,* ed. Manfred P. Fleischer (St. Louis: Concordia, 1992), 159–77 (= *Luther's Heirs Define His Legacy: Studies on Lutheran Confessionalization* [Aldershot, Eng.: Variorum, 1996], 15).

7. Erasmus Sarcerius, *Locorum communivm ex consensv divinae scripturae, & sanctorum patrum ad certum methodum . . . confirmatio* (Basel, 1557); Hieronymus Rauscher, *Loci commvnes doctrinae Christianae. Die Furnembsten Artickel Christlicher Lehre/kurtz verfast . . .* (Nuremberg: Johann von Berg and Ulrich Neüber, 1558); Job Magdeburg, *ΓΝΩΜΑΙ ΑΓΙΑΙ ΚΑΙ ΑΓΟζολικαι. Sententiae sacrae et apostolicae. Sanctorum Pauli, Petri, Iohannis, & c. Graeci & Latine in Locos Communos collectae: una cum Catechesi D. Martini Lutheri . . .* (Basel: Johann Oporinus, 1562).

8. In the preface to the first volume of the Wittenberg edition, Latin series, *WA* 54:179.

9. This situation parallels late-nineteenth-century efforts in the United States to secure the memory of Abraham Lincoln about the time the generation that had experienced his leadership was dying out.

an overview of Christian doctrine drawn from his works and Luther's. However, this overview, edited by Jacob Eisenberg, pastor in Halle, did not gather the opinions of the two Wittenberg masters from a variety of works, nor did it treat the full range of topics in the discipline of theology. Eisenberg's collection was limited to the propositions which the two Wittenberg professors had prepared for public disputations at the university; thus it was not a balanced synopsis of their teaching.[10]

In 1561 a gifted humanist who served as a deacon at Saint Peter's Church in Basel, Jacob Hertel, had produced a florilegium of Luther passages which addressed problems in biblical interpretation, particularly concerning allegory and typology.[11] The following year, at the instigation of his printer, Johannes Oporinus, he expanded this volume and added a section of Luther citations on the topics which Melanchthon had identified as the loci of Christian doctrine. However, Hertel did not attempt to present a complete overview of Luther's teaching. Under each locus he addressed a few specific questions that involved particular problems. This technique had guided his earlier effort to bring Luther's mind to bear on difficult issues of biblical interpretation. In the expanded volume the locus on God treats only seven questions: What evidence for the Trinity was there before Christ? Which are the persons of the Trinity? What is the image of God? What is the image of God in us? How are the persons of the Trinity to be distinguished? What are the two natures in Christ? When did Christ achieve the victory over sin, death, and hell? Each is answered with a single citation from Luther's Latin works. For this particular locus his lectures on Genesis and the translation of *On the Last Words of David* provided nearly all the answers.[12] Clearly, Hertel's work was limited in scope.

10. *Propositiones theologicae reverendorvm virorum D. Mart. Luth. Et D. Philippi Melanth. Continentes summam doctrinae Christianae, scriptae & disputatae Vvitebergae, inde usque ab anno 1516. de quo tempore uaticinatus est Iohannes Hilten, initium fore reformationis Ecclesiae anno 1516* (Wittenberg, 1558).

11. *Allegoriarum, typorum, et exemplorvm veteris & noui Testamenti Libri duo . . .* (Basel: Johann Oporinus, 1561). Hertel appears to have been something of a house author or compiler and editor for Oporinus. He prepared a number of classical texts for use in schools. He also assembled a theological dictionary comprising brief citations of several dozen patristic, medieval, and contemporary theologians (including prominent Lutheran and Reformed leaders): *Definitiones ac descriptiones theologicae. Ex veterum & recentiorum Theologorum monumentis collectae* (Basel: Johann Oporinus, 1564).

12. *Qvaestiones sacrarum reuerendi patris D. Martini Luther, Centuriae IIII. Libris III. distinctae: His accessit Quartus Liber, continens Quaestiones CCXXI: quibus uariae de praecipuis uerae Religionis capitibus Obiectiones summa pietate explicantur. Ex omnibus eiusdem Latinis operibus bona fide congestae* (Basel: Johann Oporinus, 1562), 544–52.

Topical Overviews of Luther's Theology

The works of Corvinus and Kirchner, of Walther and Fabricius, were different from Hertel's problem-oriented approach.[13] They aspired to offer a complete review of biblical teaching in Luther's own words—a theology of Luther in the form of *loci communes.* In so organizing and systematizing his thought, they domesticated it for use in the framework of their own particular situations and needs.

Any such collection of citations reflects the thought of the person who has selected his favorite quotations as much as it reflects the person who is being quoted. It is noteworthy that those who gathered Luther's theology into topical collections after Hertel were, for the most part, Gnesio-Lutherans. Little is known of the compiler of the first of these *Loci communes Lutheri,* but as the first attempt to press the whole of Luther's theology into Melanchthonian forms, his contribution to later use of Luther's thought is significant. Johannes Corvinus must have come from the ranks of those who followed Matthias Flacius and his Gnesio-Lutheran comrades, for his selections from Luther's writings, for example, on original sin, reflect their understanding of the subject matter. But he has left no other trace. A citation of his work in the 1582 confession of Austrian pastors of Flacian persuasion suggests that the name is not a pseudonym, but it does not surface elsewhere.[14]

Corvinus composed his *Loci communes Lutheri* for two reasons. Not only did he want to make sure that people would be able to see the clarity and order of Luther's thought, he also wanted to provide a summary and extract of Luther's works for the "pious simple people" who had not read all of them. Such a summary would enable them to judge what was at issue in the various controversies of the time and thus to determine what was true and what was false. Therefore, although no formal authority was officially accorded or ascribed to collections like Corvi-

13. They were also different from another work which employed the loci method and cited Luther extensively. A pastor from Langensalza, Nicolaus Erich, composed a compendium of quotations from Luther and Melanchthon on a wide variety of subjects, but not on the teaching of the church. It began with their comments on Aaron, Abraham, Absolution, Academia, and Adam. It was entitled *Sylvva Sententiarum, exemplorum, historiarum, allegoriarum, similitudinum, Facetiarum, Partim ex Reverendi Viri, D. Martini Lvtheri, ac Philippi Melanchthonis cum privatis tum publicis relationibus: partim ex aliorum veterum atque recentium Doctorum monumentis observata, & in Locos communes ordine Alphabetica disposita* (Frankfurt/Main: Peter Schmidt and Sigismund Feyerabend, 1566).

14. *Christlich Bekendtnuss/Einhelliger Consens/Bedencken vnd Ratschlag: Wie in dem Hochwichtigen Glaubens Artickel von der Erbsunde . . . geleret . . . Auff begeren der Lo[e]blichen zween Sta[e]nde von Herrn vnd der Ritterschaft in Oesterreich vnter der Enss/Von etlichen jhrer Gnaden darzu Beruffenen Theologen vnd Predigern in 1582. Jar verfasset* (n.p., 1587), 63^v.

nus's, they functioned in a manner somewhat similar to the confessional documents and the collections of such documents in *corpora doctrinae*. In the case of the *Loci communes Lutheri* it was no longer Luther's person nor the entire corpus of his writings that aided and guided the pastor in formulating his teaching and preaching. It was instead a construct created by followers, theologians of good will but with their own agendas.

Given that, as the proverb has it, out of sight is out of mind, Corvinus felt compelled to counteract the drift away from the teaching of the "faithful man of God, our fatherland's genuine prophet," Martin Luther. Reflecting a common Gnesio-Lutheran complaint, Corvinus was particularly disturbed by those who claimed to be Luther's disciples but were, in his view, abandoning the Reformer's teaching. Some were minimizing original sin by suggesting that it was not the substance of the fallen human creature, but only an (Aristotelian) accident. Others were defining baptism as a mere symbol or sign *(thessara)*. Others were rejecting Luther's teaching on the real presence of Christ's body and blood in the Lord's Supper, while some were conceding that the pope was the head of Christendom and that his bishops held proper jurisdiction over Lutheran pastors. Still others were teaching that the believer's righteousness consisted in the essential righteousness of God, not in God's pronouncement of righteousness through the forgiveness which Christ had won on the cross. There were also those who claimed Luther's name but were willing to compromise the faith. Corvinus's assessment of what had gone wrong with the Lutheran church of his day was typical of the Gnesio-Lutherans. These concerns compelled him to make Luther's own teaching available to more pastors and laypeople in the form of a topical handbook.[15]

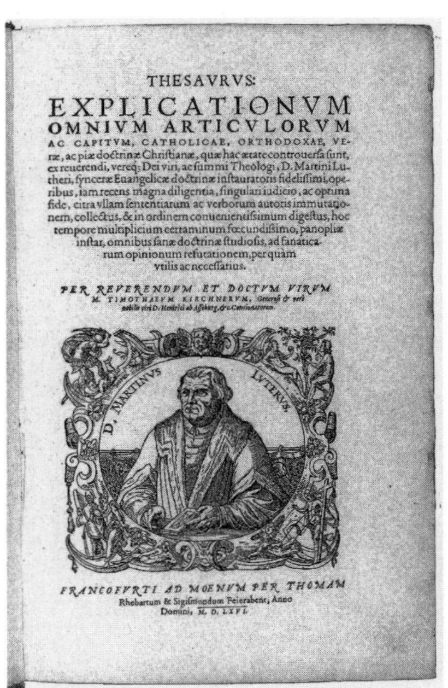

THESAVRVS:
EXPLICATIONVM
OMNIVM ARTICVLORVM
AC CAPITVM, CATHOLICAE, ORTHODOXAE, VEræ, ac piæ doctrinæ Christianæ, quæ hac ætate controuersa sunt, ex reuerendi, vereq; Dei viri, ac summi Theologi, D. Martini Lutheri, syncerae Euangelicæ doctrinæ instauratoris fidelissimi, operibus, iam recens magna diligentia, singulari iudicio, ac optima fide, citra vllam sententiarum ac verborum autoris immutationem, collectus, & in ordinem conuenientissimum digestus, hoc tempore multiplicium certaminum fœcundissimo, panopliæ instar, omnibus sanæ doctrinæ studiosis, ad fanaticarum opinionum refutationem, per quàm vtilis ac necessarius.

PER REVERENDVM ET DOCTVM VIRVM M. TIMOTHAEVM KIRCHNERVM, Generosi & veri nobilis viri D. Henrici ab Assburg, &c. Concionatorem.

FRANCOFVRTI AD MOENVM PER THOMAM Rhebartum & Sigismundum Feierabent, Anno Domini, M. D. LXVI.

Timotheus Kirchner, *Thesavrvs explicationvm omnivm articvlorvm . . .* (1566) (Concordia Seminary Library, St. Louis)

Timotheus Kirchner shared Corvinus's goals, method, and, to a large extent, perspective. He may have been working on his *Thesaurus,* which gathered Luther's teaching on all articles of the Christian faith into two massive folio volumes (one Latin, one

15. Corvinus, *Loci communes,*)(^{r}–A3^{v}.

German), even as Corvinus was preparing his collection. Or the appearance of Corvinus's work may have stimulated Kirchner's efforts, which were ready for the press by December 1565.[16] Kirchner was also a Gnesio-Lutheran, although from that wing of the party which sharply rejected Flacius's definition of original sin. Kirchner had studied at Jena and Erfurt. He had stood with Flacius in opposing the synergism of Viktorin Strigel and in 1562 suffered exile from ducal Saxony for defending his position. He was serving as court preacher in Amfurt, for the count of Asseburg, in 1565 as he compiled his *Thesaurus*. He went on to teach theology at Jena, Helmstedt, and Heidelberg—his academic career terminated in each case by exile which his dogmatic positions provoked.[17]

Deudscher THESAVRVS.
Des Hochgelerten weitberumbten vnd theuren Mans D. Mart. Luthers/ Darinnen alle Heubtartickel/ Christlicher/ Catholischer vnd Apostolischer Lere vnd Glaubens erklert vnd ausgelegt/ mit sampt bestendiger Widerlegung allerhand Irrthumen vnd Verfelschungen der reinen Göttlichen Warheit/
M. Timotheum Kirchner Ienensis Ecclesiæ Pastorem.

Gedruckt zu Franckfort am Mayn/ &c. im Jar 1570.

Timotheus Kirchner, *Deudscher Thesavrvs* . . . (edition of 1570) (Concordia Seminary Library, St. Louis)

Kirchner agreed with Corvinus's estimate of the times. Since he had only recently suffered exile for defending what he considered to be the correct interpretation of the biblical message and Luther's teaching, he wanted to combat the errors which were adulterating that teaching. By making Luther's message more readily available, he also hoped to counteract the plague of the church's ingratitude for Luther's restoration of the gospel. The dedicatory epistles of Kirchner's two volumes explain why he regarded Luther's voice as vital for the life of the church. God had used Luther to restore and cleanse the teaching of the church on every article of the catholic faith. This "Herculean man of God" had brought the light of heavenly teaching into the

16. *Thesavrvs: Explicationvm omnivm articvlorvm ac capitvm, catholicae orthodoxae, verae ac piae doctrinae Christianae, quae haec aetata controversa sunt, ex reuerendi, vereque Dei viri, ac summi Theologi, D. Martini Lutheri, syncerae Euangelicae doctrinae instauratoris fidelissimi, operibus* . . . (Frankfurt/Main: Thomas Rhebart and Sigismund Feyerabend, 1566), [b5]^r; *Deudscher Thesaurus. Des Hochgelerten weit berumbten vnd thewren Mans D. Mart. Luthers/Darinnen alle Heubtartickel/Christlicher/Catholischer vnd Apostolischer Lere vnd Glaubens erklert vnd ausgelegt* . . . (Frankfurt/Main: Peter Schmidt and Hieronymus Feierabent, 1568; Hieronymus Feierabent and Thomas Rebart, 1570).

17. On aspects of Kirchner's later career, particularly as related to the Book of Concord, see Irene Dingel, *Concordia controversa: Die öffentlichen Diskussionen um das lutherische Konkordienwerk am Ende des 16. Jahrhunderts* (Gütersloh: Gütersloher Verlagshaus, 1996), esp. 400–465 and 619–83.

darkness which the papacy had produced, and he had revealed that the papacy was the Antichrist. Luther had also clarified how the estates and orders of human life—church, state, and home—should function. He had refuted the errors and the corruptions of pure teaching which Satan had fostered through a variety of heretics and false brothers. Luther's interpretation of the Scripture surpassed the exegesis of all the Fathers, a fact which even his opponents had to concede. Finally, Luther had translated the Scriptures into German with unmatched skill and clarity.[18] Kirchner's assessment of Luther echoes that of his Gnesio-Lutheran colleagues such as Cyriakus Spangenberg and Andreas Musculus.

Kirchner was convinced that Luther fulfilled Paul's prophecy of an "instrument and mouth of God" who would come to slay the man of lawlessness, the Antichrist, with his breath (2 Thess. 2:8). Accordingly, Kirchner recommended reading Luther's commentaries on Galatians and Genesis and *On the Bondage of the Will,* along with *On the Councils and the Church* ("the best extract of Luther's teaching"), *Against Hanswurst,* and the sermons on John 14–17. In these and Luther's other writings the reader would find, Kirchner promised, "very clear, understandable, forthright, pure and correct definitions and descriptions of every element of teaching, [for Luther] did not use ambiguous and slippery terms or words." Kirchner concluded that a young theologian could not do better than to read Luther "alongside the Bible" and become accustomed to his way of speaking. New terms were being introduced into Lutheran doctrinal analysis, Kirchner complained. He and his Gnesio-Lutheran comrades took exception to phrases such as "good works are necessary for salvation," to the distinction between three kinds of righteousness—imputative, inchoate, and consummated—and to the new formulae used to treat the Lord's Supper, the law and good works, original sin, and the freedom of the will. Such terms, Kirchner feared, were creating a confused, perplexing, and ambiguous theology. So he urged his readers to return to Luther's terminology and to his way of thinking.[19] Luther's thought organized by topics seemed a worthy instrument with which Kirchner could help preserve the Reformer's message.

Andreas Musculus, professor at Frankfurt an der Oder, did not compose a *Loci communes Lutheri* as such under his own name, even though he had employed the genre in constructing three *Loci communes* out of citations of Scripture and the ancient fathers, one of which reinforced the biblical and patristic citations with quotations

18. Kirchner, *Thesavrvs,* a2^{r}–[b5]^{r}.
19. Kirchner, *Deudscher Thesaurus,* aij^{r}–[Avj]^{r}.

from Luther.[20] Musculus is to be mentioned among the editors of *Loci communes Lutheri* because he was, with Georg Coelestin, responsible for the constitution which was prepared for the church of Brandenburg in 1572. This church order contained a topical collection of Luther's thought as part of its definition of the public confession of Brandenburg.[21] Like Kirchner, Musculus opposed the Philippist party, both in his writings and in his political maneuverings against his colleague at Frankfurt, Abdias Praetorius. Musculus had assumed his position at the University of Frankfurt in 1540, after studying at Wittenberg, and he remained there as a powerful force in the church of Brandenburg until his death in 1581.

The Brandenburg church order did not explain why it set its "Explanation and Brief Excerpt" of Luther's writings alongside the Augsburg Confession and the Small Catechism as standards for public teaching. However, a deep appreciation of all that Luther had accomplished is clear from Musculus's other works.[22] In republishing his *Golden Jewel* in 1577, for example, he echoed Corvinus's and Kirchner's convictions about Luther's proclamation of the gospel. Musculus regarded Luther as "the last miraculous man, who taught pure doctrine regarding justification through faith and practiced its application and its salutary and fruitful use faithfully and diligently." He also shared their belief that pastors were turning away from Luther and his books and cared little whether their preaching agreed with Luther or not.[23] One means by which Musculus could battle the trend, at least in Brandenburg, was to create a standard of teaching drawn from Luther's own works.

The Brandenburg church order appeared in 1572. The following year a deacon at Saint Ulrich's Church in Halle, Georg Walther, issued his own *Loci communes,* a presentation of the "chief articles of Christian doctrine" constructed from citations not only from Luther's pen but

20. *Enchiridii sententariium* . . . (Frankfurt/Oder, 1552); *Loci commvnes theologici. Ex scriptvra sacra et ex Orthodoxae Ecclesiae Doctoribus collecti* (Erfurt: Georg Baumann, 1563); *Compendivm doctrinae Christianae collectvm, S. Scriptura, Ex S. Ecclesiae Patribus. S. Luthero* (Frankfurt/Oder, 1573).

21. The Musculus/Coelestin *Loci communes Lutheri* appeared in *Die Augspurgische Confession/aus dem Rechten Original . . . Der Kleine Catechismus Erklerung vnd kurtzer Ausszug aus den Postillen vnd Lehrschrifften des thewren Mans Gottes D. Lutheri/daraus zusehen/wie derselbe von fu[e]rnembsten Artickeln vnserer Christlichen Religion gelehret/ Aus verordnunge . . . Johansen Georgen . . .* (Frankfurt/Oder: Johann Eichorn, 1572). See p. 56 in the present volume.

22. See p. 55.

23. *Thesavrvs: Hochnutzlicher tewrer Schatz vnd Gu[e]lden Kleinot/aller frommen Gottes Kinder aus allen anfechtungen/streit vnd kampff des Gewissens/im leben vnd sterben/ sich zu entbrechen/Vnd endlich friedlich/fro[e]lich vnd seliglich von hinnen abzuscheiden. Aus den Bu[e]chern vnd Schrifften des heiligen Mans Gottes Lutheri/zusammen bracht* (Frankfurt/Oder: Johann Eichorn, 1577), 2^v–5^v.

also from Melanchthon's.[24] Walther was not an active participant in the strife between Gnesio-Lutherans and Philippists, although he did not shy away from conflict. In fact, his criticism of Jacob Eisenberg, court preacher for the archbishop of Magdeburg, earned him dismissal from his post in Halle. He died in 1580, not long after he subscribed the Formula of Concord.

Walther would not have assiduously assembled Luther's thought in several volumes if he had not believed that Luther should continue speaking to the pastors and people of his day. He did not, however, share Corvinus's, Kirchner's, and Musculus's view of how best to preserve Luther's teaching precisely, for, as we mentioned, he did not take part in the Gnesio-Lutheran effort to oppose the positions of the Philippists. He believed that Luther and Melanchthon shared a single viewpoint, a viewpoint which both Crypto-Philippists and their opponents in electoral Saxony tried to define, claim, and cultivate in the 1570s, specifically around 1574, the year of the crisis which brought down the Crypto-Philippist establishment there, the year following Walther's publication of his *Loci communes Lutheri et Melanchthonis*. In the calm before that storm Walther had held the firm conviction that the teaching of both men should be passed on to the new generation; he demonstrated that conviction with citations from the works of both.

Walther's collection of prophecies from Luther's pen (published fourteen years earlier) reveals that he, too, believed that the times were evil, that the gospel had fallen on bad days in the years since Luther had died; and his collection of Luther's works of consolation demonstrates his belief that the Reformer could speak to troubled consciences in later generations.[25] Convinced that a summary of Luther's and Melanchthon's teaching on the chief articles of the faith could help remedy the situation, he presented seven reasons why their understanding of the biblical message was to be preferred over the teaching of all other doctors of the church. Their teaching corresponded to the historical creed of the church, and no one had been able to prove them wrong. It had brought many to the faith. Moreover, God had sustained those who were persecuted for holding to the teaching of Luther and Melanchthon. That teaching had brought down the papacy and had comforted and strengthened troubled hearts. Finally, Walther affirmed, "no teacher has ever grasped God's Word so correctly and so clearly as did

24. *Erster [-Vierder] Theil der Heubtartickel/Christlicher Lere. In Fragestu[e]cken verfasset/vnd mit Gottes Wort/vnd fu[e]rnemen Spru[e]chen D. Lutheri/vnd D. Melanthonis erkleret vnd bekrefftiget. Allen denen/so die Bu[e]chern D. Luthers vnd D. Melanthonis nicht haben/zum dienst angestellet/damit auch diejenigen/so sie haben/alles besser finden/verstehen/und gebrauchen ko[e]nnen* (Magdeburg: Matthaeus Giseken, 1573).

25. See pp. 180 n. 83, and 167 n. 38.

Dr. [*sic*] Melanchthon, my dear preceptor, who thus produced for Christendom an indescribably great benefit, so that people can better understand and use the Bible and the magnificent books of Dr. Luther."[26] In this affirmation Walther's conception of how God had used the two Wittenbergers differed from that of Corvinus, Kirchner, and Musculus. Even though they had not criticized Melanchthon as they praised Luther in the text of their *Loci,* at least the latter two had opposed the Preceptor in the last decade of his life. They withheld the kind of praise which Walther felt free to give to Philip Melanchthon.

A generation later the son of Andreas Fabricius, a prominent Gnesio-Lutheran contemporary of Corvinus and Kirchner, published a new *Loci communes Lutheri.* Theodosius Fabricius had studied at the University of Wittenberg. He shared his father's concern for the preservation of the purity of Luther's teaching, and he suffered exile because of his refusal to submit to the Crypto-Calvinistic movement in electoral Saxony around 1590. Its adherents forced him from his pastorate in Herzberg.

For his collection of Luther's teaching, Fabricius found inspiration in a similar kind of florilegium, a collection of brief quotations from Luther's writings which could be used as aphorisms. This collection had been assembled by an aging friend of his father, the famous schoolmaster Michael Neander. Neander had studied at Wittenberg under both Luther and Melanchthon. In the 1550s he had been involved in the controversy over the definition of the law, supporting his pastoral colleagues in Nordhausen in their dispute with other Gnesio-Lutherans who accused them of being antinomian.[27]

Neander had gathered snippets of Luther's wisdom in aphoristic form. He published them not by topic in a volume of *loci communes,* but in the order in which he found them in the German and Latin series of both the Wittenberg and Jena editions of Luther's works. Neander did not aim at providing a comprehensive guide to Christian teaching. He wanted instead to improve his readers' ability to practice Christian eloquence and thus to edify themselves and—in the case of pastors and teachers—their hearers. As a practitioner of the humanistic arts he believed that such reading and hearing of aphorisms could improve both conversation and piety.

Neander dedicated his collection of Luther's maxims to Theodosius Fabricius and his brother Jonas in memory of their father, his longtime

26. *Erster Theil der Heubtartickel,* Aiij^{v}–[Aviij]^{v}.

27. Matthias Richter, *Gesetz und Heil: Eine Untersuchung zur Vorgeschichte und zum Verlauf des sogenannten Zweiten Antinomistischen Streits* (Göttingen: Vandenhoeck & Ruprecht, 1996), 273–329; Ernst Koch, "Michael Neander (1525–1595) als Theologe," in *Bekenntnis zur Kirche: Festgabe für Ernst Sommerlath zum 70. Geburtstag* (Berlin: Evangelische Verlagsanstalt, 1960), 112–25.

friend, and their two deceased brothers.[28] A decade later Theodosius Fabricius used the time afforded by his exile from Herzberg to prepare three volumes of short Luther citations arranged according to topic. The aging Georg Autumnus, superintendent of the church of Mansfeld and an associate of Fabricius's father a generation earlier, supported him in this project. Fabricius acknowledged his debt to Autumnus and those who had pioneered the genre, specifically Timotheus Kirchner.[29]

With the publication of the Book of Concord in 1580 as the standard for Lutheran confession of the faith and interpretation of the Scriptures, a new era in the history of the Lutheran church had begun more than a decade before Fabricius's *Loci communes Lutheri* appeared. Fabricius acknowledged the authority of the Book of Concord, but he also proposed that "the books of the blessed and precious man of God, Luther," be considered the "only plumb line" for reading both it and the Scriptures. For Fabricius, Luther's writings were "a beautiful and magnificent treasure of God's church." No teacher since apostolic times, Fabricius claimed, had taught with such a "rich spirit," no one had understood and explained the articles of Christian teaching so well, as had this "chosen instrument of Christ in these last times of the world." Although conceding that there was a great difference between Luther and the biblical writers, Fabricius was nonetheless certain that Luther had "remained a faithful disciple and student of Christ and his prophets and apostles at all times, and had stood fast upon the Word and the Scriptures in all articles of the Christian faith." God had raised him up to overthrow the papacy and to reprove the entire empire of hell through the power of the holy gospel. Luther had indeed been "the true miracle worker, on whom the spirit of Elijah truly rested." For in his preaching and teaching, Luther had known nothing other than Christ, his birth, suffering, death, and resurrection, his person, work, and benefits. The Reformer had also restored the proper distinction of law and gospel, which had lain for so many years in darkness. Clearly, "the Holy Spirit ruled his heart, hand, mouth, and pen."[30]

Fabricius offered a variety of reasons for extracting Luther's thought. As had his predecessors, he wanted to entice people to read more of

28. *Theologia megalandri Lvtheri Siue Aphorismi breves et sententiosi de omnibvs doctrinae Christianae capitibus* . . . (Wittenberg: Simon Groneberg, 1584), A2^{r}–B4^{r}.

29. *Loci Communes D. Martini Lvtheri viri Dei et prophetae Germanici, ex scriptis ipsius latinis forma Gnomologica & Aphoristica collecti & in quinque classes distributui* (Magdeburg: Andreas Gera, 1594),)(2^{r}–)()(2^{v}; *Loci communes. Aus den deutschen Geistrichen Schrifften/des thewren Hocherleuchten Mannes Gottes vnd waren letzten Eliae D. Martini Lvtheri* . . . (Magdeburg: Paul Donat, 1597). The Latin was reprinted in London by William Wells in 1651.

30. Fabricius, *Loci communes* (German), (?)ij^{r}–(?)v^{v}.

Luther's entire corpus of writings. He wanted to show his readers "how to use this man's magnificent and precious work with understanding and benefit for the edification of church and school." He wished to provide those who could not afford to purchase the large editions of Luther's works the opportunity to read Luther. For he believed that "especially fathers, mothers, and the dear young people" might gain "a love and desire for God's Word and pure, salutary confession of the faith, as well as rich comfort, warning, admonition, counsel and instruction" from reading Luther. Finally, the pastor in exile hoped to win over those who held Luther in low regard because of their ignorance of his work, a phenomenon he had encountered in electoral Saxony.[31]

From his father's circle Fabricius had gathered the same impressions of Luther as had Musculus and Neander from their contact with their professor. Like his predecessors Fabricius was convinced that Luther's message had to be presented anew to the church of his day. Like them he believed that using the topical form would lend clarity to that task; accordingly, he expressed his debt to Musculus, Kirchner, and others for pioneering the loci method of presenting Luther's thought.[32] To be sure, he owed them much, but the shape of his own work revealed a changing purpose for collections of Luther citations. His work offered instruction, as had its predecessors, but the sections quoted were shorter and thus gave less of the broader context and less complete instruction. Closer to Neander's anthology than were the earlier *loci communes,* Fabricius's collection was as much a resource for homiletical citation as it was for extensive learning of theology from Luther's pen.

Organizing Luther for Edification

Although they employed Luther's words and thus reproduced his theology, the fact is that the editors of the *Loci communes Lutheri* did select which words they wanted Luther to continue to speak to their readers, and they did place these words in the framework of questions they themselves posed. Thus the Luther they introduced as teacher to the reading public was a creation which grew out of their own perception and experience of the Reformer's thought. For the presentation of their own Luther they naturally chose a framework which they had learned in Wittenberg or at least from the Wittenberg tradition. They chose works with which they were most familiar and which most reflected Luther's message as they understood it.

31. Ibid., (?)vj^{r}–(?)vij^{r}.

32. Fabricius, *Der Ander Theil Locorvm commvnivm. Aus den deutschen Geistreichen Schriften/des thewren Hocherleuchten Mannes Gottes vnd waren letzten Eliae. D. Martini Lvtheri* . . . (Magdeburg: Paul Donat, 1598), (?)iij^{v} [= (?)iiij^{v}]–(?)v^{r}.

Favorites among the Reformer's works—both in terms of their appearances in all the collections under study here and in terms of frequency and importance of citation within the individual collections—were the Genesis commentary of 1545 and the Galatians commentary of 1535, various comments on the Psalms, the sermons on the Gospel of John, the Church Postil and the House Postil, and several occasional pieces of polemic or doctrinal exposition. From the earliest years of the Reformation those works which are now regarded as classics were seldom cited; Kirchner made some use of *On the Babylonian Captivity of the Church* and *On Christian Liberty* in his Latin *Thesaurus,* but the great trilogy of 1520 (these two works and the *Open Letter to the German Nobility*) was seldom employed in the other *Loci communes Lutheri.* Particularly in Kirchner's German collection and the compilations of Musculus and Walther the *Defense of All Articles of Martin Luther Condemned by the Most Recent Bull of Leo X* (1520), a summary of his views across the spectrum of Christian teaching at the time, was the much more significant representative of the early Luther. *That These Words of Christ, "This Is My Body," Still Stand,* the (Great) *Confession concerning Christ's Supper* (1528), the *Gloss on the Alleged Imperial Edict* (1531), and *On the Councils and the Church* were also frequently cited. But each editor had his own preferences, and each gathered material from an impressive range of Luther's writings. They knew their master well.

The Form of Luther's Thought according to Corvinus

The systematizers of Luther's theology fit their citations into the framework of the topics they had all learned from Melanchthon's *Loci communes theologici;* to a greater or lesser extent they all used his configuration of Christian teaching to bring order to Luther's wide-flung thoughts. Johannes Corvinus, the first of those who constructed *Loci communes Lutheri,* approached that task with his own set of experiences and concerns. Without knowing anything of his career, we nonetheless can read in his choice of topics the agenda of much of the Gnesio-Lutheran movement. First, he began with "On God's Word,"[33] a topic which Melanchthon had not included in his general headings. Even though God's Word should have been a natural starting point for those who had been trained at Wittenberg in Luther's theology of the Word, only one previous *Loci communes* had begun with that topic: the *Syntagma, or the Body of the Teaching of Christ from the New Testament, Arranged by Rational Method . . . ,* which was produced in 1558 as part of the *Magdeburg Centuries* by Johannes Wigand and Matthaeus Ju-

33. *Loci commvnes,* 1–119.

dex.[34] As members of the Gnesio-Lutheran team of theologians who constructed the *Magdeburg Centuries,* Wigand and Judex had recognized that Luther's theology begins with God's engagement of the sinner through the Word, not with the treatment of God himself. Corvinus followed their example.

Corvinus retained fewer of the Melanchthonian loci than did the *Syntagma,* but he did follow the Preceptor's general order. "God" followed "God's Word," and then "Sin" preceded "Human Powers or the Free Will." Corvinus apparently believed that the human will could not be treated apart from the context of the doctrine of sin. "The Law" came next, and Melanchthon's "Gospel" became Corvinus's "Proper Distinction between Law and Gospel." Melanchthon's "Grace and Justification" became "On Two Kinds of Faith." In accord with the model of the *Syntagma,* Corvinus placed "Prayer" immediately following "Good Works" rather than near the end of the *Loci,* where Melanchthon had situated it.

Then Corvinus discussed several topics which reflected the concerns of the Gnesio-Lutheran party, but which Melanchthon had not touched upon. Corvinus's unique topics included "A Christian Must Be Certain of His Faith," "False Teachers Are to Be Sharply Condemned," "Faithful Christian Preachers Are Bound by Their Office to Condemn the Sins of Their People," "The World neither Can nor Wishes to Tolerate the Gospel," "On Offense and Disunity in the Church," and "Whether One May Say, 'I Am a Lutheran.'"[35] Before the last of these topics Corvinus treated "Predestination."[36] This followed the lead of Melanchthon's third edition in placing the subject late in the outline. (The *Syntagma* and Melanchthon's second edition had set predestination at the heart of their presentations of the gospel.) Corvinus's locus on the cross of the Christian's suffering reflected Gnesio-Lutheran experience with exile and other forms of political persecution. He closed his work with citations from Luther on "The Church," "Church Discipline," "Ceremonies," "Political Authority," and "Marriage."[37] Thus Corvinus's outline

34. Each volume of the *Magdeburg Centuries,* the church history produced by the circle of Gnesio-Lutherans gathered in that city in the days following the Smalcald War, contained one chapter "on the teaching" of the church. The first volume of the *Centuries* was issued in two parts, the first covering the biblical material of the first century. Its chapter "on doctrine" was separately published as *ΣΥΝΤΑΓΜΑ, seu corpus doctrinae Christi, ex novo Testamento tantum, Methodica ratione, singulari fide & diligentia congestum* (Basel: Johannes Oporinus, 1558); there were five subsequent editions through 1585. The German translation (Mühlhausen, Alsace: Peter Schmidt, 1562) was expanded by Wigand and Judex with *ΣΥΝΤΑΓΜΑ, seu corpus doctrinae veri & omnipotentis Dei, ex veteri Testamento tantum, methodica ratione. . . .* (Basel: Oporinus and Herwagen, 1564).

35. *Loci commvnes,* 416–29, 429–59, 460–510, 623–50, 650–95, 709–92.

36. Ibid., 695–708.

37. Ibid., 792–1001.

for teaching the faith through Luther's words was slightly different from Melanchthon's presentation of Christian doctrine.

Corvinus's Luther spoke most extensively about the topics of the Word of God (12 percent of the total pages), the obligation of pastors to rebuke their parishioners' sins, the propriety of claiming the name "Lutheran," and the two kinds of faith (each about 10 percent of the volume). The other eighteen topics covered 60 percent of Corvinus's collection. His Luther focused on the bondage of the human will, the proper distinction of law and gospel, and the comfort of the gospel in Jesus Christ. But Corvinus's excerpts from Luther's works also reflected the turmoil and tribulation of Luther's church in the years following the Smalcald War and the Interims.

The locus "Whether One May Say, 'I Am a Lutheran,'" underscored Luther's insistence that believers are Christians, not Lutherans. At the same time the chief thrust of the nearly twenty citations under this topic is a demand for clear and sharp rejection of false teachers and false teachings.[38] The topic "Ceremonies" included citations from Luther's anti-Roman polemic branding as "cotyrants with the devil" political authorities who force Christians into certain practices. This was a direct attack on the Philippist position in the Leipzig Interim.[39] The locus "That a Christian Must Be Certain of His Faith and Look to God's Word Alone and Be Christ's Disciple" reinforced this criticism of the Philippist tendency toward compromise.[40] "That False Teachers Are to Be Sharply Condemned" denounced the Philippist belief that Lutheran unity could best be restored by a "forgetting" *(amnēstia)* of past mistakes, a clearing of the slate without condemning, as the Gnesio-Lutherans demanded, specific false teachings and false teachers.[41] "Faithful Christian Preachers Are Bound by Their Office to Condemn the Sins of Their People" had a similar message regarding life at the parish level.[42] As he dealt with the problems of heresy and sin within the church, however, Corvinus also had Luther remind his readers that believers are saints and sinners at the same time; this reminder, rich in pastoral concern, was drawn from the House Postil's sermon for Easter Tuesday.

"On the Holy Cross," "That the World neither Can nor Wishes to Tolerate the Gospel," and "On Offense and Disunity in the Church" all treated aspects of the persecution which Gnesio-Lutherans—and other contemporary evangelicals as well—had suffered as a result of both

38. Ibid., 709–92.
39. Ibid., 867–88.
40. Ibid., 416–29.
41. Ibid., 429–59.
42. Ibid., 460–510.

Emperor Charles's attempt to eliminate Lutheranism from his empire and the efforts of Lutheran princes and city councils to bring independent-minded pastors under the discipline of a centralizing authority, efforts that were part of the absolutizing development of the early modern period that led to seventeenth-century absolutism.

Corvinus's outline of Christian teaching in one thousand quarto pages did not touch all the topics which Melanchthon had deemed important. Its list of loci was unique, and its agenda had clearly been shaped by the events and concerns which formed and drove the Gnesio-Lutherans. Corvinus had fashioned from the raw material of Luther's works an image of the Luther he believed would have instructed the church of the 1550s and 1560s had the Reformer lived: a prophetic teacher, anchored in God's Word, proclaiming law and gospel. Considering the milieu in which this work was assembled, two topics are particularly noticeable by their absence. Corvinus dealt little with Christology and not at all with the sacraments. Without knowing more about the man, it is impossible to suggest why this is the case. His presentation of Luther spoke to the concerns of his time, but his readers encountered an incomplete Luther.

The Form of Luther's Thought according to Kirchner

To a great extent the content of the teaching of Timotheus Kirchner's Luther resembled that of Corvinus's reformer. But Kirchner presented Luther's thought on more topics and drew material from both his German and Latin works (Corvinus's compilation contained only German quotations). Kirchner's Luther was a more balanced expositor of the whole counsel of God than was Corvinus's. That is, Kirchner's loci are, unlike Corvinus's, roughly equal in length, with one exception. In his German *Thesaurus* the topic "The Lord's Supper" covers almost 15 percent of the volume. No other topic comes close. That may reflect his sacramental piety; it almost certainly reflects the increasing conflict he was experiencing with spiritualizing views of the Lord's Supper in German evangelical churches.

In form or structure Kirchner's exposition of each topic is similar to the approach taken in the *Syntagma* and its Melanchthonian model. In the Latin volume Kirchner often began a locus with "What it is [Quod sit]," in the German, with "the several names for ——— [Mancherley Namen]." Within each locus he followed the pattern of dialectical analysis which Lutheran students of his generation had learned from Melanchthon's textbooks if not from Melanchthon himself.

Kirchner drew material for his Latin *Thesaurus* from Luther's Latin works, for his German *Thesaurus* from the German works. His association with the organizers of the Jena edition may have influenced this decision, for they, too, resolved to use Luther's works only in their original language. Occasionally Kirchner, like the Jena editors, made an exception and used a translation when, to complete a point, he needed a quotation from a work originally published in the other language. This general principle of citing works only in their original language dictated that certain themes were stressed in one volume but absent from the other. Kirchner used more than three dozen different works by Luther in compiling his Latin collection and over one hundred separate tracts or books for the German version, a reflection of the ratio between Luther's Latin and German titles.

The Latin *Thesaurus* was drawn overwhelmingly from biblical commentary in either lecture or sermon form. Eighty percent of Kirchner's Latin loci used at least one citation from the Genesis lectures, and over sixty percent drew on the Galatians commentary of 1535. Luther's comments on various Psalms were equally important, and the Isaiah commentary was not far behind in the number of topics to which it contributed. Luther's Latin sermons on Matthew's Gospel also provided material for a dozen topics. His treatments of Hosea, Joel, and Micah were each cited in at least eight loci, often several times within the locus. None of his occasional writings was cited nearly this much. Kirchner apparently preferred Luther's biblical studies. On the other hand, the German *Thesaurus* did not rely on exegetical material as heavily as did the Latin volume; it employed a much wider range of writings, reflecting the linguistic profile of Luther's total opus.

Like Corvinus's *Loci communes Lutheri,* Kirchner's work represents the developing tradition of Christian teaching among the Gnesio-Lutheran students and followers of the Reformer, albeit a more moderate version of that tradition. Kirchner's treatment of the Holy Scriptures and the rules for their interpretation ("On God's Word," which in German was expanded to "On God's Word or the Holy Scripture") was more extensive than that of Corvinus. He also addressed questions which Corvinus apparently found irrelevant, such as the forms in which God's Word had come to the people of the Old Testament—dreams, visions, and prophecies. Whereas Corvinus had directed Luther's words to the pressing issues of the day, Kirchner attempted to cover a wider area, including questions which the church had asked in the past and might again in the future. He also cited Luther on themes which the Reformer had loved and favored, such as the authority and certainty of the Scriptures and the power and effect of the Word as it becomes living and active in the proclamation of preachers.[43] Kirchner included polemic against the Roman Catholic and Schwenck-

43. *Thesavrvs,* 1–32; *Deudscher Thesaurus,* 1ʳ–18ʳ.

feldian attitudes toward the Scriptures as well. In contrast to Corvinus, Kirchner treated questions of Christology quite extensively under the topic "On God." He cited *On the Last Words of David* at length (some four folio pages) on "the two natures in Christ and the communication of attributes,"[44] a reflection that in the 1560s a controversy over Christology was beginning within the Wittenberg camp.

The controversy over Flacius's definition of original sin as the substance of the fallen human creature (understood in Aristotelian terms) lay in the future. A decade later Kirchner would oppose that definition. In his German *Thesaurus* he quoted Luther's sermons on 1 Corinthians 15 to demonstrate that "sin is not the human substance and nature itself created by God, but a terrible corruption and contamination of it." In citing Luther's sermon on Genesis 1 he used language which would later cause Flacius severe difficulty: "The human creature must be either in God's image or in the devil's." Kirchner also entitled a section taken from Luther's treatment of Hosea 2 (in a discussion of characteristics which original sin imposes upon the sinner) "The Loss of God's Image and the Acquisition of the Image of Satan." In the German *Thesaurus* the topic "The Powers of Free Will in the Sinful Human Creature" was placed in the midst of the loci on anthropology, preceding the loci on sin. In the Latin *Thesaurus* the corresponding locus was entitled "On the Bound Will," and found at the end of the loci on sin. In both cases Luther's arguments were marshaled in defense of the position for which Kirchner had suffered exile. He made it quite clear that in spiritual matters the human will had lost all its capacity for turning to God. The Latin treated the issue in particular detail, with citations from *On the Bondage of the Will,* but also from Luther's comments on Genesis, Hosea, Galatians, and Psalm 51.[45]

Kirchner's Latin analysis of God's law did not present its third use (as a guide for the lives of believers); the German did. In both, the theological use of the law, its accusing function, was emphasized. The Latin locus was entitled "On the Moral Law," and the German "On the Law of Ceremonies and the External Regulations of the People of Israel." In regard to the moral injunctions found in the Old Testament both stressed that "Moses and nature are one thing [the same]." That both also reprinted Luther's *Theses against the Antinomians* reflects Kirchner's concern that the law of God be preached effectively.[46]

The 1535 Galatians commentary provided much of the material for Kirchner's Latin exposition of the concept of the gospel and the proper

44. *Deudscher Thesaurus,* 31^{r}–39^{v}.

45. *Thesavrvs,* 154–201; *Deudscher Thesaurus,* 75^{v}–78^{v}.

46. *Thesavrvs,* 272–327; *Deudscher Thesaurus,* 99^{v}–112^{r}.

distinction of gospel from law. Similarly, the interpretation of Galatians 3 provided the German audience with a careful analysis of the distinction between law and gospel. Kirchner's Luther attacked misunderstandings of the gospel even as he proclaimed God's gracious promise in Christ. Kirchner made certain that his readers would understand the power of the gospel and its effect. Appropriate citations from Luther's biblical exposition in both languages emphasized the nature and role of faith at the center of the believer's life.[47]

The thesauruses continued their presentation of the gospel with a locus on predestination. Here Luther's pastoral concern for those afflicted with doubts about their status before God and his warnings against speculation in regard to God's hidden will complement his proclamation of God's unconditional grace and favor toward his chosen children.[48]

Longer loci on justification through faith follow in each volume. Typically Kirchner begins by orienting the reader to the terminology. Citing Luther's preface to the 1535 Galatians commentary, the Latin *Thesaurus* distinguishes between two kinds of righteousness, God's and human, a distinction vital for a proper understanding of the Scriptures. In the German this distinction is drawn from Luther's comments on the seven penitential psalms and John 16. Kirchner then couples antipapal polemic with a careful presentation of Luther's pastoral application of the forgiveness of sins and the justification of the sinner in God's sight.[49]

Good works flow from justification, Kirchner was convinced, and so he continued with a locus "On New Obedience or Good Works," which stressed their origin in faith. He continued with a locus on "Prayer," which in the German *Thesaurus* preceded treatments of four additional good works which are not found in the Latin *Thesaurus,* but which are grouped together under one topic in the *Syntagma:* "confession of biblical teaching," "love for the neighbor," "Christian almsgiving," and "Christian fasting."[50]

Following "On Repentance," which contained extensive polemic against medieval practices,[51] Kirchner treated the sacraments: baptism, absolution (this section was entitled "On the Office and Power of the Keys" in German), and the Lord's Supper. Here polemic against Anabaptists and Sacramentarians was coupled with the proclamation of the gospel through the sacraments. Citing a wide range of Luther's

47. *Thesavrvs,* 328–63 (= 353); *Deudscher Thesaurus,* 112ʳ–25ʳ.
48. *Thesavrvs,* 363 (= 353)–64; *Deudscher Thesaurus,* 125ᵛ–27ᵛ.
49. *Thesavrvs,* 364–451; *Deudscher Thesaurus,* 127ᵛ–58ᵛ.
50. *Thesavrvs,* 452–540; *Deudscher Thesaurus,* 159ʳ–91ᵛ.
51. *Thesavrvs,* 540–62; *Deudscher Thesaurus,* 191ᵛ–202ᵛ.

works on the Lord's Supper and other works as well, the German *Thesaurus* discussed at great length the presence of Christ's body and blood in the sacraments and its effects in the life of the believer.[52]

The locus on the church contained some antipapal polemic along with an emphasis on God's drawing his people to Christ through Word and sacrament. The following locus, which dealt with the public ministry of the Word, reflected the Gnesio-Lutheran insistence on the independence of the church, and thus of its ministers, from the political authorities. Luther's comments on the importance of the ministerial office and its functions were augmented with suitable warnings against subjecting the pastors of the church to earthly authorities.[53]

Kirchner was presenting the whole of Christian doctrine, as the heirs of Melanchthon understood it, and so he continued with the topics which Philip had set in place for his church: Christ's kingdom, Christian liberty, the cross, miracles, the Antichrist, human traditions, ceremonies and adiaphora, offense. With the exception of the cross in the life of the church and believers, none of these topics received much attention. Not so, however, with the next two topics, marriage and governmental authority, the latter of which cited Luther on the godliness of the ruler's calling and the virtues which God expects from those whom he has placed in the offices of temporal power. The German *Thesaurus* recalled Luther's hesitance, in a letter to Wenzeslaus Linck, regarding use of the sword to suppress heresy.[54]

In following Melanchthon in creating a locus on the cross in the Christian life, Kirchner treated the cross of illness, but gave more extensive attention to the "calamities which befall the church" and particularly its pastors, a subject reflecting his own exile because of the position he espoused in the synergistic controversy.[55] The German *Thesaurus* also included a separate locus on confessing the faith.[56] Nonetheless, Kirchner's work is not dominated by the same sort of concern for public confession that absorbs the latter half of Corvinus's *Loci*.

Like Corvinus, Kirchner wanted to make Luther available and useful to pastors and to preserve his teaching through their ministries. Thus their *Loci communes Lutheri* resemble each other to a great extent, though Kirchner's is more complete and more oriented toward the historical catholic dogmatic tradition than toward the burning issues of

52. *Thesavrvs,* 563–609; *Deudscher Thesaurus,* 203^{r}–302^{r}.
53. *Thesavrvs,* 610–58; *Deudscher Thesaurus,* 302–53^{r}.
54. *Thesavrvs,* 659–823; *Deudscher Thesaurus,* 353^{v}–402^{r}.
55. *Thesavrvs,* 676–706; *Deudscher Thesaurus,* 376^{v}–95^{r}.
56. *Deudscher Thesaurus,* 183^{v}–84^{v}.

the day. For Kirchner encountered Luther in the quiet of his study, while Corvinus called on Luther's words for support on the barricades of religious controversy.

The Form of Luther's Thought according to the Brandenburg Theologians

The *Loci communes Lutheri* which Andreas Musculus and Georg Coelestin assembled to reinforce their colleagues' commitment to the Augsburg Confession and Luther's Small Catechism was similar in its content though much shorter. Its stated intention was "to explain the Augsburg Confession and the Small Catechism with durable, clear instruction, based on God's Word, regarding the most important points of our religion and Christian faith from the postils and doctrinal writings of the venerable and precious man of God, Dr. Martin Luther,"[57] the same goal as that of the Formula of Concord.

Luther's two postils provided a majority of the citations by which the Brandenburg church order guided pastors into the proper understanding of the pressing issues of the time. These issues, rather than the entire conception of Christian teaching, shaped the Brandenburg extract of Luther's thought. In this way it resembles Corvinus's *Loci communes Lutheri.* Its pages also reflect the Gnesio-Lutheran positions which particularly Musculus had defended in controversy at the University of Frankfurt an der Oder. These selections reveal above all Musculus's individual understanding of the uses of the law in the Christian life. He believed that Christians perform good works not because of a special use of the law in their lives, but apart from all necessity and "with a free and merry spirit." In the Brandenburg collection of Luther citations the topic "On the Law" presents the functions and powers of the law along with its incapacity to save. Only through faith can the law be kept, the extracts from Luther reminded the Brandenburg pastors. Musculus's so-called antinomian views undoubtedly influenced the selection of citations from the postils and from the preface to the sermons on the Sermon on the Mount. In line with Musculus's views, no discussion of any third use of the law is found here.[58]

The document's treatment of repentance reflects the peculiar developments in Brandenburg, where the antinomian Johann Agricola had found refuge after he fled Wittenberg in 1540.[59] Although not sharing

57. *Die Augspurgische Confession,* leaf between 31 and 32.

58. Ibid., 58^{r}–78^{r}. On Musculus's view of the law see Richter, *Gesetz und Heil,* esp. 208–50.

59. *Die Augspurgische Confession,* 102^{r}–19^{v}. On the controversy around Agricola, see Timothy J. Wengert, *Law and Gospel: Philip Melanchthon's Debate with John Agricola of Eisleben over* Poenitentia (Grand Rapids: Baker, 1997).

his position, Musculus, as Agricola's brother-in-law, had unavoidably been influenced to a certain extent by his framing of the issue. The church order of 1572 thus found passages in Luther which showed how the gospel can reveal God's wrath as well as his grace. At the same time it demonstrated how the law calls believers to repentance throughout their earthly lives. The topic "On Good Works" reflects Musculus's position in the controversy over the proposition that good works are necessary for salvation; his presentation is quite similar to those of Kirchner and Corvinus. The Brandenburg collection quotes Luther against the proposition and at the same time provides instruction on how the Holy Spirit produces the mortification of the flesh and the fruits of faith in believers.[60]

On the doctrine of original sin the Brandenburgers, while citing Luther to give witness to the total corruption of the heart of humanity, avoided a Flacian definition of original sin as the essence of the fallen human creature. The locus on baptism focused on defending infant baptism, but also reminded readers of the power of baptism in daily life. This locus was drawn entirely from four postil sermons. The Lord's Supper, treated thoroughly and in the same depth and breadth as "The Law" and "Good Works," reproduced material from the *Confession concerning Christ's Supper* of 1528.[61] On the issues and concerns which Lutherans in Brandenburg faced in the early 1570s, the new ecclesiastical constitution reflected the understanding of Luther that was held by Brandenburg's leading theologians, Andreas Musculus and Georg Coelestin. Like Corvinus and Kirchner, they regarded Luther as a unique teacher. They had the power to obligate the pastors of Brandenburg to their interpretations of Luther's positions, for the pastors had to vow to abide by the teaching of the new constitution. Musculus and Coelestin were willing to exercise this power because they believed that no one else had presented the pattern of sound teaching so clearly, accurately, and effectively as Luther had.

The Form of Luther's Thought according to Walther

In the *Chief Articles of the Christian Teaching . . . Explained with God's Word and Fine Passages from Dr. Luther and Dr. Melanchthon . . .*, compiled by Georg Walther, Luther teaches in the company of others, above all Philip Melanchthon. In the six octavo volumes Luther takes the lead in teaching the reader, but Melanchthon, Johannes Brenz, Johannes Bugenhagen, Urbanus Rhegius, and other Lutheran theologians are occasionally cited. Walther's compilation reflects a general Melanchtho-

60. *Die Augspurgische Confession,* 120^r–40^r.

61. Ibid., 32^r–40^r, 140^r–47^r, 147^v–68^r.

nian flavor, avoiding the controversial positions of some of Melanchthon's followers in the Philippist party while also not embracing special Gnesio-Lutheran concerns. In general, Walther followed Melanchthon's outline of Christian doctrine in organizing citations of the Reformer for the guidance of parish pastors.

The locus on the Lord's Supper was Walther's longest, spreading over 226 octavo pages (the topics of justification, the cross and tribulation, and marriage are each roughly 100 pages short of this total; the others are shorter yet). On the topic of the Lord's Supper Melanchthon was ignored almost completely—apart from the treatment of communion in both kinds and a catena of patristic quotations which he had assembled. Instead, Brenz and Bugenhagen offered modest support for extensive citations from Luther. The sacramentarian wing of the Philippist party found no backing from Walther here. Rather, he marshaled citations from Luther's sacramental writings—such as *On Communion in Both Kinds; That These Words of Christ, "This Is My Body," Still Stand; Against the Heavenly Prophets;* both Confessions on the Lord's Supper; and the *Open Letter to the Christians in Frankfurt am Main.* He did fail to raise one critical point which Lutherans regarded as essential to a complete definition of the real presence: that the unworthy or the impious also receive Christ's body and blood in the sacrament. But in Luther's words and his own Walther made it clear that Christ's body and blood are received "through the mouth" and that Christ is present "in a sacramental mode," two test phrases for the Lutheran understanding of the real presence of Christ's body and blood in the sacrament.[62] Walther clearly belonged to those admirers of Melanchthon who had no qualms about signing the Formula of Concord.

Throughout, Walther distinguished himself from the earlier editors of *Loci communes Lutheri* by his extensive use of Melanchthon, his occasional use of patristic citations, and his quotations from Brenz, Rhegius, and Bugenhagen. Like Kirchner, Walther's organization of material shows some signs of the influence of Melanchthon's rhetorical and dialectical tools, such as the syllogism, an influence not found in the works of Corvinus and the Brandenburgers. Walther did not view Luther's authority as unique by any means. He revered him as an important teacher of the church, whose insights could enrich contemporary preaching and teaching. But he viewed Luther and Melanchthon as two more or less equal members of a team, which included Rhegius, Brenz, and Bugenhagen as well. Walther's *Chief Articles of the Christian Teaching* demonstrates that in the 1570s some did not understand Luther to be a unique spokesman of God, even though they cherished

62. *Vierder Theil der Heubtartickel,* b^{r-v}.

him as a teacher of the church. For Walther it sufficed that God had given the church teachers of the power and insight of Luther—and Melanchthon.

The Form of Luther's Thought according to Fabricius

Theodosius Fabricius lived in a radically altered situation. Although controversy continued in the 1590s (indeed, he lost his parish in Saxony because he opposed the Crypto-Calvinists), Fabricius's church had clearly defined its lines of authority. In the process of establishing the Book of Concord as their secondary authority, the Lutherans of Fabricius's era had reverently but quite firmly set Luther to one side. For Fabricius he remained a voice with authority, but not the voice of God's authority. Thus Luther was no longer the adjudicator of disputes within the church, as he had been for Corvinus and Musculus—and remained for Cyriakus Spangenberg, who had opposed the introduction of the Book of Concord.

Fabricius followed the model of Neander in providing his readers with short selections from Luther's writings, somewhat longer than Neander's aphorisms to be sure, but seldom more than a paragraph. Demonstrating a broad and thorough knowledge of Luther's works, he relied very heavily on Luther's expositions of the Scripture in lecture, commentary, and sermon. Fabricius covered a broader range of subjects than did any of his predecessors. His *Loci communes Lutheri* reflects both the changing situation of German Lutheranism in the closing decades of the sixteenth century and the convictions of his father's circle of Gnesio-Lutheran pastors a generation earlier.

Fabricius's Luther conformed to the theology of the Formula of Concord. Theodosius reflected his father's rejection of Flacius's doctrine of original sin[63] (though the elder Fabricius had been Flacius's comrade in earlier battles after Luther's death), but he abandoned his father's rejection of the third use of the law and opted instead for the position of the Formula.[64] He devoted eight pages of his Latin loci to holding high "the dignity, necessity, and utility" of the proper distinction of law and gospel.[65] He followed the model of the *Syntagma* by turning next to predestination, providing his readers with brief but clear expressions of Luther's comfort for those who struggled with this teaching as well as the comfort which God's election of his own brings. Fabricius also cited Luther's warning against unseemly curiosity regarding the hidden will of God.[66]

63. *Loci communes* (German), 32^{v}–33^{r}; section 2, 58^{v}–59^{v}; (Latin), 2:27–29.
64. *Loci communes* (German), 38^{r}–39^{r}; section 2, 62^{v}–63^{r}; (Latin), 2:57–60.
65. *Loci communes* (Latin), 2:71–87.
66. *Loci communes* (Latin), 2:87–95.

In the second section of Fabricius's collection baptism receives a relatively long treatment. It includes both a defense of infant baptism and an application of God's promise in baptism to daily life.[67] Fabricius's own experience of conflict with the Crypto-Calvinists in Herzberg undoubtedly helped shape his handling of the locus "On the Lord's Supper." Particularly in the German volumes Fabricius drew extensively on Luther's polemic against the Sacramentarians in order to support the Lutheran understanding of Christ's body and blood in the Lord's Supper. He did not ignore, however, the application of the gospel of the sacrament to the daily life of the Christian. His treatment of the "benefits and power" of the Lord's Supper was drawn largely from Luther's sermons but also from some of his polemical writings.[68]

Fabricius's third section, which concerns the Christian life, begins with a long treatment of faith. He very effectively catches Luther's manner of grounding the believer's daily life in trust in Christ, and then moves on to show how faith produces a life of love for the neighbor. Fabricius also shows his readers how faith fights temptations to insecurity and despair. In a faithful synopsis of the basis of Luther's piety Fabricius collects a variety of Luther's observations on prayer, persecution, spiritual tribulations, on Christian joy, the mortification of the flesh, and struggles with weakness of faith. This section then treats a long series of virtues and provides words of comfort for the suffering and dying.

The fourth section of Fabricius's *Loci communes Lutheri* reviews Luther's teaching on the three estates of human society, with attention given to the Christian's calling in the home, the church, and the state. After introductory comments on God's establishment of the three estates, Fabricius treats the struggles of believers in carrying out their callings in face of the ingratitude of the world and the enmity of Satan. Fabricius cites Luther's admonition to people of high and low estate to fulfil their godly callings in humility and fear of God, recognizing and using the gifts which God has given them.

Fabricius's collection concludes by treating every evil imaginable. The fifth section gives extensive coverage to Satan's kingdom and to Satan himself and then quickly surveys Luther's critiques of papists, Turks, Jews, Anabaptists, Sacramentarians and Zwinglians, and antinomians. Tyrants and other governmental officials who persecute God's church are also criticized. Every kind of vice which Luther had condemned is reviewed. And just as the third section concludes its treatment of the Christian life with eschatological topics, including the

67. *Loci communes* (German), 52^{r}–55^{r}; section 2, 81^{r}–85^{v}; (Latin), 2:113–25.
68. *Loci communes* (German), 55^{r}–62^{v}; section 2, 85^{v}–89^{v}; (Latin), 2:140–49.

resurrection of the pious to glory and life everlasting, so the fifth section concludes the entire work with the locus "Hell."

Fabricius did not intend his *Loci communes Lutheri* to be read from beginning to end. Nor did he gather his materials in the form of a textbook of Christian teaching, as had Corvinus, Kirchner, and Walther. Instead, his work offered a handy reference in which pastors could find words from Luther on any and every topic which they might want to address in preaching and teaching. In addition, Fabricius presented a Luther whose proclamation of the biblical message conformed to the theology of the new Lutheran secondary authority, the Book of Concord.

Fabricius also conformed to the structure imposed by the Melanchthonian loci. His contemporaries apparently found most useful those works that employed Melanchthon's method purely and simply, that is, expositions of Lutheran teaching that used Philip's rhetorical and dialectical tools to analyze biblical materials; dogmatic works of the era contained only occasional reference to Luther. As valuable as Luther was for Fabricius's contemporaries as their father in the faith, he had lost his position as the authoritative interpreter of the Scripture. The nature of his instruction obviously changed when others excerpted his words. In the *Loci communes Lutheri* the citations are long enough to permit the Reformer's voice to be heard quite clearly, although Fabricius's quotations are briefer than those in the other works (the shortness of the citations tended to put interpretation in the hands of the readers). Doctor Luther continued to teach from the pages of these works, but his teaching was limited to the questions posed and to selected words.

Fabricius was not the last person to produce a compilation of Luther citations for the reference shelf of the Lutheran pastor. In 1611 and 1613 Andreas Praetorius, Andreas Musculus's grandson, published two volumes, *Luther Reborn* and *The Posthumous Luther, or Luther's Heart,* at the behest of the Frankfurt printer Henning Gross. Praetorius followed the pattern of Michael Neander, excerpting in the order of their appearance the best quotations from the Wittenberg and the Eisleben editions respectively.[69] In 1614 Philip Gräter, provost in Herbrechtingen in Württemberg, prepared a "treasure chest of Luther" for laity. His introduction of Luther to the people was divided into five topics: Luther's confrontation with the papacy, his doctrinal writings, the

69. *Luther Redivivus Oder Geistreiche Schatzkammer/Aus allen deutschen Schrifften D. Martini Lutheri Mit grosser Arbeit vnd Fleiss zusammen getragen* (Leipzig: Michael Lantzenberger, 1611); and *Lutherus posthumus sive Cor Luther. Das ist/Das Lutherische hertz. Oder Nu[e]tzlicher Ausszug aus den deutschen Eisslebischen Tomis vnd Bu[e]chern/D. Martini Lutheri p.m.* (Leipzig: Michael Lantzenberger, 1613).

devil's attacks on evangelical teaching, polemical writings against all foes, and the story of his death.[70] Almost a half century later the superintendent of the church in Regensburg, Erasmus Gruber (1609–84), organized Neander's short quotations from Luther's works into fifty-two "articles." This compendium of loci ranging from "God's Word" to "Eschatology" proved useful to pastors in their preaching and teaching.[71] At the end of the seventeenth century a series of loci on the theology of the Augsburg Confession was drawn from Luther's words in the Altenburg edition and cast into a dialogue between Studiosus Theologiae (S.T.) and Luther Redivivus (L.R.); in the course of the dialogue Luther defends the theological positions of Philip Jakob Spener, who wrote a preface for the work.[72] The tradition of collecting Luther citations for handy use by parish pastors and others continued into the twentieth century.[73]

That such collections continued to appear in the seventeenth century suggests that the church—pastors and laity—had a need and found use for anthologies of excerpts from Luther's writings. That almost all of these works appeared in only one edition suggests that none of the editors solved the problem of providing enduring auxiliary material for pastors' sermons and laypeople's meditation. The evolution of the genre from doctrinal textbook to rhetorical thesaurus suggests that Luther's words were increasingly being fit into previously conceived molds that were formed by a host of factors, Luther's reformatory insights among them.

Melanchthon's method of organizing learning, particularly theological learning, made collections of Luther citations by topic natural for

70. *Schatzkammer Luther. Aller Geschichten vnd Schrifften Lutheri kurtzer Begriff vnd Erklerung in fu[e]nff Theilen . . . Alles zu klarem Verstand der letsten Engel in S. Joannis Offenbarung* (Lauingen: Jacob Winter, 1614).

71. *Theologia Luther In kurtzen ausserlesenen Spru[e]chen/von den fu[e]rnemsten Articuln Christlicher lehr fu[e]rgestelt/vnd aus des theuren see: [seeliger] Manns lateinischen vnd Teutschen Schrifften gezogen* (Regensburg: Christoff Fischer, 1657). Gruber went on to publish similar works: *Luther redivivvs, Oder Das . . . Theologische Schatz-ka[e]stlein . . .* (Frankfurt/Main: Johann Niclas Hummer and Johann Gerlin, 1665), and *Spicilegium sacrum, Oder Außerlesene Aphorismi und Spru[e]che von allerley denkwu[e]rdigen Theologischen Materien/aus denen Stucken vnd Schrifften deß theuren seeligen Mannes Gottes/D. Martini Lutheri . . .* (Tübingen: Johann Heinrich Reiß, 1670).

72. *Luther Redivivus Oder Des fu[e]rnehmsten Lehrers der Augspurgischen Confession Herrn D. Martini Luthers . . . Hinterlassene Schrifftliche Erkla[e]rungen Aus welchen ungezweiffelt zu vernehmen/Was der Augspurgischen Confession eigentliche Meinung vnd Verstand in allen Articuln allezeit gewesen/vnd noch sey . . .* (Halle: Christoph Salfeld, 1697).

73. E.g., *Lutherlexikon,* ed. Kurt Aland, 4th ed. (Göttingen: Vandenhoeck & Ruprecht, 1983); *What Luther Says: An Anthology,* ed. Ewald Plass (St. Louis: Concordia, 1959). Both of these volumes constitute a collection of aphorisms handy for inclusion in a sermon; they do not present a systematic treatment of Christian doctrine.

the people of the following generation. Corvinus and Kirchner, Musculus and Walther, proceeded to gather quotations and organize them into *loci communes* with the conviction that they were letting Luther speak to the changing landscape of church and society in their generation. They did not reflect on how to make objective allowance for their own concerns and prejudices. They simply pursued the task of presenting Luther to the public of their day. In so doing, particularly those compilers whose citations were longer did indeed let the Reformer speak on his own terms, even though he spoke to the questions posed by the individual editor's conception of the biblical message.

Most editions of the *Loci communes Lutheri* did not make claims for Luther's prophetic authority. No explicit definition of his words as secondary authority is found in any of these volumes apart from the Brandenburg collection, which was explicitly designed to have that kind of authority. The others left to their readers the decision on how to use the material assembled and organized in their pages. Clearly, however, readers were to recognize Luther as the first and foremost teacher of the church in all ages.

Although the collections of aphorisms, such as Neander's and Fabricius's, delivered little more than ornamentation for teaching and preaching, the longer excerpts gathered by Corvinus, Kirchner, Musculus, and Walther did indeed convey much of Luther's thought. For those who wanted to learn his theology within the framework of the method taught by the theological faculties of the era, these works undoubtedly served a valuable purpose. The *Loci communes Lutheri* permitted the Reformer to continue teaching into succeeding generations.

Conclusion

Theander Luther

Five hundred years after his birth Martin Luther continues to engage and fascinate those who encounter him. The testimony of his biography and his writings continues to cast "reflections of his form in water of different depths and hues," as Horst Stephan commented nearly a century ago.[1] Modern scholars have formed their own judgments of Luther and have put his thoughts to their own use on bases different from those that motivated his contemporaries. Apt is Mark Edwards's observation that twentieth-century accounts often give a false representation of sixteenth-century perceptions, "not because the historian knows too little but because the historian knows too much."[2] This is the case because historians have a view "from above"—a more comprehensive view of Luther's context, of his impact, even of the corpus of his writings—a view which none of Luther's contemporaries, nor Luther himself, could have had. For instance, as Edwards observes, "we forget that, except perhaps for a few of Luther's students, no contemporary read Luther's works in light of his pre-Reformation lectures on Psalms, Galatians, and Romans."[3] In fact, the few who had read manuscript notes on these lectures preferred his later works, which more reflected what they had heard from him.

On the other hand, when modern historians come to what Luther wrote and wrought, they do not bring the yearnings and longings shaped by the spirit of medieval apocalyptic nor the humanistic adventure of return to the sources. Instead, we bring our own conceptual framework and our own questions and goals to the texts and story of Martin Luther. Further, it is impossible to return to the pristine sources of the 1510s, 1520s, and 1530s uninfluenced by the interpretations of Luther forged by his students and contemporaries and those who followed them in the succeeding two generations.

1. Horst Stephan, *Luther in den Wandlungen seiner Kirche* (Giessen: Töpelmann, 1907), 127.

2. Mark U. Edwards Jr., *Printing, Propaganda, and Martin Luther* (Berkeley: University of California Press, 1994), 4.

3. Ibid.

From the perspective of the sixteenth century, Luther had seven heads or more. To a remarkable if not unique degree this monk and professor became a fixation for foes and friends alike. Whatever the reasons (as assessed by twentieth-century scholars) may have been, this widespread fixation developed less on the strength of political power or economic resources or social status than on the strength of his ideas and through the public presentation and projection of these ideas. His disciples perceived him to be an authoritative prophet or an insightful teacher or a national and cultural hero, or one who combined two or all of these roles.

As Luther's supporters praised him by recounting his heroic deeds or by repeating his insightful instruction or by putting his image and ideas to use in the life of church and society, they inevitably cast the raw material of his life into forms dictated by the challenges and concerns of their own times. Around 1520 a host of images were marshaled to describe this prophetic figure. In the first decade of his emergence in public he was seen as an authority for determining the proper exposition of biblical truth, the new teacher of the church for the last times, and a hero who would end papal tyranny. All three representations of the Wittenberg professor continued to be in vogue throughout his life and in the years immediately after his death. Gradually, however, his role as adjudicatory authority, which was transferred from his person to his writings, appeared ever less able to serve effectively as a means of deciding and defining public teaching. The national hero he remained, ever more simplified and stylized but not less important because of that, particularly as the shadow of the Counter-Reformation grew heavier over evangelical Germany. His role as teacher continued as well, albeit in limited and adapted form. Changing times meant changing use of the individual who had been thought to personify the message of God and to satisfy the longings of the people.

Not all of Luther's followers put him to use as a substitute for popes and councils, as a secondary authority who could adjudicate disputes over the gospel and the practice of the church. Many did, for the church always needs such a secondary authority. The conviction that the papacy was Antichrist and that councils and the Fathers were fallible produced a crisis of authority in the churches of the Reformation. Among Luther's followers biblical authority prevailed unchallenged as the primary authority for determining truth in the presentation of the gospel. The Fathers and councils had also schooled the thinking of the Wittenberg disciples, although they reckoned with the possibility of errors in patristic and conciliar writings and thus dismissed them as secondary authorities. Accordingly, some certain standard for adjudication of disputes over the interpretation of the biblical message was needed.

Luther's prophet-like appearance on the late medieval scene and his own dynamic concept of the Word of God—as it is repeated in the mouths of living speakers of the biblical message—prompted his contemporaries to attribute adjudicatory authority to him. Medieval apocalyptic hopes and humanist convictions regarding the power of effective oral communication combined with his own understanding of the power of God in the living voice of the gospel to create a belief that he was a special tool of God. As such, it was believed, he spoke God's word of condemnation against the deceiving tyrants of the papal system and announced God's word of grace and mercy in Jesus Christ, and he did so with an authority which he had received along with the gift of clear interpretation of the biblical message. But even while he lived, appeals to his authority were restricted to those circles that accepted him as God's authoritative prophet for the latter day. Furthermore, once he died and could no longer directly apply God's Word to current situations, and the church had to rely on the written works he had left behind, it ceased to be practical—and possible—to regard him as a secondary, adjudicatory authority in the church. The written corpus was too bulky. It contained contradictions. It became politically delicate to emphasize Luther so strongly.

The negative side of Luther's proclamation—in defense of the gospel and in opposition to papal oppression—had made him a hero of Herculean proportions to his contemporaries around 1520; and a hero for nation and people, for freedom and humanity, he remained, particularly as the Roman Catholic prelates and princes became increasingly aggressive and the political tensions within the empire mounted—culminating in the Thirty Years' War. In the following centuries, pressed into a variety of images and forms by the governments of divine-right monarchies and by fans of the Enlightenment, by theologians of diverse perspectives and by politicians of various ideologies,[4] Luther's persona continued to prove itself a useful symbol—a hero of one kind or another—even when his authority and indeed his theology were rejected by his partisans. More often than not, misunderstanding of the hero—occasionally perhaps deliberate, often innocent—separated the historical figure of the Reformer from the Luther myths created ever anew for some purpose or another.

Luther has found enduring use as a teacher of the church as well. To a remarkable extent his thought continued to determine the agenda of theological discussion in many parts of Christendom in succeeding generations. Those who claimed his name could not escape addressing the emphases of his theology—justification, the Word of God as means

4. For literature on this subject, see p. 10 n. 4.

of grace, the authority of Scripture, the nature and effect of the sacraments, to name but a few of his doctrinal accents. Nonetheless, from the beginning his followers' understanding of his teaching was influenced by the medieval heritage which continued to echo through the minds of his contemporaries, by the agenda of polemic set by his foes as well as his friends, by their individual pastoral or professorial concerns, and by the method and theology of his Wittenberg colleague Philip Melanchthon. Melanchthon's practice of theology schematized the thinking of students into the forms dictated by the loci method, and they could recognize no alternative to placing Luther's thought into these Melanchthonian forms.

The dogmatic tradition which ran from Melanchthon through Martin Chemnitz's commentary on his *Loci communes theologici* to Johann Gerhard and the dogmatic works of Lutheran orthodoxy became the standard expression of what Lutherans believed and taught. Other sources may have shaped preaching, catechetical instruction, and pastoral care, but the conceptual framework into which graduates of Lutheran theological faculties placed materials from Luther's pen and the pens of other theologians came from the Melanchthonian dogmatic tradition. Modern scholars may express chagrin or regret over this fact; indeed, they may find Luther more refreshing or relevant than the works of his followers. But his epigones did fulfil the calling of all theologians: they applied the biblical message and the tradition of their church to the lives of their parishioners in their own generation. And however they may have adapted Luther, they adopted what they understood the heart of his message to be, even if from later perspectives they may have sacrificed too much of its peculiar insights.

There are grounds for such judgments. The topical method for formulating theology had no place for introductory prolegomena providing orientation to the theological process and setting forth the presuppositions which guided Luther's thought. Thus it was difficult for his followers to incorporate explicitly into their theological method his distinction between the two kinds of righteousness as well as the several elements comprehended in his theology of the cross.[5] His students often grasped such elements of his conceptual framework, but the *loci communes* tradition and the polemic of the period narrowed the usage of Luther to those topics and citations that fit into the Melanchthonian scheme and were relevant to the new issues of a new day.

Indeed, Luther's followers focused above all on those issues to which the polemics of the period gave the most attention and on the concep-

5. See Robert Kolb, "The Ordering of the *Loci Communes Theologici:* The Structuring of the Melanchthonian Dogmatic Tradition," *Concordia Journal* 23 (1997): 321–23.

tualization of those issues that was dictated by the polemical fronts. Thus Luther's doctrine of justification, somewhat dehydrated in the course of two generations of polemic but nonetheless retaining its fundamental form, remained at the heart of Lutheran self-definition, but the Reformer's understanding of the atonement, not under dispute, was not taken as seriously already in the generation of his own students.[6] Also a certain change of focus took place in sacramental theology in the decades following his death. Luther's rich baptismal theology received far less attention from his followers than he had given it himself, and the continuing battles against the Roman mass and Reformed views of the real presence highlighted polemical issues—although pastoral concerns for consolation and pious living were not absent from the ongoing Lutheran treatment of the Lord's Supper. That Luther's complaint about the medieval church—that it de-emphasized baptism and disregarded its effects on daily life[7]—came to apply to his own disciples even as they emphasized the Lord's Supper may reflect not only the polemical situation, but also the staying power of medieval habits of thought.

Furthermore, that the hero Luther could be honored and celebrated by being cited in formulaic ways made it unnecessary for young pastors to read his writings and glean the fullness of his unique exposition of the biblical message. The dynamic of his homiletical teaching was placed into forms which limited the ways in which Luther could continue to teach his church. The sermonic ways in which he treated and conveyed the biblical message were set aside. The full scope of his teaching was channeled for the usage of a new day.

Indeed, Luther's teaching for the early sixteenth century needed to be reshaped and readdressed to changing patterns of church life and new issues as well as old. In the course of that inevitable process the vigor and vitality of the prophetic teacher were tamed even as the content of his teaching was preserved within the forms which his followers found useful for conveying his message in their generations. At the outset of the seventeenth century Luther continued to teach, particularly through the most practical of his writings: the postils and the commentaries which could aid preaching, his catechisms, his devotional meditations. His followers regarded him as the greatest of their teachers

6. See Robert Kolb, "'Not without the Satisfaction of God's Righteousness': The Atonement and the Generation Gap between Luther and His Students," *Archiv für Reformationsgeschichte,* supp. vol., *Die Reformation in Deutschland und Europa: Interpretation und Debatten,* ed. Hans R. Guggisberg und Gottfried G. Krodel (Gütersloh: Gütersloher Verlagshaus, 1993), 136–56.

7. *WA* 6:527. See also Mark David Tranvik, "The Other Sacrament: The Doctrine of Baptism in the Late Lutheran Reformation" (Th.D. diss., Luther Northwestern Theological Seminary, 1992).

even if they received his teaching through a grid constructed by others, above all Philip Melanchthon. Luther's prophetic authority as a substitute for popes and councils in adjudicating disputes over the biblical message had waned. Although its memory echoed through certain expressions of praise during the closing decades of the sixteenth century and the opening years of the seventeenth, the Book of Concord had become the secondary authority for a majority of Lutheran churches. The authority of Luther's person, and then the corpus of his writings, had been replaced by the authority of his church's confessional documents. Even those images which had given substance to the claim for his authority—above all, angel of the apocalypse and prophet—were by the end of the sixteenth century no longer used as grounds on which to justify his adjudication of doctrinal differences or to define public teaching, but were used instead to focus attention on his heroic deeds of resistance to papal oppression, deeds out of which the new and final revelation of the gospel had appeared.

Nonetheless, the vibrant interest in Luther's person and career, as well as the availability of much of the corpus of his writings, ensured that his voice continued to inform and form the faith and the life of the people of his church. Even though the extravagant appraisal of his contemporaries had been tamed, for most Lutherans of the early modern period this prophet and teacher loomed over their lives as a unique hero of the faith and of God's Word.

Appendix

The Printing History of the Wittenberg and Jena Editions of Luther's Works

Wittenberg Edition

German Volumes

Volume	Years							
1	1539	1539	1551	1552	1556	1567	1578	1602
2	1548	1551	1557	1567	1569	1570	1588	
3	1550	1553	1560	1566	1581			
4	1551	1553	1568	1569	1581			
5	1552	1556	1557	1573	1603			
6	1553	1558	1559	1570	1589			
7	1554	1561	1562	1563	1572	1583		
8	1556	1568	1569	1583				
9	1557	1558	1569	1590	1593			
10	1558	1564	1569	1593				
11	1558	1562	1565	1566	1572	1593		
12	1559	1572	1603					

Latin Volumes

Volume	Years						
I	1545	1550	1551	1558	1582		
II	1546	1551	1562				
III	1549	1553	1583				
IV	1552	1574					
V	1554						
VI	1555	1556	1557	1561	1562	1563	1580
VII	1557	1558					

Jena Edition

German Volumes

Volume	Years						
1	1555	1560	1564	1567	1575	1590	1615
2	1555	1558	1558	1563	1565	1572	1595	1613
3	1556	1560	1565	1573	1585	1588	1611
4	1556	1560	1565	1566	1573	1574	1586	1606
5	1557	1561	1565	1566	1575	1577	1588
6	1557	1561	1568	1578	1604		
7	1558	1562	1568	1578	1581	1598	
8	1558	1562	1568	1580	1600		

Latin Volumes

Volume	Years			
I	1556	1564	1579	
II	1557	1566	1581	1600
III	1557	1567	1582	1603
IV	1558	1570	1583	1611[1]

1. The printing history has been compiled from *Verzeichnis der im deutschen Sprachbereich erschienen Drucke des XVI. Jahrhunderts,* ed. Bayerische Staatsbibliothek (Munich) and Herzog August Bibliothek (Wolfenbüttel), part 1, vol. 12 (Stuttgart: Hiersemann, 1988), 14–39; and Kurt Aland, *Hilfsbuch zum Lutherstudium* (Witten: Luther, 1970), 549–81.

Bibliography

Primary Sources

Agricola, Johann. *Epistola S. Pavli ad Titum. . . .* Hagenau: Johannes Secer, 1530.

Amsdorf, Nikolaus von. *Das die zu Wittenberg im andern teil der bucher Doctoris Martini im buch das diese wort Christi (Das ist mein Leib etc.) noch fest stehen mehr denn ein blat vier ganzter Paragraphos vorsetzlich aussgelassen haben wie folget.* Magdeburg, 1549.

———. *Das Doctor Martinus kein Adiaphorist gewesen ist/vnd Das D. Pfeffinger vnd das buch on namen ihm gewalt vnd vnrecht thut.* Magdeburg: Christian Rödinger, 1550.

———. *Etliche spruche aus Doctoris Martini Luther Schriften/Darinne er/als ein Adiaphorist sich mit dem Bapst hat vergleichen wollen.* N.p., 1551.

Andreae, Jakob. *Fu[e]nff Predigten: Von dem Wercke der Concordien/Vnd endlichen Vergleichung der vorgefallenen streitigen Religions Artickeln. . . .* Dresden: Gimel Bergen, 1580.

———. *Passional Bu[e]chlein/Das ist/Die Historia des bittern vnd thewren leiden vnd sterbens/auch der fro[e]lichen Aufferstehung vnsers Herrn Jhesu Christi. . . .* Wittenberg: Johann Krafft, 1577.

Antwerp ministerium. *Confessio ministrorum Jesu Christi, in ecclesia Antwerpiensi, quae Augustanae Confessioni adsentitur.* N.p., 1567.

Apologia, Oder Verantwortung dess Christlichen Concordien Buchs/In welchen die ware Christliche Lehre/so im Concordi Buch verfasset/mit gutem Grunde heiliger Go[e]ttlichen Schrifft vertheydiget. . . . Dresden: Matthes Stoeckel, 1584.

Aslaksen, Konrad. *Oratio theologico-historica. De religionis per D. Martinum Lutherum reformatae origine & progressu in Germania; & ejusdem in hisce Regnis Danicae & Norvegiae, elapso hac centenario, videlicet ab Anno 1517. ad Annum 1617. . . .* Copenhagen: Heinrich Waldkirch, 1621.

Die Augspurgische Confession/aus dem Rechten Original . . . Der Kleine Catechismus Erklerung vnd kurtzer Ausszug aus den Postillen vnd Lehrschrifften des thewren Mans Gottes D. Lutheri/daraus zusehen/wie derselbe von fu[e]rnembsten Artickeln vnserer Christlichen Religion gelehret/Aus verordnunge . . . Johansen Georgen. . . . Frankfurt/Oder: Johann Eichorn, 1572.

Austrian ministerium. *Christlich Bekendtnuss/Einhelliger Consens/Bedencken vnd Ratschlag: Wie in dem Hochwichtigen Glaubens Artickel von der Erbsunde . . . geleret . . . Auff begeren der Lo[e]blichen zween Sta[e]nde von Herrn vnd der Ritterschaft in Oesterreich vnter der Enss/Von etlichen jhrer Gnaden darzu Beruffenen Theologen vnd Predigern in 1582. Jar verfasset.* N.p., 1587.

———. *Confessio. Christliche Bekentnis des Glaubens/etlicher Euangelischen Prediger in Oster-Reich*. Eisleben: Gaubisch, 1567.

Autumnus, Georg. *Vom Freien Willen vnd Bekerung des Menschen zu Gott. Warhafftige/bestendige/vnd in Gottes wort wol gegrundte Lehr vnd meinung/der heiligen Schrifft/Autoritet der Va[e]ter/vnd anderen Einreden vnd gegenwu[e]rffe/so die Schutzherrn des nichtigen Freen willens pflegen zu gebrauchen. . . .* Eisleben: Andreas Petri, c. 1565.

Balduin, Friedrich. *De disputatione Lvtheri cum Diabolo: in controversia de privata Missa, Tractatio theologica et Scholastica Apologetici loco. . . .* Eisleben: Jacob Gubisius, 1605.

———. *Parentatio Anniversaria pro D. Martino Lvthero P.M. qva ostenditur Beatissim. illum Patrem Verum fuisse Episcopum & Evangelistam Germaniae. . . .* Wittenberg: Zacharias Lehmann, 1599.

Beringer, Michael. *Rettung der Teutscher Biblischen Dolmetschung D. Martin Luthers: Wider die offenbar vnua[e]rschampte Vnwarheit des Melchior Zanger . . . damit er gedachte D. Luthers Biblische Translation/allerley beschwerlicher fa[e]hrlicher Irrthumben ohne Grund beschuldiget. . . .* Tübingen: Dietrich Werlin, 1613.

Bolschenius, Heinrich. *Cvrrvs et avriga Lvtheri, denuo recognitus*. Magdeburg: Meisner, 1600.

Braunschweig-Lüneburg ministerium. *Bedencken oder Censura der Theologen im Fu[e]rstenthumb Lu[e]neburg/von dem Newen Wittenbergischen Catechismo*. Jena: Richtzenhan, 1571.

———. *Corpvs doctrinae. Das ist/Die Summa/Form vnd vorbilde der reinen Christlichen Lehre/welche aus der heiligen Go[e]ttlichen Schrift der Propheten vnd Apostel zusammen gezogen ist. . . .* Uelzen: Michael Kröner, 1576.

Braunschweig-Wolfenbüttel ministerium. *Kirchenordnung Vnser/von Gottes Gnaden/Julij Hertzogen zu Braunschweig. . . .* Wolfenbüttel: Conrad Horn, 1569.

———. *Vom Catechismo etlicher Wittenbergischen. Der Lerer im Land zu Braunschweig Bedencken*. Jena: Richtzenhan, 1571.

Bremen ministerium. *Warhaffte Vnd Christliche verantwortung/der Prediger zu Bremen/auff die jhnen zugemessene Artickel vnd Puncten . . . Als Nemlich: I. Von der Person Christi. II. Von der heyligen Tauff. III. Von dem H. Abendmal. IIII. Von der Go[e]ttlichen Wahl. V. Von der Ceremonien*. Bremen: Arend Wessel and Dietrich Gloichstein, 1581.

Buck, Thomas. *Ehespiegel. Ein sehr lustige vnd lehrhaffte Comedi/darinnen angezeigt wu[e]rdt: Wie die Eltern jhre Kinder auffziehen vnd verheyraten: Vnd welcher massen das jung Gesind/beides im ledigen Stand/vnd hernach in wehrenden Ehe sich verhalten solle. Aus dem lebendigen kra[e]fftigen Wort Gottes/den Schrifften Lutheri/vnd andern guten Bu[e]chern gezogen. . . .* Tübingen: Georg Gruppenbach, 1598.

Bugenhagen, Johannes. *Eine Christliche Predigt Vber der Leich vnd Begrabnus/Weiland des Ehrwurdigen/Achtbarn vnd Hochgelarten Herrn D. Martini Lutheri Seeliger Gedechtnis. . . .* Wittenberg: Paul Helwig, 1546.

Bullinger, Heinrich. *Repetitio et dilvcidior explicatio consensvs veteris orthodoxae catholicaeque Christi Ecclesiae in doctrina prophetica & apostolica de inconfusis proprietatibus naturarum Christi Domini. . . .* Zurich: Christoph Froschauer, 1564.

Carion, Johannes. *Chronica.* Wittenberg, 1532.

Catalogus oder Register aller Bu[e]cher vnd schrifften/D. Mart. Luth. durch jn ausgelassen/vom jar M.D. XVIII. bis jns XXXIII. Wittenberg: Hans Lufft, 1533.

Chytraeus, David. *Historia der Augspurgischen Confession.* Rostock: Lucius, 1576.

Cochlaeus, Johannes. *Commentaria Ioannis Cochlaei, de actis et scriptis Martini Lvtheri Saxonis. . . .* Mainz: Franz Behem, 1549.

———. *Septiceps Lutherus, vbique sibi, suis scriptis, contrarius in Visitationem Saxonicam.* Leipzig: Valentin Schumann, 1529.

Coelestin, Johann Friedrich. *Von Buchhendlern/Buchdruckern vnd Buchfu[e]rern: Ob auch one su[e]nde/vnd gefahr jrer Seligkeit/Vnchristliche/Ketzerische/Bepstische/Vnzu[e]chtige/oder sonst bo[e]se Bu[e]cher drucken/vnd offentlich feil haben/oder von andern kauffen/vnnd widerumb/one vnterscheidt/menniglich verkauffen mo[e]gen. Auch Allen andern Christen/sonderlich Kremern/Kauff/Handels vnd Handwerckleuten/zu diesen gefehrlichen zeitten nu[e]tzlich zulesen.* N.p., 1569.

Columben, Peter. *No[e]tiger vnd Christlicher Bericht aus heiliger Go[e]ttlicher Schrifft vnd Lutheri Bu[e]chern zusammen gezogen/wie wir uns in Pestilentzischer Straffe/vnd geferlicher Todeszeit gegen unsern Frommen getrewen Gott/vnsern Nehesten/auch vnsere Seele vnd Leib (auff das Gott nicht ferner mu[e]ge erzu[e]rnet werden) verhalten sollen.* Magdeburg: Paul Donat, 1598.

Corvinus, Johannes. *Loci commvnes Doct: Mart: Lutheri totius Doctrinae Christianae. Das ist/Heubtartikel Vnsers Christlichen Glaubens/vnd rechtschaffener Lere/aus D. Mart. Luthers Schrifften/mit seinen eigenen worten/Einfeltiglich vnd trewliche zusamen getragen. . . .* Ursel: Nicolaus Henricus, 1564.

Cuno, Samuel. *Lvthervs Rediuiuus. Das ist D. Martini Lutheri Sententz vnd Bedencken/von der formula Concordiae, vnd aller hierzu geho[e]rigen handel/welche sich in diesen viertzig Jahren in den Kirchen der Augspurgischen Confession zugetragen. . . .* Mühlhausen: Andreas Hantzsch, 1595.

Dietrich, Konrad. *Vlmisches Evangelisches Jubelfest . . . durch das Ministerium oder Predigampt daselbsten.* Ulm: Johann Medern, 1618.

Dinckel, Johannes. *Heiliges lehr vnd trostreiches Bett bu[e]chlein D. Martini Lutheri. . . .* Erfurt: Zacharias Zimmer, 1592.

Dresser, Martin. *De festis & praecipvis anni partibvs Liber. . . .* Wittenberg: Simon Gronenberg, 1584.

———. *Martini Lvtheri historia . . . .* Leipzig: Franz Schnelbatz, 1598.

———. *Millenarius Sextus Isagoges historicae. . . .* Jena: Tobias Steinmann, 1591.

Eichmann, Johann. *Von dem ytzigen Sterben oder Pestilentz. . . .* Marburg: Andreas Collien, 1554.

Eisenberg, Jacob, ed. *Propositiones theologicae reverendorvm virorum D. Mart. Luth. Et D. Philippi Melanth. Continentes summam doctrinae Christianae, scriptae & disputatae Vvitebergae, inde usque ab anno 1516. de quo tempore uaticinatus est Iohannes Hilten, initium fore reformationis Ecclesiae anno 1516.* Wittenberg, 1558.

Erich, Nicolaus. *Sylvva Sententiarum, exemplorum, historiarum, allegoriarum, similitudinum, Facetiarum, Partim ex Reverendi Viri, D. Martini Lvtheri, ac Philippi Melanchthonis cum privatis tum publicis relationibus: partim ex aliorum veterum atque recentium Doctorum monumentis observata, & in Locos communes ordine Alphabetica disposita.* Frankfurt/Main: Peter Schmidt and Sigismund Feyerabend, 1566.

Erklerung aus Gottes Wort/vnd kurtzer bericht/der Herren Theologen/auff dem Tag zu Lu[e]neburg/im Julio des 61. Jars gehalten. Regensburg, 1562.

Faber, Basilius. *Allerley Christliche/no[e]tige vnd nu[e]tzliche vnterrichungen/ von den letzten Hendeln der Welt/Als: Vom Ju[e]ngsten tage/vnd wie man sich darzu bereiten sol. Vom Sterben. Von aufferstehungen der Todten. Vom ju[e]ngsten Gericht. Vom Himel vnd ewigen leben. Vnd von der Helle. Mit angehenckten warnungen vnd Prophezeiungen D. Mart. Luthers/Deutschland betreffende.* Eisleben: Urban Gaubisch, 1565.

Faber, Zacharias. *100 Vnwarheiten. Welche die Caluinisten begehen an der H. Schrifft/der H. Va[e]tern/der Augspurgischen Confession, Christlichen Concordienbuch/vnd dem theuren Manne Luthero/etc. Colligirt aus der Apologia des Christlichen Concordienbuchs.* Wittenberg: Johann Krafft, 1598.

———. *Verzeichnis mehr denn Vierhundert Offendlicher vnd Schendlicher Lu[e]gen/welche die Calvinsten in jhren/in offenen Druck Publicirten, Bu[e]chern/in die gantze Christenheit fu[e]r die reine Seligmachende warheit Go[e]ttliches Worts/gantz Vnuerschempt spargirn vnd ausstrewen/vnnd darmit Vnsa[e]glichen Seelen schaden stifften.* Wittenberg: Johann Krafft d. Jungere, 1600.

Fabricius, Andreas (of Nordhausen). *Die Hauskirche. Das ist: Wie ein Hausvater neben dem o[e]ffentlichen Predigtampt auch daheime sein Heufflein zu Gottes Wort vnd dem lieben Catechismo reitzen soll.* Eisleben: Andreas Petri, 1572.

Fabricius, Theodosius. *Loci communes. Aus den deutschen Geistrichen Schrifften/des thewren Hocherleuchten Mannes Gottes vnd waren letzten Eliae D. Martini Lvtheri. . . .* Magdeburg: Paul Donat, 1597.

———. *Loci Communes D. Martini Lvtheri viri Dei et prophetae Germanici, ex scriptis ipsius latinis forma Gnomologica & Aphoristica collecti & in quinque classes distributui.* Magdeburg: Andreas Gera, 1594.

Fabricius Leodus, Andreas. *Harmonia Confessionis Augustanae, doctrinae evangelicae consensvm declarans.* Cologne: Maternus Cholinus, 1573.

Finck, Caspar. *Lvthervs redivivus, Das ist/Widerlegung aller Argumenten/welche die Calvinisten vnsere Stieffbru[e]der heutiges tages vom H. Abendemal fu[e]hren/auss den Schrifften vnd Bu[e]chern dess seligen H. D. Martini Lutheri. Auch Beweiss Dass heutiges tages die gedachte Calvinisten vnd Zwinglianer nichts auff die bahn bringen/welches nicht zuvor gru[e]ndlich vom Herrn Luthero widerleget sey. . . .* Frankfurt/Main, 1614.

Flacius Illyricus, Matthias. *Catalogus testium veritatis, qui ante nostram aetatem reclamarunt Papae. . . .* Basel: Oporinus, 1556.

———. *Etliche Klare vnd treffliche Zeugnussen/D. Martini Luthers/von dem bo[e]sen Wesen . . . oder Gestalt des jrdischen todten Adams. . . .* N.p., 1574.

———. *Gru[e]ndliche verlegung aller Sophisterey/so Juncker Isleb/D. Interim/ Morus/Pfeffinger/D. Geitz in seinem grundlichem bericht vnd jhre gesellen/die andere Adiaphoristen/das Leipsische Interim zu bescho[e]nen gebrauchen.* N.p., n.d.

———. *Eine schrifft widder ein recht epicurisch buch/darin das Leipzische Interim verteidiget wird sich zu hu[e]ten fu[e]r der verfelschern der waren Religion.* . . . N.p., 1549.

——— (or his circle). *Tro[e]stliche Gegenspru[e]ch des Ernwirdigen Herren Doctoris Martini Lutheri/vnd Matthie Jllyrici/wider des Rabe Osiandri Primarij spruch.* . . . Magdeburg: Rödinger, 1552.

———. *Warhafftige vnd bestendige meinung vnd zeugnis/Von der Erbsu[e]nde vnd dem freien willen . . . D. Martin Luthers Aus allen seinen schrifften trewliche vnd mit vleis zusamen gezogen.* . . . Jena: Thomas Rebart, 1560, 1561.

———. *Widder den ausszug des Leiptzischen Interims/oder das Kleine Interim.* Magdeburg: Christian Rödinger, 1549.

Flasch, Sebastian. *Augenscheinliche Erweisung auss D. Martin Luthers aigenen Bu[e]chern vnd worten/dass er kain heiliger Prophet Teutschlands/sondern ein rechter Vnflat gewesen.* . . . Ingolstadt: David Sartorius, 1577.

———. *Zwey vnd zwaintzig Vrsachen/Des . . . Sebastiani Flaschij von Manssfeldt Warumb er die Lutherisch Ketzerey/darinn er geboren/vnd von Jugend aufferzogen/verlassen hab. Daneben auss D. Martini Luthers aigenen Bu[e]chern vnd Worten augenscheinlich erweisung/dass er kein heiliger Prophet Teutschlandts/sondern ein rechter Vnflat gewesen.* Munich: Adam Berg, 1584.

Forster, Johann. *Vindiciae Lutheri: id est, Orationes dvae, pro Luthero Theologorum omnium, ab Apostolorum aetate, Phosphoro aduersus conuitia & calumnias Jesuitarum, Nicolae Serarii imprimis.* . . . Wittenberg: Johann Gormann, 1609.

Franz, Wolfgang. *Historische Erzehlung Der Beyden Heiligthu[e]men/nemblich eines/So in der Schlosskirchen zu Wittenberg im anfang der Reformation Herrn D. Lutheri vorhanden gewesen. . . . Aus Welcher Historischen Erzehlung alle fromme Christen . . . anfingen zu greiffen/Auch jhren Nachkommen hinderlegen/vnd demselben also zu wiessen machen ko[e]nnen/mit was fu[e]r grossen Betrug vnsere liebe Vorfahren/vnter dem dicken Babstumb geplaget worden/dakegen was der Ewige Gott durch die Reformation Herrn D. Lutheri fu[e]r grosse Barmhertzigkeit allen Menschen erzeiget habe.* Wittenberg: Paul Helwig, 1618.

Geistliche Lieder/D. Mart. Luth. vnd anderer frommen Christen/nach Ordnung der Jarzeit mit Collecten vnd Gebeten. Frankfurt/Oder: Johann Eichorn, 1575.

Gisen, Johannes. *Catechismus B. Lutheri est parva Biblia, Idque ostenditvr praecipuis Scripturae Sacrae dictis Doctrinae Christianae sedem, & fundamentum continentibus.* Strassburg: Paul Ledertz, 1620.

Glaser, Peter. *Hundert vnd zwanzig Propheceyunge/oder Weissagung/des Ehrwirdigen Vaters Herrn Doctoris Martini Luthers/von allerley straffen/so nach seinem tod vber Deutschland von wegen desselbigen grossen/vnd vielfaltigen Su[e]nden kommen solten.* . . . Eisleben: Urban Gaubisch, 1557. Revised as *Zwey Hundert Propheceyunge oder weissagunge/des thewren Mans D. Martini Lutheri/von allerley Straffen/welche Deutschland nach seinem Tode/von wegen desselbigen vielfaltigen vnd grossen Su[e]nden vberfallen sollen.* Bautzen: Michael Wolrab, 1574.

Glaser, Theophilus. *Wie der thewre Mann D. Martin Luther/Wider die Sacramentirer gelehrt/geprediget/vnd geschrieben/ausserhalb derer Bu[e]cher/darinnen er insonderheit vnd durchauss wider sie handelt. Daraus kla[e]rlich zu befinden/ das er in seinen Lehrschrifften eben diss biss an sein ende gelehrt vnd bekent habe/Was er in seinen Streitbu[e]chern wider die Sacramentirer erstritten. . . .* Leipzig: Abraham Lamberg, 1603.

Gloccer, Georg. *Warhafftige Historia/Vnd gru[e]ndlicher Summarischer Bericht/ von der Lehr/Leben/Beruff/vnd seligen Abschiedt des thewren Gottes Manns Doctoris Martini Lutheri/fu[e]r einfeltige Christen/auss bewerten vnd glaubwu[e]rdigen Scribenten auff das ku[e]rtzest zusammen gezogen.* Strassburg: Anton Bertram, 1586.

Gobler, Caspar (pseud.). *Wieder die lesterliche Calumnia des vngelerten Esels M. Flachens/eines Manßfeldischen Jesuiters/von D. Martino Luthero. Bericht/ Daraus zu sehen/das Gott durch D. Lutherum der gantzer Christenheit wunderbarlich aus Papistischer Finsternis geholffen. . . .* "Christlingen," 1591.

Grandmundt, Christopher. *D. Martini Lutheri Seeligen Lehr vnd Meinung/Von der Person Christi. Von seiner Himmelfahrt. Vom Sitzen zur Rechten Gottes. Auss welchem der christliche Leser/so Frieden vnd Wahrheit liebet/zusehen/ dass Doctor Jacobe Andreae (genant Schmidlin) vnnd seiner mithelffer/Newe Lehr von Obgesetzten puncten/mit der Heiligen vnd Allgemeinen Christlichen Kirchenlehre/auch Doctor Luthero/wie sie des die Leut zübereden gedencken/ mit nichten vbereinstimmet. Alles auss den schrifften D. Martini Lutheri vnd zum theil Johan Brentij/zusammengetragen/vnd in 100 Propositiones gefasset. . . .* Neustadt/Hardt: Matthaeus Harnisch, 1581.

Gräter, Philip. *Schatzkammer Luther. Aller Geschichten vnd Schrifften Lutheri kurtzer Begriff vnd Erklerung in fu[e]nff Theilen . . . Alles zu klarem Verstand der letsten Engel in S. Joannis Offenbarung.* Lauingen: Jacob Winter, 1614.

Gruber, Erasmus. *Luther redivivvs, Oder Das . . . Theologische Schatzka[e]stlein. . . .* Frankfurt/Main: Johann Niclas Hummer and Johann Gerlin, 1665.

———. *Spicilegium sacrum, Oder Außerlesene Aphorismi und Spru[e]che von allerley denkwu[e]rdigen Theologischen Materien/aus denen Stucken vnd Schrifften deß theuren seeligen Mannes Gottes/D. Martini Lutheri. . . .* Tübingen: Johann Heinrich Reiß, 1670.

———. *Theologia Luther In kurtzen ausserlesenen Spru[e]chen/von den fu[e]rnemsten Articuln Christlicher lehr fu[e]rgestelt/vnd aus des theuren see: [seeliger] Manns lateinischen vnd Teutschen Schrifften gezogen.* Regensburg: Christoff Fischer, 1657.

Gruntlicher vnd Warhafftiger Bericht der vorigen vnd jetzigen/für vnd nach dem Kriege ergangen Handlungen/von den Adiaphoris oder Mitteldingen. . . . Leipzig: Bapst, 1550.

Hartmann, Andreas. *Erster Theil/des cvrricvli vitae Lvtheri. Das ist: Warhafftige vnd kurtze Historische Beschreibung/der Geburt vnd Ankunfft/Auch Lehr/Lebens/Wandels/Beru[e]ffs/Standes vnd Ampts/Vnd sonderlich der beharlichen vnd standhafftigen Glaubens Bekendtnis/bey reiner Euangelischer Warheit/*

vnd in Summa/der gantze Laufft/beydes Lebens vnd Sterbens/Des Ehrwurdigen/Hocherleuchten/Gottseligen vnd Tewren Mannes Gottes/Herrn D. Martini Lutheri/etc. Heiliger Geda[e]chtnuss. . . . N.p., 1601.

Heerbrand, Jacob. *Rettung Des kleinen Catechismi D. Luthers/Vnd Bericht Auff vnnd wider der Jesuiter zu Gratz/bosshafftige/du[e]ckische verbo[e]serung/verfa[e]lschung vnnd verstu[e]mplung desselbigen.* Tübingen: Georg Gruppenbach, 1587.

Heilbrunner, Philip. *Der Vnschuldige Luther/Das ist/Augenscheinliche Beweisung/Das alles das jenige/so die Iesuiter, in jhren jungst aussgesprengten Lesterschrifften/wider weyland D. Martin Luthers Person/aus seinen eignen Schrifften (die reine Lehre dess H. Euangelij dadurch verda[e]chtig zu machen) auffbringen/von jhnen vbel angezogen/bosshafftig verkehrt/vnd lauter Betrug sey.* . . . Lauingen: Leonhart Reinmichel, 1599.

Hertel, Jacob. *Allegoriarum, typorum, et exemplorvm veteris & noui Testamenti Libri duo.* . . . Basel: Johann Oporinus, 1561.

———. *Definitiones ac descriptiones theologicae. Ex veterum & recentiorum Theologorum monumentis collectae.* Basel: Johann Oporinus, 1564.

———. *Qvaestiones sacrarum reuerendi patris D. Martini Luther, Centuriae IIII. Libris III. distinctae: His accessit Quartus Liber, continens Quaestiones CCXXI: quibus uariae de praecipuis uerae Religionis capitibus Obiectiones summa pietate explicantur. Ex omnibus eiusdem Latinis operibus bona fide congestae.* Basel: Johann Oporinus, 1562.

Hesshus, Tilemann. *Klare vnd helle Zeugnissen Doctoris Martini Lutheri. Das Die Erbsu[e]nde nicht sey das wesen des Menschen.* . . . Jena, 1572.

Hirtzwig, Heinrich. *Lutherus Drama.* . . . Frankfurt/Main: Sigismund Latomus, 1617.

Höe von Höenegg, Matthias. *Martinalia Sacra Pragensis. Das ist: D. Hoe unvermeidenliche Rettung/Der Ehr/Person/Lehr vnd Gaben des heiligen Thewren hocherleuchten Mannes Gottes/Herren Doctoris Lutheri seligen/wider allerley Jesuitische Lu[e]gen vnd Lesterungen.* . . . Leipzig: Abraham Lamberg, 1613.

———. *Pro beato Luthero, Avgvstana Confessione, et veritate historica, Adversus Iohannis Lampadii . . . horrendas calumnias, criminationes, blasphemias, & crassissima mendacia . . . Apologia maxime necessaria.* . . . Leipzig: Abraham Lamberg, 1611.

———. *Sanctus Thaumasiander et Triumphator Lutherus. Das ist/Bericht von dem heiligen Wundermanne/vnd wieder das Bapsthumb/auch andere Rotten vnd Secten/Triumphierenden Ru[e]stzeug Gottes/Herrn D. Martini Luthero . . . Wie hoch er von Gott vnd den Menschen geehret: Welche reine heilige vnu[e]berwindliche Lehr er gefu[e]hret: Vnd in Summa/wie er sich als einen trewen Evangelisten vnd hochgewu[e]nschten dritten Eliam erzeiget habe.* . . . Leipzig: Abraham Lamberg and Caspar Closemann, 1617.

Hugo, Johann. *Gru[e]ndlicher vnd Klarer bericht von der Erbsu[e]nde/Was dieselbe eigendliche sey. Aus des tewren Mans Gottes D. Luthers Schrifften gezogen.* . . . Eisleben, 1573.

Hunger, Albert. *Orationes dvae, vna, de fide ac religione magni illius Athanasii Alexandrini . . . altera, de homologia sive consensv concentvqve theologiae Lutheri cum Philosophia Epicvri.* . . . Ingolstadt: Weissenhorn, 1582.

Irenaeus, Christoph. *Prognosticon Aus Gottes Wort no[e]tige Erinnerung/Vnd Christliche Busspredigt zu dieser letzten bo[e]sen Zeit . . . Auf den Cometen/so von Martini des 1577. Jars/biss zum Eyngang des 1578. Jars gesehen. . . .* N.p., 1578.

Jonas, Justus, and Michael Coelius. *Zwo Trostliche Predigt vber der Leich D. Doct. Martini Luther zu Eissleben den XIX. vnd XX. Februarii gethan durch D. Doct: Justum Jonam, M. Michaelem Celium, Anno. 1546.* Wittenberg: Georg Rhau, 1546.

Judex, Matthaeus. *De typographiae inventione et de praelorvm legitima inspectione, libellvs brevis et vtilis.* Copenhagen: Johannes Zimmermann, 1566.

Julius, Michael. *Christus redivivvs. Das ist: Der Ostergesang/Christ lag in Todesbanden/von der Passion vnd Aufferstehung Jesu Christi/Aus dem 4. Capit. der Epistel an die Ro[e]mer/vnd dem Oster sequentz/Victimae Paschali laudes, in deutsche Reimen gebracht durch D. Martin. Luth. P. M.* Erfurt: Johann Beck, 1602.

———. *Das scho[e]ne Pfingst vnd Trostliedt Nun bitten wir den heyligen Geyst/ec. Welches der theure Mann Gottes D. Martinus Lutherus auss dem lateinischen Sequentz vnd Prosa genommen/vnnd in deutsche Reimen verfasset. . . .* Erfurt: Zacharias Zimmer, 1595. Reprinted under the title *Pfingst Sequentz oder Prosa.* Erfurt: Johann Beck, 1603.

———. *Sechs kurtze Predigten: In welchen das herrliche scho[e]ne Kinderliedt: Erhalt vns Herr bey deinem Wort/etc. erkleret vnd ausgelegt ist. . . .* Erfurt: Esaias Mechler, 1589.

Kielmann, Heinrich. *Tetzelocramia, dass ist, Eine lustige Comoedie von Johan Tetzels AblassKram. Wie Gott der Herr denselben/Jtzo fu[e]r Hundert Jahren durch sein erwehltes Ru[e]stzeug, D. Martinum Lutherum in krafft des Heiligen Evangelii/vmbestossen vnnd aussgetrieben. . . .* Wittenberg: Johann Mathaeus, 1617.

Kirchner, Timotheus. *Deudscher Thesaurus. Des Hochgelerten weit berumbten vnd thewren Mans D. Mart. Luthers/Darinnen alle Heubtartickel/Christlicher/ Catholischer vnd Apostolischer Lere vnd Glaubens erklert vnd ausgelegt. . . .* Frankfurt/Main: Peter Schmidt and Hieronymus Feierabent, 1568; Frankfurt/Main: Hieronymus Feierabent and Thomas Rebart, 1570.

———. *Index oder Register der die Achte deutsche Tomos/Ersten vnd andern Drucks/aller Bu[e]cher vnd Schrifften des thewren vnd seligen Mans Gottes/ Doctor Martini Lutheri. . . .* Jena: Donatus Richtzenhayn and Thomas Rebart, 1564.

———. *Thesavrvs: Explicationvm omnivm articvlorvm ac capitvm, catholicae orthodoxae, verae ac piae doctrinae Christianae, quae haec aetata controversa sunt, ex reuerendi, vereque Dei viri, ac summi Theologi, D. Martini Lutheri, syncerae Euangelicae doctrinae instauratoris fidelissimi, operibus. . . .* Frankfurt/Main: Thomas Rhebart and Sigismund Feyerabend, 1566.

Kreuch, Andreas. *Sigillum Lutheri. Eine Christliche vnd einfeltige Predigt/Vom Sigill vnd Merckzeichen/des Hocherleuchten vnd Gottseligen Mannes Gottes/D. Martini Lutheri, welches gewesen Ein Rot Hertz/mit einem schwartzen Creutze/in einer Weissen Rosen: Darinnen vnser gantz Christenthumb abgebildet. . . .* N.p., 1579.

Laelius, Lorenz. *Rettung D. Martin Luthers/seeligen/Lehr/ehr/vnd guten Namens: Wider D. Sixti Sartorii . . . in den Causis Motivis seines Abfals/angehefften Schmachreden.* Onaltzbach: Paul Bohem, 1614.

Lampadius, Johannes. *Mellifici historici pars tertia. . . .* Marburg: Paul Egenolph, 1611.

Lapaeus, Johann. *Practica vnd Prognosticon/Oder erschreckliche Propheceyhung Doct. Martini Luthers/des ausserwehleten Ru[e]stzeugs vnd Propheten des Deutschlands/Vnd der letzten Posaunen Gottes. . . .* Lübeck: Johann Balhorn, 1595.

———. *Propheceiung Des Thewren Propheten vnd seligen Mannes Gottes D. Martini Lutheri/Darinnen er vns Deutschen ernstlich erinnert/vnserer 1. Gnedigen Heimsuchung 2. Schrecklichen Vndancks 3. Kleglichen zustands der Religion 4. Grewlichen straffen Gottes/mit angehengter 5. Warnung zur buss/Vnd Verku[e]ndigung des Ju[e]ngsten tages. . . .* Eisleben: Urban Gaubisch, 1592.

———. *Warhafftige Prophezeiungen des thewren Propheten/vnd Heiligen Manns Gottes/D. Martini Lutheri seliger Gedechtnis Darinnen er den jetzigen kleglichen Zustandt Deutscher Nation/die Zersto[e]runge der Kirchen/Verfelschunge der Lere/vielerley grewliche Straffen Gottes/den Ju[e]ngsten tag/vnd anders dergleichen mehr eygentlich zuuor verku[e]ndiget hat. . . .* Ursel: Nicolaus Henrici, 1578.

Lomonymus, Sicomorobans (pseud.). *Christi Jesu des HERRN aller Herrn/ durch Doctorn Lutherum. Gewiss vnd vbergewiss Defension, Sieg vnd Triumph Werck . . . auss Christi vnd Lutheri Rustkammer vnd Schrifften colligirt vnd verfasset.* N.p., 1619.

Loyseleur de Villiers, Pierre. *Ratio ineundae Concordiae inter Ecclesias Reformatas. . . .* N.p., 1579.

Luther, Martin. Complete works, Wittenberg edition, German. *Der Erste Teil der Bucher D. Mart. Luth. vber etliche Epistel der Aposteln,* etc. 12 vols. Wittenberg: Hans Lufft, 1539–59.

———. Complete works, Wittenberg edition, Latin. *Tomvs primvs omnivm opervm Reverendi Domini Martini Lutheri . . . ,* etc. 7 vols. Wittenberg: Hans Lufft, 1545–57.

———. Complete works, Jena edition, German. *Der Erste Teil aller Bu[e]cher vnd Schrifften des thewren/seligen Mans Doct: Mart: Lutheri/vom XVII. jar an/ bis auff das XXII.,* etc. 8 vols. Jena: Christian Rödinger, 1555–58.

———. Complete works, Jena edition, Latin. *Tomvs primvs omnivm opervm Reuerendi Patris D. M. L. quae vir Dei ab Anno XVII. vsque ad Anni vicesimi aliquam partem scripsit & edidit . . . ,* etc. 4 vols. Jena: Christian Rödinger, 1556–58.

———. Complete works, Eisleben supplement. *Der erste Theil Der Bu[e]cher/ Schrifften/vnd Predigten des Ehrwirdigen Herrn/D. Martin Luthers . . . ,* etc. 2 vols. Eisleben: Urban Gaubisch, 1564–65.

———. *Der Achte Psalm Davids/gepredigt vnd ausgelegt durch Martin Luther/ Anno 1537. Vor nie in Druck ausgangen. . . .* Mühlhausen: Hantzsch, 1572.

———. *Das achtzehend vnd neunzehend Capitel/vnd ein Stu[e]k aus dem zwentzigsten S. Johannis von dem Leiden/Sterben/vnd Aufferstehung vnsers Herrn*

Jhesu Christi. Gepredigt vnd ausgelegt durch Doc. Mart. Luther. . . . Jena: Heirs of Christian Rödinger, 1557.

———. *Acta Concordiae. Das ist/Was sich in Dem Tractat vnd handel der Concordien . . . vber dem stritt desz heiligen Nachtmals Christi . . . verloffen.* Heidelberg, 1572. Republished under the title *Antwort vnd Widerantwort/Herrn Doctor Martin Luthers/Vnd Herrn Philippi Melanchthonis . . . Auff der Schweitzerischen Reformirten Evangelischen Sta[e]tten.* . . . Marburg: Paul Egenolff, 1614.

———. *Ad Leonem X. pontificem maximvm, Resolutiones.* . . . Basel: Johann Froben, 1518.

———. *Ad Leonem X. pontificem maximvm, Resolutiones.* . . . Strassburg: Matthias Schürer, 1519.

———. *Der ander Psalm Dauids.* . . . Magdeburg: Christian Rödinger, 1550.

———. *Argvmenta Vnd Gru[e]nde/der Sacramentirer/damit sie jhre meinunge zubeweisen gedencken/Vnd kurtze Widerlegung derselbigen. Aus den Streitbu[e]chern Lutheri.* . . . Dresden: Gimel Bergen, 1578.

———. *Auslegung des Glaubens/Gepredigt durch D. Martinum Lutherum/zu Schmalkalden/Anno 1537. Itzund zum ersten mal im Druck ausgangen.* Eisleben: Urban Gaubisch, 1562.

———. *Auslegung/etzlicher Trostspruche/so der Ehrwirdige Herr/Doctor Martinus Luther/jnn seiner lieben Herrn/vnd guten Freunden Biblien vnd Postillen/mit eigner handt . . . geschrieben.* Erfurt: Wolfgang Sturmer, 1547; Nuremberg: Johann Petreius, 1547.

———. *Bestendige Lehr D. Martini Luthers/Vom Vrsprung dess Glaubens.* . . . Amberg: Michael Forster, 1598.

———. *Brevis ac ervdita enarratio Psalmi XXII. et XXIII. a reverendo viro D. Doctore Martino Lvthero sanctae memoriae, conscripta anno xxxi. Nvnc primvm edita.* . . . Leipzig: Valentin Babst, 1551.

———. *Christliche Einhellige Lehr vnd Bekentnis. Von der Person Jesu Christi vnsers Herrn/etc. Von seiner Himmelfart/vnd sitzen zur rechten Hand des Vaters. Vom Heiligen Hochwirdigen Abentmal des Herrn. Laut heiliger Go[e]ttlicher Schrifft, Aus den Streit/vnd Lehrschrifften D. Martini Lutheri.* . . . Wittenberg: Simon Groeneberg, 1583(?).

———. *Christliche Geseng Lateinisch vnd Deudsch zum Begrebnis. D. Martinus Luther.* Leipzig: Jacob Berwaldt, 1552; also Nuremberg, 1560, 1563.

———. *Eine Christliche Hochzeit Predigt vber den Spruch zun Hebreern am dreyzehenden Capitel.* . . . Jena: Johann Weidner, 1608.

———. *Christliche/tro[e]stliche Auslegung/D. Mart. Luthers/u[e]ber die Wort Genesis am 15. Capit. Vom Tode Abrahe. Aus der newen letzten Auslegung/u[e]ber dasselbige Buch/durch Vitum Dietrich/seligen/ausgangen.* . . . Leipzig: Wolf Guenter, 1551.

———. *Ein Christliche/Tro[e]stliche/vnd sehr Nu[e]tzliche Ausslegung/vber den Propheten Micham. Auss der Lectionibus des Ehrwirdigen Herrn vnd Vatters/Doctor Martini Luthers/seliger gedechtnus/zusammen ordentlich getragen vnd ins Latein gebracht/Erstlichen durch Herrn Veit Dieterich . . . Jetzt mit fleiss auss dem Latein verdeutscht.* . . . Königsberg: Johann Daubmann, 1555.

———. *Ein Christlich Vrtheyl D. Martin Luthers von seinem eigen Buchern. Sampt einer Vnterricht/was darzu geho[e]re/wenn man jnn der heiligen Schrifft recht studirn/vnd darnach gutte Bucher schreiben will.* Nuremberg: Leonhart Milchthaler, 1539; Augsburg: Philip Ulhart, 1540.

———. *Comment/Oder Ausslegung/weiland des Ehrwirdigen Herren Doctor Martin Luthers/vber den CXXVII. Psalm . . .* , trans. Erhardt Krauss. Strassburg: Christian Mueller, 1563.

———. *D. Martini Luthers auslegung/vber den 129. Psalm Verdeutscht/zu diesen betru[e]bten zeiten fast nutzlich zu lesen.* Magdeburg: Michael Lotter, 1550.

———. *Das der freye Wille nichts sey. Antwort/D. Martini Lutheri/an Erasmum Roterodamum/Verdeudscht durch D. Justum Jonam/Zuuor niemals allein im Druck ausgangen. . . .* Regensburg: Heinrich Geissler, 1559.

———. *Das diese wort Christi. . . .* Magdeburg: Paul Donat, 1582; Frankfurt/Main: Johann Spies, 1586; Lauingen: Leonhart Reinmickel, 1589.

———. *De Concilijs et ecclesia, liber. Germanice scriptus iam olim a Reverendo patro D. D. Martino Lutero. . . .* Basel: Johann Oporinus, 1557.

———. *De logica Ex fidei regno excludenda epistola Reverendi patris Martini Lutheri ex primo tomo epistolarum anno 1556. Jhenae excusarum excerpta, qua Ostenditur non novvm neque temerarium esse certamen, quod Hofmanno cum Caelianis intercedit.* Lemgo: Conrad Grothe's heirs, 1600.

———. *De personali vnione dvarvm natvrarvm in Christo, et ascensv Christi in coelvm. . . .* Tübingen: Ulrich Morhardt's widow, 1561.

———. *De vsvra taxanda ad pastores ecclesiarum commonefactio D. Mart. Lutheri.* Frankfurt/Main: Peter Brubach, 1554.

———. *Defensio . . . verborum coenae: accipite, comeditae: hoc est corpus meum. Contra Phanaticos Sacramentiorum spiritus, aedita Germanice a Luthero. . . .* Nuremberg: Johann vom Berg and Ulrich Neüber, 1556.

———. *Eine Disputation des thewren Mann Gottes D. Mart. Luth. sa[e]liger gedechtnu[e]ss/von den guten Wercken/Darin der jrrthumb/das die guten Werck zur Sa[e]ligkeyt no[e]tig sein/verworffen wirdt,* ed. Matthias Flacius. Strassburg: Jacob Frohlich, 1557.

———. *Disputatio Reuerendi patris D. Martini Lutheri de operibus legis & gratiae . . .* , ed. Albert Christian. Magdeburg: Michael Lotther, 1553.

———. *Ein einfeltige weise zu beten fu[e]r einen guten freund.* Leipzig: Jacob Berwald, 1546.

———. *Enarratio 53. Capitis Esaiae prophetae ex praelectionibus Reuerendi D. Martini Lutheri. . . .* Magdeburg: Lotther, 1550.

———. *Epistolae aliquot D. Martini Lutheri cum alijs testimonijs illius de Philippo Melanthone & eius scriptis. . . .* Görlitz: Ambrose Fritsch, 1579.

———. *Epistolarvm Reverendi patris Domini D. Martini Lutheri, Tomus primus continens scripta viri Dei, ab anno millesimo quingentesimo septima, vsqve ad annum vicesimum secundum.* Jena: Christian Rödinger, 1556. Vol. 2, Eisleben: Andreas Petri, 1565.

———. *Ein erinnerung vnd ermanung D. Martini Luthers des Man Gottes/Von den letzten schweren zeyten geschryben.* Nuremberg, 1554; Schleusingen, 1555.

———. *Erklerung D. Mart. Lutheri von der frage/die Notwehr belangend.* Magdeburg: Michael Lotther, 1547; Wittenberg: Hans Lufft, 1547.

———. *Etliche fu[e]rneme Schrifften/Doct. Martin Luth. Darin die reine Christliche lehr vnd bekandtnuss vom H. Abentmal vnsers Herrn Jesu Christi begriffen ist. . . .* Nuremberg: Johann vom Berg and Ulrich Neüber, 1561; Nuremberg: Kauffmann, 1597.

———. *Etliche Schlu[e]sse D. Mart. Luth. Das man dem Bapst vnd seinem Schutzherrn wider vnrechte gewalt vnd Kriege/widerstand thu[e]n sol.* Wittenberg: Georg Rhau, 1546.

———. *Etliche scho[e]ne Trostschriffte/des Ehrwirdigen Herrn Doctoris Martini Lutheri/So er an den Durchleuchtigsten Fu[e]rsten vnd Herrn/Hertzog Joannes/Churfu[e]rsten zu Sachsen/Gottseliger gedechtnis/Vnd an andere seine Herrn vnd gute Freunde gethan. . . .* Erfurt: Wolfgang Sturmer, 1547.

———. *Etliche Trostschrifften vnd Predigten des Ehrwird. Herrn Doct. Mart. Luth. fu[e]r die so in Todes/vnd ander not vnd anfechtung sind/ . . . von newen zugericht/vnd . . . gemeret. . . .* Jena: Christian Rödinger, 1554.

———. *Etliche Trostschrifften vnd predigten/für die so in tods vnd ander not vnd anfechtung sind. Doct. Mar. Luth.* Wittenberg: Hans Lufft, 1544; Wittenberg: Veit Creutzer, 1546, 1548.

———. *Etliche warhafftige weissagung/vnd fu[e]rneme spruche des Ehrwirdigen Vaters/Hern Doctor Martini Luthers . . .*, trans. Albert Christian. Magdeburg: Michael Lotter, 1552.

———. *Etlicke scho[e]ne Predigen/Vth der ersten Epistel S. Johannis von der Leue. D. Mart. Luth.* Lübeck: Johann Ballhorn, 1551.

———. *Etlike Sehr scho[e]ne Trostschrifften vnd Predigeden D. Mart. Luth. an sinen leuen Vader Johan Luther in syner kranckheit/Anno 1535. geschreuen. Insunderheit sehr nu[e]tte vnd tro[e]stlick vor de/so in dodes vnd ander nodt vnd anfechtinge sint. . . .* Hamburg: Heinrich Binder, 1590.

———. *Fu[e]nff Predigten D. Martini Lutheri/von den fu[e]nff Heubtsu[e]nden . . . das vmb solcher Su[e]nde willen Gott jtziger zeit Deudschland billich straffe.* Jena: Christian Rödinger, 1554.

———. *Die fu[e]rnemsten vnd besten Schrifften des Hocherleuchten vnd Geistreichen Mannes Gottes/Herrn Doctoris Martini Lutheri/Von den beiden Sacramenten des Newen Testaments. . . .* Wittenberg: Hans Lufft, 1575.

———. *Der Garaus Von dem Endchrist/seinem Reich vnd Regiment/aus dem Propheten Daniel gezogen vnd gestellet/wider das gantze Bapsthumb vnd seinem Anhang.* Ursel: Nicolaus Henricus, 1574.

———. *Das Gebet Mose/des Mans Gottes. Der XC. Psalm. . . .* Wittenberg: Rhau, 1546.

———. *Ein geistlich Lied Von vnser heiligen Tauff Darin fein Kurtz gefasset Was sie sey? Wer sie gestifftet habe? Was sie nutze? . . .* Regensburg: Hans Kohl, c. 1554.

———. *Ein Gu[e]lden Kleinod . . . Anno 1524 . . . den Bu[e]rgermeistern vnnd Rathern/allen Sta[e]dte Deutsches Landes insonderheit verehret hat. . . .* Nuremberg: Alexander Dietrich, c. 1590; Nuremberg, 1600.

———. *Heerpredigt D. Martin Luthers/wider den Tu[e]rcken. . . .* N.p., 1593. Reprinted in *Weissagung Des heiligen Propheten Obadiae von dem endlichen vntergang der Edomiter . . . Desgleichen Eine Heerpredigt wider den Tu[e]rcken. . . .* Ursel: Nicolaus Henricus, 1594.

———. *Herrlich Bedencken/Des tewren Mannes Gottes Lutheri seligen/von dem jetzund newen Bepstischen Calender/Daraus grundlich zuuernemen/Das der Mann/als ein rechter Prophet/die aus jtzigen Bepstischen Calender entstehende zuru[e]ttunge/vnd verbitterunge der hertzen/zuuor im Geist geschehen. . . .* N.p., 1584.

———. *Die Heubtartikel des Christlichen glaubens/Wider den Bapst/vnd der Hellen pforten zu erhalten. Sampt dem Bekentnis des glaubens/D. Mart. Lu. . . . Die drey Symbola oder Bekentnis des Christliche glaubens. . . .* Wittenberg: Veit Creutzer, 1548.

———. *Der CXXVIII. Psalm . . . Vom heiligen Ehestande. . . .* Leipzig: Wolfgang Guenter, 1552.

———. *Kurtz Bekentnis Doct. Mart. Luthers/vom heiligen Sacrament . . . .* Ursel: Nikolaus Heinrich, 1559; Wittenberg: Hans Lufft, 1567, 1574; Lauingen: Leonhart Reinmichel, 1589; and Magdeburg: Johann Franck, 1592. Also published as *Offentliche gemeine Bekentniss vom Abendmal des Herrn. D. Martini Lutheri vnd derer Kirchen . . . Letzte Bekentnis D. Martini Lutheri/von dem hochwirdigen Sacrament. Anno 1544.* Leipzig: Ernst Voegelin, 1562.

———. *Libellus Martini Lutheri, de constituendis scholis Latine redditus. . . .* Hildesheim: Gossel, 1620.

———. LOGOI DUO . . . *Dvae orationes Martini Lvtheri, vna de precatione: altera de praeparatione ad mortem pie obeundam. . . .* Magdeburg: Matthaeus Giseken, 1572.

———. *Martini Luthers der waren go[e]ttlichen schrifft Doctors/Augustiner zu Wittenbergk/mancherley bu[e]chlin vnd tractetlin. . . .* Basel: Andreas Cratander, 1520.

———. *Martini Luthers . . . mancherley bu[e]chlin vnnd tractetlin. . . .* Strassburg: Matthias Schürer, 1520.

———. *Nu[e]tzliche vnd zu diesen gefehrlichen zeiten no[e]tige erklerung Der Lehre von der Person Christi/D. Martini Lutheri . . . vber auslegung der wort des 14. Cap. Joan. . . .* Wittenberg: Zacharias Lehmann, 1591.

———. *Ob man fu[e]r dem sterben fliehen mu[e]ge. Martin Luther. Geschriben im Jar M.D. XXVII. . . .* Königsberg: Hans Lufft, 1549.

———. *Passio/Vnsers Herrn Jhesu Christi/Auss den vier Euangelisten gezogen. Mit scho[e]nen Figuren gezieret . . . Item/Das Symbolum der heiligen Aposteln . . . aussgelegt.* Frankfurt/Main: Sigismund Feierabendt, 1570.

———. *Praefatio methodica totius scripturae in epist: Pauli ad Romanos e vernacula Doct: Mart: Luth: 1523. in latinum. . . .* Berlin: Michael Hentzker, 1579.

———. *Eine Predigt aus dem Comment des heiligen vnd trewen Dieners Christi Lutheri vber das fu[e]nfft capitel Hosee gezogen in rechtschaffenen vnd falscher Busse.* Jena: Donatus Richtzenhan, 1562.

———. *Ein Predigt aus den Schrifften Lutheri vber die Propheten gezogen. Das Deudsche land wie Israel Judea vnd Jerusalem wird zersto[e]rt vnd verwu[e]stet werden vmb gleicher Su[e]nde willen.* Jena: Thomas Rebart, 1562.

———. *Eine Predigt D. Martini Lutheri/Vber diese Wort/Jm Anfang war das Wort/ etc. Johannis j. . . .* Wittenberg, 1562.

———. *Eine Predigt D. Martini Luthers. Von Nu[e]chterkeit vnnd Messigkeit Widder vo[e]llerey vnd Trunckenheit. Aus der Epistel S. Petri. . . .* Erfurt: Barbara Sachsse, 1552.

———. *Prima [Secvnda . . .] pars opervm Reverendi patris, ac sacrae theologiae Doctoris Martini Lvtheri. . . .* Basel: Andreas Cratander, 1519.

———. *Der Prophet Joel durch Doct. Mart. L. in Latinischer sprach gelesen vnd ausgelegt Vnd newlich verdeudscht etc.* Jena, 1553.

———. *Propositiones disputatae, Wittembergae pro doctoratu eximiorum D. Hieronymi Weller, & M. Nicolai Medler. . . .* Eisleben: Urban Gaubisch, 1585.

———. *R. P. Doct. Martini Lvtherii . . . lvcvbrationvm pars vna. . . .* Basel: Adam Petri, 1520.

———. *Reuerendi Viri D. Martini Lvteri missa ad theologos Norimbergenses (orta quadam inter ipsos dissensione) pia et vere Apostolica Epistola. . . .* Leipzig: Voegelin, 1572.

———. *Ein Rhatschlag Doctoris Martini Luther/Ob dem Keiser/so er jemants mit gewalt/des Evangelij halben/vberziehen wolte/mit rechte widerstandt geschehen mo[e]ge. . . .* Berlin: Hans Weiss, 1546.

———. *Ain scho[e]ne Christliche Prophetische Sermon vnd Predig/vor etlichen iaren von einem Gotsgelerten mann vnd Apostel der Teutschen gepredigt/von der zersto[e]rung Jerusalem. Das auch das Teutschland also zersto[e]rt werden solle/wo es die zeyt seiner heimsuchung nicht erkennet. Was der Tempel Gottes sei. D. M. L.* N.p., 1547.

———. *Das scho[e]ne Confitemini an der zal der CXVIII. Psalm. . . .* Wittenberg: Hans Lufft, 1546.

———. *Ein scho[e]ner Sermon oder predigt vonn dem Ehestande/durch den Ehrwirdigen Vater Doctorem Martinum Lutherum/heiliger vnd seliger gedechtnis/ zu Wittenberg gepredigt/vormals desgleichen nie ausgangen oder gedruckt worden.* Berlin: Georg Buchholzer, 1560.

———. *Septvaginta propositiones dispvtandae. De tribus hierarchijs, Ecclesiastica, Politica, Oeconomica: & quod Papa sub nulla istarum sit, sed omnium publicus hostis.* Basel, 1546.

———. *Ein Sermon D. Martini Luthers/Auff das Evangelium Marci am. letzten Da die Elff zu Tisch sassen/offenbart sich jn der HERR Christus/vnd schalt jren vnglauben vnd jres hertzen hertigkeit. . . .* Wittenberg: Clemens Schleich and Anton Schoen, 1574.

———. *Das XVII. Capitel S. Johannis/Von dem Gebet Christi.* Magdeburg: Andreas Ghene, 1568.

———. *Der Spruch Christi Matthei am xx. Capitel. Viel sind beruffen: aber wenig sind auserwelt.* Augsburg: Hans Zimmerman, 1548.

———. *Der Spruch Esaie am XXXV. Ausgelegt aus den Schrifften D. Martini Luth. seliger gedechtnis.* Magdeburg: Michael Lotter, 1548.

———. *Der Spruch Jhesu Christi Johan. am iij. Cap. Also hat Gott die Welt geliebet etc. Ausgelegt/durch D. Mart. Luther. . . .* Wittenberg: Georg Rhau, 1546.

———. *Testimonia D. Martini Lvteri de socio laborvm et pericvlorvm svorvm Philippo Melanchthone. . . .* Görlitz: Ambrose Fritsch, 1580.

———. *Thesaurus thesaurorum sive Fontes consolationvm. Die überaus scho[e]ne vnd herrliche Valet Predigt des Sohns Gottes wie dieselbe von dem heiligen Evan-*

gelisten Johanne in seinem XIV. XV. XVI. vnd XVII. Cap. beschrieben vnd von Martino Luthero . . . ausgelegt. Leipzig: Lamberg, 1624.

———. *Tischreden Oder Colloquia Doct. Mart: Luthers/So er in vielen Jaren/gegen gelarten Leuten/auch frembden Gesten/vnd seinen Tischgesellen gefuret/Nach den Heuptstucken vnserer Christlichen Lere/Zusammen getragen. . . .* Eisleben: Urban Gaubisch, 1566.

———. *Trewhertzige Vermahnung/An die Bu[e]rgermeister vnd Rhatherrn aller Sta[e]dte Deutsches Landes/das sie Christliche Schulen auffrichten vnd halten sollen/Mart. Luth. Doct. . . .* Magdeburg: Wendelin Pohl, 1621.

———. *Vber die ersten fu[e]nff vnd zweintzig vnd etliche folgende Psalmen/kurtze vnd richtige Ausslegungen/des Ehrwirdigen Herrn/D. Mart. Luth. Mit Christlichem fleiss durch M. Vitem Dietrich . . . Vnd vormals nie in Truck aussgangen. Auss dem Latein trewliche verdeutscht.* Nuremberg: Johann von Berg and Ulrich Neüber, 1560.

———. *Van dem Hochwerdigen Sacrament des Liues vnd Blodes Jhesu Christi/Eine scho[e]ne Predige des Erwirdigen vnd Seligen D. Mart. Luther. . . .* Hamburg: Johann Wickrodt the Younger, 1557.

———. *Vera et propria enarratio dicti Christi Ioannis VI. Caro non prodest quicquam &c. a Reverendo viro sanctae memoriae D. Martino Luthero scripta contra Sacramentarios. . . .* Frankfurt/Main: Peter Brubach, 1554.

———. *Verzeichnus etliche/der fu[e]rnember Spru[e]ch/ausser den Bu[e]chern Doctor Martini Lutheri seelig/darinnen der recht Verstandt/von der Gegenwu[e]rtigkeit des waren Leibs vnd Bluts Christi/in dem heiligen Abentmal/auch von der Himmelfart Christi . . . erkla[e]rt wu[e]rdt.* Tübingen: Ulrich Morhart's widow, 1560.

———. *Vier Predigten/Von der Todten Aufferstehung/vnd letzten Posaunen Gottes/Aus dem 15. Cap. der 1. Epistel S. Pauli/an die Corinther/Gepredigt von dem Ehrwirdigen Herrn vnd thewren Mann Gottes/D. Martin Luther zu Wittenberg/Anno 1544. vnd 45. . . . Vor nie im Druck ausgangen/Vnd jetzt newlich aus M. Georgen Ro[e]rers geschriebenen Bu[e]cher zusamen bracht.* Erfurt: Georg Baumann, 1564.

———. *Das XIIII. vnd XV. Capitel S. Johannis: durch D. Mart. Luther Gepredigt vnd ausgelegt.* Wittenberg: Georg Rhau, 1548.

———. *Vom Kriege Wider den Turcken Doct. Mart. Luth. Anno XXVIII. Mit einer Vorrede Doct. Georg. Maior.* Wittenberg: Hans Lufft, 1566.

———. *Vom wucher vnd widerkeufflichen Zinsen.* Magdeburg: Michael Lotter, c. 1552.

———. *Von Abendmal Christi Bekandtniss.* Lauingen: Leonhart Reinmickel, 1589.

———. *Von den Ju[e]den vnd jren Lu[e]gen. Vom Schem-Hamphoras der Ju[e]den/vnd von Geschlecht Christi. Wider die Sabbather/vnd der Ju[e]den Lu[e]gen vnd betrug. . . .* Leipzig: Heirs of Jacob Berwald, 1577.

———. *Von Ehesachen D. Mart. Luth. Jtem. Vom Ehebruch vnd Weglauffen D. Johaņ Bugenhagen.* Wittenberg: Georg Muller, 1592.

———. *Von Jhesu Christo/Warem Gott vnd Menschen/vnd von seinem Ampt vnd Reich/so er fu[e]hrt in der Christenheit. Zwo Predigten D. Martini Lutheri/aus der Epistel S. Pauli/Colos: Cap. 1. Gepredigt zu Wittenberg/Anno Domini.*

1537. Vor dem Munde Lutheri auffgefangen sind/zusammenbracht/vnd in Druck verfertigt. Mühlhausen: Georg Hantzsch, 1579.

———. *Von Kauffhandlung vnd wucher Martinus Luther. Auff das Newe Gedruckt.* Hamburg: Hans Binder, 1579.

———. *Von unser seligen Hoffnung/Aus der Epistel S. Pauli/Tit. 2. Cap. Durch D. Martinum Luther/gepredigt zu Kemberg/xix. Augusti/Anno M.D. XXXI. Vnd jtzt allererst aus M. Georgen Ro[e]rers/seliger/geschriebenen Bu[e]cheren/zusamen bracht vnd zugericht/Vor nie im druck ausgangen.* Erfurt: Georg Baumann, 1561.

———. *Warnunge D. Martini Luth. An seine lieben Deudschen.* Augsburg: Valentin Otmar, 1546. Also published under the titles *Hertzenswuntsch vnd allergetreuste Warnung des hocherleuchten Manns Gottes . . . Martin Luthers an seine liebe Teutschen . . . aus bemelter Warnung vnd andern . . . Schrifften Martin Luthers extrahirt*, n.p., 1620; and *Alter Deutsche Trew/Lautere Warheit/vnd Wahre Auffrichtigkeit. Allen Getrewen Patrioten der Deutschen Redligkeit/vnd hertzen Freunden der Go[e]ttlichen Warheit/bey jtzigen Kriegsu[e]chtigen Zeiten wiederumb zu gute herfu[e]r gerbracht. . . .* Wittenberg, 1627.

———. *Warnungsschrifft Doct. Martin Luthers/an die zu Franckfurt am Mayn/ Anno 1533. aussgangen. . . .* Lauingen: Leonhart Reinmickel, 1589.

———. *Was Geistliche vnd Weltliche Obrigkeit/wider die offentliche Laster/zu thun schuldig ist/mit vnterscheidt beider Obrigkeit Ampt/vnd straffen. Aus der Hausspostil D. Lutheri. . . .* Eisleben: Urban Gaubisch, 1559.

———. *Der Weg zum Ewigen Leben. Johannis am xiiij. . . .* Leipzig: Nikolaus Berwald, c. 1550.

———. *Wider das Bapstum zu Rom/vom Teuffel gestifft/ein notwendige schrifft D.M. Lutheri. . . .* N.p., 1565.

———. *Wider die alte/grobe/Heydnische Lu[e]gen der Papisten/vom Fegfewer . . . I. Doctor Martinus Luther seligen/von jm geschrieben Anno 1530. . . .* Frankfurt/Main: Nikolaus Basse, 1570.

———. *Wie der thewre Man D. Martinus Lutherus/wider die Sacramentirer gelehret/gepredigetvnd geschrieben/ausserhalben derer Bu[e]cher/darinnen er insonderheit vnd durchaus wider sie handelt. . . .* Leipzig: Jacob Berwald's heirs, 1577.

———. *Zeugniss Des Herrn D. Martini Lutheri/von der Vernunfft vnnd dero Meisterin Philosophia . . . Auss Lutheri Schrifften zusammen getragen.* Magdeburg: Andreas Duncker, 1600.

———. *Das Zwelffte Capitel Danielis/mit der Auslegung D. Martini Lutheri/vom Antichrist vnd seinem Reich. . . .* Regensburg: Heinrich Giessler, 1560.

Lysthenius, Johann. *Florilegium sacrolutheranum, Das ist, Lutherisch Paradiessga[e]rtlein/Darinnen die furnemsten Spru[e]chlein Altes vnd Neues Testaments/sampt derselbigen Auslegungen von den H. Va[e]tern/wie dieselben im Register verzeichnet. Insonderheit aber/Des thewren Mannes/letzten Propheten/vnd dritten Eliae D. Martini Lutheri zu finden.* Leipzig: Gregor Risch, 1630.

Magdeburg, Job. ΓΝΩΜΑΙ ΑΓΙΑΙ ΚΑΙ ΑΓΟζολικαι. *Sententiae sacrae et apostolicae. Sanctorum Pauli, Petri, Iohannis, & c. Graeci & Latine in Locos Commu-*

nos collectae: una cum Catechesi D. Martini Lutheri. . . . Basel: Johann Oporinus, 1562.

Magdeburg ministerium. *Bekentnis Vnterricht vnd vermanung der Pfarhern vnd Prediger der Christlichen Kirchen zu Magdeburgk.* Magdeburg, 1550.

———. *Confessio et apologia pastorum et reliquorum ministrorum ecclesiae Magdeburgensis. . . .* Magdeburg, 1550.

Mansfeld ministerium. *Bedencken das diese Proposition oder Lere nicht nu[e]tz/not/noch war sey/vnnd one ergernis in der Kirchen nicht mo[e]ge geleret werden. Das gute werck zur seligkeit no[e]tig sind. Vnd vnmu[e]glich sey, one gute werck selig werden.* Magdeburg: Lotther, 1553.

———. *Bekendtnis der Prediger in der Graffschafft Mansfelt/vnter den jungen Herren gesessen. Wider alle Secten/Rotten/vnd falsche Leren/wider Gottes wort/die reine Lere Luthers seligen/vnd der Augspurgischen Confession/an etlichen o[e]rtern eingeschlichen/mit notwendigen widerlegungen derselbigen.* Eisleben, 1560.

———. *Confessio et sententia ministrorum verbi in comitatu Mansfeldensi, de dogmatis quorundam proximo triennio publice editis.* Eisleben: Gaubisch, 1565.

———. *Der Prediger in der Herrschafft Mansfelt antwort/auff Stephani Agricole . . . aussgegangene schlussreden vnd schmeschrifften/die newen lere in vnsern Kirchen/Das gut werck zur seligkeit no[e]tig sein/belangende.* Magdeburg: Lotther, 1553.

Marsteller, Gervasius. *Kurtzer vnd einfeltiger Bericht Wie man/so viel Gott gefellig/sich fu[e]r der grawsamen vnd schrecklicher Pestilentz bewaren. . . .* Uelzen: Michael Kroener, 1577.

Mathesius, Johann. *Historien/Von des Ehrwirdigen in Gott Seligen thewren Manns Gottes, Doctoris Martini Luthers/anfang/lehr/leben vnd sterben. . . .* Nuremberg: Johann vom Berg's heirs and Ulrich Neüber, 1566.

Melissander, Caspar. "Viel schoner Trostbrieffe vnd geistriche Rathschlege . . . Mart: Lutheri begriffen . . . zusamen geordnet." In Tilemann Hesshus and Simon Musaeus, eds., *Trostbuchlein Jn hohen geistlichen Anfechtungen/vnd schwermutiger Trawrigkeit. . . .* Jena: Ernst von Gera, 1572.

Mörlin, Joachim. *Enchiridion. Der Kleine Catechismus Doc. Martini Lutheri/Sampt der Haustafel/in mehr Fragestu[e]ck vorfasset.* Magdeburg: Michael Lotther, 1554; Leipzig: Heirs of Valentin Bapst, 1560.

———. *Wider die Landlu[e]gen der Heidelbergischen Theologen.* Eisleben: Andreas Petri, 1565.

———. *Wie die Bu[e]cher vnd Schrifften/des tewren vnd Seligen Manns Gottes D. Martini Luthers nu[e]tzlich zu lesen Fu[e]r einfeltige frome Pfarherrn vnd andere Christen Liebhaber vnd Leser/der Bu[e]cher D. Martini Lutheri. . . .* Eisleben: Adam Petri (1565).

Musculus, Andreas. *Compendivm doctrinae Christianae collectvm, Ex S. Scriptura, S. Ecclesiae Patribvs, S. Luthero.* Frankfurt/Oder: Johann Eichorn, 1573.

——— (or his circle). *Drei Sermon D. Martini Lutheri/darin man spu[e]ren kan wie ein Herlicher Prophetischer Geist in dem manne gewesen ist/das er das/was *itzt vngo[e]tliche/vom Andrea Osiandro geleret wird/lengst zuuor/als wu[e]rd es bald geschehen gesehen hat*. Frankfurt/Oder: Johann Eichorn, 1552.

———. *Das Guldene Kleinod. Wie ein Christ in Geistlicher anfechtung/sonderlich aber im Todtbett/sich von der Sund/Gesetz/Gottes zorn vnd gericht . . . entbrechen*. . . . Erfurt: Georg Baumann, 1561, 1562, 1570. Volume 1 reissued by Baumann, 1566; Berlin: Michael Hentzsken, 1578 reprint (all four volumes).

———. *Loci commvnes theologici. Ex scriptvra sacra et ex Orthodoxae Ecclesiae Doctoribus collecti*. Erfurt: Georg Baumann, 1563.

———. *Thesavrvs, Hochnutzlicher tewrer Schatz vnd gulden Kleinot*. . . . Frankfurt/Oder: Johann Eichorn, 1577; Frankfurt/Oder: Friedrich Hartmann, 1595 reprint.

———. *Von der vnzertrennlichen voreynigung in einer Person beider naturn vnsers Herrn Jesu Christi Gottes vnd Marien Son/Docto. Martini. Lutheri bekentnis/Glaub/vnd Leere/aus seinen bu[e]chern zusamen getragen/wieder den neulichen erregten Nestorischen vnd Eutichischen miesvorstandt vnd jrrthum*. Frankfurt/Oder: Johann Eichorn, 1553.

———. *Von des Teufels Tyranney/Macht vnd Gewalt/Sonderlich in diesen letzten tagen/vnterrichtung*. Erfurt: Georg Baumann, 1561. Republished in *Teufelbücher in Auswahl*, ed. Ria Stambaugh, 4:191–95. Berlin: De Gruyter, 1978.

———. *Von Guten Wercken/vnterrichtung. Aus des thewren vnd seliger Lehrers/D. Martin Lutheri Bu[e]chern/trewliche vnd fleissig zusamen getragen*. Erfurt: Georg Baumann, 1562.

MVSICA DIVINA, Das ist/Die Geistreichen Doctoris Martini Lutheri, vnd etlicher anderer Christlichen Lehrer/Teutsche/fu[e]rnembste Gesa[e]nge/So in der christlichen Versamlung durchs gantze Jahr gesungen werden. . . . Wolfenbüttel: Elias Holwein, 1620.

Myconius, Friedrich. "Historia Reformationis vom Jahr Christi 1517. bis 1542." Edited by Ernst Salomon Cyprian. In Wilhelm Ernst Tentzel, *Historischer Bericht vom Anfang und ersten Fortgang der Reformation Lutheri*, 2:1–23. Leipzig: Gleditsch and Weidmann, 1718.

Mylius, Georg. *Parentatio Lvtheri. Eine Christliche Predigt Vom Herrn Martino Luther/Was Gott durch diesen seligen thewren Mann/vnd ausserwehlten Ru[e]stzeug ausgerichtet/vnd gemeiner Christenheit fu[e]r Edele Wolthat erzeigt habe*. . . . Wittenberg: Matthes Welack, 1592.

———. *ΤΕΤΡΑΒΙΒΛΟΣ ΑΝΤΙΔΕΙΠΝΟΣΟ-φισικη Martini Lvtheri: continens librorvm 1. Secundi, qui* αὐτιπροφήλικοι *inscribitur. 2. Cui titulus est* περὶ τοῦ ῥητοῦ *in verbis Co[e]nae. 3. Maioris Homologetici. 4. Minoris Homologetici. Analysin*. Jena: Tobias Steinmann, 1591.

Neander, Michael. *Theologia megalandri Lvtheri Siue Aphorismi breves et sententiosi de omnibvs doctrinae Christianae capitibus*. . . . Wittenberg: Simon Groneberg, 1584.

Newe Zeitung. Eine warhafftige Geschicht/welche sich zugetragen hat zu Mu[e]nchen im Beyerland/von der Jesuuitischen Rotte/wie sie Doctor Luthern sein Ebenbild: welcher in Gott seligen lengest vorschieden ist/mit seinem Bu[e]chern vorbrendt haben. Was aber fu[e]r vnglu[e]ck daraus entstanden ist/werdet jhr in dieser Geschicht lesen. . . . Lübeck(?): Johann Balhorn der Jüngere(?), 1580.

Nezenius, Abel. *D. Mart. Lutheri Operationum Biblicarum singularis exercitationis Pars Prima. Super quinque Mosis libros, legales. . . .* Jena: Christoph Lippold, 1610.

Opitz, Joshua. *Kinder-Bibel/Der Kleine Catechismus D. Martini Lutheri mit scho[e]nen Spru[e]chlein heiliger Schrifft erklert. . . .* Büdingen, 1583.

Osiander, Andreas. *Christlicher vnd Gru[e]ndtlicher bericht/Von der Rechtfertigung des Glaubens/Einwonung Gottes vnd Christi in vns . . . D. Martini Luthers . . . Johannis Brentzij . . . Vrbani Regij. . . .* Nuremberg: Johann Daubmann, c. 1550.

———. *Etliche schon Spruche/von der Rechtfertigung des Glaubens/Des Ehrwirdigen Hochgelerten D. Martini Luther heiliger gedechtnis Welche aus den vornemisten vnd besten desselben Bu[e]chern zusamen gezogen. . . .* Königsberg: Hans Lufft, 1551.

———. *Excerpta qvaedam dilvcide et perspicve dictorvm de ivstificatione fidei, in commentario, super Epistolam Pauli ad Galatas, reverendi patris, domini Martini Lvtheri.* Königsberg: Hans Lufft, 1551.

Osiander, Lucas. *Der kleine vnd der grosse Catechismus/Herrn D. Martini Luthers/seliger geda[e]chtnus. Aus welchen ein Christ fein kurtz vnd gru[e]ndlicht erlernen kan/was D. Luther seliger von allen vnd jeden Articuln vnd Stucken der Christlichen Religion Geglaubt vnd gelehret . . . Sampt Einer aussfu[e]rlichen Vorred D. Lucas Osianders/in denen gru[e]ndtlich angezeigt wu[e]rdt/wie vnbillich die Jesuiter/vnd jhres gleichen Papistische Scribenten/die reine Christliche Lehr/vnd die Person D. Luthers/mutwillig calumnieren/verkehren/vnd verla[e]stern. . . .* Tübingen: Georg Gruppenbach, 1599.

Otto, Anton. *Eine Einfeltige vnnd Christliche Trostschrifft . . . an die Christen/so hin vnd wider vmb der Reinen Religion Jesu Christi willen/von den Papisten verfolget werden. Item/Ein Trostschrifft D. M. Lutheri/an die verjagten Christen/ec.* Eisleben: Andreas Petri, 1564.

———. *Etliche Propheceyspru[e]che D. Martini Lutheri/Des dritten Elias.* Magdeburg: Michael Lotter, 1552.

Palatine ministerium. *Verantwortung Wider die vngegrundten aufflagen vnd verkerung/mit welchen der Catechismus Christlicher lere zu Heidelberg jm Jar M.D.LXIII. aussgangen/ . . . beschweret ist . . . Item/D. Martini Luthers meinung vom Brotbrechen im H. Abendmal. . . .* Heidelberg: Johann Maier, 1564.

Pauli, Simon. *Avsslegung der Deutschen Geistlichen Lieder/so von Herrn Doctore Martino Luthero vnd anderen Gottseligen Christen gemacht/oder aus dem Latein ins Deutsche vbersetzet vnd gebracht sind . . . ordentlich nach dem gantzen text erkleret.* Magdeburg: Ambrosius Kirchner, 1588.

Pfeil, Johann. *Schatzkammer Vnd Heuratsteur dess heiligen Geistes Darinnen zu lehrnen alles was einem jeden Christen Menschen vom heiligen Ehestande zu wissen von no[e]ten ist/Auss den Operibus dess Ehrwirdigen Hochgelarten Herrn/Doctor Martini Lutheri . . . gezogen. . . .* Frankfurt/Main: Paul Reffeler, 1565.

Poach, Andreas. *Vom Christlichen Abschied aus diesem sterblichen Leben des lieben thewren Mannes Matthei Ratzebergers der Artzney Doctors Bericht. . . .* Jena: Thomas Rebart, 1559.

Policarius, Johannes. *Trostspiegel der armen Sunder. Das ist/Vom warhafftigen Erkendtnus vnsers Herrn Jheus Christi/vnd vom seligen Trost/Fried vnd Freud desselbigen/wider die verzweifflung/angst/trawrigkeit/vnd anfechtung des hertzens vnd Gewissens . . . Aus den Buchern . . . Martini seligers zusammen gezogen.* Leipzig: Jacob Berwald, 1556.

Pomeranian ministerium. *Des Ehrwirdigen vnd Geistreichen Mans Gottes/Doctoris Martini Lutheri Schrifften/wider die Sacramentirer vnd falsche Lere vom heiligen Abendmal vnsers Herrn Jesu Christi. Zu welchen sich die Pomerischen Kirchen vnd Landen je vnd alle wege bekant vnd noch bekennen/vnd hinfuro bestendiglich dabey zu beharren/durch Gottes gnade vnd hu[e]lff bedacht sein.* Stettin: Andreas Kelner, 1573.

Porta, Conrad. *Des Heiligenn Catechismi: oder Leyen Bibel/Nutz vnd hoheit. Aus den geistreichen Bu[e]chern D. Martini Lutheri des Mans Gottes/Vnd anderer Furtrefflicher Theologen bedencken . . . in Frage vnd Antwort verfasset. Allen trewen Predigern/vleissigen Schulmeistern/vnd frommen Hausuetern/gehorsamen Kindern vnd Gesinde/nu[e]tzlich zu wissen vnd zu lesen.* Halle: Urban Gaubisch, 1578.

———. *Oratio continens adhorationem, ad assidvam Lectionem scriptorum Reverendi Patris & Praeceptoris nostri D. Martini Lvtheri vltimi Eliae & Prophetae Germaniae.* Jena: Donatus Richtzenhan, 1571.

———. *Pastorale Lvtheri. Das ist/Nvtzlicher vnnd no[e]tiger Vnterricht/von den fu[e]rnembsten Stu[e]cken zum heiligen Ministerio geho[e]rig/Vnd richtige Antwort auff mancherley wichtige Fragen/von schweren vnd gefehrlichen Casibus, so in demselbigen fu[e]rfallen mo[e]gen. Fu[e]r anfahende Prediger vnd Kirchendiener zusamen bracht. . . .* Eisleben: Andreas Petri, 1582.

Praetorius, Abdias. *De bonorvm opervm et novae obedientiae necessitate testimonia Ex Sacris literis. Ex Luthero. Ex Melanthone. Ex Confessionibus. Ex Patribus. Ex Scriptoribus recentioribus. . . .* Frankfurt/Oder: Johann Eichorn, 1562.

Praetorius, Andreas. *Luther Redivivus Oder Geistreiche Schatzkammer/Aus allen deutschen Schrifften D. Martini Lutheri Mit grosser Arbeit vnd Fleiss zusammen getragen.* Leipzig: Michael Lantzenberger, 1611.

———. *Lutherus posthumus sive Cor Luther. Das ist/Das Lutherische hertz. Oder Nu[e]tzlicher Ausszug aus den deutschen Eisslebischen Tomis vnd Bu[e]chern/D. Martini Lutheri p.m.* Leipzig: Michael Lantzenberger, 1613.

Praetorius, Peter. *Der Kleine Catechismus Doctoris Martini Lutheri Fu[e]r die Jugent vnd Einfeltigen der Christlichen Gemeine/in Ko[e]nigsbergk/zu derselben jerlichen vnterweisung die Fasten.* Wittenberg: Heirs of Georg Rhau, 1563.

Praetorius, Zacharias. *Libellvs cantionvm Lutheri.* Eisleben: Andreas Petri, 1571.

Probus, Anton. *Oratio de vocatione et doctrina Martini Lvtheri doctoris magni & Prophetae Germaniae vltimi, co[e]lesti & divina recitata publice Islebij in patria S. Lutheri: & opposita Epicureae orationi Alberti Hungeri . . . de homologia, sive consensu doctrinae Lutheri cum Philosophia Epicuri.* Leipzig: Heirs of Jacob Baerwald, 1583.

———. *Renovalia Lvtheri. Von der Gnadenreichen Offenbarung des Heiligen Evangelij/Vnd der grewlichen Abgo[e]tterey des Bapsthumbs/aus den Schrifften des thewren vnd seligen Mannes Gottes/D. Martini Lvtheri/vnd andern Scribenten zusamengebracht. Die erste Predigt. . . .* Jena: Tobias Steinmann, 1590.

Rabus, Ludwig. *Der Heyligen ausserwo[e]hlten Gottes Zeugen, Bekennern vnd Martyrern . . . Historien . . .* 4. Strassburg: Samuel Emmel, 1556.

———. *Historien der Martyrer* 2. Strassburg: Josias Rihel, 1572.

Rauscher, Hieronymus. *Loci commvnes doctrinae Christianae. Die Furnembsten Artickel Christlicher Lehre/kurtz verfast. . . .* Nuremberg: Johann von Berg and Ulrich Neüber, 1558.

Reuss-Schönburg ministerium. *Confessionschrifft. Etlicher Predicanten in den Herrschafften/Graitz/Geraw/Schönburg/vnd anderer hernach vnterschriebenen. . . .* Eisleben, 1567.

Rinckhart, Martin. *Der Eisslebische Christliche Ritter/Eine newe vnd schone/ Geistliche Comoedia/darinnen nicht allein die Lehr/Leben vnd wandel des letzten deutschen Wundermans Luther/sonder auch seiner/vnd zu forderst des Herrn Christi zweyer vornemsten Hauptfeinden/Papst vnd Calvinisten . . . abegemahlet vnd auffgefuhret.* Eisleben, 1613.

———. *Indulgentiarius Confusus/oder Eislebische Mansfeldische Jubel-Comoedia Von der offentliche/Wundermachtigen Beschamung des grossen vnd grewlichen Gottslesterers Johann Tezels: Sampt der vnverschambten/Bapstischen Ablass-Crahmerey: Wie noch des gantzen Romischen vnd Anti Christlichen Bapstthumbs: So Gott/die hohe Majestat/durch die hellklingende/Evangelische Jubel Posaun seines hierzu auserwehlten/hochfliegenden Posaun Engels/des Deutschen/Mansfeldischen Wunder-Propheten/D. Martini Lutheri/nunmehr vor hundert Jahren glucklich anfahen.* Eisleben: Heirs of Jakob Gaubisch, 1618.

———. *Monetarius Seditiosus sive Incendia Rusticorum Bellica/& reliqua ejus lustri memorabilia . . . Der Müntzerische Bawren Krieg . . . Vnd was Gott die Hohe Maj. durch jhren dazu sonders auserwehlten Rustzeug Doct. Martinum Lutherum dabey gethan vnd verrichtet. . . .* Leipzig: Elias Rehfeld and Johann Gross, 1625.

Rivander, Zacharias. *Lvthervs redivivvs. Eine newe Comoedia Von der langen vnd ergerlichen Disputation bey der Lehre vom Abendmal/derer so man Lutherisch vnd Calvinisch/So wol der andern/die man Philippisch vnd Flacianisch heisst. Darinnen Historischer Bericht/wenn/von wem/vnd wie solch erbermlich wesen Anno 24. angefangen/vnd gefu[e]ret worden biss zum ende des 92. Jahres. Aus denen daruon ausgegangenen mehr als drey hundert Streitschrifften mit fleis colligiret/vnd menniglichen zur Lehr/Trost/Warnung vnd Vermahnung/keinen Theil weder zu lieb noch zu leid/auffs aller glimpflichst fu[e]r augen gestellet.* N.p., 1593.

Rosinus, Johannes, ed. *Antiturcica Lutheri: Das ist/Vom Kriege vnd Gebet wider den Tu[e]rcken/vnd von desselben Alcoran: etliche Schrifften/dess thewren vnd werthen Mannes Gottes/Doctoris Martini Lutheri . . . Sampt angehengten etlichen dess Herren D. Lutheri Propheceyungen/von dem ku[e]nfftigen grossen Vnglu[e]ck vber Deutschland.* Leipzig, 1595.

Sarcerius, Erasmus. *Locorum communivm ex consensv divinae scripturae, & sanctorum patrum ad certum methodum . . . confirmatio.* Basel, 1557.

Sartorius, Sixtus. *Causae motiuae . . . conuersionis rationes. . . .* Ingolstadt: Andreas Angermann, 1602.

Saxon (ducal) ministerium. *Confutationes . . . etlicher . . . zu wider . . . Gottes wort . . . Corruptelen. . . .* Jena: Rebart, 1559.

———. *Corpvs doctrinae Christianae. Das ist/Summa der Christlichen lere/aus den Schrifften der Propheten vnd Aposteln/fein kurtz/rundt vnd gru[e]ndtlich/durch D. Martinum Lutherum sonderlich/vnd andere dieser Lande Lerer zusamment gefasset. . . .* Jena: Christian Rödinger's heirs, 1570.

———. *. . . solida & ex Verbo Dei sumpta Confutatio & condemnatio praecipuarum Corruptelarum. . . .* Jena: Rebart, 1559.

Saxon (electoral) ministerium. *Kurtz Bekentnis vnd Artickel vom heiligen Abendmahl des Leibs vnd Bluts Christi. . . .* Wittenberg: Hans Lufft, 1574.

Schilter, Zacharias. *Orationes dvae . . . Altera. Continens apologiam . . . patris DD. Martini Lutheri, repurgatoris doctrinae Co[e]lestis celeberrimi, praeclarissimique de Republica Christiana meriti. . . .* Leipzig: Johann Steinmann, 1583.

Schipper, Hermann. *Lvthervs Exvlans. Der ins Elend vnschuldig vertriebene Luther. . . .* Strassburg: Christoph von der Heyden, 1623.

Schlüsselburg, Conrad. *Postilla, Das ist: Ausslegung der Episteln vnd Evangelien. . . .* Frankfurt/Main: Johann Saur, 1604.

Schoppe, Andreas. *Rettung Des Heiligen Catechismi wider den Schwarm der newen Manicheer vnd Substantijsten.* Jena: Donatus Richtzenhan, 1572.

Schütz, Johannes. *Schilt des Glaubens/Wider die Sicherheit vnd verzweiffelung/ auch wider die Anfechtung von der Versehung/Vnd ob Gesichten vnd Offenbarung in diesen/letzten zeiten zu trawen sey . . . Aus D. Mart. Lutheri Schrifften/ kurtzliche zusamen gebracht.* Wittenberg: Simon Gronenberg, 1583.

Schwan, Sebastian. *De megalandro D. Martino Lvthero, sincerae religionis instauratore, eiusque praeclare gesto officio, ac piae obitu Oratio ad recolendam et praesertim hoc anno jubilaeo evangelico celebrandam operum Dei magnificentiam, ac beneficiorum Germaniae. . . .* Hamburg: Heinrich Carstens, 1618.

Schwob, Sigismund. *Index omnium scriptorvm Reverendi patris D. Martini Luther: accommodatus & ad 19. Tomos Vitebergenses & 12. Ihenenses. . . .* Breslau: Crispin Scharffenberg, 1563; Wittenberg: Peter Seitz, 1564, 1573.

———. *Register aller Schrifften des Ehrwirdigen Herrn D. Martini Lutheri/gerichtet zugleich auff die XIX. Wittembergischen/vnd XII. Jhenischen Tomos. . . .* Breslau: Crispin Scharffenberg, 1563; Wittenberg: Peter Seitz, 1564.

Seidel, Paul. *Historia vnd Geschicht Des Ehrwirdigen vnsers in Gott lieben Vaters/Herrn Doctoris Martini Lutheri, seliger gedechtnuss/wie durch Gottes Geist getrieben/vnd sich anfenglich aus sonderlicher schickung des Allmechtigen zwischen jm vnd dem Bapst der Streit erhoben/domit das selige Liecht des heiligen Euangelij in diesen letzten zeiten wider an tag gegeben/Vnd wie es bis auff diese stund/nach vielen vnd mancherley eingeschlichenen Corruptelen/ heimlichen vnd offentlichen Verfelschungen/wunderbarer weis erhalten/vnd jtzt in die new auffgerichte Formulam Concordiae rein vnd vnverfelscht ist gebracht worden. Aus seinen eigenen Schrifften vnd andern Historien vmb gemeiner Leute besserer nachrichtung willen/zu Trost Warnung vnd Vermanung. . . .* Wittenberg: Heirs of Hans Krafft, 1582.

Selnecker, Nikolaus. *Historica narratio et oratio de D. D. Martino Luthero, postremae aetatis Elia, & initijs, causis, & progressu Confessionis Augustanae, atque Lutheri ac Philippi omonoia sancta. . . .* Leipzig: Heirs of Jacob Baerwald, 1575.

———. *Historica Oratio. Vom Leben vnd Wandel des Ehrwirdigen Herrn/vnd thewren Mannes Gottes/D. Martini Lutheri. Auch von einhelliger vnd bestendiger Eintrechtigkeit Herrn Lutheri vnd Philippi. . . .* Leipzig: Johannes Rhambau, 1576.

———. *Notatio . . . De studio sacrae Theologiae.* Leipzig: Johann Rhamba, 1579.

———. *Oratio historica de initiis, cavsis, et progressv confessionis Augustanae, et de vita ac laboribus D. D. Martini Lvtheri, postremae aetatis Eliae. . . .* Jena: Tobias Steinmann, 1592.

———. *Recitationes aliqvot . . .* (4. "De avtoritate Lvtheri et Philippi . . ."). Leipzig: Georg Defner, 1581.

———, ed. *Sententiae consolatoriae, collectae ex scriptura coelesti, quibus utimur, cum ad sacram communionem accedimus, quibus etiam D. Doctor Martinus Lutherus usus est.* Nuremberg: Johann Daubmann, 1553. Translated as *Tro[e]stliche scho[e]ne Spru[e]che aus heiliger Schrifft gezogen/ausgelegt/vnd von newem vbersehen vnd gebessert/Allen Christen zu dieser elenden zeit/ sonderlich den betru[e]bten gewissen zu gut/mit vielen Gebetlin zugerichtet vnd verfertiget.* Dresden: Matthes Stoeckel, 1565. Reissued as *Sehr scho[e]ne Trostspru[e]che/auss Heiliger Go[e]ttlicher Schrifft gezogen/Fu[e]r die angstigen gewissen. Durch Veit Dietrich.* Nuremberg: Ludwig Lochner, 1618.

Sententia ministrorvm in Ecclesia Lubecensi, Hamburgensi, Lüneburgensi & Magdeburgensi, de corruptelis doctrinae iustificationis, quibus D. Georg. Maior adserit. . . . Magdeburg: Lotther, 1553.

Serarius, Nikolaus. *Apologiae pro discipvlo et magistro, Lvthero et diabolo. . . .* Mainz: Balthasar Lipp, 1605.

———. *Dass Luthers Nachtliecht/das ist/Kurtzer Warhafftiger/besta[e]ndiger vnd gru[e]ndlicher Bericht/von der grossen vnd ersten/vornembsten vnd wunderbarlichen Erleuchtung/durch welche dem thewren vnd hochgelehrten Mann D. Martin Luther seine Lehr im anfang offenbaret worden. . . .* Ingolstadt: Andreas Angermayer, 1603.

———. *De Lutheri magistro, vt digito possit monstrari et diceri hic est ad Lutheranos praedicantes non belli sed pacis ergo, in vnius ex eorum numero, Frid Balduini. . . .* Mainz: Balthasar Lipp, 1604.

———. *Lvtherotvrcicae orationes qvarvm, post praefationem, indicvlvs.* Mainz: Balthasar Lipp, 1604.

———. *Lvthervs theosdotos Rostochiensi rhetori revissvs, Cum Discipulo suo Calvino. . . .* Mainz: Balthasar Lipp, 1607.

Simon, Johann. *Apologeticvs, in quo Nicolai Serarii S. J. presbyteri tum theosdoto remisso, tum Orationi de Disputatione Diaboli cum Luthero, respondetur.* Rostock: Stephen Myliander, 1608.

———. *Lvthervs Theosdotos. Oratio, Mendacijs Papisto-Turcici cujusdam Jesuitae, origenem doctrinae co[e]lestis, cujus ὑποφήτης interpres & doctor diuinibus excitatus fuit MARTINUS LUTHERUS, Diabolo blaspheme ascribentis.* Rostock: Stephen Myliander, 1606.

———. *Parentatio Lvtheri oratio de Beneficijs, quae Deus per electissimum Spiritus Sancti organum Martinvm Lvthervm generi humano exhibuit. . . .* Rostock: Stephan Myliander, 1596.

Sleidanus, Johannes. *Commentariorvm de statv religionis & Reipublicae, Carolo Quinto Caesare, Libri XXVI.* Strassburg: Theodosius Rihel, 1559.

Spalatin, Georg. "Annales Reformationis, oder Jahr-Buecher von der Reformation Lutheri." Edited by Ernst Salomon Cyprian. In Wilhelm Ernst Tentzel, *Historischer Bericht vom Anfang und ersten Fortgang der Reformation Lutheri,* 2:1–7. Leipzig: Gleditsch and Weidmann, 1718.

Spangenberg, Cyriakus. *Cythara Lvtheri. Die scho[e]nen/Christlichen/trostreichen Psalmen vnd Geistlichen Lieder/des Hochwirdigen thewren Lerers vnd Diener Gottes/D. Martini Luthers. Der Erste [–Vierder] Theil.* Erfurt: Georg Bawmann, 1570.

———. *Die dritte Predigte/von dem heiligen Gottes Manne/Doctore Martino Luthero/Sonderlich von seinem Prophetenampt. . . .* Erfurt: Georg Baumann, 1564.

———. *Die sechste Predigt. Von dem werden Gottes Lerer: Doctor Martin Luther/ Das er ein rechter Pavlvs gewesen.* Erfurt: Georg Baumann, 1565.

———. *Die Siebende Predigt. Von dem Hocherleuchten Gottesmanne/Doctor Martin Lvther/Das er ein warer Evangelist/vnd rechter Ioannes gewesen.* Erfurt: Georg Baumann, 1566.

———. *Theander Lutherus. Von des werten Gottes Manne Doctor Martin Luthers Geistliche Haushaltung vnd Ritterschaft. . . .* Ursel: Nikolaus Heinrich, 1589.

———. *Die vierde Predigt/Von dem grossen Propheten Gottes/Doctore Martino Luthero/Das er ein rechter Helias gewesen. . . .* Erfurt: Georg Baumann, 1564.

———. *Warhafftige/gewisse/bestendige/der heiligen Schrifft gemesse/vnd in Gottes Wort gegru[e]ndte Lere/von der Erbsu[e]nde. Doctor Martini Luthers/Daraus klar zusehen/das dieselbige nicht sey ein Accidens.* Eisleben: Andreas Petri, 1572.

———. *Warhafftiger Bericht von den wolthaten/die Gott durch Martin Luther seligen/fu[e]rnemlich Deudschland erzeigt/vnd von der Schendlichen groben vndanckbarkeit/fu[e]r solche grosse gaben geschrieben.* Jena: Thomas Rhebart, 1561.

———. *Die Zehende Predigt/Von dem thewren Bekenner Gottes. D. Martini Lvther. . . .* Eisleben: Petri, 1568.

Spangenberg, Johann. *Der Gros Catechismus vnd Kinder Lehre D. Mart. Luth. Fu[e]r die jungen Christen/in Fragestu[e]cke verfasset. . . .* Frankfurt/Main: Johann Wolf, 1565.

———. *Des kleinen Catechismi kurtzer begrieff und der Haustaffel/wie man sie in aller gemeine zu Halle/für die Kinder handelt. . . .* Halle: Hans Frischmut. 1542.

Spener, Philip Jakob, ed. *Luther Redivivus Oder Des fu[e]rnehmsten Lehrers der Augspurgischen Confession Herrn D. Martini Luthers . . . Hinterlassene Schrifftliche Erkla[e]rungen Aus welchen ungezweiffelt zu vernehmen/Was der Augspurgischen Confession eigentliche Meinung vnd Verstand in allen Articuln allezeit gewesen/vnd noch sey. . . .* Halle: Christoph Salfeld, 1697.

Statius, Martin. *Lutherus redivivus. Das ist: Lutheri Christenthumb Darinn der wahre lebendige Glaube/sein Vrsprung/Natur/Krafft vnd Wirckung/der waren*

Christen Majestaet/Herrligkeit/Heiligkeit vnd Vereinigung mit Christo/wie auch jhr ungeferbte Liebe/vnd Christlichs leben/mit Lutheri gantz herrlichen vnd geistrichen worten fu[e]r augen gestellet wird. . . . Thorn: Franciscus Schnellboltz, 1626.

Stolz, Johann. *Brevis defensio viri Dei Martini Lvtheri, in modvm somnij opposite somniatori Adiaphoristico.* Regensburg: Johann Kohl, 1555.

Sylvius, Emericus, ed. *Beweyss/Das Magister Cyriacus Spangenberg vnd seine Mitbekenner inn der Lehre von der Erbsu[e]nde/mit Luthero durchauss vbereinstimmen. . . .* N.p., 1579.

Tettelbach, Johann. *Das Gu[e]lden Kleinod. D. Mart. Lutheri Catechismus/In kurtze Frage vnd antwort gefasset/Vnd der lieben Jugend einfeltigklich aussgelegt.* Frankfurt/Main: Catherina Rebart and Kilian Han, 1571.

Timann (Amsterdam), Johann. *Prophetiae aliqvot verae: Et sententiae insignes reuerendi patris, Domini Doctoris Martini Lutheri, Tercij Helie: De calamitatibus, defectione, & Tenebris, Germaniae obuenturis, eo in Domino mortuo, & perpetuo viuente.* N.p., 1550; Magdeburg: Michael Lotther, 1552.

Ursinus, Zacharias. *Catechismus Oder Kurtzer vnterricht Christlicher Lehr. . . .* Neustadt/Hardt: Matthaeus Harnisch, 1592, 1595.

Varnbuller, Anton. *Auff M. Sebastiani Flaschen von Mansfeldt/vnd anderer seines gleichen Bapstischen Scribenten/verklerungen vnd lo[e]sterungen: da sie auss D. Luthers seeligen Schrifften (wie die gifftigen spinnen) etwas heraus saugen/vnd daraus beweisen wo[e]llen/das D. Martin Luther/kein heyliger Prophet dess Teutschlandts/sonder ein rechter vnflat gewesen sein soll.* Tübingen: Alexander Hock, 1585.

Verzeichnung vnd Register aller Bu[e]cher vnd schrifften D. Mart. Luther/durch yn aussgelassen/vom Jar 1518. bis yns acht vnd zwentzigst. N.p., 1528(?).

Voigt, Balthasar. *Echo Jubilaei Lutherani. Das ist Ein Christlich Gedicht vnd Widerschall vom Lutherischen Jubelfest/so des abgewichenen 1617. Jahrs in der Christlichen Catholischen vralten vnd Lutherischen Kirchen Celebriert worden. . . .* N.p., 1618.

Walther, Christoph. *Register aller Bu[e]cher vnd Schrifften des Ehrnwirdigen Herrn Doctoris Martini Lutheri seliger gedechtnis. . . .* Wittenberg: Hans Lufft, 1556, 1558.

Walther, Georg. *Beicht vnd Bettbu[e]chlein/Darin scho[e]ne vnd Kurtze erklerung/in Frag vnd antwort/auss dem Catechismo Lutheri vnd andern Schrifften gezogen/so vormals nie getruckt/jetzund erst aussgangen. . . .* Frankfurt/Main: Sigismund Feyerabent, 1581.

———. *Erster [–Vierder] Theil der Heubtartickel/Christlicher Lere. In Fragestu[e]cken verfasset/vnd mit Gottes Wort/vnd fu[e]rnemen Spru[e]chen D. Lutheri/vnd D. Melanthonis erkleret vnd bekrefftiget. Allen denen/so die Bu[e]chern D. Luthers vnd D. Melanthonis nicht haben/zum dienst angestellet/damit auch diejenigen/so sie haben/alles besser finden/verstehen/und gebrauchen ko[e]nnen.* Magdeburg: Matthaeus Giseken, 1573.

———. *Prophezeiungen D. Martini Lutheri. Zur erinnerung vnd anreitzung zur Christlichen Busse/ordentlich vnd mit vleis zusamen getragen.* Wittenberg: Lorentz Schwenck, 1559.

———. *Trostbuchlein Auss der heiligen Schrifft/vnd D. Martini Lutheri Bu[e]chern von Wort zu Wort gestellet.* Nuremberg: Ulrich Neüber, 1560. Reissued as *Das Erste [Ander . . .] Theil der Trostspruche D. Martini Lutheri. Angefochtenen vnd Betrubten Christen zum Trost verordnet. . . .* Bautzen: Johann Wolrab, 1571.

Waltper, Otto. *Oratio pro defensione Lvtheri Lvtheranorumque doctrina: opposita orationi Albert Hvngeri Iesviticae sectae professoris et procancellari & Academiae Ingolstadiensis, in qua malitiose conatus est Theologiam Lutheri, Caluini, aliquorumque, vt ipse ait, Nouatorum, cum Philosophia Epicuri comparare. . . .* Marburg: Paul Egenolff, 1590.

Weller, Hieronymus. *Der Christliche vnd gemein Kirchen Gesang. Gott der Vatter wohn vns bey/ec. . . .* Nuremberg: Johann von Berg and Ulrich Neüber, c. 1555.

Westphal, Joachim. *Des Ehrwirdigen vnd thewren Mans Doct. Marti. Luthers seliger gedechtnis meinung von den Mitteldingen.* Magdeburg: Michael Lotther, 1550.

———. *Sententia reverendi viri D. M. Luth. Sanctae memoriae de Adiaphoris ex scriptis illius collecta.* Magdeburg: Michael Lotther, 1549.

———. *Verlegung des Gru[e]ndlichen Berichts der Adiaphoristen zu diesen bo[e]sen zeiten.* N.p., 1551.

Wigand, Johannes. *Commonefactio de fravdibvs qvorvndam sacramentariorum. . . .* N.p., n.d.

———. *Confession oder Bekentnis Gotlicher reiner/heilsamer Lere von den fu[e]rnemesten Artickeln des Glaubens/sampt etlicher widerwertigen Lere/Corruptelen vnd Irthum/kurtze vnd gegru[e]nte widerlegung.* Erfurt: Isaiah Melchler, 1582.

———. *1. De abstracto theologico Methodus. 2. Collatio de nova Controuersia. 3. Synodvs Prvtenica de hac re. 4. Cavsae, cvr Locvtiones & doctrinae &c. sint scandalosae & falsae per se.* Königsberg: Georg Osterberg, 1578.

———. *De confessione in doctrina divina, & necessarijs factis.* Jena: Rödinger, 1569.

———. *Ob Die Newen Wittenberger/stets bis daher/einig mit den alten geleret: Vnd ob Lutheri vnd Philippi schriften/durch aus gantz einig vnd einhellig . . . Christliche Vnd Notwendige Erinnerung vnd bericht.* Königsberg: Bonifacius Daubman, 1575.

———. *Oratio de doctrina et praecipuis certaminibus Lutheri.* Jena: Günther Hüttich, 1571.

———. *Von der Erbsu[e]nde/Lere aus Gottes Wort/aus dem Du[e]ringischen Corpore Doctrinae/vnd aus D. Luthers Bu[e]chern. . . .* Jena: Donatus Richtzenhan, 1571.

———. *Wider den blawen dunst eines newen Propheten.* Königsberg: Georg Osterberg, 1578.

Wigand, Johannes, and Matthaeus Judex. ΣΥΝΤΑΓΜΑ, *seu corpus doctrinae Christi, ex novo Testamento tantum, Methodica ratione, singulari fide & diligentia congestum.* Basel: Johannes Oporinus, 1558.

———. ΣΥΝΤΑΓΜΑ, *seu corpus doctrinae veri & omnipotentis Dei, ex veteri Testamento tantum, methodica ratione. . . .* Basel: Oporinus and Herwagen, 1564.

Wittenberg theological faculty. *De praecipvis horvm temporvm controversiis propositiones, orationes et qvaestiones, continentes svmmam confessionis ac Academiae Vvitebergensis, congruentem cum perpetua sententia purioris & orthodoxae antiquitatis. Scriptae et propositae publice Vvitebergae, Anno Christi 1570.* Wittenberg: Johannes Schwertel, 1571.

———. *Endlicher Bericht vnd Erklerung der Theologen beider Vniuersiteten/Leipzig vnd Wittemberg Auch der Superintendenten der Kirchen in des Churfu[e]rsten zu Sachsen Landen/belangend die Lere/so gemelte Vniuersiteten vnd Kirchen von anfang der Augspurgischen Confession bis auff diese zeit/laut vnd vermu[e]ge derselben/zu allen Artickeln gleichfo[e]rmig/eintrechtig vnd bestendig gefu[e]ret haben/vber der sie auch durch hu[e]lff des allmechtigen Gottes gedencken fest zu halten.* Wittenberg: Hans Lufft, 1570.

———. *Kurtze vnd gru[e]ndliche Erkla[e]rung/in welchen Puncten D. Luther/ vnd die so man Caluinische nennet/in der Lehr vom H. Abendmal/einig vnd auch strittig sein/Auss Herrn Lutheri eigen Schrifften aussgezogen. . . .* N.p., 1577.

———. *Von der person vnd Menschwerdung vnsers HERRN Jhesu Christi/Der waren Christlichen Kirchen Grundfest/Wider die newen Marcioniten/Samosatener/Sabellianer/Arianer/Nestorianer/Eutychianer vnd Monotheleten/vnter dem Flacianischen hauffen. Durch die Theologen zu Wittemberg/aus der heiligen Schrifft/aus den Symbolis/aus den fu[e]rnemesten Concilijs vnd einhelligem Consenss aller bewerten Lerer. Widerholet vnd Gestellet/zu trewer lere vnd ernster verwarnung an alle frome vnd Gottselige Christen. Neben warhaffter vorantwortung/auff die gifftigen vnd boshaftigen verleumbdungen/so von den Propositionibus vnd Catechismo zu Wittemberg ausgangen/von vielen dieser zeit ausgesprenget werden. . . .* Wittenberg: Hans Lufft, 1571.

Wolffhart, Bartholomaeus. *Der Kleine Catechismus Lutheri: durch etliche Kurtze vnd Kindische Fragestu[e]ck erkleret/damit jhn die Jugent desto besser verstehen mo[e]ge.* Ursel: Nicolaus Henricus, 1566.

Zanger, Melchior. *Examen versionis Lutheri in Biblia. . . .* Mainz: Johann Weiss, 1605.

Ziegler, Bernhard. *Zwo Predigten des Ehrwirdigen herren Doctoris Martini Lutheri. . . .* Leipzig: Hantzsch, 1551.

Edited Sources

Album Academiae Vitebergensis ab A. Ch. MDII usque ad A. MDCII. 2. Halle: Niemeyer, 1894.

Allen, P. S., ed. *Opus epistolarum Des. Erasmi Roterodami* 1. Oxford: Clarendon, 1906.

Die Bekenntnisschriften der evangelisch-lutherischen Kirche. 5th ed. Göttingen: Vandenhoeck & Ruprecht, 1963.

Luther, Martin. *Dr. Martin Luthers Werke.* 65 vols. Weimar: Böhlau, 1883–1993.

Luther, Martin. *Luther's Works.* 55 vols. St. Louis and Philadelphia: Concordia and Fortress, 1958–86.

Mehlhausen, Joachim, ed. *Das Augsburger Interim von 1548.* Neukirchen-Vluyn: Neukirchener Verlag, 1970.

Melanchthon, Philip. *Corpus Reformatorum. Philippi Melanchthonis opera quae supersunt omnia.* Edited by Karl Bretschneider and Heinrich Bindseil. 28 vols. Braunschweig: Schwetschke, 1834–60.

Neudecker, C. G., ed. *Die handschriftliche Geschichte Ratzebergers über Luther und seine Zeit.* Jena: Mauke, 1850.

Rembe, Heinrich, ed. *Der Briefwechsel des M. Cyriakus Spangenberg.* 2 vols. Dresden: Naumann, 1887–88.

Reu, Johann Michael, ed. *Quellen zur Geschichte des kirchlichen Unterrichts in der evangelischen Kirche Deutschlands zwischen 1530 und 1600.* 9 vols. in 3. Gütersloh: Bertelsmann, 1902–24.

Rogge, Joachim, ed. *Luther in Worms, 1521–1971: Ein Quellenbuch.* Berlin: Evangelische Verlagsanstalt, 1971.

Sachs, Hans. *Hans Sachsens ausgewählte Werke.* Vol. 1, *Gedichte.* Frankfurt/Main: Insel, 1961.

Schubart, Christof, ed. *Die Berichte über Luthers Tod und Begräbnis.* Weimar: Böhlau, 1917.

Schulz, Frieder, ed. *Die Gebete Luthers: Edition, Bibliographie und Wirkungsgeschichte.* Gütersloh: Mohn, 1976.

Wackernagel, Philipp, ed. *Das deutsche Kirchenlied von der ältesten Zeit bis zu Anfang des XVII. Jahrhunderts.* 5 vols. Leipzig: Teubner, 1864–77.

Zwingli, Ulrich. *Corpus Reformatorum. Huldreich Zwinglis Sämtliche Werke.* Edited by Emil Egli et al. 14 vols. (88–101). Zurich: Berichthaus, 1959–68.

Secondary Sources

Aland, Kurt. *Hilfsbuch zum Lutherstudium.* Witten: Luther, 1970.

———. *Lutherlexikon.* 4th ed. Göttingen: Vandenhoeck & Ruprecht, 1983.

Bagchi, David V. N. *Luther's Earliest Opponents: Catholic Controversialists, 1518–1525.* Minneapolis: Fortress, 1991.

Balzer, Bernd. *Bürgerliche Reformationspropaganda: Die Flugschriften des Hans Sachs in den Jahren 1523–1525.* Stuttgart: Metzler, 1973.

Barnes, Robin Bruce. *Prophecy and Gnosis: Apocalypticism in the Wake of the Lutheran Reformation.* Stanford: Stanford University Press, 1988.

Bäumer, Remigius. *Johannes Cochlaeus (1479–1552): Leben und Werk im Dienst der katholischen Reform.* Münster: Aschendorff, 1980.

Benkert, J. A., ed. *Deutsche Luthersagen.* Berlin: Eckart, 1937.

Benz, Ernst. "Der Traum Kurfürst Friedrichs des Weisen." In *Humanitas-Christianitas: Walther v. Loewenich zum 65. Geburtstag,* edited by Karlmann Beyschlag, Gottfried Maron, and Eberhard Wolfel, 134–49. Witten: Luther, 1968.

Bornkamm, Heinrich. *Luther im Spiegel der deutschen Geistesgeschichte.* Heidelberg: Quelle & Meyer, 1955.

Brecht, Martin. *Martin Luther: His Road to Reformation, 1483–1521.* Translated by James L. Schaaf. Philadelphia: Fortress, 1981.

Brückner, Wolfgang. "Historien und Historie: Erzählliteratur des 16. und 17. Jahrhunderts als Forschungsaufgabe." In *Volkserzählung und Reformation,* edited by Wolfgang Brückner, 3–75. Berlin: Schmidt, 1974.

———. "Loci Communes als Denkform, Literarische Bildung und Volkstradition zwischen Humanismus und Historismus." *Daphnis* 4 (1975): 1–12.

———. "Luther als Gestalt der Sage." In *Volkserzählung und Reformation,* edited by Wolfgang Brückner, 261–94. Berlin: Schmidt, 1974.

———, ed. *Volkserzählung und Reformation.* Berlin: Schmidt, 1974.

Christensen, Carl C. *Art and the Reformation in Germany.* Athens, Ohio: Ohio University Press, 1979.

———. *Princes and Propaganda: Electoral Saxon Art of the Reformation.* Kirksville, Mo.: Sixteenth Century Journal, 1992.

Daniel, David P. "Publishing the Reformation in Habsburg Hungary." In *Habent sua fata libelli, Books Have Their Own Destiny: Essays in Honor of Robert V. Schnucker,* edited by Robin B. Barnes, Robert A. Kolb, and Paul L. Presley, 47–60. Kirksville, Mo.: Thomas Jefferson University Press, 1998.

Dingel, Irene. "Ablehnung und Aneignung: Die Bewertung der Autorität Martin Luthers in den Auseinandersetzungen um die Konkordienformel." *Zeitschrift für Kirchengeschichte* 105 (1994): 35–57.

———. *Concordia controversa: Die öffentlichen Diskussionen um das lutherische Konkordienwerk am Ende des 16. Jahrhunderts.* Gütersloh: Gütersloher Verlagshaus, 1996.

———. "The Echo of Controversy: Caspar Fuger's Attempt to Propagate the Formula of Concord among the Common People." *Sixteenth Century Journal* 26 (1995): 515–31.

———. "Melanchthon und die Normierung des Bekenntnisses." In *Der Theologe Melanchthon,* edited by Heinz Scheible, 195–211. Sigmaringen: Thorbecke, 1999.

Edwards, Mark U., Jr. *Luther and the False Brethren.* Stanford: Stanford University Press, 1975.

———. *Luther's Last Battles, Politics and Polemics 1531–1546.* Ithaca: Cornell University Press, 1983.

———. *Printing, Propaganda, and Martin Luther.* Berkeley: University of California Press, 1994.

Eisenstein, Elizabeth L. *The Printing Press as an Agent of Change, Communications and Cultural Transformations in Early-Modern Europe.* 2 vols. Cambridge: Cambridge University Press, 1979.

Evans, R. J. W. *Rudolf II and His World: A Study in Intellectual History, 1576–1612.* Oxford: Clarendon, 1973.

Fraas, Hans-Jürgen. *Katechismustradition: Luthers kleiner Katechismus in Kirche und Schule.* Göttingen: Vandenhoeck & Ruprecht, 1971.

Gericke, Wolfgang. *Glaubenszeugnisse und Konfessionspolitik der Brandenburgischen Herrscher bis zur Preussischen Union, 1540 bis 1815.* Bielefeld: Luther, 1977.

Grane, Leif. *Martinus Noster: Luther in the German Reform Movement, 1518–1521.* Mainz: Zabern, 1994.

Greschat, Martin. *Melanchthon neben Luther: Studien zur Gestalt der Rechtfertigungslehre zwischen 1528 und 1537.* Witten: Luther, 1965.

Grimm, Claus, et al., eds. *Lukas Cranach, Ein Maler-Unternehmer aus Franken: Katalog zur Landesausstellung. . . .* Augsburg: Haus der Bayerischen Geschichte, 1994.

Gruppe, Heidemarie. "Katalog der Luther- und Reformationssagen des 19. Jahrhunderts." In *Volkserzählung und Reformation,* edited by Wolfgang Brückner, 295–311. Berlin: Erich Schmidt, 1974.

Hägglund, Bengt. "Die Rezeption Luthers in der Konkordienformel." In *Luther und die Bekenntnisschriften,* 107–20. Erlangen: Martin Luther, 1981.

Hase, Hans Christoph von. *Die Gestalt der Kirche Luthers: Der Casus Confessionis im Kampf des Matthias Flacius gegen das Interim von 1548.* Göttingen: Vandenhoeck & Ruprecht, 1940.

Hasse, Hans Peter. "Die Lutherbiographie von Nikolaus Selnecker: Selneckers Berufung auf die Autorität Luthers im Normenstreit der Konfessionalisierung in Kursachsen." *Archiv für Reformationsgeschichte* 86 (1995): 91–123.

Headley, John M. *Luther's View of Church History.* New Haven: Yale University Press, 1963.

Heim, Karl. *Das Gewissheitsproblem in der systematischen Theologie bis zu Schleiermacher.* Leipzig: Hinrich, 1911.

Henze, Barbara. *Aus Liebe zur Kirche Reform: Die Bemühungen Georg Witzels (1501–1573) um die Kircheneinheit.* Münster: Aschendorff, 1995.

Herrmann, Johannes. "Augsburg–Leipzig–Passau (Das Leipziger Interim nach Akten des Landeshauptarchivs Dresden, 1547–1552)." Th.D. diss., University of Leipzig, 1962.

Herrmann, Wolfgang. "Die Lutherpredigten des Cyriacus Spangenberg." *Mansfelder Blätter* 39 (1934/1935): 7–95.

Herte, A. *Die Lutherkommentare des Johannes Cochläus.* Münster: Aschendorff, 1935.

Holl, Karl. *Gesammelte Aufsätze zur Kirchengeschichte.* Vol. 1, *Luther.* Tübingen: Mohr (Siebeck), 1921.

Junghans, Helmar. *Der junge Luther und die Humanisten.* Göttingen: Vandenhoeck & Ruprecht, 1985.

Kastner, Ruth. *Geistlicher Rauffhandel: Illustrierte Flugblätter zum Reformationsjubiläum.* Mikrokosmos 11. Frankfurt/Main: Peter Lang, 1982.

Kaufmann, Thomas. "Die Konfessionalisierung von Kirche und Gesellschaft: Sammelbericht über eine Forschungsdebatte." *Theologische Literaturzeitung* 121 (1996): 1008–25, 1112–21.

Keller, Rudolf. *Die Confessio Augustana im theologischen Wirken des Rostocker Professors David Chyträus (1530–1600).* Göttingen: Vandenhoeck & Ruprecht, 1994.

Klaus, Bernhard. "Die Lutherüberlieferung Veit Dietrichs und ihre Problematik." *Zeitschrift für bayerische Kirchengeschichte* 53 (1988): 33–47.

Klein, Thomas. *Der Kampf um die zweite Reformation in Kursachsen, 1586–1591.* Cologne: Böhlau, 1962.

Koch, Ernst. "Auseinandersetzungen um die Autorität von Philipp Melanchthon und Martin Luther in Kursachsen im Vorfeld der Konkordienformel von 1577." *Lutherjahrbuch* 59 (1992): 128–59.

———. "Lutherflorilegien zwischen 1550 und 1600: Zum Lutherbild der ersten nachreformatorischen Generation." *Theologische Versuche* 16 (1986): 105–17.

———. "Michael Neander (1525–1595) als Theologe." In *Bekenntnis zur Kirche: Festgabe für Ernst Sommerlath zum 70. Geburtstag,* 112–25. Berlin: Evangelische Verlagsanstalt, 1960.

Kolb, Robert. *Confessing the Faith: Reformers Define the Church, 1530–1580.* St. Louis: Concordia, 1991.

———. "The Fathers in the Service of Lutheran Teaching: Andreas Musculus' Use of Patristic Sources." In *Auctoritas patrum,* edited by Leif Grane, Alfred Schindler, and Markus Wriedt, 2:105–23. Wiesbaden: Steiner, 1998.

———. *For All the Saints: Changing Perceptions of Martyrdom and Sainthood in the Lutheran Reformation*. Macon, Ga.: Mercer University Press, 1987.

———. "Georg Major as Controversialist: Polemics in the Late Reformation." *Church History* 45 (1976): 455–68.

———. "The Influence of Luther's Galatians Commentary of 1535 on Later Sixteenth-Century Lutheran Commentaries on Galatians." *Archiv für Reformationsgeschichte* 84 (1993): 156–84.

———. "Jakob Andreae's Concern for the Laity." *Concordia Journal* 4 (1978): 58–67.

———. "The Layman's Bible: The Use of Luther's Catechisms in the German Late Reformation." In *Luther's Catechisms—450 Years: Essays Commemorating the Small and Large Catechisms of Dr. Martin Luther,* edited by David P. Scaer and Robert D. Preus, 16–26. Fort Wayne, Ind.: Concordia Theological Seminary Press, 1979.

———. "Luther, Augsburg, and the Late Reformation Concept of Confession." In *Controversy and Conciliation: The Reformation and the Palatinate 1559–1583,* edited by Derk Visser, 33–49. Allison Park, Pa.: Pickwick, 1986.

———. "Luther, the Master Pastor: Conrad Porta's *Pastorale Lutheri,* Handbook for Generations." *Concordia Journal* 9 (1983): 179–87.

———. *Luther's Heirs Define His Legacy: Studies on Lutheran Confessionalization.* Aldershot, Eng.: Variorum, 1996.

———. "Matthaeus Judex's Condemnation of Princely Censorship of Theologians' Publications." *Church History* 50 (1981): 401–14.

———. *Nikolaus von Amsdorf (1483–1565): Popular Polemics in the Preservation of Luther's Legacy.* Nieuwkoop: B. De Graaf, 1978.

———. "'Not without the Satisfaction of God's Righteousness': The Atonement and the Generation Gap between Luther and His Students." *Archiv für Reformationsgeschichte.* Supp. vol., *Die Reformation in Deutschland und Europa: Interpretation und Debatten,* edited by Hans R. Guggisberg und Gottfried G. Krodel, 136–56. Gütersloh: Gütersloher Verlagshaus, 1993.

———. "The Ordering of the *Loci Communes Theologici:* The Structuring of the Melanchthonian Dogmatic Tradition." *Concordia Journal* 23 (1997): 317–37.

———. "'Perilous Events and Troublesome Disturbances': The Role of Controversy in the Tradition of Luther to Lutheran Orthodoxy." In *Pietas et Societas: New Trends in Reformation Social History: Essays in Memory of Harold J. Grimm,* edited by Kyle C. Sessions and Phillip N. Bebb, 181–201. Kirksville, Mo.: Sixteenth Century Journal, 1985.

———. "Philipp's Foes but Followers Nonetheless: Late Humanism among the Gnesio-Lutherans." In *The Harvest of Humanism in Central Europe: Essays in Honor of Lewis W. Spitz,* edited by Manfred P. Fleischer, 159–77. St. Louis: Concordia, 1992.

———. "Sixteenth-Century Lutheran Commentary on Genesis and the Genesis Commentary of Martin Luther." In *Théorie et pratique de l'exégèse: Actes du troisième colloque international sur l'histoire de l'exégèse biblique au XVIe siècle,* edited by Irena Backus and Francis Higman, 243–58. Geneva: Droz, 1990.

———. "Die Umgestaltung und theologische Bedeutung des Luthersbildes im späten 16. Jahrhundert." In *Die lutherische Konfessionalisierung in Deutschland: Wissenschaftliches Symposion des Vereins für Reformationsgeschichte 1988,* edited by Hans-Christoph Rublack, 202–31. Gütersloh: Mohn, 1992.

Körsgen-Wiedeburg, Andrea. "Das Bild Martin Luthers in den Flugschriften der frühen Reformationszeit." In *Festgabe für Ernst Walter Zeeden zum 60. Geburtstag am 14. Mai 1976,* edited by Horst Rabe, Hansgeorg Molitor, and Hans-Christoph Rublack, 153–77. Münster: Aschendorff, 1976.

Kremer, Ulrich Michael. "Martin Luther in the Perspective of Historiography." In *Seven-Headed Luther: Essays in Commemoration of a Quincentenary, 1483–1983,* edited by Peter Newman Brooks, 207–29. Oxford: Clarendon, 1983.

Kruse, Martin. *Speners Kritik am Landesherrlichen Kirchenregiment und ihre Vorgeschichte.* Witten: Luther, 1971.

Kunst der Reformationszeit, Staatliche Museen zu Berlin. . . . Berlin: Elefanten, 1983.

Lienhard, Marc. "Held oder Ungeheuer? Luthers Gestalt und Tat im Lichte der zeitgenössischen Flugschriftenliteratur." *Lutherjahrbuch* 45 (1978): 56–79.

Lohse, Bernhard. *Martin Luther: Eine Einführung in sein Leben und sein Werk.* 2d ed. Munich: Beck, 1983.

Luther mit dem Schwan, Tod und Verklärung: Katalog zur Ausstellung in der Lutherhalle Wittenberg anläßlich des 450. Todestages von Martin Luther. Wittenberg: Lutherhalle and Schelzky & Jeep, 1996.

Martin Luther, 1483 bis 1546: Katalog der Ausstellung in der Staatlichen Lutherhalle Wittenberg. Wittenberg: Lutherhalle, 1983.

Martin Luther und die Reformation in Deutschland: Ausstellung zum 500. Geburtstag Martin Luthers veranstaltet vom Germanischen Nationalmuseum Nürnberg. . . . Frankfurt/Main: Insel, 1983.

Mattox, Mickey L. "Martin Luther's Interpretation of the Women of Genesis in the Context of the Christian Exegetical Tradition." Ph.D. diss., Duke University, 1997.

Maurer, Wilhelm. *Der junge Melanchthon zwischen Humanismus und Reformation.* Vol. 2, *Der Theologe.* Göttingen: Vandenhoeck & Ruprecht, 1969.

Meinhold, Peter. *Die Genesisvorlesung Luthers und ihre Herausgeber.* Stuttgart: Kohlhammer, 1936.

Meusel, O. "Die Reussische oder Reussisch-Schönburgische Konfession von 1567." *Beiträge zur sächsische Kirchengeschichte* 14 (1899): 149–87.

Moeller, Bernd. "Das Berühmtwerden Luthers." *Zeitschrift für historische Forschung* 15 (1988): 65–92.

———. *Deutschland im Zeitalter der Reformation.* 2d ed. Göttingen: Vandenhoeck & Ruprecht, 1981.

———. "Luther in Europe: His Works in Translation, 1517–1546." In *Politics and Society in Reformation Europe: Essays for Sir Geoffrey Elton on His Sixty-Fifth Birthday,* edited by E. I. Kouri and Tom Scott, 235–51. New York: St. Martin's, 1987.

———. "Die Rezeption Luthers in der frühen Reformation." *Lutherjahrbuch* 57 (1990): 57–71.

———, ed. *Luther in der Neuzeit: Wissenschaftliches Symposion des Vereins für Reformationsgeschichte.* Gütersloh: Gerd Mohn, 1983.

Mühlenberg, Ekkehard, and Franz Brunhölzl. "Florilegien." In *Theologische Realenzyklopädie,* 9:215–21. Berlin: de Gruyter, 1983.

Mühlhaupt, Erwin. "Martin Luther oder Thomas Müntzer—und wer ist der rechte Prophet?" *Luther* 45 (1974): 55–71.

Nischan, Bodo. "Reformation or Deformation? Lutheran and Reformed Views of Martin Luther in Brandenburg's 'Second Reformation.'" In *Pietas et Societas: New Trends in Reformation Social History: Essays in Memory of Harold J. Grimm,* edited by Kyle C. Sessions and Phillip N. Bebb, 203–15. Kirksville, Mo.: Sixteenth Century Journal, 1985.

Pelikan, Jaroslav, ed. *Interpreters of Luther: Essays in Honor of Wilhelm Pauck.* Philadelphia: Fortress, 1968.

Pesek, Jirí. "Protestant Literature in Bohemian Private Libraries *circa* 1600." In *The Reformation in Eastern and Central Europe,* ed. Karin Maag, 36–49. Aldershot, Eng.: Scolar, 1997.

Peterson, Luther D. "The Philippist Theologians and the Interims of 1548: Soteriological, Ecclesiastical, and Liturgical Compromises and Controversies within German Lutheranism." Ph.D. diss., University of Wisconsin, 1974.

Peuckert, Will Erich. *Die Grosse Wende, Geistesgeschichte und Volkskunde.* Darmstadt: Wissenschaftliche Buchgesellschaft, 1966.

Piepkorn, Arthur Carl. "The Lutheran Symbolical Books and Luther." In *Luther for an Ecumenical Age: Essays in Commemoration of the 450th Anniversary of the Reformation,* edited by Carl S. Meyer, 242–70. St. Louis: Concordia, 1967.

———. "Suggested Principles for a Hermeneutics of the Lutheran Symbols." *Concordia Theological Monthly* 29 (1958): 1–24.

Plass, Ewald, ed. *What Luther Says: An Anthology.* St. Louis: Concordia, 1959.

Polisensky, J. V. *The Thirty Years War.* Translated by Robert Evans. Berkeley: University of California Press, 1971.

Preger, Wilhelm. *Matthias Flacius Illyricus und seine Zeit.* 2 vols. Erlangen: Bläsing, 1859, 1861.

Preuss, Hans. *Martin Luther: Der Prophet.* Gütersloh: Bertelsmann, 1933.

Rehermann, Ernst Heinrich. "Die Protestantischen Exempelsammlungen des 16. und 17. Jahrhunderts." In *Volkserzählung und Reformation,* edited by Wolfgang Brückner, 579–645. Berlin: Schmidt, 1974.

Richter, Matthias. *Gesetz und Heil: Eine Untersuchung zur Vorgeschichte und zum Verlauf des sogenannten Zweiten Antinomistischen Streits.* Göttingen: Vandenhoeck & Ruprecht, 1996.

Schilling, Johannes. "Bibliographie der Tischreden-Ausgaben." *WA* 59:748–49.

Schnell, Hugo. *Martin Luther und die Reformation auf Münzen und Medaillen.* Munich: Klinkhardt & Biermann, 1983.

Schönstädt, Hans-Jürgen. *Antichrist, Weltheilsgeschehen und Gottes Werkzeug, Römische Kirche, Reformation und Luther im Spiegel des Reformationsjubiläums 1617.* Wiesbaden: Steiner, 1978.

———. "Das Reformationsjubiläum 1617, Geschichtliche Herkunft und geistige Prägung." *Zeitschrift für Kirchengeschichte* 92 (1982): 5–57.

Schwiebert, Ernest G. *The Reformation.* Minneapolis: Fortress, 1996.

Scribner, R. W. *For the Sake of Simple Folk: Popular Propaganda for the German Reformation.* Cambridge: Cambridge University Press, 1981.

———. "Incombustible Luther: The Image of the Reformer in Early Modern Germany." *Past & Present* 110 (Feb. 1986): 39–68.

———. "Luther-Legenden des 16. Jahrhunderts." In *Martin Luther, Leben, Werk, Wirkung,* edited by Günter Vogler et al., 377–90. Berlin: Akademie-Verlag, 1986.

Seeberg, Erich. *Studien zu Luthers Genesisvorlesung.* Gütersloh: Bertelsmann, 1932.

Sommer, Wolfgang. "Luther—Prophet der Deutschen und der Endzeit: Zur Aufnahme der Prophezeiungen Luthers in der Theologie des älteren deutschen Luthertums." In *Zeitenwende—Zeitenende: Beiträge zur Apokalyptik und Eschatologie,* edited by Wolfgang Sommer, 109–28. Stuttgart: Kohlhammer, 1997.

Spahn, Martin. *Johannes Cochläus: Ein Lebensbild aus der Zeit der Kirchenspaltung.* Berlin: Dames, 1898.

Spitz, Lewis W. "The Third Generation of German Renaissance Humanists." In *Aspects of the Renaissance: A Symposium,* edited by Archibald R. Lewis, 105–21. Austin: University of Texas Press, 1967.

Stephan, Horst. *Luther in den Wandlungen seiner Kirche.* Giessen: Töpelmann, 1907.

Strauss, Gerald. *Luther's House of Learning: Indoctrination of the Young in the German Reformation.* Baltimore: Johns Hopkins University Press, 1978.

Tranvik, Mark David. "The Other Sacrament: The Doctrine of Baptism in the Late Lutheran Reformation." Th.D. diss., Luther Northwestern Theological Seminary, 1992.

Verzeichnis der im deutschen Sprachbereich erschienen Drucke des XVI. Jahrhunderts. Edited by the Bayerische Staatsbibliothek (Munich) and the Herzog August Bibliothek (Wolfenbüttel). Part 1, vol. 12. Stuttgart: Hiersemann, 1988.

Volz, Hans. *Die Lutherpredigten des Johannes Mathesius: Kritische Untersuchung zur Geschichtsschreibung im Zeitalter der Reformation.* Halle: Waisenhaus, 1929.

———. "Magister Peter Treuer aus Coburg, 'Exul Christi' und erster Sammler von Luthergebeten." *Zeitschrift für bayerische Kirchengeschichte* 39 (1970): 238–58.

———. "Der Traum Friedrichs des Weisen vom 30./31. Oktober 1517: Eine bibliographisch-ikonographische Untersuchung." *Gutenberg-Jahrbuch* 45 (1970): 174–211.

———, and Eike Wolgast. "Geschichte der Lutherbriefeditionen des 16. bis 20. Jahrhunderts." *WA Br* 14:400–408.

Waldeck, Oskar. "Die Publizistik des Schmalkaldischen Krieges." *Archiv für Reformationsgeschichte* 7 (1909–10): 1–55; 8 (1910–11): 44–133.

Wallmann, Johannes. "Die Rolle der Bekenntnisschriften im älteren Luthertum." In *Theologie und Frömmigkeit im Zeitalter des Barock: Gesammelte Aufsätze,* 46–60. Tübingen: Mohr/Siebeck, 1995.

Wartenberg, Günther. "Philipp Melanchthon und die sächsisch-albertinische Interimspolitik." *Lutherjahrbuch* 55 (1988): 60–80.

Weiss, James Michael. "Erasmus at Luther's Funeral: Melanchthon's Commemorations of Luther in 1546." *Sixteenth Century Journal* 16.1 (1985): 91–114.

Wengert, Timothy J. "Caspar Cruciger (1504–1548): The Case of the Disappearing Reformer." *Sixteenth Century Journal* 20 (1989): 417–41.

———. "Georg Major (1502–1574): Defender of Wittenberg's Faith and Melanchthonian Exegete." In *Melanchthon in seinen Schülern,* edited by Heinz Scheible, 129–56. Wiesbaden: Harrassowitz, 1997.

———. *Law and Gospel: Philip Melanchthon's Debate with John Agricola of Eisleben over* Poenitentia. Grand Rapids: Baker, 1997.

———. "Martin Luther's Movement toward an Apostolic Awareness as Reflected in His Early Letters." *Lutherjahrbuch* 61 (1994): 71–92.

Wingren, Gustaf. *Luther on Vocation.* Translated by Carl C. Rasmussen. Philadelphia: Muhlenberg, 1957.

Wolgast, Eike. "Biographie als Autoritätsstiftung: Die ersten evangelischen Lutherbiographien." In *Biographie zwischen Renaissance und Barock: Zwölf Studien,* edited by Walter Berschin, 41–71. Heidelberg: Mattes, 1993.

———. "Geschichte der Luther-Ausgaben vom 16. bis zum 19. Jahrhundert." In *WA* 60:431–60.

———. "Der Streit um die Werke Luthers im 16. Jahrhundert." *Archiv für Reformationsgeschichte* 59 (1968): 177–202.

———. "Die Wittenberger Luther-Ausgabe: Zur Überlieferungsgeschichte der Werke Luthers im 16. Jahrhundert." *Archiv für Geschichte des Buchwesens* 11.1–2:1–336.

Zabel, Amalie. *Lutherdramen des beginnenden 17. Jahrhunderts.* Ph.D. diss., University of Munich, 1911.

Zeeden, Ernst Walter. *Martin Luther und die Reformation im Urteil des deutschen Luthertums: Studien zum Selbstverständnis des lutherischen Protestantismus von Luthers Tode bis zum Beginn der Goethezeit.* 2 vols. Freiburg/B: Herder, 1952.

Index

Robert Kolb is missions professor of systematic theology at Concordia Seminary, St. Louis, Missouri. He is the author of several books, including *For All the Saints: Changing Perceptions of Martyrdom and Sainthood in the Lutheran Reformation; Luther's Heirs Define His Legacy: Studies on Lutheran Confessionalization;* and *Nikolaus von Amsdorf (1483–1565): Popular Polemics in the Preservation of Luther's Legacy.*